# Acclaim for Eric Alterman's *What Liberal Media?*

"Compelling . . . Dead-on, and ought to be heard." —*The Washington Monthly*

"Meticulously researched . . . Fair-minded and persuasive."
  —*The Santa Fe New Mexican*

"Makes a powerful case for how the news media have shifted dangerously to the right. . . . Eric Alterman is to be thanked for fully engaging the conservative media horde that has overrun the citadels of American communications."
  —*Salon*

"A welcome, lonely voice in our current political and media climate."
  —*The Columbus Dispatch*

"With extensive documentation and persuasive logic, [Alterman] shows that wherever you turn unabashed conservatives dominate the media. On talk radio, political opinion approaches a level of uniformity only seen in totalitarian societies." —*Boston Herald*

"An exhaustively documented puncturing of the conservative mantra . . . Each well-footnoted point, each unassailable statistic, resounds with the dull thwack of meat on concrete, as facts always hit harder than mere assertions."
  —*The Village Voice*

"Often humorous and acerbic . . . Well worth the read."
  —*The Charlotte Observer*

"Alterman argues persuasively that far from reflecting a liberal bias, the media are more likely guilty of being beholden to business interests and the status quo than to any political ideology." —*The Sacramento Bee*

"Not only a superb piece of polemical reporting—one done so well that no one surely will hereafter be able to talk about liberal bias in the news with a straight face—it's also fun to read. . . . Alterman, who ends with an impassioned essay on the crucial importance of high-quality journalism in a democratic society, shows that much more than liberal or conservative victory is at stake."
  —*South Florida Sun-Sentinel*

"Long overdue . . . [Alterman] does a masterful, painstakingly documented job."
—*Milwaukee Journal Sentinel*

"Produces a powerful effect. . . . In this detailed and comprehensive examination of nearly every facet of the American news-commentary industry, Alterman presents an impressive refutation of the liberal-media myth."
—*The American Prospect*

"Alterman hits the nub. . . . A sobering reminder that TV long ago abandoned serious journalism and that watchdogs and skeptics are thin on the ground in all media."
—*Kirkus Reviews*

"Alterman delivers well-documented, well-argued research in compulsively readable form. . . . Whether readers agree with Alterman or not, his writing on the business of opinion making is eye-opening. This book will be required reading for anyone in politics or journalism, or anyone curious about their complicated nexus."
—*Publishers Weekly*

"At a time when media ownership in the United States is more or less limited to six major conglomerates, this is an extremely important book."
—*The Tucson Citizen*

"Alterman, a serious journalist with several political books to his name, methodically proves his case. . . . There is one chapter that alone is worth the price of the book."
—*The Hartford Courant*

"Exhaustively researched, the book presents a mountain of evidence to debunk the myth in a convincing fashion. . . . While the notion of a Left-leaning press may be just an illusion, Alterman demonstrates that the perception is perhaps more important than the reality." —*The Providence Journal*

"Intelligent and exhaustively researched . . . Alterman's facts will be difficult to dispute. Hopefully, they will be just as difficult to ignore." —*Boston Review*

# WHAT LIBERAL MEDIA?

## ALSO BY ERIC ALTERMAN

*Sound & Fury:*
*The Making of the Punditocracy*
(1992, 2000)

*Who Speaks for America?*
*Why Democracy Matters in Foreign Policy*
(1998)

*It Ain't No Sin to Be Glad You're Alive:*
*The Promise of Bruce Springsteen*
(1999, 2001)

*When Presidents Lie:*
*Deception and its Consequences*
(2004)

Published by Basic Books,
A Member of the Perseus Books Group

Hardcover edition first published by Basic Books in 2003.
Paperback edition first published by Basic Books in 2004.

*Designed by Jeff Williams*
Set in 10.5-point Adobe Garamond

Library of Congress has catalogued the hardcover edition as follows:
Alterman, Eric.
    What liberal media? : the truth about *Bias* and the news / Eric Alterman.
        p.    cm.
    Includes bibliographical references and index.
    ISBN 0–465-00176-9 (hc)
    ISBN 0–465-00177-7 (pbk)
    1. Journalism—Objectivity.    2. Journalistic ethics.    I. Title.

PN4784.O24 A44 2003
306.44—dc21
                                                                            2002152568

04 05 06/ 10 9 8 7 6 5 4 3 2 1

# WHAT LIBERAL MEDIA?

## *The Truth About* Bias *and the News*

Eric Alterman

BASIC
BOOKS

A Member of the
Perseus Books Group
New York

To my girls,
Diana Roberta, Eve Rose, and Ruthie . . .
and to my father, Carl,
with deep love and profound gratitude.

My dear fellow, a journalist is a juggler, and he must accustom himself to the difficulties of his profession.

—HONORE DE BALZAC,
ILLUSIONS PERDUES, 1837–1843

—◀○▶—

Still a man hears what he wants to hear
and disregards the rest...

—PAUL SIMON, "THE BOXER"

# CONTENTS

# PREFACE TO THE
# PAPERBACK EDITION

My publisher asks that I say a few words about how this book was first received and what kind of impact this had on my thesis. Lest I be accused of whining (I do, but only in private), the book's reception was pretty terrific. Not only were reviews largely favorable and intelligent, the mail was intensely gratifying. I suppose 90 percent of life is timing, and indeed I am lucky to have timed my message to a moment when so many people were eager to hear it.

Still, the way in which a book is received tells an author a number of things. Much of the book's early success, in my view, is attributable to the enthusiasm with which it was received not in the media per se but in the liberal blogosphere. My argument that even the genuinely "liberal" media is not nearly so liberal as the conservatives are conservative, that it is not organized as a political movement—and that indeed, much of it has been cowed into adopting conservative assumptions and arguments if only unconsciously—was more than borne out by the collective yawn with which these ideas were met by some of the media's most liberal constituents. After all, if the media were so liberal, than the really liberal part of it likely would have embraced a book designed to prove the opposite case—the better to get on with its work of being liberal in the extreme under the radar of the unsuspecting masses. Alas, this did not take place.

*What Liberal Media?* went unreviewed in three genuinely liberal newspapers—the *Boston Globe*, the *Seattle Post-Intelligencer*, and the *San Francisco Chronicle*—even though it made it into single digits on all three of those newspapers' local best-seller lists. It also went unreviewed even in the liberal *The New Republic*. The neoliberal *Washington Monthly* turned the book over to a writer whose work I strongly criticized, both in the book and elsewhere. Gene Lyons of *Harper's* was less than crazy about it, while over at *The Atlantic* my good friend Ben Schwarz, its terrific literary editor, let it pass without a word. No word either in *New York. Slate* gave the book to its dyspeptic media critic, Jack Shafer, who ignored its contents, except to take a swipe at a silly debate in which I participated on *National Review* Online. (The latter, by the way, appeared bent on welching on the $100 plus a fleece sweatshirt I was promised for my participation, until its editors were inundated with e-mail missives from loyal Altercation readers. Thanks guys.) The *New York Observer* assigned a front-page hatchet-job profile to the very writer who found himself charmed and delighted by Ann Coulter's remark about how much fun it would have been had Timothy McVeigh blown up the *New York Times*. He quoted me referring to women as "chicks" when in fact I was pointing to baby chicks painted on my daughter's wall, among a few no less egregious misrepresentations. Remember, these are actual liberals in the media, where I have actual friends. If the genuinely liberal media worked in any way remotely comparable to the conservative media as presented in the following, little of what I describe here would have been even theoretically possible.

Meanwhile, with the exception of an extremely thoughtful review in *Columbia Journalism Review*, the alleged alpha males of watchdog journalism also saw fit to ignore this book, for reasons about which I can only speculate. *Washington Post* and *CNN* media reporter Howard "Conflict of Interest" Kurtz doubly ignored it. (I was a regular in Howie's media notes column before the book was published; nevermore.) *American Journalism Review*'s editors did not think it merited a review. Fox News Channel's "fairly balanced" media program *Fox Newswatch* could not spare a moment of mention; neither could communist NPR's program *On the Media*. Given the (gratifying) attention that the book's argument received on Jim Romenesko's Media News web site as well as favorable reviews in such places as the *New York Times*, the *Sunday New York Times Book Review*, the *Los Angeles Times*, and *The New Yorker* (see front and back cover blurbs), it's hard to argue that these failures even to address the topic were not conscious decisions.

Meanwhile, the conservative media certainly did their job. *What Liberal Media?*, I am proud to say, completely stinks in the opinion of Andrew Sullivan, Jonah Goldberg, Bernard Goldberg, David Horowitz, the *Wall Street Journal* editorial page, *Commentary*, *American Enterprise*, the *American Spectator*, *The Hill*, all of right-wing talk radio, and most of cable TV (where I was almost always paired with an extremist conservative lest my views infect viewers if not disputed within thirty seconds). Whatever else it may have accomplished, this book was certainly a boon to the facetime media careers of the likes of William McGowan and the folks at Brent Bozell's Media Research Center.

On broadcast television and in national newsweeklies, again, the book was unheard of. Nothing at all on any of the networks or PBS, save for an excellent forty-minute debate on the Iraq war with Christopher Hitchens on *The Charlie Rose Show*. This overall lack of attention might not be so remarkable were it not for the fact that Ms. Coulter is embraced by this particular constituency in spite of her frequent jokes about how funny it would be if journalists were murdered by terrorists and comparing Katie Couric—a mother and widow—to both Eva Braun and Joseph Goebbels.

All in all, indeed, I have precious little about which to complain. I remain extremely heartened and encouraged by the manner in which the book was initially received
and discussed in many significant media circles. Given the ever decreasing role to
which books are allotted in our tabloid culture, any serious author of course would
be thrilled with the degree and quality of attention this book has received, and I am
certainly no exception. Yet whatever the degree of notice—favorable or unfavorable—
to blame (or thank) "liberals" for it would be more than a bit nutty; that's all I want
to say. That and, oh yeah—I hear O'Reilly wears a rug. If you don't like it big guy,
sue me.

E. R. A.
November 2003
New York City

# PREFACE TO THE
# HARDCOVER EDITION
# AND ACKNOWLEDGMENTS

It's a bit complicated psychologically to write a book that so perfectly contradicts conventional wisdom by arguing that the bias of the American media is more conservative than liberal. I suppose I am a natural for it, but still, it's hard to do without allies. Fortunately, I was lucky in mine.

But before I start thanking people, I should mention a couple of the circumstances that helped fuel the work, since they seem relevant to the book's genesis. First, while working on it, I was also putting the finishing touches on a nearly decade-long effort to complete my dissertation in the history department at Stanford. My topic was presidential lying. In reading and rereading my data, I continued to be struck by how little even the best and most admired journalism of the period in question—no matter what period it was—really understood about what happened behind closed doors with regard to presidential decisions, and how easily they swallowed the most transparent deceptions. This was particularly true with regard to matters of war and peace. This knowledge steeled my resolve in calling attention to what I believe is a deeply misguided consensus on the notion of "liberal media" today.

My resolve was further strengthened by the personal anomaly that, until I began work on this book, I had studied history virtually my entire life without ever reading the work of Robert Caro on either Robert Moses or Lyndon Johnson. I rectified this unforgivable omission in my education by devouring all of Caro's books in an unbroken string. (Actually, I listened to them on tape, unabridged, for a period of about a year, something I recommend to all those who find themselves in a similar state of ignorance, but without a lot of time for reading for pleasure.) In any case, one of the many points I found continually beaten into my head during my long walks or short Stairmaster sessions was the same one that had struck me in doing my own research on past presidencies. Throughout the amazingly well-documented careers of both Moses and LBJ, the contemporary journalism of the period served mainly to confuse the reality of what actually took place, and almost always in the service of power. Read 3,850 pages of Robert Caro, dear reader, and you will find that you actually can fool most of the people most of the time—at least for a period of a half century or so. If so many people could be so wrong so frequently about figures as important as these, it does not tax my imagination to believe the possibility that many of the people who write and speak about the media are wrong today.

Success or failure, I cannot say, but this book has many fathers (and mothers). In some ways, it is a sequel to my first book, *Sound & Fury*, published originally in 1992, for which many are to blame. In some ways it is a natural outgrowth of my work as a media columnist for the *Nation* and everything columnist/Weblogger for MSNBC.com. Victor Navasky and Katrina vanden Heuvel may be held responsible for inviting me to undertake the former and Joan Connell and Merrill Brown, the latter. I originally began research specifically for a book on media, the role of ideas in society, and the power that money has to help shape both, at the suggestion of my good friend Bill Moyers, in his capacity as president of the Florence and John Schumann Foundation. Thanks too, to Hamilton Fish and Taya Grobow of the Nation Institute for help in facilitating the research grants, among other things. I will always be grateful for the foundations' generosity.

I was working merrily on that earlier book on September 11, 2001, when, in the shock of what took place, I suddenly lost my excitement for it and began floundering. Todd Gitlin came to my rescue with what now seems like an obvious idea. It was so obvious, in fact, that it took Todd only nine words to make his point. His e-mail read in its entirety: "You should write a book called *What Liberal Media?*" Fortunately much of my research for the former work proved relevant to this one. So thanks to Todd, I got my mojo working again and didn't lose any time or waste much effort on the wrong book, which is something so valuable you can't even buy it with an American Express Centurian card.

Todd did a bit more after sending the e-mail, giving me a tough-minded read on the early drafts and helping me tease out ideas that would have forever stayed buried in my subconscious. Given the fact that Todd has now done this on about every book I've written, I calculate my debt to him as unpayable. So I won't try. Michael Waldman had nothing to do with the idea of the book but was just as helpful in its execution. His reading of it saved me from many errors and inspired numerous ideas and examples to be found in the text. Michael has also helped me with previous books, and, as with Todd, I am indeed fortunate to have such friends.

Much of the book was originally researched for *Nation* columns I've written over the past few years and to the degree that the facts are correct, I am indebted to editor Betsy Reed and an army of *Nation* fact-checkers. First among equals of these is Mica Rosenberg. Thanks people, especially to Mica. Karen Abrams did some first-rate proofreading, giving generously of her time and talents.

Given the nature of the book, it is also incumbent on me to point out that it relies rather heavily on the work of many other writers and reporters, all of whom, I hope, are duly credited in both the footnotes and the text. Of these, however, two stand out for special mention. The reporter whose work I borrow most heavily is almost certainly Eric Boehlert of Salon. I had no idea how good he is—or in fact, that anyone at all was this good—until I began to do systematic searches on the topics about which I planned to write. Almost every time, Eric got there first, and often, best. I also, to my own surprise, found myself relying quite frequently on the reporting of Howard Kurtz of CNN and the *Washington Post*. I mention my surprise because, as the reader will soon see, I am rather critical of Kurtz on political grounds in the text. I stand by that, of course, but he is an insanely energetic reporter and I think, in the main, a reliable one. As a media critic and historian, I am grateful for the body of work he has produced. As a writer who is also employed by two separate media organizations, I have considerable sympathy for the conflict-of-interest quandaries in which Kurtz is impossibly enmeshed. My situation is easier than his because I write only about what I choose, whereas neither the media reporter of the *Washington Post* nor the host of CNN's *Reliable Sources* is free to ignore important issues and stories. Still I should be held accountable on these issues as I hold Kurtz accountable and I hope that the (constructive) criticism I offer my employers in this work speaks to this point. I do admit to being a bit easier on people who happen to be my friends than I might otherwise be. How could it be otherwise? It would be better if I could identify my relationship to each and every individual in this book, but it would also be impossible. Ultimately, I think I am fair (and balanced) in my judgments to both friend and foe. Readers are obviously invited to make their own judgments.

Meanwhile, I also relied on the work of a few key journalistic watchdog institutions, and I should like to salute them as well. These include the editors and writers of the *Columbia Journalism Review*. Thanks tremendously to whoever made the decision to put its enormously valuable archives on the Web. The work published in *American Journalism Review* was quite helpful. So too was the material published and/or transmitted by the Pew Charitable Trust's Project for Excellence in Journalism and by the Committee of Concerned Journalists. And, as a regular writer on media-related topics, I am perhaps most grateful to Jim Romenesko and the people at the Poynter Institute who support his invaluable work. Doing this book without Media News would have added years to my research. Thanks also to the German Marshall Fund for generously funding my research on European media views and to the Aspen Institutes, Italia and Berlin.

Finally, the actual book owes its reality to the support and expertise of my crack editors at Basic, Vanessa Mobley and John Donatich; no less to the work of my

Superagent, Tina Bennett, who—and I do not say this lightly—is to agents what the E Street Band is to rock and roll. Thanks also to my careful copy editor, Judy Serrin. To be honest, the book would have been completed a little bit earlier without the efforts of my family, the (equally) beautiful and talented Diana Roberta Silver, and Eve Rose Alterman to get me to do other stuff; it would also have been no fun. While I do not yet know what they are, I imagine this book contains its fair share of mistakes. I blame my parents.

ERA  
NYC, 8 November 2002

# WHAT LIBERAL MEDIA?

# 1

## Introduction

### *Bias, Slander, and BS*

ONLY A LIBERAL would be dumb enough to title a book, *What Liberal Media?*
Listen to just about anyone and the answer is obvious: "What, are you stupid? Just
pick up a newspaper or turn on your TV." Should that fail to convince, bemusement
can turn to anger, or at best, pity, as in "There are none so blind as those who will
not see." America's argument about media bias features just two points of view. The
right argues that the media is biased toward leftists. The other side responds, to quote
David Broder, "dean" of the Washington press corps, "There just isn't enough ideology in the average reporter to fill a thimble."[1] The idea that the media might, for reasons of ownership, economics, class, or outside pressure, actually be more sympathetic to conservative causes than to liberal ones is widely considered to be simply
beyond the pale.

Social scientists talk about "useful myths," stories we all know are not necessarily
true, but that we choose to believe anyway because they seem to offer confirmation
of what we already know (which raises the question, if we already know it, why the
story?). Think of the wholly fictitious but illustrative story about little George
Washington and his inability to lie about that cherry tree. For conservatives, and even
more many journalists, the "liberal media" is just that: a myth, to be certain, but a
useful one. If only it were true, we might have a more humane, open-minded, and
ultimately effective public debate on the issues facing the nation. Alas, if pigs could
fly. . . .

Republicans of all stripes have done quite well for themselves during the last five
decades fulminating about the liberal cabal/progressive thought-police who spin, sup-
plant, and sometimes suppress the news we all consume. Indeed, it's not only conservatives who find this whipping boy to be an irresistible target. Dwight David
Eisenhower received one of the biggest ovations of his life when, at the 1964
Republican convention, he derided the "sensation-seeking columnists and commentators" who sought to undermine the Republican Party's efforts to improve the

nation.[2] The most colorful example of this art form, however, is probably a toss-up between two quips penned by William Safire when he was a White House speech-writer for Vice President Spiro Agnew, who denounced both the "nattering nabobs of negativism" and the "effete corps of impudent snobs" seeking to sink the nation's morale.[3] His boss, Richard Nixon (who had been Ike's VP), usually held his tongue in public, but complained obsessively in private to the evangelist Billy Graham of "a terrible liberal Jewish clique" that "totally dominates the media" and "erodes our confidence, our strength."[4] Just about everyone wants to get in on the fun. Even Bill Clinton whined to *Rolling Stone* that he did not get "one damn bit of credit from the knee-jerk liberal press."[5] The presidency's current occupant, George W. Bush, continues this tradition, complaining that the media "are biased against conservative thought."[6] On a trip to Maine in January 2002, he quite conspicuously carried a copy of the best-selling book, *Bias*, by Bernard Goldberg, as if to the give the so-called "liberal media"—hereafter, SCLM—a presidential thumb in the eye.[7]

But while some conservatives actually believe their own grumbles, the smart ones don't. They know mau-mauing the other side is a just a good way to get their ideas across—or perhaps to prevent the other side from getting a fair hearing for theirs. On occasion, honest conservatives admit this. Rich Bond, then the chair of the Republican Party, complained during the 1992 election, "I think we know who the media want to win this election—and I don't think it's George Bush."[8] The very same Rich Bond also noted during the very same election, however, "There is some strategy to it [bashing the 'liberal' media] . . . . If you watch any great coach, what they try to do is 'work the refs.' Maybe the ref will cut you a little slack on the next one."[9] Bond is hardly alone. That the SCLM were biased against the administration of Ronald Reagan is an article of faith among Republicans. Yet James Baker, perhaps the most media-savvy of them, owned up to the fact that any such complaint was decidedly misplaced. "There were days and times and events we might have had some complaints [but] on balance I don't think we had anything to complain about," he explained to one writer.[10] Patrick Buchanan, among the most conservative pundits and presidential candidates in the republic's history, found that he could not identify any allegedly liberal bias against him during his presidential candidacies. "I've gotten balanced coverage, and broad coverage—all we could have asked. For heaven sakes, we kid about the 'liberal media,' but every Republican on earth does that,"[11] the aspiring American ayatollah cheerfully confessed during the 1996 campaign. And even William Kristol, without a doubt the most influential Republican/neoconservative publicist in America, has come clean on this issue. "I admit it," he told a reporter. "The liberal media were never that powerful, and the whole thing was often used as an excuse by conservatives for conservative failures."[12] Nevertheless Kristol apparently feels no compunction about exploiting and reinforcing ignorant prejudices of his own constituency. In a 2001 subscription pitch to conservative potential subscribers of his

Rupert Murdoch–funded magazine, the *Weekly Standard,* Kristol complained, "The trouble with politics and political coverage today is that there's too much liberal bias. . . . There's too much tilt toward the left-wing agenda. Too much apology for liberal policy failures. Too much pandering to liberal candidates and causes."[13] (It's a wonder he left out "Too much hypocrisy.")

In recent times, the right has ginned up its "liberal media" propaganda machine. Books by both Ann Coulter, a blond bombshell pundette, and Bernard Goldberg, former CBS News producer, have topped the best-seller lists, stringing together such a series of charges that, well, it's amazing neither one thought to accuse "liberals" of using the blood of conservative children for extra flavor in their soy-milk decaf lattes. While extremely popular with the media they attack, both books are so shoddily written and "researched" that they pretty much refute themselves. Their danger derives less from the authors' respective allegations than the "where there's smoke, there's fire" impression they inspire. In fact, barely any of the major allegations in either book stands up to more than a moment's scrutiny. The entire case is a lie, and, yes, in many instances, a slander. Although I abhor the methods of both authors, I do not feel they can go unanswered. Ideas, particularly bad ones, have consequences. The myth of the "liberal media" empowers conservatives to control debate in the United States to the point where liberals cannot even hope for a fair shake anymore. However immodest my goal, I aim to change that.

---

I first met Ann Coulter in 1996 when we were both hired to be pundits on the new cable news station, MSNBC. Still just a right-wing congressional aide, she had been hired without even a hint of journalistic experience but with a mouth so vicious she made her fellow leggy blond pundit, Laura Ingraham, look and sound like Mary Tyler Moore in comparison. Coulter was eventually fired when she attacked a disabled Vietnam veteran on the air, screaming, "People like you caused us to lose that war."[14] But this was just one of many incidents where she had leaped over the bounds of good taste into the kind of talk that is usually reserved for bleachers or bar fights. In her columns, published in one of the most extreme of all conservative publications, *Human Events,* she regularly referred to the president of the United States, Bill Clinton, as a "pervert, liar, and a felon" and "a flim-flam artist." She termed the first lady to be "pond scum" and "white trash"[15] and the late Pamela Harriman a "whore." Coulter said these things all the while appearing on air in dresses so revealing they put one in mind of Sharon Stone in the film *Basic Instinct.*

The greater Coulter's fame, the more malevolent grew her hysteria. In her 1998 book, *High Crimes and Misdemeanors: The Case Against Bill Clinton,* she wrote, "In this recurring nightmare of a presidency, we have a national debate about whether he 'did it,' even though all sentient people know he did. Otherwise there would be debates only about whether to impeach or assassinate."[16] Such was the wisdom of the alleged "constitutional scholar" whose work George Will quoted on ABC's *This Week*. (Will is not very particular about his sources. I counted exactly one work of history in Coulter's copious footnotes. Coulter has also been accused of plagiarism by a former colleague, but denies the charge.)[17]

Shortly after 9/11, Coulter became famous again when she suggested, in a column published by National Review Online, after seeing anti-American demonstrators in Arab nations, that we "invade their countries, kill their leaders and convert them to Christianity."[18] Coulter's column was dropped by the magazine, but not because the editors objected to its content. Editor Jonah Goldberg explained, "We ended the relationship because she behaved with a total lack of professionalism, friendship, and loyalty." (Coulter had called the editors "girly boys.")[19] Coulter remained unbowed. At a meeting of the National Political Action Conference, speaking of the young American who converted to militant Islam and fought for the Taliban, Coulter advised, "We need to execute people like John Walker in order to physically intimidate liberals, by making them realize that they can be killed too. Otherwise they will turn out to be outright traitors."[20] She also joked about the proposed murder of the U.S. secretary of transportation, Norm Mineta.[21]

In her second book-length primal scream, published in the summer of 2002, Coulter compared Katie Couric of the *Today* show to Eva Braun. (She would later add Joseph Goebbels after Couric challenged her in an interview.) She termed Christie Todd Whitman, the former governor of New Jersey and then head of the Environmental Protection Agency, a "dimwit" and a "birdbrain." Sen. Jim Jeffords is a "half-wit." Gloria Steinem is a "termagant" and "deeply ridiculous figure," who "had to sleep" with a rich liberal to fund *Ms.* magazine.[22] But the errors are even more egregious than the insults, and her footnotes are, in many significant cases, a sham.[23] The good folks at the *American Prospect*'s Web log "Tapped" went to the trouble of compiling Coulter's errors chapter by chapter. The sheer weight of these, coupled with their audacity, demonstrates the moral and intellectual bankruptcy of a journalistic culture that allows her near a microphone, much less a printing press.[24] (If you doubt this, put down this book and log on right now to www.whatliberalmedia.com, and follow the clicks to Appendix One.)[25]

Coulter's view of the U.S. media can be summed up as follows: "American journalists commit mass murder without facing the ultimate penalty, I think they are retarded." In the *New York Observer*, published in one of the two cities attacked on 9/11, Coulter joked about how wonderful it would have been if Timothy McVeigh had blown up the *New York Times* building and murdered all of its inhabitants. Apparently nothing—not even the evocation, serious or not, of the mass murder of journalists—could turn Coulter's love affair with the SCLM sour.

For such comments, she is celebrated and rewarded. While promoting *Slander*, Coulter was booked on *Today*, *Crossfire* (as both a guest and guest host), *Hardball*, *The Big Story with John Gibson*, and countless other cable and radio programs. She was lovingly profiled in *Newsday*, the *New York Observer*, and the *New York Times* Sunday Styles page, while also enjoying a seat at the White House Correspondents Association Dinner as a guest of the *Boston Globe*. She was even invited on ABC's *Good Morning America* as an election analyst in November 2002. In the *Wall Street Journal*—a newspaper that had actually been destroyed by terrorists, and whose reporter, Daniel Pearl, had been murdered by them—Melik Kaylan defended her comments in Coulter-like fashion. He argued, "We have been programmed to think that such impassioned outrage, and outrageousness, are permissible only on the left from counter-culture comedians or exponents of identity politics." He also compared Coulter's alleged "humor" to that of Lenny Bruce, Angela Davis, and the Black Panthers. Too bad, therefore, as Charles Pierce pointed out, the conservative media darling has yet to be "arrested and jailed for what she said (Lenny Bruce), prosecuted in federal court (Angela Davis), or shot to ribbons in her bed (the Black Panthers)."[26]

---

Bernard Goldberg's book *Bias* suffers from many of the same weaknesses as Coulter's, though he lacks her colorful flair for murderous invective. Still *Bias* proved a smashing success. The *New York Times*'s publishing columnist, Martin Arnold, termed its sales to be "the most astonishing publishing event in the last 12 months."[27] Indeed, with its publisher claiming more than 440,000 copies in print, the book's sales figures alone are taken by many to be evidence of the truth of its argument.[28] In many ways, the conservative side was hardly better served in its arguments by Goldberg than by Coulter. To those who do not already share Goldberg's biases, his many undocumented, exaggerated assertions have the flavor of self-parody rather than reasoned argument. Among these are such statements as: "Everybody to the right of Lenin is a 'right-winger' as far as media elites are concerned." Opposition to the flat tax, he claims, comes from the same "dark region that produces envy and the seemingly unquenchable liberal need to wage class warfare."[29] Roughly 72 of the 232 pages of *Bias* are devoted to attacks or score-settling with Dan Rather, whom Goldberg believes to have ruined his career. "If CBS News were a prison instead of a journalistic enterprise, three-quarters of the producers and 100 percent of the vice-presidents would be Dan's bitches," Goldberg says.[30] Much of the rest of *Bias* consists of blasts at unnamed liberals who are accused of exaggerating data and manipulating the truth for their own purposes. How strange, therefore, that Goldberg seeks to make his case with statements about: "America's ten-trillion-page tax code," tuition fees that are "about the same as the cost of the space shuttle," and Laurence Tribe's "ten million"[31] appearances on CBS News during the 1980s.[32]

Taking the conservative ideology of wealthy white male victimization to hitherto-unimagined heights, Goldberg employs an extended Mafia metaphor to describe his departure from CBS. He speaks of having broken his pledge of "omerta"[33] by writing an op-ed in the *Wall Street Journal* attacking his colleagues. "So what happened?" he writes. "Well, as Tony Soprano might put it to his old pal Pussy Bompensiero in the Bada Bing! Lounge: Bernie G. opened his big mouth to the wrong people—and he got whacked."[34] You believe this heartbreaking tale until you discover that CBS had every right to fire him for violating the terms of his contract by attacking the network news program in a public forum. Instead, his superiors found him a comfortable job where he was allowed to quietly qualify for a higher pension. (On *The Sopranos*, and indeed, in most Mafia lore, the term "to whack" carries rather different connotations, as evidenced by Big Pussy's undisturbed slumber with "the fishes.")

During the course of over 220 pages of complaining, Goldberg never bothers to systematically prove the existence of liberal bias in the news, or even define what he means by the term. About as close as we get is: "I said out loud what millions of TV news viewers all over America know and have been complaining about for years: that too often, Dan and Peter and Tom and a lot of their foot soldiers don't deliver the news straight, that they have a liberal bias, and that no matter how often the network stars deny it, it is true."[35] A few of his examples, such as those involving corporate self-censorship in the event that a certain segment might offend the audience or advertisers, or the preference for interviewees with blond hair and blue eyes over people of color, actually serve to make the opposite case. With a keen eye to his likely audience of conservative talk-show hosts and book-buyers, the author simply assumes the existence of a liberal bias in the media to be an undisputable fact.

This same undocumented assumption characterized the conservative celebration of the book. The editors of the *Wall Street Journal* thundered: "There are certain facts of life so long obvious they would seem beyond dispute. One of these—that there is a liberal tilt in the media. . . ."[36] *U.S. News and World Report* columnist John Leo added, in praise of *Bias*, that "the reluctance of the news business to hold seminars and conduct investigations of news bias is almost legendary."[37] Glenn Garvin, television critic of the *Miami Herald*, added, "That newsrooms are mostly staffed by political liberals is pretty much beyond dispute, although a few keep trying to argue the point." That newspaper's executive editor, Tom Fielder, was said to be so impressed by *Bias* that he invited Goldberg to lunch with top members of his staff. He told Garvin, "I hate to say there's a political correctness that guides us, but I think there is. We tend to give more credibility to groups on the liberal side of the spectrum than on the conservative side."[38]

If, in an alternative universe, all of Goldberg's claims somehow turned out to be justified, the crux of his argument would nevertheless constitute a remarkably narrow indictment. Goldberg did not set out to prove a liberal bias across the entire media, nor even across all television news. He concerned himself only with the evening news broadcasts, and not even with politics, but with social issues. Moreover, he appears to have done little research beyond recounting his own experiences and parroting the complaints of a conservative newsletter published by Brent Bozell's Media Research Center.[39] It is hard to see what so excited conservative readers about the book. The broadcasts in question represent a declining share of viewers' attention, and, increasingly, an old and, at least from advertisers' standpoint, undesirable audience. It is possible that these particular news programs—if not their very format—will not survive the retirement ages of the current generation of anchors.[40]

Goldberg appears to consider this fact. However, he attributes the relative decline in viewership of the network nightly news to viewer unhappiness with the widespread liberal bias he claims to have uncovered. "It's as if the Berlin Wall had come down," he explains. "But instead of voting with their feet, Americans began voting with their remote control devices. They haven't abandoned the news. Just the news people they no longer trust." "How else can we account for Bill O'Reilly and *The O'Reilly Factor* on The Fox News Channel? . . . As far as I'm concerned, the three people Bill owes so much of his success to are Tom Brokaw, Peter Jennings, and Dan Rather."[41]

The logic of the above argument is genuinely difficult to fathom. Goldberg is correct to note that all three networks have seen a significant decline in their ratings for their news programs. But so has just about everything on network programming, due, quite obviously, to the enormous rise in viewer choice—the result of the replacement of a three-network television universe with one that features hundreds of choices on cable and satellite TV and the Internet. Viewership for all four networks—ABC, CBS, NBC, and Fox—during the ratings period September 24, 2001, to March 3, 2002, for instance, made up only 43 percent of TV watchers, compared with more than twice that percentage for just three networks two decades earlier.[42] Still the network news programs' numbers remained impressive. The combined audience of the three network news programs is well over thirty million Americans, and better than fifteen times the number tuning into Mr. O'Reilly. It is also more than ten times the combined total prime-time audience for Fox News Channel, CNN, and MSNBC.[43] These ratios render Goldberg's logic entirely nonsensical. Had he, or anyone related to the book, had enough respect for his readers to bother with even ten minutes of research, this claim would have never made it into print.

Not all of Goldberg's arguments are quite as easy to disprove, but most are no less false or misleading. One of the claims that many critics and television interviewers have considered the strongest in the book was the one the author credited with having inspired his initial interest in the topic:

> not because of my conservative views but because what I saw happening violated my liberal sense of fair play. Why, I kept wondering, do we so often identify conservatives in our stories, yet rarely identify liberals? Over the years, I began to real-

ize that this need to identify one side but not the other is a central component of liberal bias. There are right-wing Republicans and right-wing Christians and right-wing radio talk show hosts. The only time we journalists use the term "left-wing" is if we're talking about a part on an airplane.

Goldberg illustrates his point with an example taken from the Clinton impeachment proceedings, during which, he claims, Peter Jennings identified senators as they came to sign their names in the oath book. According to Goldberg, Jennings described Mitch McConnell of Kentucky as a "very determined conservative," Rick Santorum of Pennsylvania as "one of the younger members of the Senate, Republican, very determined conservative," and Bob Smith of New Hampshire as "another very, very conservative Republican" but did not describe liberals accordingly. Goldberg also complained that CBS identifies the radical feminist Catharine MacKinnon as a "noted law professor" while Phyllis Schlafly is a "conservative spokeswoman." Rush Limbaugh, says Goldberg, is the "conservative radio talk show host" but Rosie O'Donnell is not described as the liberal TV talk show host. "Robert Bork is the 'conservative' judge. But liberal Laurence Tribe, who must have been on *CBS Evening News* ten million times in the 1980s," is identified simply as a "Harvard law professor."[44]

Well, it would be interesting if true. And many of even the sharpest SCLM critics of Goldberg's book assumed it to be true, perhaps out of the mistaken belief that he must have done at least this much research. Both Howard Kurtz and Jeff Greenfield failed to challenge it on CNN. Jonathan Chait accepted it in his extremely critical cover story on the book in the *New Republic* but then went on to explain why, aside from liberal bias, it might be the case.[45] And the then-dean of the Columbia School of Journalism, Tom Goldstein, writing in the *Columbia Journalism Review,* mocked Goldberg's ad hominem claims but nevertheless credited Goldberg for "get[ting] down to specifics . . . [that] have the ring of truth" on this point.[46]

In fact, all were overly generous. Goldberg presents no testable evidence and his arguments bear little relationship to the truth. At a 2002 book-store appearance broadcast on C-Span, a political science professor asked Goldberg something almost no television interviewer had bothered to inquire: Did he have any systematic data to back up this point? The author scoffed at the very idea of evidence. "I didn't want this to be written from a social scientist point of view," Goldberg explained. "I have total confidence that the point here is accurate."

Another audience member then challenged him on this point and here, Goldberg got a bit testy:

Let me say this. And I want to say this as clearly as I can. You are dead wrong. Dead wrong. Not even close about Teddy Kennedy. You have not, almost every time they mention his name, heard "liberal." I will say this—you have heard the word "liberal" almost never mentioned when they say his name, on the evening newscasts. They just don't. That part—I mean you gave me an easy one, and I appreciate that. It doesn't happen.[47]

Goldberg seems to think that such statements become true by emphatic repetition. In fact, they are testable and it is Bernard Goldberg who is "dead wrong." On the small, almost insignificant point of whom Peter Jennings identified with what label on a single broadcast, Goldberg's point is a partial, and deliberately misleading, half-truth. As the liberal Daily Howler Web site pointed out, "the incident occurred on January 7, 1999, and Jennings did not identify 'every conservative' as the senators signed the oath book." He identified only three of them as such, failing to offer the label of conservative to such stalwarts as Senators Gramm, Hatch, Helms, Lott, Mack, Thurmond, Lugar, Stevens, Thompson, and Warner.[48] Most of the labels had nothing to do with politics and were peppered with personal asides about a given senator's age, interests, or personality. On the larger point regarding a liberal bias in the labeling of conservatives, but not liberals, Goldberg could hardly be more wrong, even using the very examples he proposes. For instance, Ted Kennedy does not appear on the news with much frequency, but during the first six months of 2001, when he did, it was almost always accompanied by the word "liberal."[49] As for the "million" respectful references to Laurence Tribe that appeared without the appendage "liberal," the indefatigable Howler checked those as well. According to Lexis, Howler found, Tribe has appeared on the *CBS Evening News* just nine times since 1993, almost always identified with a liberal label. On one occasion, May 14, 1994, CBS News even used Tribe and Robert Bork together, described as "legal scholars from both ends of the political spectrum."[50]

The above anecdotes are reinforced by some careful research on the topic by Geoffrey Nunberg of the Center for the Study of Language and Information at Stanford University and its department of linguistics. The results of these are reprinted in Appendix Two, available at www.whatliberalmedia.com, and I urge you to examine them if you believe Goldberg has even a shred of credibility remaining.

---

Given the success of Fox News, the *Wall Street Journal*, the *Washington Times*, *New York Post*, *American Spectator*, *Weekly Standard*, *New York Sun*, *National Review*, *Commentary*, and so on, no sensible person can dispute the existence of a "conservative media." The reader might be surprised to learn that neither do I quarrel with the notion of a "liberal media." It is tiny and profoundly underfunded compared to its conservative counterpart, but it does exist. As a columnist for the *Nation* and an independent Weblogger for MSNBC.com, I work in the middle of it, and so do many of my friends. And guess what? It's filled with right-wingers. Unlike most of the publications named above, liberals, for some reason, feel compelled to include the views of the other guy on a regular basis in just the fashion that conservatives abhor.

Take a tour from a native: *New York* magazine, in the heart of liberal country, chose as its sole national correspondent the right-wing talk-show host Tucker Carlson. During the 1990s, the *New Yorker*—the bible of sophisticated urban liberalism—chose as its Washington correspondents the Clinton/Gore hater Michael Kelly and the soft, Democratic Leadership Council neo-conservative Joe Klein. At least half of the "liberal *New Republic*" is actually a rabidly neoconservative magazine (see chapter 3) and has been edited in recent years by the very same Michael Kelly, as well as the conservative liberal hater Andrew Sullivan. Its rival on the "left," the *Nation*, happily published the free-floating liberal hater Christopher Hitchens until he chose to resign, and also invites Alexander Cockburn to attack liberals with morbid predictability. The *Atlantic Monthly*—a mainstay of Boston liberalism—even chose the apoplectic Kelly as its editor, who then proceeded to add a bunch of *Weekly Standard* writers plus Christopher Hitchens to *Atlantic*'s anti-liberal stable. What is the hysterically funny but decidedly reactionary P. J. O'Rourke doing in both the *Atlantic* and the liberal *Rolling Stone?* Why does liberal *Vanity Fair* choose to publish a hagiographic Annie Leibovitz portfolio of Bush administration officials designed, apparently, to invoke notions of Greek and Roman gods? Why does the liberal *New York Observer* alternate *National Review*'s Richard Brookhiser with the Joe McCarthy-admiring columnist, Nicholas von Hoffman—both of whom appear alongside editorials that occasionally mimic the same positions taken downtown by the editors of the *Wall Street Journal.* The tabloid-style liberal Web site Salon gives free reign to the McCarthyite impulses of both Andrew Sullivan and David Horowitz. The neoliberal Slate also regularly publishes both Sullivan and Christopher Caldwell of the *Weekly Standard* and has even opened its pixels to such conservative evildoers as Charles Murray and Elliott Abrams. (The reader should know I am not objecting to the inclusion of conservatives in the genuinely liberal component of the media. In fact, I welcome them. I'd just like to see some reciprocity on the other side.)

Move over to the mainstream publications and broadcasts often labeled "liberal" and you see how ridiculous the notion of liberal dominance becomes. The liberal *New York Times* op-ed page features the work of the unreconstructed Nixonite William Safire and for years accompanied him with the firebreathing-if-difficult-to-understand neocon A. M. Rosenthal. Current denizen Bill Keller also writes regularly from a soft, DLC neoconservative perspective. Why was then-editorial page editor, now executive editor, Howell Raines one of Bill Clinton's most vocal adversaries during his entire presidency?[51] Why is this alleged bastion of liberalism, on the very morning I wrote these words, offering words of praise and encouragement to George W. Bush and John Ashcroft for invoking the hated Taft-Hartley legislation on behalf of shipping companies, following a lock-out of their West Coast workers?[52] (Has the

*Wall Street Journal* editorial page ever, in its entire history, taken the side of American workers in a labor dispute?) It would later endorse for re-election the state's Republican/Conservative governor, George Pataki, over his capable, if unexciting, liberal Democratic African-American opponent, Carl McCall. The *Washington Post* editorial page, which is considered less liberal than the *Times* but liberal nevertheless, is just swarming with conservatives, from Mr. Kelly to George Will to Robert Novak to Charles Krauthammer, among many more. On the morning before I finally let go of the draft manuscript of this book, the paper's lead editorial is endorsing the president's plan for a "pre-emptive" war against Iraq.[53] The op-ed page was hardly less abashed in its hawkishness. A careful study by Michael Massing published in the *Nation* found, "Collectively, its editorials, columns and Op-Eds have served mainly to reinforce, amplify and promote the Administration's case for regime change. And, as the house organ for America's political class, the paper has helped push the debate in the Administration's favor. . . ."[54] If you wish to include CNN on your list of liberal media—I don't, but many conservatives do—then you had better find a way to explain the near ubiquitous presence of the attack dog Robert Novak, along with those of neocon virtuecrat William Bennett, *National Review*'s Kate O'Beirne, *National Review*'s Jonah Goldberg, the *Weekly Standard*'s David Brooks, and Tucker Carlson. This is to say nothing of the fact that among CNN's most frequent guests are Ann Coulter and the anti-American telepreacher Pat Robertson. Care to include ABC News? Again, I don't but, if you wish, how do you deal with the fact that the only ideological commentator on its Sunday interview show is the hardline conservative George Will? Or how about the fact that its only explicitly ideological reporter is the deeply journalistically challenged conservative crusader John Stossel? How to explain the entire career of Cokie Roberts, who never met a liberal to whom she could not condescend? What about *Time* and *Newsweek*? In the former, we have Mr. Krauthammer holding forth and in the latter Mr. Will.

I could go on almost indefinitely here, but the point is clear. Conservatives are extremely well represented in every facet of the media. The correlative point here is that even the genuine liberal media is not so liberal. And it is no match—either in size, ferocity, or commitment—for the massive conservative media structure that, more than ever, determines the shape and scope of our political agenda.

A Tom Tomorrow cartoon makes this point more cogently that I can in just four panels simply by (implicitly) asking readers to undergo a thought experiment. What if there really were a "liberal media"? Imagine, "an expansive network of left-wing think thanks which are of course bankrolled by secretive left-wing financiers seeking to advance their radical agenda." Now imagine "blatantly left-wing cable news networks and op-ed pages that then promote (left-wing) ideas relentlessly." Had enough? What about "angry liberals" debating these left-wing proposals with weak, mealy-mouthed conservatives on the Sunday talk shows? Want more? How about an entire universe of left-wing talk radio hosts spending endless hours devoting themselves to hammering these left-wing notions into the heads of tens of millions of listeners across the land? Why, poor President Bush and Vice President Cheney wouldn't have a chance.[55]

But to divide the media into their conservative, liberal, or centrist aspects misses a larger point and can do more to obscure than illuminate. The media make up a vast and unruly herd of independent beasts. Given their number and variety, it can be difficult for anyone to speak accurately about all of them simultaneously. Can one usefully compare Thomas Friedman to Larry Flynt? What about Garry Wills and Matt Drudge? Charlie Rose and Jerry Springer? Bill Moyers and Bill O'Reilly? Does *Foreign Affairs* share a single subscriber with the *National Enquirer*? Indeed, even the *New York Times* and the *New York Post* are not really in the same business. They have differing audiences, differing mandates, and differing professional standards, thank goodness. Marshall McLuhan was wrong, or at least woefully inexact: The medium is only the message if you're not paying close attention. *

Perhaps the most frequently made argument in defense of the SCLM thesis is the populist one. In a letter to the *New Republic*, for instance, Bernard Goldberg wrote, "Let's assume I'm dead wrong in my book, that there is no liberal bias in the big-time media. Then I can be easily dismissed. But what about the millions and millions of Americans—including many liberals—who think I'm right . . . Are they all stupid? Or delusional? Are they under some kind of mass hypnosis, doing the dirty work of right-wing nuts who are pulling the strings? These strike me as important questions."[56]

According to a September 2002 Gallup poll, 47 percent of Americans questioned believe the media are "too liberal."[57] This is an even smaller percentage of Americans than voted for George W. Bush. But even so, it hardly constitutes any form of normative proof or evidence. (Thirteen percent believe the media are biased toward conservatives.) Moreover the "millions and millions of people believe" is not a terribly convincing argument no matter what. Millions also believe in ghosts, extra-terrestrial visitations, and Osama bin Laden's promise of seventy-two virgins. That "millions and millions" of people think Goldberg is right about the media is likely an indication that much of what the public sees and reads confirms their belief that liberal bias does exist. Or it could mean that most media reporters believe that a great percentage of Americans share this view and so don't wish to confuse them. Conservatives, lest we forget, are much more energetic and better-funded complainers about media bias

---

*For the purposes of our discussion, we may assume that the relevant media are the elite national media, located largely in the networks, the nation's top five national newspapers, the newsweeklies, the opinion magazines, the executives who run these companies along with the sources, both on- and off-air who supply them with information and opinions. With a few important exceptions, these media's inhabitants can largely be found living and working in New York or Washington, with an entertainment subsidiary in Los Angeles.

than are liberals. They are extremely vocal and well-organized in their pressure tactics, and they've done an impressive job over the years in convincing many people that any view that does not comport with a conservative ideological viewpoint is by definition "liberal." In a careful 1999 study published in the academic journal *Communications Research*, four scholars examined the use of the "liberal media" argument and discovered a four-fold increase in the number of Americans telling pollsters that they discerned a liberal bias in their news. But the evidence, collected and coded over a twelve-year period, offered no corroboration whatever for this view. The obvious conclusion: News consumers were responding to "increasing news coverage of liberal bias media claims, which have been increasingly emanating from Republican Party candidates and officials."[58]

The right is working the refs. And it's working. Much of the public believes a useful, but unsupportable, myth about the SCLM and the media itself have been cowed by conservatives into repeating their nonsensical nostrums virtually nonstop. As the economist/pundit Paul Krugman observes of Republican efforts to bully the media into accepting the party's Orwellian arguments about Social Security privatization: "The next time the administration insists that chocolate is vanilla, much of the media—fearing accusations of liberal bias, trying to create the appearance of "balance"—won't report that the stuff is actually brown; at best they'll report that some Democrats claim that it's brown."[59]

No single work can compensate for the enormous advantage conservatives enjoy in their fight with liberals to control the fate of American politics. But if people are willing to examine the question of media bias in an open-minded fashion, perhaps we can even up the sides a bit.

# 2

## You're Only As Liberal As the Man Who Owns You

"REPEAT SOMETHING often enough and people will believe it" goes the adage, and this is nowhere truer than in American political journalism. As four scholars writing in the *Journal of Communication* observed in a study of the past three elections, "claiming the media are liberally biased perhaps has become a core rhetorical strategy by conservative elites in recent years." As a result, these unsupported claims have become a "necessary mechanism for moving (or keeping) analytical coverage in line with their interests."[1] Another way of saying this is that conservatives have successfully cowed journalists into repeating their baseless accusations of liberal bias by virtue of their willingness to repeat them . . . endlessly.

The psychological effects of conservatives' persistent attacks on the SCLM are significant. In seeking to explain why, well before 9/11, President Bush's life was "more pleasant than Clinton's ever was, even at the start of his presidency," *Washington Post* White House reporter John Harris pointed to "one big reason for Bush's easy ride: There is no well-coordinated corps of aggrieved and methodical people who start each day looking for ways to expose and undermine a new president." Harris expanded on the difference:

> There was just such a gang ready for Clinton in 1993. Conservative interest groups, commentators and congressional investigators waged a remorseless campaign that they hoped would make life miserable for Clinton and vault themselves to power. They succeeded in many ways. One of the most important was their ability to take all manner of presidential miscues, misjudgments or controversial decisions and exploit them for maximum effect. Stories like the travel office firings flamed for weeks instead of receding into yesterday's news. And they colored the prism through which many Americans, not just conservative ideologues, viewed Clinton. It is Bush's good fortune that the liberal equivalent of this conservative coterie does not exist.[2]

It does not matter that the evidence for liberal bias often disintegrates upon careful scrutiny. It works anyway. To be fair, it is enormously difficult to design an intellectually respectable study that tells us much of significance about journalistic bias because no one can control for events. George W. Bush earned enormously more generous coverage in the aftermath of the 9/11 attacks than he had in nine previous months of his presidency. But the composition of the press corps was obviously unchanged. Did reporters turn less liberal overnight—in which case, the entire argument about the SCLM is now consigned to history's proverbial dustbin? Or did the composition of the relevant issues change? And in an atmosphere of constantly changing issues, how is it possible to measure, scientifically, the treatment the issues receive in the media?

Another problem with accusations of liberal bias in the media is definitional. Just what constitutes a "liberal" bias anyway? The folks at Fox News Channel stake the network's identity on the claim that its programs are "fair and balanced," rather than "conservative." Whenever a reporter inquires about this, Fox's chairman and CEO, Roger Ailes, dismisses the question as itself evidence of liberal bias and says something like: "Fox is not a conservative network! I absolutely, totally deny it." According to Ailes, Fox's mission is no more controversial than "to provide a little more balance to the news" and "to go cover some stories that the mainstream media won't cover."[3] No one believes this; in fact, it's hard to believe that even Ailes does, which helps explain why he felt free to send memos to Karl Rove offering post–9/11 political advice to George W. Bush. But the tendency to insist that reality is whatever happens to comport with one's own ideological bias is not restricted to conservatives. The British reporter Robert Fisk is perhaps the most anti-American correspondent employed by a major English-language newspaper. His reports in the London-based *Independent* are no less biased than the average FNC broadcast, albeit in the opposite direction. But Fisk sees the problem with the other side as simply "the cowardly, idle, spineless way in which American journalists are lobotomizing their stories." Like his opposite numbers at Fox, Fisk seems to believe that the problem of truth is no more complex than the fact that he gets it and the other guys don't. "Why do we journalists try so hard to avoid the truth?" he asks. "All we have to do is tell the truth."[4]

But no content study can measure truth. Philosophers cannot even define it. Most, therefore, do not even try. Content studies, therefore, are rarely "scientific" in the generally understood connotation of the term. Many are merely pseudoscience, ideology masquerading as objectivity. When, in the spring of 2002, an independent Web site ran some numbers and pronounced the *New York Times*'s Paul Krugman—also an economist at Stanford, Princeton, and MIT—to be the most partisan of newspaper pundits by virtue of the mathematical ratio of the number of remarks critical of the Bush Administration per word published, Krugman made the following argument in response:

Suppose, just for the sake of argument, that the Bush administration was, in a fundamental way, being dishonest about its economic plans. Suppose that the numbers used to justify the tax cut were clearly bogus, and that the plan was in fact obviously a budget-buster. Suppose that the Social Security reform plan simply ignored the system's existing obligations, and thus purported to offer something for nothing. Suppose that the Cheney energy report deliberately misstated the nature of the country's actual energy problems, and used that misstatement to justify subsidies to the energy industry. Suppose also that I found myself writing an economics column as these plans were being sold—and that I was a highly competent economist, if I say so myself. Suppose that as an economist able to do my own analysis, not obliged to rely on conflicting quotes from the usual suspects, I was in a position to spot right away that some of the stuff being peddled made no sense—and clued in enough to get hold of experts who could tell me what was wrong with the other stuff. Suppose that I had been repeatedly proved right in my critiques of the Bush administration's assertions, even in cases where nobody else in the media was willing to take my criticisms seriously—for example, suppose that, because I understand microeconomics a lot better than your average columnist, I realized that economists who said that California's electricity crisis had a lot to do with market manipulation were probably right, more than a year before conventional wisdom was willing to contemplate the possibility. In this hypothetical situation, what sort of columns should I have been writing? Does the ideal of "nonpartisanship" mean that I should have mixed my critiques of Bush policies with praise, or with attacks on the hapless, ineffectual Democrats, just for the sake of perceived balance? Given what I knew to be the truth, would that even have been ethical?[5]

Because these kinds of objections are well known, some researchers seeking to demonstrate the liberal bias of the elite press corps have turned to other means to try to prove that reporters are liberals who vote Democratic and look down their noses at people who don't. The right's Rosetta Stone in this regard is the now famous poll of "Washington bureau chiefs and congressional correspondents" released in 1996 by the Freedom Forum. "Ever since a now-legendary poll from the Media Studies Center showed that 89 percent of Washington journalists voted for Clinton in 1992, it has been hard to deny that the press is 'liberal,'" wrote Christopher Caldwell, a *Weekly Standard* writer, in the *Atlantic Monthly*, in one typical rendering. Caldwell's rendering could stand for thousands more such assertions.[6]

The conservative pundit James Glassman employed these results to declare in the *Washington Post*: "The people who report the stories are liberal Democrats. This is the shameful open secret of American journalism. That the press itself . . . chooses to gloss over it is conclusive evidence of how pernicious the bias is."[7] Here Glassman makes a common tautological claim, insisting that the denial of crime is evidence of guilt. In addition he equates Clinton voters with "liberal Democrats," again positing no evidence. Such carelessness ought to be intellectually indefensible to anyone who takes a moment to consider it. Bill Clinton ran in 1992 quite self-consciously as a "New Democrat," heavily supported by the centrist Democratic Leadership Council. He hailed from a conservative Southern state. He supported the death penalty, "free trade," and "an end to welfare as we know it." In foreign policy, his hawkish views won him the support of right-wingers like William Safire and many hard-line neo-conservatives. The only way to conclude that a Clinton voter is de facto a "liberal Democrat" is by refusing to make any distinctions between the words "liberal" and "Democrat"—a distinction that keeps the Democrats in office in much of the southern and western parts of the nation.

Taken outside of the singular context of U.S. politics, moreover, the insistence that "Democrat" equals "liberal" grows even more problematic. The entire context of American politics exists on a spectrum that is itself well to the right of that in most industrialized democracies. During the 1990s, Bill Clinton was probably further to the right than most ruling West European conservatives, such as Germany's Helmut Kohl and France's Jacques Chirac. Indeed, virtually the entire axis of political conversation in the United States takes place on ideological ground that would be considered conservative in just about every nation in democratic Western Europe.[8]

In late October 2002, I took a trip to five cities in France, Spain, Italy, and Germany to meet with dozens of influential writers, editors, and cultural voices, both individually and in groups, in these four countries. Everywhere people voiced considerable admiration and affection for "America" in the abstract and a deep, if sometimes baffling, attraction to American culture, both popular and literary. The once-reflexive anti-Americanism inspired by the Vietnam War and the Cold War romance with communism among these elites had been entirely dispelled. Almost all expressed solidarity with America vis-à-vis the 9/11 attacks. Alessandro Portelli, editor of an Italian literary magazine, voiced the hope that America's recognition of its own vulnerability might help the nation develop some empathy for the vulnerable elsewhere in the world, who lack the ability to act on the world stage with impunity. Yet the primary response, as Portelli saw it, as voiced in the media and among well-known American intellectuals, has "a rhetoric of the exceptionalism of American sorrow," with a ready-made accusation of "anti-Americanism" employed to silence anyone who questions the views of the current administration.[9] Similarly, in Paris, Jacques Rupnik of the Centre d'Etudes et de Recherches Internationales—a close friend and adviser to both ex-Prime Minister Lionel Jospin as well as the powerfully pro-American Czech President Vaclav Havel—endorsed the U.S. military response in both Afghanistan and the Balkans, expressing sincere gratitude. But, as with virtually everyone to whom I spoke, he took profound offense at "the extraordinary, almost staggering moral self-righteousness of this administration" toward the good opinion of the rest of the democratic world.[10]

Virtually no one in high European media and cultural circles appeared willing to support or even defend the manner in which the Bush administration chose, unilaterally and without any prior consultation, to withdrawal from the Kyoto Protocol on global warming. Nor was anyone to be found who thought it wise for the United States to refuse to accept the jurisdiction of the nascent International Criminal Court. Without questioning Israel's right to live freely and securely within internationally recognized boundaries, nobody at all in these nations had a good word for the administration's unstinting support for the campaign of Israel's Ariel Sharon to expand Israeli settlements beyond the "Green Line," isolate Yasir Arafat, destroy the Palestinian Authority, and re-occupy Palestinian lands. Nor could I find anyone among the many dozens of people I met who thought it wise or prudent for the United States to engage in a pre-emptive war in Iraq, though Saddam Hussein and his brutal regime inspired neither excuses nor illusions. The very idea of the administration's campaign to legitimate its declared right of "pre-emption" filled most of my fellow discussants with horror and dread. Europeans were also virtually unanimous in their disapproval of Bush's enthusiasm, while governor of Texas, for the death penalty, and shocked in particular at what they deemed to be the moral callousness of his comments regarding the frequency with which he was willing to employ it.

In the U.S. media, such views are routinely dismissed as the products of old-fashioned European anti-Americanism at best, anti-Semitism at worst, or frequently, both. But these views were repeated to me across the political spectrum by conservatives as well as liberals, by "pro-American" writers and thinkers as well as those who had traditionally been aligned with resistance to American power; they were spoken in nations whose leadership had agreed to support the administration in its efforts to organize the global community for war in Iraq as well as in those that opposed it, by Jews and gentiles alike. Whether one shares these views or not, the conclusion is inescapable: in autumn 2002, a consensus had formed across the Atlantic on virtually every significant issue facing the U.S.-Atlantic community that located itself well to the left of the mainstream views that dominated debate in America's SCLM. The neoconservative domination of the U.S. media's foreign policy debate is hardly atypical. Suffice to say that the domestic fault line within European media and intellectual circles is far enough to the left to be considered off the map in our own SCLM.

Fundamental European assumptions across the political spectrum regarding the value of social welfare programs, cultural Puritanism, labor rights, gun control, public financing of elections, public goods for all, and the need to invest in public education might place most editors closer to the center of gravity of a *Nation* magazine editorial board meeting than "responsible" opinion in respectable SCLM circles.

Indeed, the right's ideological offensive of the past few decades has succeeded so thoroughly that the very idea of a genuinely philosophically "liberal" politics has come to mean something quite alien to American politics.

Contemporary intellectual definitions of liberalism derive by common accord from the work of the political theorist John Rawls. The key concept upon which Rawls bases his definition is what he terms the "veil of ignorance"; the kind of social compact based on a structure that would be drawn up by a person who has no idea where he or she fits into it. In other words, such a structure would be equally fair if judged by the person at the bottom as well as the top; the CEO as well as the guy who cleans the toilets.[11] In real-world American politics, this proposition would be considered so utopian as to be laughable. In 2001, the average CEO of a major company received $15.5 million in total compensation, or 245 times, on average, what they paid their employees.[12] The steps that would need to be taken to reach a Rawlsian state in such a situation are politically unthinkable, beginning (and ending) with a steeply progressive income tax, to say nothing of making universally available, high-quality health care, education, housing, public parks, beaches, and last but not least, political power. The ethical philosopher Peter Singer notes, moreover, in his study of the morals of globalization that even Rawls' demanding standards do not take into account our responsibilities as citizens to those who live beyond our borders, in places where starvation, disease, and child mortality are rampant. These too are fundamental liberal causes, almost entirely unmentionable in a society that offers the world's poor barely one-tenth of one percent of its gross domestic product in development aid.[13] Judged by this standard, even to begin to argue on behalf of a genuinely liberal political program is to invite amused condescension . . . at best.

But if we put the question of ideology aside for a moment, it is not hard to see that in 1992 journalists had strong self-interested reasons to prefer Bill Clinton to George Bush. A second Bush administration, peopled with many of the same figures who had served in the three administrations that preceded it, would have meant a full sixteen years without a break during which journalists would be forced to cover the same old guys saying the same old things about the same old issues. What could possibly be the fun in that? More than enough careers had already been made during the Reagan/Bush years, and it was time now to give a new bunch of people a chance to show their stuff.

I would not deny that I sensed a great deal of excitement among the press corps in Little Rock on Election Day 1992, but it had little to do with ideology. Part of the thrill was generational. Bush was part of Reagan's generation; Clinton was, like most reporters, a baby boomer. Part of the exhilaration was substantive. Clinton was king of the political policy wonks, armed and ready with blueprints for a decade's worth of ambitious programs. He and his advisers would make politics fun again in a way that Republican, button-down CEOs could not. Moreover, Democrats generally admit to liking journalists and enjoy both leaking to, and socializing with, them.

They are also not terribly good about disciplining themselves when they disagree with one another—which is most of the time—and hence, prove to be talkative sources. In addition, lest we forget, Clinton's reputation as the world's biggest horndog was by this time well known to all of us. Careers could be made in scandal reporting—just look at David Brock. Paul Gigot, the fiercely conservative columnist, now editor of the *Wall Street Journal's* editorial page, has quipped, "Clinton was a gold mine. I often joke that if I had known back in 1992 what he would do for my career, I probably would have voted for him."[14]

Even with all of these caveats, the case is not closed on the Freedom Forum poll. The study itself turns out to be based on only 139 respondents out of 323 questionnaires mailed, a response rate so low that most social scientists would reject it as inadequately representative. What's more, the responders were not the right 139. Independent investigative journalist Robert Parry contacted the Roper Center in Connecticut, where the results were tabulated, and was given a list of the company affiliations of the original recipients. This too proved problematic. Fewer than 20 percent of the questionnaires were sent to the major elite media outlets such as the *New York Times*, *Washington Post*, CBS, NBC, ABC, *Time*, and *Newsweek*. The bulk went to middle-sized-market papers such as the *Modesto Bee*, the *Denver Post*, and the *Dallas Morning News*. Roughly a quarter went to small-circulation newspapers where the job "bureau chief" actually means "entire bureau." These included the 58,000-circulation *Green Bay (Wis.) Press-Gazette*, the 27,000-circulation *Sheboygan (Wis.) Press*, the *Mississippi Press*, *Fort Collins Coloradoan*, *Grand Junction (Colo.) Daily Sentinel*, and the *Thibodaux (La.) Daily Comet*. The same was true, Parry found, regarding the magazines included. *Time* and *Newsweek* were statistically overshadowed by publications like *Indian Country Today*, *Hill Rag*, *El Pregonero*, *Senior Advocate*, *Small Newspaper Group*, *Washington Citizen*, *Washington Blade*, and *Government Standard*. Interestingly, Parry noted, "What was most dramatically missing from the list were many of the principal conservative journals." This is due, he reasoned, to the fact that many conservative journals are organized as nonprofit corporations in order to be able to solicit tax-deductible donations. While many writers for conservative journals are extremely influential in the national media, they often cannot secure credentials from the congressional press gallery.[15] The net result was that this particular survey, with its tiny numbers and somewhat randomly created data base, could easily have underestimated the conservatives' presence. It certainly overemphasized the influence of people without much influence in the national debate.

Then again, let's not kid ourselves. The percentage of elite journalists who voted for Bill Clinton in 1992 was probably consistent with the percentage he received among all well-educated urban elites, which was pretty high. Most people who fit this profile do indeed hold socially "liberal" views on issues like gun control, abortion, and school prayer, and I have no doubts that most journalists do too. The journalists whose alleged biases concern conservatives, live, according to the current parlance, in "blue" states and, when it comes to social issues, carry with them typical "blue state" values. The vast majority are pro-choice, pro-gun control, pro-separation of church and state, pro-feminism, pro-affirmative action, and supportive of gay rights.

Most journalists, as the sociologist Herbert Gans explained, are also congenitally "reformist." They believe in the possibility of improving things or they would not have chosen the profession in the first place.[16] But both reformist sympathy and the "elite" association can cut more than one way, in political terms. Beginning with the 1980 election of Ronald Reagan and accelerating with the "Gingrich Revolution" of 1994, conservatives began to capture the language of reformism, in opposition to what Gingrich termed "reactionary liberalism." Much of the media bought into this etymological transformation and hence, a bias toward "reform" gives little clue about a person's ideology anymore. Journalists were naturally in sympathy with liberal (and in the case of John McCain, conservative) efforts to reform our campaign finance laws. But they also appeared quite well-disposed to conservative efforts to "reform" the nation's Social Security system so as to introduce private stock market accounts— at least before the Nasdaq crashed.

Also, lest we forget, journalists are not entirely immune to the seductions of affluence. While they are not nearly as well paid as the nation's corporate, legal, or medical elite, high-level Washington and New York journalists do make considerably more money than most Americans. They have spouses who do too, and hence, live pretty well. According to a study conducted by the sociologist David Croteau, 95 percent of elite journalists' households earned more than $50,000 a year, and 31 percent earned more than $150,000. He points out, "High levels of income tend to be associated with conservative views on economic issues such as tax policy and federal spending."[17] And journalists are no different. The journalists' views on economic matters are generally consistent with their privileged position on the socioeconomic ladder, and, hence, well to the right of most Americans. They are more sympathetic to corporations, less sympathetic to government-mandated social programs, and far more ideologically committed to free trade than to the protection of jobs than are their fellow citizens.[18] Polls, of course, are always of limited value, and comparing ones taken at different moments in history, based on differently worded questions, invites rhetorical abuse. I would not take any of these individual statistics to the bank. Nevertheless the overall pattern is undeniably consistent, and it is not "liberal."

But if top Washington journalists are personally social liberals and economic conservatives, one must still ask what it means insofar as identifying a bias in coverage. The answer to that question has to be, "it is not entirely clear."

When it comes to news content, the journalists are often the low people on the totem pole. They are "labor," or if they are lucky, "talent." They are not "management." They do not get to decide by themselves how a story should be cast. As *Washington Post* columnist Gene Weingarten put it in a column he wrote about an editorial disagreement with his bosses:

> My company is a large, liberal-minded institution that thrives on convivial collegial consensus among persons who—as human people professionally partnered in common goal-oriented pursuits—are complete coequals right up to the time an actual disagreement occurs. At this point, the rules of the game change slightly. We go from Candy Land to rock-paper-scissors. Editors are rock. Writers are those gaily colored wussy plastic paper clips. In short, I was given a choice: I could see the lucent wisdom of my editors' point of view and alter the column as directed, or I could elect to write a different column altogether, or (in an organization this large and diverse, there are always a multitude of options) I could be escorted to the front door by Security.[19]

Weingarten is a much-beloved columnist and so is given quite a bit of freedom. Moreover, he does not cover politics—this column was published in the Style section, which affords him even more latitude. But even so, print journalists have editors who have editors above them who have publishers above them who, in most cases, have corporate executives above them. Television journalists have producers and executive producers and network executives who worry primarily about ratings, advertising profits, and the sensibilities of their audience, their advertisers, and their corporate owners. When it comes to content, it is these folks who matter, perhaps more than anyone.

Examine, for a moment, the corporate structure of the industry for which the average top-level journalist labors. Ben Bagdikian, former dean of the journalism school at the University of California at Berkeley, has been chronicling the concentration of media ownership in five separate editions of his book, *The Media Monopoly*, which was first published in 1983 when the number of companies that controlled the information flow to the rest of us—the potential employment pool for journalists—was fifty. Today we are down to six.[20]

Consider the following: When AOL took over TimeWarner, it also took over: Warner Brothers Pictures, Morgan Creek, New Regency, Warner Brothers Animation, a partial stake in Savoy Pictures, Little Brown & Co., Bullfinch, Back Bay, Time-Life Books, Oxmoor House, Sunset Books, Warner Books, the Book-of-the-Month Club, Warner/Chappell Music, Atlantic Records, Warner Audio Books, Elektra, Warner Brothers Records, Time-Life Music, Columbia House, a 40 percent stake in Seattle's Sub-Pop records, *Time* magazine, *Fortune, Life, Sports Illustrated, Vibe, People, Entertainment Weekly, Money, In Style, Martha Stewart Living, Sunset, Asia Week, Parenting*, Weight Watchers, *Cooking Light*, DC Comics, 49 percent of the Six Flags theme parks, Movie World and Warner Brothers parks, HBO, Cinemax, Warner

Brothers Television, partial ownership of Comedy Central, E!, Black Entertainment Television, Court TV, the Sega channel, the Home Shopping Network, Turner Broadcasting, the Atlanta Braves and Atlanta Hawks, World Championship Wrestling, Hanna-Barbera Cartoons, New Line Cinema, Fine Line Cinema, Turner Classic Movies, Turner Pictures, Castle Rock productions, CNN, CNN Headline News, CNN International, CNN/SI, CNN Airport Network, CNNfi, CNN radio, TNT, WTBS, and the Cartoon Network. The situation is not substantially different at Disney, Viacom, General Electric, the News Corporation, or Bertelsmann.[21]

The point of the above is to illustrate the degree of potential conflict of interest for a journalist who seeks to tell the truth, according to the old *New York Times* slogan, "without fear or favor," about not only any one of the companies its parent corporation may own, but also those with whom one of the companies may compete, or perhaps a public official or regulatory body that one of them may lobby, or even an employee at one of them with whom one of his superiors may be sleeping, or divorcing, or remarrying, or one of *their* competitors, or competitors' lovers, ex-lovers, and so on. While the consumer is generally unaware of these conflicts, the possibilities are almost endless—unless one is going to restrict one's journalism to nothing but preachy pabulum and celebrity gossip. The natural fear for journalists in this context is direct censorship on behalf of the parent's corporate interests. The number of incidents of even remotely documented corporate censorship is actually pretty rare. But focusing on examples of direct censorship in the U.S. media misses the point. Rarely does some story that is likely to arouse concern ever go far enough to actually need to be censored at the corporate level. The reporter, the editor, the producer, and the executive producer all understand implicitly that their jobs depend in part on keeping their corporate parents happy.

Television viewers received a rare education on the corporate attitude toward even the slightest hint of criticism of the big cheese when, on the morning after Disney took over ABC, *Good Morning America* host Charles Gibson interviewed Thomas S. Murphy, chairman of Capital Cities/ABC, and Disney's Michael D. Eisner. "Where's the little guy in the business anymore?" Gibson asked. "Is this just a giant that forces everybody else out?" Murphy, now Gibson's boss, replied, "Charlie, let me ask you a question. Wouldn't you be proud to be associated with Disney? . . . I'm quite serious about this."[22]

While some editors and producers profess to be able to offer the same scrutiny to properties associated with their own companies that they offer to the rest of the world, in most cases, it taxes one's credulity to believe them. Journalists, myself included, are usually inclined to give their friends a break. If you work for a company that owns a lot of other companies, then you automatically have many such friends in journalism, in business, and in government. Michael Kinsley, the founding editor of Slate.com, which is funded entirely by the Microsoft Corporation, did the world a favor when he admitted, "Slate will never give Microsoft the skeptical scrutiny it requires as a powerful institution in American society—any more than *Time* will suffiently scrutinize Time Warner. No institution can reasonably be expected to audit itself. . . . The standard to insist on is that the sins be of omission, not distortion. There will be no major investigations of Microsoft in Slate."[23] Eisner said much the same thing, perhaps inadvertently, when he admitted (or one might say, "instructed"), "I would prefer ABC not to cover Disney. . . . I think it's inappropriate."[24]

Media magnates have always sought to reign in their reporters, albeit with mixed success. In 1905, Standard Oil baron John D. Rockefeller predicted of the New York *World*, in 1905, "The owner of the *World* is also a large owner of property, and I presume that, in common with other newspaper owners who are possessed of wealth, his eyes are beginning to be opened to the fact that he is like Samson, taking the initiative to pull the building down upon his head."[25] Similarly, advertisers have always attempted to exert pressure on the news and occasionally succeeded. What has changed is the scale of these pressures, given the size and the scope of the new media conglomerates, and the willingness of news executives to interfere with the news-gathering process up and down the line. One-third of the local TV news directors surveyed by the Pew Project for Excellence in Journalism in 2000 indicated that they had been pressured to avoid negative stories about advertisers, or to do positive ones.[26] Again, by the time you get to actual pressure on an editor or writer, a great many steps have already been taken. A 2000 Pew Research Center study found that more than 40 percent of journalists felt a need to self-censor their work, either by avoiding certain stories or softening the ones they wrote, to benefit the interests of the organizations for which they work.[27] As the editors of the *Columbia Journalism Review* put it: "The truth about self-censorship is that it is widespread, as common in newsrooms as deadline pressure, a virus that eats away at the journalistic mission."[28] And it doesn't leave much room for liberalism.

Conservative critics of the SCLM often neglect not only the power of owners and advertisers, but also the profit motive to determine the content of the news. Any remotely attentive consumer of news has noticed, in recent years, a turn away from what journalists like to term "spinach," or the kind of news that citizens require to carry out their duties as intelligent, informed members of a political democracy, toward pudding—the sweet, nutritionally vacant fare that is the stock in trade of news outlets. The sense of a news division acting as a "public trust," the characterization of the major networks throughout the Cold War—has given way to one that views them strictly as profit centers, which must carry the weight of shareholder demands the same way a TV sitcom or children's theme park must.

The net result has been the viral growth of a form of "news" that owes more to sit-coms and theme parks than to old-fashioned ideas of public and civic life. Instead of John Kennedy and Nikita Khrushchev as the iconic images of the world of "news," we are presented the comings and goings of Madonna, O. J. Simpson, Princess

Diana, Gary Condit, and Chandra Levy. Again, this tabloid contagion, which afflicts almost all commercial news programs and newspapers, has many unhappy implications, but one obvious one is that the less actual "news" one covers, the less opportunity alleged liberals have to slant it.

Moreover, the deeply intensified demand for profit places renewed pressure on almost all media outlets to appeal to the wealthiest possible consumer base, which pretty much rules out the poor and the oppressed as the topic of investigative entrepreneurship. As *New York*'s Michael Wolff observed of the creation of two new "leisure" sections in the *New York Times* and the *Wall Street Journal,* "They don't want to be old-fashioned newspapers at all, but information brands, sensibility vehicles, targeted upscale-consumer media outlets. . . . The battle that has been joined is for the hearts and minds of the 2 million or 3 million wealthiest and best-educated people in the nation." In the not-so-distant past, Wolff notes, this kind of market-driven, consumerist definition of news would have inspired journalistic purists into principled opposition. But, "There's very little of that now: Any journalist with any career prospects is also a marketer, and packager, and all-around design- and demographic-conscious media professional. Every journalist is also a worried journalist, united with the business side in concerns about 'being viable.'"[29] Even in a tough year like 2001, media companies were demanding—and receiving—profit margins in the 20 percent range.[30] There is not much room for an overriding liberal bias on the great issues of the day between that particular rock and hard place, I'm afraid, even with the best (or worst) of intentions. Reporters could be the most liberal people on earth. But for all the reasons discussed above, it would hardly matter. They simply do not "make" the news.

The intensified emphasis on profits of recent years has resulted in a few high-profile scandals in the business. The *Los Angeles Times* sold its soul to the Staples Center in exchange for a pittance in paid advertising, offering to share advertising revenue in a phony magazine supplement designed to look like a genuine news report. Meanwhile, ABC News almost gave Ted Koppel, its most distinguished journalist, his walking papers for a comedy program with lower ratings but higher advertising profits. *San Jose Mercury-News* publisher Jay Harris resigned in a loud and eloquent protest against Knight Ridder's adherence to the "tyranny of the markets" that he said was destroying his newspaper.[31] But no less important than the scandals are the non-scandals, the ones that are perhaps even more egregious in terms of the news values but, for whatever reason, are never brought before the public.

These priorities were never more evident than in the winter of 2002 during the long, drawn-out debate over campaign finance reform. The dramatic events in question dominated domestic coverage for weeks, if not months—a fact that many conservatives attributed to liberal media bias, since Americans, while supportive of reform, did not appear to be passionately interested in the story. But even within this avalanche of coverage, virtually no one in the media thought it worthwhile to mention that media industry lobbyists had managed to murder a key provision of the bill that would have forced the networks to offer candidates their least expensive advertising rates.[32] True, it was a hard story for which to create snappy visuals; "Dead behind the eyes" in Dan Rather's parlance.[33] But why is that not viewed as a challenge rather than a cause for capitulation? Political campaigns have become a get-rich-quick scheme for local television station owners, whose profit margins reflect the high rates they charge for political advertisements. This is no small factor in the mad pursuit of money that characterizes virtually every U.S. political campaign and makes a mockery of our claims to be a "one-person, one-vote" democracy.

Estimates of the income derived from these advertisements are up to $750 million per election cycle and continue to rise.[34] The provision in question, originally passed by the Senate by a 69 to 31 margin, died in the House of Representatives following a furious lobbying campaign by the National Association of Broadcasters and the cable television industry. After the House vote, *Broadcasting & Cable* magazine reported, "Back in their headquarters, the National Association of Broadcasters popped the champagne, deeply appreciative of the strong bipartisan vote stripping the [advertising provision]." The broadcasters' victory left the United States alone among 146 countries, according to one study, in refusing to provide free television time to political candidates.[35]

The silent treatment given the advertising amendment was, in many ways, a repeat of the non-coverage of an even more significant story: The 1996 Telecommunications Act. When the Republicans took over Congress in 1994, the party leadership invited telecommunications corporate heads to Washington, sat down with them, and asked, "What do you want?"[36] The result, after many millions of dollars worth of lobbying bills, was a milestone of deregulation that vastly increased the ability of the big media conglomerates to increase (and combine) their market share in almost every medium. This expansion came, virtually without exception, at the expense of the smaller voices in those markets. The net result turned out to be a significant diminution in the opportunities for citizens to experience, and participate in, democratic debate.[37] Based on a quick perusal of TV listings for 1995, apparently not one of the major TV news magazines of Westinghouse/CBS (*48 Hours, 60 Minutes*), Disney/Cap Cities/ABC (*Primetime Live, 20/20*), or General Electric/NBC (*Dateline NBC*) devoted even a minute of their 300 or so hours of airtime to the bill or the issues that lay beneath it.[38] Where, one might ask, were the SCLM when their corporate owners were rewriting the rules of democratic debate to increase their own profits?

Ultimately, as Tom Johnson, former publisher of the *LA Times* and later president of CNN, would observe,

It is not reporters or editors, but the owners of the media who decide the quality of the news . . . produced by or televised by their news departments. It is they who most often select, hire, fire, and promote the editors and publishers, top general managers, news directors, and managing editors—the journalists—who run the newsrooms. . . . Owners determine newsroom budgets, and the tiny amount of time and space allotted to news versus advertising. They set the standard of quality by the quality of the people they choose and the news policy they embrace. Owners decide how much profit should be produced from their media properties. Owners decide what quality levels they are willing to support by how well or how poorly they pay their journalists.[39]

To ignore the power of the money at stake to determine the content of news in the decisions of these executives—given the role money seems to play in every other aspect of our society—is indefensibly childish and naive. The two heads of AOL Time Warner, Gerald Levin and Steve Case, took home a combined $241 million in 2001. Michael Eisner of Disney pulled down nearly $73 million.[40] Leave aside the fact that stocks of each of these companies performed miserably in the same years, something you will probably not find discussed much in the myriad media properties they control. Ask yourself if the men and women who earn numbers like these are really sending forth aggressive investigators of financial and political malfeasance, charged, as the saying goes, to "afflict the comfortable and comfort the afflicted"? As longtime editor Harold Evans pointed out, in a situation like the current one, "The problem that many media organizations face is not to stay in business, but to stay in journalism."[41]

# 3

## The Punditocracy One

### *Television*

YOU CAN ARGUE ON VARIOUS FRONTS, with different degrees of nuance, that in some instances, bias skews liberal and in others, conservative. But the punditocracy is another matter. This group of commentators who, together with the White House, define the shape and scope of public debate in the elite media is dominated by two qualities: ignorant belligerence and sitcom-like silliness. The pundits are the conservatives' shock troops. Even the ones who constantly complain about alleged liberal control of the media cannot ignore the vast advantage their side enjoys when it comes to airing their views on television, in the opinion pages, on the radio, and on the Internet.

Take a look at the Sunday talk-shows, the cable chat fests, the op-ed pages and opinion magazines, and the radio talk shows. It can be painful, I know, but try it. How many liberals do you see compared with conservatives? With the exception of Bill Moyers, who appears only on PBS, the most liberal commentator on the broadcast network news for the past half decade has been George Stephanopoulos. When he was appointed to succeed Sam Donaldson and Cokie Roberts on ABC's *This Week*, Dick Morris, a Fox News analyst (and Stephanopoulos's former rival as a Clinton Administration adviser), complained that the appointment "represents the final enshrinement of the liberal establishment media at ABC. Discarding even the pretense of nonpartisanship, the network hires a liberal politician, not even journalist, as its new anchor."[1] But as Paul Glastris, editor of the neoliberal *Washington Monthly*, observed, before Stephanopoulos was appointed anchor, "Stephanopoulos is supposed to be the liberal counterweight to George Will on ABC's *This Week*. He performs the role well when he chooses to, often puncturing Will's sophisms with the sharp edge of a well-chosen fact. Just as often, however, Stephanopoulos's palpable desire to be accepted as a journalist leads him to value-neutral how-the-game-is-played analysis, or to gestures of unreciprocated fair-mindedness ('You know, I have to agree with George Will on this one')."[2] Just before he was elevated to be the host of ABC's Sunday program, Stephanopoulos received the praise of the *Wall Street*

*Journal*'s far-right editorial page. Its television columnist, Tunku Varadarahan, termed him "a good egg" and a "a figure of loathing in Clintonite circles."[3] Yet even this "liberal" voice appears to have been eliminated by ABC by virtue of Stephanopoulos's ascension to the host's chair.

On the debut program of ABC's *This Week with George Stephanopoulos*, the program contained the extremely conservative George F. Will, but no liberals at all. Condoleezza Rice, the Bush administration's national security adviser, was respectfully questioned, as was Democratic Senate Majority Leader Tom Daschle, though the latter was asked to respond to an extremely critical editorial about the Democrats' position on Iraq from the hard-line neoconservative editors of the *New Republic*. During the program's round table, conservatives were represented by Will and *Newsweek*'s Fareed Zakaria. The nonpartisan ABC News reporter Michel Martin—another regular—joined as well. Stephanopoulos moderated from a disinterested political perspective. Not a single liberal syllable was spoken during the entire program. And while President Bush's desire to engage Iraq in a war had been opposed for months by top former members of his father's administration, numerous retired top military officers, and extremely influential members of the Republican Party in Congress—to say nothing of virtually every world leader save Israel and England—not a single guest or regular panelist spoke up on behalf of these objections.[4]

The same circumstances held a week later when the guest panelist was Peter Beinart, editor of the Iraq-obsessed *New Republic*. Zakaria returned for week three and was soon signed up as a permanent member. The *Wall Street Journal* political editor, John Harwood, was invited to drop by for week four. Meanwhile, viewers hoping to hear a single panelist take issue with George Bush's (or George Will's) constant drumbeat for war were still waiting in vain. While a lineup of just hawkish conservatives and straight reporters is, in punditocracy terms, unremarkable, its opposite—one of just liberals and reporters, is barely imaginable. While media cops like Howard Kurtz examined the program for evidence of "lean[ing] toward the Democrats"—forever in the grip of the SCLM myth—no one in the media even mentioned the absence of a liberal or dovish voice.[5] And why should they? It's the norm.

Across virtually the entire television punditocracy, unabashed conservatives dominate, leaving lone liberals to offer themselves up to be beaten up by gangs of marauding right-wingers, most of whom voice views much further toward their end of the spectrum than does any regularly televised liberal. Grover Norquist, the right's brilliant political organizer, explains his team's advantage by virtue of the mindset of modern conservatism. "The conservative press is self-consciously conservative and self-consciously part of the team," he noted. "The liberal press is much larger, but at the same time it sees itself as the establishment press. So it's conflicted. Sometimes it thinks it needs to be critical of both sides." Indeed, Glastris observes, "liberal pundits . . . seem far more at ease on journalistic neutral ground, analyzing the strengths and weaknesses of both sides, rather than in vigorously defending Democrats."[6] Think about it. Who among the liberals can be counted upon to be as ideological, as relentless, and as nakedly partisan as George Will, Bob Novak, Pat Buchanan, Bay Buchanan, William Bennett, William Kristol, Fred Barnes, John McLaughlin, Charles Krauthammer, Paul Gigot, Ben Wattenberg, Oliver North, Kate O'Beirne, Tony Blankley, Ann Coulter, Sean Hannity, Tony Snow, Laura Ingraham, Jonah Goldberg, William F. Buckley Jr., Bill O'Reilly, Alan Keyes, Tucker Carlson, Brit Hume, CNBC's roundtable of the self-described "wild men" of the *Wall Street Journal* editorial page, and on and on? In fact, it's hard to come up with a single journalist/pundit appearing on television who is even remotely as far to the left of the mainstream spectrum as most of these conservatives are to the right. These people, as Glastris noted, "are ideological warriors who attempt with every utterance to advance their cause."[7] To find the same combination of conviction, partisanship, and ideological extremism on the far left, a network would need to convene a "roundtable" featuring Noam Chomsky, Alexander Cockburn, Vanessa Redgrave, and Fidel Castro. Meanwhile, Novak—who has enjoyed at least three shows at a time for decades and sometimes seems to show up at least twenty times a week, and who earned a reputation as the most ideological half of a duo nicknamed "Errors and No-Facts"—insists with a straight face that ABC's consideration of Stephanopoulos to head the Sunday show in the spring of 2002 "prove[d] that the liberals control the media."[8]

It is perhaps indicative of how few liberal pundit/journalists have been given the opportunity to develop their television talents that, when CNN decided to revitalize *Crossfire* in the spring of 2002, the network chose two political operatives, Paul Begala and James Carville, to oppose the right-wing journalists Novak and Tucker Carlson. (The liberals were replacing another political operative, Bill Press, who replaced the brilliant, but not-so-liberal, journalist, Mike Kinsley. Before Kinsley, the job was held by Tom Braden, an aging, ex-CIA agent.) Shortly after the arrival of Begala and Carville, Novak lamented that previously, he could "do [the show] in my sleep," and now worried it would "take a few years to get used to" the new situation.[9] Also significantly, as soon as Begala and Carville joined up, Republicans tried to start a boycott of the program, so shocked were they by the experience of actually being asked tough questions. The coda to this story is that MSNBC followed up CNN's move by hiring Press and Buchanan to host their own two-hour show together. Once again the "respectable" continuum of views on television was displayed for all to see: a likable, establishment Washington-based liberal, and a likable, radical right-wing populist with a soft spot for Nazis.[10] All was well in the land of the punditocracy.

Done well, punditry can serve a crucial function in our democracy. This is, in part, an accident of American journalistic history. The media of most nations do not profess much faith in the notion of objective news-gathering. Journalists in Europe, for instance, freely mix fact and opinion to create a richer context for their reports and trust readers and viewers to know the difference and make up their own minds. Newspapers are more explicitly ideological there and readers generally choose their paper according to the view that matches their own. By and large, those nation's elite media offer fewer pundits but more sophisticated journalism.

But where journalism adopts the pretense of reporting only "the facts ma'am," the need for "opinion writers," dedicated to placing the news in a larger and more useful context for readers, rises accordingly. If reporters are doing their best to stick to a strict definition of facts—or, what is more common, the quotes of politicians and their press secretaries who attempt to spin these facts—then the creation of an understandable context for these facts, be it historical, political, sociological, economic, or even psychological, must be left to someone else. Even people who devote themselves to trying to remain informed cannot do so on every issue of importance—not if they have jobs, families, or lives that require them to occasionally turn off the TV, the computer, or put down their newspaper. Pundits can be particularly influential in the United States owing to the amazing degree of ignorance and/or apathy many Americans share regarding politics and public affairs. In a nation where six of ten high school students lack what the Department of Education terms "even a basic knowledge of U.S. history," and where more people can give pollsters the names of all three Stooges than any three members of the Supreme Court, the importance of someone helping out with a reasoned and intelligent contextual view of events can hardly be overstated.[11]

This being America, much of our punditry takes place on television. The phenomenon, which had been a drizzle during the golden age of print pundits in the 1950s and early 1960s, grew rapidly in the 1980s and, with the explosion of cable news in the mid-1990s, became a kind of flood.[12] As recently as 1992, the world punditry encompassed was still quite small. In a book published that year that gave the punditocracy its name, I defined its television members as the chairs on NBC's *McLaughlin Group* and *Meet the Press*, CBS's *Inside Washington*, ABC's *This Week*, and CNN's *The Capital Gang*, and *Crossfire*. Its print portfolio consisted of "the op-ed columns of the *New York Times*, the *Washington Post*, the *Wall Street Journal*, the top editorships of the *New Republic* and a few newsweekly columnists." Various experts, ex-officials, and think-tank mavens fleshed out its outer circle. Not many people outside academia had yet heard about the World Wide Web (as it was originally called), and cable news, which included only CNN, was still pretty much devoted to, well, news. In the mid-1990s, however, the advent of three all-news cable stations, coupled with the nearly overnight explosion of the Net, vastly inflated the punditocracy's numbers. As with major league baseball, the quality fell as the numbers rose. Players who should have ended their careers in high school or college ended up in the majors, and the level of public discourse catapulted south.

Few people, one imagines, give much thought to just what qualifies someone to be a television pundit. In fact, the criteria upon which network executives and news producers base their choices largely relies on television "Q-ratings" rather than knowledge or expertise. For pundit chat, these qualities usually include: not being too fat or too ugly; the ability to speak in short sentences and project an engaging personality; and a willingness to speak knowingly about matters about which one knows little or nothing. Believe it or not, ignorance is actually an advantage, since it allows you to ignore the inherent complexity of any given problem with a concise quip and a clear conscience. As *Capital Gang* panelist Margaret Carlson observed, "The less you know about something, the better off you are. . . . They're looking for the person who can sound learned without confusing the matter with too much knowledge. I'm one of the people without too much knowledge. I'm perfect."[13] Carlson's honesty is rare and engaging. More typical is Fred Barnes, executive editor of the *Weekly Standard*, who once boasted, "I can speak to almost anything with a lot of authority." It was on this epochal program that John McLaughlin conducted a roundtable in which he asked his guests to "give a grade to the planet earth." McLaughlin gave it a "B," and I quote his justification in its entirety: "Overcoming nationalism and a general spirit of internationalism."[14] The ability to say such things on television with a straight face is considered prima facie qualification for the job of network television pundit.

Owing to its tangled roots in personal journalism, political commentary, and television production values, the punditocracy never developed a recognizable code of ethics. This situation was further complicated by the entry into the profession in the early 1980s of large numbers of political operatives who could not even pretend to consider themselves journalists. No longer a reward for the profession's most distinguished members, the job opened up to political deal-makers, speechwriters, press flacks, and professional ideologues. Moreover, there were almost no rules of professional conduct. George Will felt free to coach Ronald Reagan on his debating technique and then praise his student's "thoroughbred performance" on ABC News immediately following the debate. Morton Kondracke and Fred Barnes of Fox News Channel's *The Beltway Boys* sell their dinner conversation to wealthy American Express Platinum Card holders "by invitation only." Robert Novak hosts pricey off-the-record briefings by Cabinet officials for corporate executives, refusing admission to journalists.

The money available to celebrity journalists for corporate appearances is fantastic. Steve and Cokie Roberts, for instance, commanded $45,000 for a joint appearance at a banking conference in Chicago in 1994. They also accepted a paid gig from the Philip Morris tobacco corporation, though Cokie claimed to be sick at the last moment and Steve went alone. Buckraking journalists are understandably reluctant to discuss this aspect of their lives. A spokesman responded to a journalist's inquiry that Cokie Roberts's corporate speaking fees were "not something that in any way, shape, or form should be discussed in public."[15] Though Roberts is certainly among the most enthusiastic of buckrakers, she is hardly alone. Television personalities can augment their income by hundreds of thousands of dollars this way, and there is almost no work involved, beyond attending a cocktail party and giving a canned speech. The obvious ethical problem involved with a journalist who covers Congress taking money from corporations that lobby Congress has received considerable atten- tion and many media companies have banned the practice. What has gone relatively unnoticed, however, is the manner in which the mere existence of this money skews the media rightward. Journalists are not being paid tens of thousands to give a single speech by public school children, welfare mothers, individual investors, health-care consumers, or even (in most instances) unions. They are taking it from banks, insur- ance companies, investment houses, and all manner of unindicted CEOs. If they want to continue to be invited, they had better not write anything that might offend these people. It is a rule of thumb that speaking bureaus prefer to represent conser- vatives because it is they who command interest from corporations. For an aspiring pundit, eager for the most lucrative possible career, speaking fees act as a built-in ide- ological incentive to side with big business over the "little guy." James Fallows quotes ex-*Washington Post* editor Ben Bradlee making the point in typically blunt fashion: "If the Insurance Institute of America, if there is such a thing, pays $10,000 to make a speech, don't tell me you haven't been corrupted. You can say you haven't and you can say you will attack insurance issues in the same way, but you won't. You can't." Alan Murray of the *Wall Street Journal*, a frequent television commentator, added, "You tell me what is the difference between somebody who works full time for the National Association of Realtors and somebody who takes $40,000 a year in speaking fees from Realtor groups. It's not clear to me there's a big distinction."[16]

For the past two decades, the most influential example in the pundit world has undoubtedly been the *McLaughlin Group*.[17] More than twenty years old, the show flatters itself—and its corporate sponsor, GE—that it is providing some kind of pub- lic service. It is even offered on PBS in many cities, and its Web site features such faux educational trappings as classroom guides and discussion-group questions, along with $50 golf shirts. And while ratings have dropped steadily and precipitously for the past few years, this is due largely to the fact that its very format has nearly taken over our media world. Entire cable networks are devoted to the ethos of the *McLaughlin Group*, and even the old reliables of respectable political discourse—like NBC's *Meet the Press* and CBS's *Face the Nation*—are dancing to its dissonant tune.

In addition to debasing the culture of journalism, the *McLaughlin Group* also aided its corporate sponsors and conservative friends in shifting the foundation of political debate in the heartland of Reagan country—where it remains to this day. The group set up a center of gravity in which two extreme right-wing ideologues, Buchanan and Novak, were "balanced" by the wishy-washy neoconservatism of Kondracke and the bourbon-laced, no-nonsense nonpartisanship of Germond—a down-the-line reporter with liberal leanings but few political axes to grind. The conservative McLaughlin acted—and I do mean "acted"—as referee. The net result was to bestow respectability on views that had only recently been the exclusive property of the caveman right and to marginalize liberalism beyond "responsible" debate. In this regard, McLaughlin both inspired and continues to reflect the political makeup of the contemporary punditocracy. As *Weekly Standard* writer Andrew Ferguson described it, the debate's final form—at least on the polite shows—went something like this:

> Sitting side by side before the camera, host and pundit enter into an unwritten compact. The guest gives pithy answers of rock-solid certitude. The host agrees never again to mention what those answers are. Exceptions are permitted, when, for example, the guest makes some outlandishly implausible guess—say, Alan Keyes will sweep 50 states in the presidential election next November—that, God help us, proves correct. Otherwise, pundits' opinions are supposed to sail through the air, bounce off the satellites, enter the viewer's home, roil around a minute, then disappear into the ether where they belong.[18]

The most influential of conservative television personalities is probably ABC's George F. Will, who is also a columnist for *Newsweek* and the *Washington Post*, and formerly a panelist on *Agronsky and Company* until ABC made him give it up.[19] Will's first editor, the *Washington Post's* Philip Geyelin, noted that Will observed that when he began as a columnist, he never had the chance to develop even an "elementary sense of journalistic propriety," and this has frequently marred his career. When informed that his trial period had ended and the *Washington Post* Writers Group was ready to syndicate him nationally, Will asked, "Does this mean I have to stop writing speeches for Jesse Helms?"[20] Will failed to let his editors know of a purloined copy of the other side's debate preparation materials in the possession of a Reagan aide and Will confidant, David Stockman, and even touched up the occasional speech by President Reagan. Many years later, in May 1995, Will spoke up on ABC's *This Week* against the Clinton administration's plan to impose a tariff on Japanese luxury cars without mentioning that his wife, Mari Maseng, was being paid $200,000 a year as a registered foreign agent for the Japan Automobile Manufacturers Association. Will thought the potential for conflict of interest over a mere $200,000 was "just too silly" for comment.[21] Well, perhaps, but isn't that interesting as well?

As a pundit, Will wears his learning—puffed up by a staff of "quote-boys"—with a kind of comic self-assurance, peppering his columns with aphorisms by famous writers and philosophers whether relevant or not, flaunting his close friendships to presidents and presidential contenders, and practically daring anyone to challenge him. Will is a complete wash-out as a Lippmann-like political philosopher. His most significant attempt to write a book-length tome on "statecraft versus soulcraft" read, as one *Washington Monthly* reviewer put it, "like Monty Python's shooting script of Bartlett's."[22] But the truth is, for all the journalistic corruption Will's personal and professional relationships suggest, he is quite a good pundit. He works hard to make complex issues understandable and writes with considerable felicity. He has a gift for speaking concisely and memorably on television and makes no bones about his ideological obsessions. While he has a thuggish streak intellectually, this may be as much a function of the brevity demanded of the form in which he operates as it is of his proclivity for the ideological cheap shot.

But Will's conservative colleagues who dominate the chat-show airwaves and cable lines cannot honestly be said to hold to even his compromised standards. Cable TV networks love to broadcast pundit chat shows because they are so cheap to produce. As Tim Rutten explained it in the *Los Angeles Times*, all that is necessary is to "build a sound stage, install a performing pundit with more predictable opinions than ideas and encourage as much snarling as possible. Even if one of your personalities becomes successful enough to command a salary in the millions, it's still cheaper by far than maintaining bureaus and paying field reporters and experienced producers to gather and broadcast news."[23]

The undisputed King of Cable today is Fox's Bill O'Reilly, who has successfully cast himself as the tribune of average America. "I understand working-class Americans. I'm as lower-middle-class as they come," says O'Reilly, host of the top-rated political talk show on cable, a number one best-selling author, and a popular radio host as well. "We're the only show from a working-class point of view," he once told the *Washington Post*.[24] "Class," boasts O'Reilly, is his "bottom line."[25] But O'Reilly has a few confusing ideas about what the words "working class" and "middle class" imply to most people. His Fox News contract is estimated to be worth $20 million, which would make it hard to keep in touch with working-class financial woes.[26] He does not go to bars, where the kinds of workers he professes to admire tend to congregate, and while he proudly claims to drive a second-hand car, it's a Lexus. O'Reilly claims to be a political independent but he is a registered Republican, long unknown to most Americans as the working-class party. O'Reilly is pro-gun control, pro-choice, and willing to consider measures to control global warming. So his views are genuinely more nuanced than the typical Limbaugh-style dittohead. But there are plenty of reasons to question his boast that he is "the first person in this country to command a national audience and bring working-class sensibility to the program."[27]

In addition to his alleged affection and connection to working stiffs without $20 million paychecks, O'Reilly is deeply relaxed about the factual basis for the arguments he makes on TV. He even goes as far as to mock his better-informed guests when they insist on offering evidence to refute his baseless assertions. Fairness and Accuracy in Reporting compiled a host of these examples, and to the degree that any of O'Reilly's fans would like to believe him to be an honest and fair-minded interlocutor, it is not a pretty sight. Among the highlights compiled by Peter Hart:

- During an interview with National Organization for Women president Kim Gandy (*O'Reilly Factor*, February 5, 2002), O'Reilly claimed that "58 percent of single-mom homes are on welfare." When Gandy questioned that figure, O'Reilly held firm: "You can't say no, Miss Gandy. That's the stat. You can't just dismiss it. . . . It's 58 percent. That's what it is from the federal government." But by the next broadcast (February 6, 2002), O'Reilly was revising his accounting: "At this point, we have this from Washington, and it's bad. Fifty-two percent of families receiving public assistance are headed by a single mother, 52 percent." Not only is that a different number, it's the converse of the statistic he offered the previous night—not the percentage of households headed by single mothers that receive welfare, but the percentage of families receiving public assistance headed by single mothers. That's a distinction that O'Reilly did not attempt to clarify; rather, he seemed unapologetic about emphatically putting forward an inaccurate statistic the night before. The following night (February 7, 2002), O'Reilly came up with more solid figures, but they bore no resemblance to his original numbers: About 14 percent of single mothers receive federal welfare benefits—less than one-fourth of his earlier claim. (He suggested that food stamps ought to be considered a kind of welfare, but that only gets him to 33 percent—still 25 percentage points short.) O'Reilly explained that "It's really hard to get a stat to say how many single moms percentage-wise get government assistance," though he'd found it easy enough to pull one out of the air just three nights earlier.

- O'Reilly re-wrote diplomatic history during an interview with James Zogby of the Arab American Institute (April 2, 2002). After Zogby argued that Israeli settlements were an obstacle to peace between Israel and Palestine, O'Reilly countered that, during the Camp David negotiations in July 2000, the offer made by Israeli Prime Minister Ehud Barak "would have given 90 percent of those settlements back"—an idea he credited to "what every single American expert who has seen that says." In fact, O'Reilly got the proportion of settlements Barak was prepared to give up almost backward: Barak promised Israelis that any deal with the Palestinians would involve "80 percent of the settlers in settlement blocks under our sovereignty" (*Jerusalem Post*, September 13, 2000). When Zogby pointed out O'Reilly's error, the host said he would welcome any former diplomats who could prove him wrong: "I'll put them on tomorrow," he said—but didn't.

- O'Reilly frequently refuses to believe his guests—even when they cite a source. When one *Factor* guest remarked (March 1, 2002) that "60 percent of all people will live in poverty for one year of their life," O'Reilly shot back: "Not in the United States . . . No, that's bogus. I mean, that's a socialist stat. You can believe it if you want to, but it's not true." When the guest explained that the number comes from research at Cornell University, O'Reilly shot back: "Well, what more do I have to say?"—as if any information coming from an Ivy League institution had to be wrong.[28]

These are just the highlights of FAIR's report. And even it does not include the foolish complaints O'Reilly makes about the alleged persecution he suffers at the hands of the SCLM. For instance, during his 2002 book tour, O'Reilly continually complained about National Public Radio's liberal "bias" and whined that he could not get himself booked on its programs. Well, perhaps O'Reilly forgot that he did a twenty-minute interview on April 24, 2002, with Brian Lehrer on *New York & Company* on WNYC, which is an NPR affiliate. He was also frequently invited on the NPR program *On the Media* but declined to appear, according to its producer.[29] Drawing a distinction between NPR and an NPR affiliate is a mighty fine line—especially when they're taped at the same station.[30]

Conveniently for a man making eight figures, O'Reilly's brand of class-based populism contains not a hint of concern for issues of economic equity. He terms universal health care "socialist, old Democrat" and worries frequently about the effects of the estate tax, which affects only well-to-do Americans, and the wealthiest Americans the most. We hear lots of complaints about Hillary Clinton and Rosie O'Donnell—whom O'Reilly managed to compare to Joseph Goebbels—but nothing about issues of a tax system skewed toward the wealthy, an increasingly top-weighted distribution of wealth and income, or minimal public investment in education, transportation, worker-training, or universal health care, to say nothing of Enron-style corporate malfeasance and its accompanying official indulgence.[31] When Patricia Ireland, former president of the National Organization for Women, worried on his program that George Bush's economic policies were likely to increase the wage gap between the rich and poor, O'Reilly responded like an ignorant drunk: "You can always move to Cuba, where everybody is the same, and everyone is poor. You can always go there. They would love to have you, Ms. Ireland!"[32] When a University of North Carolina professor assigned his students to read a book about the origins of the Koran, O'Reilly called this "unbelievable." He compared it to assigning *Mein Kampf* during the Second World War, and wondered why in the world students should be required to study "our enemy's religion."[33] But when it came to tax cuts for the wealthiest Americans, O'Reilly was positively enamored of the idea. "How on earth could 38 Democratic senators vote against it? . . . This is not a big tax cut. . . . A tax cut that puts money in the pockets of all working Americans is a good thing, period."[34] Never mind over half the benefits were earmarked for fewer than 1 percent of Americans—a percent that happened to include O'Reilly.[35] To a guy making twenty million, the top 1 percent of American earners qualify, no doubt, as "middle class." O'Reilly's voice is, recall, the dominant voice on cable news in America.

Much of what can be said about O'Reilly also applies to his competitor, MSNBC's Chris Matthews. Matthews is very much a showman, rather than a journalist. His career, before he became a pundit, was made on the "other side of the street" as a paid spokesperson for Democratic House Speaker Tip O'Neill, which would indicate a certain attachment to old-fashioned liberalism. But Matthews's program demonstrates him to be all over the map politically as well as journalistically.

During the impeachment scandal, Matthews, while interviewing Kathleen Willey, who had accused Clinton of fondling her in the Oval Office, made a startling accusation that a man who threatened Willey while jogging near her home was actually Cody Shearer, the well-known writer and friend of the president. Rush Limbaugh then picked up the accusation, and Matthews repeated it on a second night, again with no evidence. Suddenly Shearer, who had been in California when the alleged incident took place, was deluged with threatening phone calls. (He even faced an intruder at his house—who turned out to be Pat Buchanan's emotionally troubled brother, Hank—wielding a gun and demanding to see him.) Matthews—who had not even tried to verify Willey's story or Shearer's identity—refused to apologize, until he received a threatening letter from Shearer's attorney.[36]

As Noam Scheiber noted in the *New Republic*, "In the course of a typical hour of *Hardball*, which he hosts five nights per week on CNBC, Matthews denigrates Ivy League elitists, scolds politicians who forget they serve real working people."[37] Like O'Reilly, Matthews's shtick has made him fantastically rich. He tells inquiring journalists that his salary is "more than you can imagine."[38] Again his millionaire brand of working-class populism is without discernible economic context. Scheiber notes that for both O'Reilly and Matthews, the term "working class" is defined "not by income but by cultural values such as hard work, devotion to family, and respect for authority and tradition." It's fair to point out, as Scheiber does, that such values go a good distance toward explaining the hostility felt in many middle-class areas toward the Clintons and the Gores, why welfare retains the ability to inflame, and why George Bush did so well with voters whose economic interests Democrats more fairly represent. Both O'Reilly and Matthews would much prefer to talk about personalities rather than issues. Here, for instance, is Matthews's evocation of George W. Bush's leadership skills in the wake of the al-Qaeda attack:

There are some things you can't fake. Either you can throw a strike from 60 feet or you can't. Either you can rise to the occasion on the mound at Yankee Stadium with

56,000 people watching or you can't. On Tuesday night, George W. Bush hit the strike zone in the House that Ruth Built. He did it sporting the most revered insignia in America today: that of the New York Fire Department. This is about knowing what to do at the moment you have to do it—and then doing it. It's about that "grace under pressure" that Hemingway gave as his very definition of courage.[39]

(Based on Matthews' criteria for presidential leadership, it's a wonder how the nation made it through World War II, when, readers may recall, the country was led by a man who could not have thrown a strike if his life depended on it.)

Like so many talk-show hosts, both O'Reilly and Matthews are obsessed with Hillary Clinton. O'Reilly complains that her "demeanor is one of elitism, that she's a Yale-educated, very liberal, lives-in-her-mind-rather-than-in-the-real-world person." O'Reilly admits to keeping a doormat with the former First Lady's face on it beneath his desk.[40] Matthews, who frequently refers to New York's junior senator as "Evita," screams, "I look at this woman as a person who has, for whatever reason, a deep sense of entitlement . . . expecting the peasants to bring her bouquets of flowers. . . . Where did she get the idea the public should worship her as almost a goddess?" When speaking of Hillary Clinton, Matthews, like O'Reilly, strikes a faux macho pose. "You're not going to see Hillary Clinton on my show," he told one interviewer. "She'll never come on, because she knows she can't answer the two questions I'm gonna ask . . . . I'm gonna ask her, 'Are you ambitious?' And, 'Are you a politician?'"[41]

As with O'Reilly, the millionaire Matthews pays little if any attention to issues of economic equity, nor to the myriad instances in which the Bush administration has given the back of its hand to working-class Americans in favor of the corporate elite. Many Catholic politicians have forged entire careers on the connections between a church-based cultural conservatism and a populist progressive economic agenda. *TNR*'s Scheiber mentions former House Speaker Tip O'Neill—with whom Matthews began his career—and former House Majority Whip David Bonior (D-Mich.) as examples. But there are also Representatives David Obey (D-Wisc.), Dennis Kucinich (D-Ohio), and Jim McGovern (D-Mass.)—all of whom are among the most progressive people in national politics, and among the most progressive people in Congress. E. J. Dionne of the *Washington Post* writes an extremely eloquent and intellectually challenging political column from this point of view. Michael Harrington, and Dorothy Day before him, helped to galvanize a political movement and an entirely new attitude toward the poor in this nation on this basis of just this philosophical connection. But both Matthews and O'Reilly act as if they never heard of the Catholic social justice movement or its hundred-year history of poor and working-class solidarity. In the O'Reilly/Matthews universe, the poor are, at best, an annoyance and at worst, moral inferiors. And the working-class economic interest appears to lie only in the pursuit of larger and larger tax breaks for the wealthy. In this regard O'Reilly and

Matthews replicate, albeit in exaggerated form, the most basic prejudice of the rest of the media: their narrow condescension toward America's have-nots and those the so-called "new economy" leaves behind.

Matthews is, in the words of his station's president, Erik Sorensen, MSNBC's "flagship face of prime time."[42] In June 2002 he was awarded a salary reported to be in the area of $2 million annually after rumors appeared in the media that he was considering running for Senate in Pennsylvania as well as being considered to replace the departing Bryant Gumbel on CBS. In September 2002, Matthews was given his own show on NBC. He is, in other words, an extremely successful and influential media personality by any conceivable measure. But as Bill Kovach and Tom Rosenstiel note in their study of the media, *Warp Speed: America in the Age of Mixed Media*, "*Hardball* has no grounding in reporting, no basic news function, is not designed to elicit facts or explore issues with policy-makers."[43] While a great number of people do not actually watch these shows, the rest of the media does, and that gives them a degree of influence well beyond their numbers. Orville Schell, dean of the University of California at Berkeley's School of Journalism, likened such programs to a "virus implanted on the American media's hard drive." While "the actual number of people they've infected so far is small [given their low ratings], they're steadily contaminating the rest of the media. They've created a template on how to get more viewers and readers. They've succeeded in contriving a common wisdom, that if you don't imitate them in some way, you're falling behind in the race for market share."[44]

Yet another contender for O'Reilly's cable crown is Fox's Sean Hannity, whose *Crossfire*-like program *Hannity and Colmes* allows him to slap around liberals on a nightly basis. Hannity, while extremely popular on both TV and radio, is no more enamored with facts and evidence than are his talk-show brethren. Like O'Reilly and Limbaugh, among many others in the business, Hannity is remarkably nonchalant in his approach to facts. Ben Fritz and Bryan Keefer of the Web site Spinsanity performed a merciless autopsy on Hannity's book *Let Freedom Ring* (2002) and discovered a mass of wild allegations and accusations unsupported by even a remote connection to reality. To borrow a few examples from their research, they note that Hannity repeats a frequently made (in conservative circles) lie about Bill Clinton, insisting that when the president gave a speech to Georgetown University shortly after the 9/11 attacks, he "seemingly blamed the vicious terrorist attacks on you and me and all Americans." By noting that Clinton had mentioned the Crusades and slavery in his speech, Hannity claimed he was offering a "justification for radical Islamic terrorism" and an "apology for terrorism." But Clinton did nothing of the sort. The context of the speech itself clearly demonstrates that he simply explained to the audience that the murder of innocent noncombatants is not exactly new. Either Hannity didn't look at the original speech or he didn't care. The author also gives voice to a common conservative complaint that Clinton is guilty of "not effectively going after

Osama bin Laden" and suggests Clinton should have sent "a covert team over to the Middle East to take out bin Laden." To say this, Hannity must ignore not only that in fact Clinton did attack bin Laden with cruise missiles in 1998, but also that Clinton's national security staff readied a plan to go after bin Laden in a much more concerted way in 2000, but that plan was rejected by the incoming administration of George W. Bush.

With regard to tax policy, the millionaire Hannity sounds a lot like his fellow millionaires O'Reilly and Matthews. He claims "the tax burden on American families is at a record high, having skyrocketed during the Clinton-Gore years." In fact, the Center on Budget and Policy Priorities found that the share of income paid in federal taxes by the middle 20 percent of families declined from 1995 to 2000, when it stood at its lowest level since 1979. While paying tribute to Ronald Reagan, Hannity tries to argue, "Had all of Reagan's budgets been adopted federal spending would have been 25 percent less on a cumulative basis." Apparently he is confused by his own book's data. Hannity's claim is accompanied by a chart demonstrating the difference between federal budgets enacted from 1982 through 1989 and those proposed by Reagan. The actual difference: 2.7 percent.[45] (But what's a 1,000 percent error between conservatives?) It goes on. In support of Bush's desire to drill in the Arctic, Hannity claims that the U.S. Geological Survey said the Arctic National Wildlife Refuge could yield up to 16 billion barrels of oil. A geologist interviewed in the *Washington Post*, however, put the number at 3.2 billion barrels. Even the Republican senator from Alaska, Frank Murkowski, arguing for the drilling on the Senate floor, could not bring himself to claim much more than ten billion.[46]

Another semi-successful star in the cable political punditocracy is Laura Ingraham, a pretty blond ex-clerk to Supreme Court Justice Clarence Thomas who first came to public attention not for her trenchant legal analytical abilities, but because she had the good sense to wear a leopard-skin miniskirt for a *New York Times Magazine* cover shoot. Before becoming a pundit, Ingraham's professional journalistic experience was largely earned in college, where she helped write and edit the infamous *Dartmouth Review*, a conservative student newspaper that specialized in publishing the contents of secretly taped meetings of gay students—thereby outing them involuntarily— along with Sambo-style parodies of African-American speech patterns. I first met her on the set of MSNBC during the first few hours of the network's first day on the air in July 1996. We were asked to interview then ex-Israeli Prime Minister Shimon Peres in the aftermath of a mysterious plane crash of TWA Flight 800, bound for Paris, off the coast of East Moriches, Long Island. Right off, Laura asked Peres if he thought it a good idea for the U.S. to bomb Syria or Libya in response to the crash. Recall that no one yet had any idea why the plane had gone down. (The cause was later deemed to be mechanical failure.) Shortly thereafter, CBS News hired Ingraham to join former senator and future presidential candidate Bill Bradley as half of a "he said, she said" pundit tag-team. She also kept her MSNBC job, thereby becoming the only person in the media to negotiate simultaneous contracts with both NBC and CBS. She also turned up regularly on Imus, the *McLaughlin Group, Politically Incorrect*, and all the nation's gossip pages, flying off with Robert DeNiro, dining with Dustin Hoffman. Eventually, Ingraham was given her own show on MSNBC, which flopped quite publicly, as she missed commercial breaks, flubbed lines, and invited her old friends for boring reminiscing and catty innuendo. Nevertheless she landed on her feet and soon made a career (quite ironically, given her good looks) on talk radio.

While Ingraham was politically quite conservative, her analysis tended to focus on people's personal appearances more than the political substance of their remarks or actions, decrying fat and ugly people on the basis of what she assumed to be her own widely shared taste. When a male pundit complained of the "objectification" of women by *Sports Illustrated*'s annual swimsuit issue, she demanded "What does that mean?" five times in succession before declaring, "No one wants to see fat people on the cover of magazines in swimsuits." (When asked about the importance of her own looks, Ingraham responded, "No one wants to see Quasimodo up there.")[47] Even today, Ingraham continues to judge past and potential presidential candidates on this basis. Here, for instance, was her analysis of Al Gore's speech before a Florida Democratic convention on CNN's *Reliable Sources* in spring 2002: "He came out and did his very best to, you know, get that sort of gravelly thing back in his voice, and to be so energetic that he—his perspiration was, I mean . . . it was quite unpleasant."[48] She was back on the show just a few weeks later, displaying this same talent for fashion-conscious analysis with this observation about the quality of the nightly news: "I think one of the worst things that's happened to news is this sort of open-collared shirt, no tie, you know, do you take the jacket off? That whole, you know, undress thing on television. . . ."[49]

With the success of Ingraham, cable executives were on the hunt for look- and soundalikes, who, paradoxically, in the words of one MSNBC producer, "cut against the cliché." Laura, he explained, was "young, smart, hip and conservative. She's sort of the perfect image of somebody different."[50] Little Lauras began sprouting up all over the media, spouting right-wing anti-feminist politics as they brushed their peroxide blond locks back and straightened out their own leopard miniskirts on camera. (Jennifer Grossman, another MSNBC right-wing blond, did actually wear a leopard mini-skirt on the air. She insisted to me that Ingraham had borrowed hers for the famous photo shoot.)

While Ingraham may have been nasty, ignorant, and frequently silly on television, the worst thing that can be said about her is that she inspired TV producers to go searching for someone like Ann Coulter to cash in on the right-wing blond fashion craze.[51] But even with Ingraham, Coulter, and (the now forgotten) Fitzgerald on the loose, the evolutionary endpoint of questionable pundit qualifications may finally have manifested itself in the person of young Heather Nauert, yet another young blond called upon to twirl her locks before the camera while sounding off on national affairs. Nauert appeared on PBS's *To the Contrary*, ABC's *Politically Incorrect with Bill Maher*, MSNBC, CBC, the BBC, and quite frequently, Fox News Channel, where her views on the nation's "heinous tax system," presidential elections, gun control, foreign policy, and the latest Dixie Chicks video were much sought after. While Nauert is reasonably articulate and quite easy on the eyes—one reporter described her as looking like the younger sister of Heather Locklear—she enjoyed precious few professional qualifications, even by the considerable non-standards of the cable punditocracy. Nauert had never worked in journalism or politics before being cast as a pundit on TV, nor worked as a law clerk or a Congressional staffer. Fox would occasionally refer to her as a "GOP consultant" or a "GOP strategist," ignoring the fact that Nauert had never consulted nor strategized for Republicans at any time in her short life. "From the time I was 16, I knew I wanted to do something on TV," Nauert explained to the *Washington Post*'s Paul Fahri. That really is all there is to it, apparently, if you are conservative and look like Heather Locklear's sister. Nevertheless, Nauert notes, it's not all fun and games. "Reporters are so serious that I have a hard time connecting with them," she complained.[52]

Nauert, the imaginary "strategist," was not invented by producers as a pundit by accident, of course. She is pretty. She is articulate. And most important perhaps, like ancient ancestors Ingraham and Coulter, she is conservative. It remains a curious fact that until MSNBC decided to give Phil Donahue his own show in the summer of 2002, not a single liberal had been recruited by a cable network to host a solo talk show. It is perhaps a measure of how successful the conservative propaganda offensive on this point has been that NBC's Katie Couric felt compelled to ask Donahue whether a "lot of people might say, 'Gosh, we really don't need another liberal spouting his views on national television.'"[53] In the real world, even Republicans acknowledged the obvious. "It's affirmative action," quipped Patrick Buchanan.[54]

Clearly the success of Fox News demonstrates a strong preference on the part of many cable viewers for a version of news that is biased toward the right. CNN chief Walter Isaacson obviously noticed this and began signing up conservatives like Bill Bennett and Jonah Goldberg, and even making a run at Rush Limbaugh. MSNBC, too, shows itself willing to offer conservative extremists like Ingraham, Alan Keyes, and others the honor of having their own shows, while Donahue, cable's lone solo liberal host, was clearly forced to clear a far higher bar—boasting literally decades of experience as a talk-show host—before he was invited to join the six-year-old network. Why is this, given that repeated opinion polling on the issues demonstrates a preference for centrist and frequently "liberal" positions over those of the hard right? Bill O'Reilly postulates conservative dominance of the talk-show format to be the result of the relative complexity of conservative and liberal worldviews. "Conservative people tend to see the world in black and white terms, good and evil," O'Reilly explains. "Liberals see grays. In any talk format, you have to pound home a strong point of view. If you're not providing controversy and excitement, people won't listen, or watch."[55]

Jeffrey Scheuer, the author of a scholarly work on television and conservatism, concurs with O'Reilly. "A sound bite society," he wrote, "insists on simplicity, and simplicity is an inherent characteristic of conservative politics. Differences over the respective roles and limits of government and the market constitute defining watersheds . . . of the simpler and more complex political visions. Laissez-faire is a simpler model of society than the welfare state. Arguments about types and degrees of regulation and redistribution of wealth are more complex than arguments against regulation and redistribution as such." The liberal argument, Scheuer noted, demands complexity "not just of government but, inferentially, of society and of causality itself." Even when liberal voices for change are "simplistic or sloganeering, demanding peace, jobs, equality, or a greener planet, the underlying values are more inclusive and far-reaching." Television quite obviously has no use for this kind of thing. It atomizes, compartmentalizes, manipulates, disjoins, disintegrates, wrenches from context, ignores, and changes the subject whenever it feels like it. It does not sit still for complex arguments. "Television," Scheuer noted, "systematically 'keeps it simple, stupid.'"[56] The net result is a disaster for democracy, as intelligent debate under these circumstances becomes impossible, and a dream medium for a conservative carrying a simple, sensible-sounding solution to all that appears to ail us. For liberals, this is a problem with no easy solution.

# 4

# The Punditocracy Two

*Print*

EVEN WITH THE REDUCED INFLUENCE of network news and the relatively small numbers of people who watch cable, television remains the news source from which the vast majority of Americans received their news. But that does not necessarily make it the most influential. Television is a medium that is not merely indifferent to ideas but actively hostile to them. But ideas need to originate from somewhere if pundits are going to have anything to say between commercial breaks, and standard practice inside the television punditocracy is to "borrow" them from print. For television pundits who are also writers, this usually means nothing more disreputable than speaking aloud what they have already published in print.

Most television pundits, as indicated earlier, are strong conservatives. So, therefore, are most television pundits who are also print pundits. Of the most prominent liberals writing in the nation's newspapers and opinion magazines—Frank Rich, Garry Wills, E. J. Dionne, (the now retired) Anthony Lewis, Richard Cohen, Bob Kuttner, Robert Scheer, Paul Krugman, Bob Herbert, William Greider, Mary McGrory, Hendrik Hertzberg, Nicholas Kristof, Molly Ivins—not one enjoys or has ever enjoyed a prominent perch on television. Michael Kinsley did for a while, but only as the liberal half of *Crossfire*'s tag-team, and Kinsley, by his own admission, is not all that liberal. While the *Weekly Standard* and *National Review* editors enjoy myriad regular television gigs of their own, and are particularly popular as guests on the allegedly liberal CNN, with the possible exception of editor Katrina vanden Heuvel, the only *Nation* writer to appear on television with any regularity was Christopher Hitchens, who finally quit the magazine in September 2002, because he had developed into a hard-line conservative on many issues. Columnists Mark Shields and Al Hunt also play liberals on television, but always in opposition to conservatives and almost always on the other team's ideological field, given the conservatives' ability to dominate television's "he said, she said" discourse virtually across the board.

For print pundits who are not also television pundits, the situation is far more complex. Many are indeed conservatives, but many are also centrists who lean left or right depending on the issue. Print pundits generally have a higher standard of truth-telling than do television pundits because the (relatively) lasting quality of their work makes errors far more costly to their respective reputations then merely mouthing off on a television program that disappears into the ether when the credits roll. Print punditry obviously lends itself to a great deal more complexity and nuance than does television, and rewards thoughtfulness, research, and eloquence rather than good looks and acting ability. Liberals are not as rare in the print punditocracy as in television, but their modest numbers nevertheless give lie to any accusations of SCLM domination.

Again, any discussion of bias is riddled with definitional problems, owing to the considerable degree of conservative success in moving the fifty-yard line deep into what not long ago was already their own territory. Richard Nixon was a conservative in his day but the positions he took in 1968 were well to the left of those taken by Al Gore in the 2000 election. Dwight Eisenhower's views on the defense budget as enunciated in his famous farewell address in 1961 can barely find a home in the left-wing fringe of the Democratic Party today. And President George H. W. Bush was well to the left of his son on most issues. The principled conservatism of politicians like the late Barry Goldwater and his fellow Arizonian, John McCain, is treated as the "liberal" position on a whole host of issues, with liberals relegated to arguing amongst themselves in the political equivalent of Siberia. Obviously this ideological transformation has many roots and is both a cause and an effect of the rightward shift in political discourse that has taken place during the past few decades. Conservative assumptions have come to rule the roost of insider debate almost entirely. And they do so not merely because of conservative domination of the punditocracy but also because of conservative colonization of the so-called "center"—where all action in American politics is deemed to take place. Nowhere is this transformation better illustrated than in the work of the "dean" of American political reporting and punditry, the *Washington Post*'s David Broder.

Allow me to dwell on Broder's status and achievement for a moment because, more than any other example, I believe it demonstrates what kind of values are admired and emulated at the top of the profession today. "Dean" Broder is revered by elite journalists exactly for his alleged ability to ignore ideological blinders and bluster and speak to what is understood to be the common-sense "middle ground" of American politics. The fact that he does so frequently on untested and occasionally false conservative assumptions does not seem to adversely affect the universal renown he enjoys. This may be because these assumptions are so universally held in the first place—or it may be the result of the influence he enjoys. Or it may be a combination of the two. It's impossible to know for certain, but its presence is undeniable.

The veteran of nearly a half century of political reporting and punditry, Broder is not simply the most admired print reporter in America, a position he has occupied for more than thirty years; after Walter Lippmann, and perhaps James Reston, he is almost certainly the most widely admired political reporter of the century.

Broder's position inside Washington is absolutely unique. In the mind of the Washington insider establishment, he is virtue itself. He is a sacred cow in a business of beefeaters. Ted Koppel might be equally respected, but his political views remain a mystery. Broder's opinions are influential on both the center-right and center-left. He has occupied the position of "high priest" of political journalism—as named in Timothy Crouse's *The Boys on the Bus* over thirty years ago—because, not in spite, of his opinions. To examine Broder is to study the jewel in journalism's crown.

When asked to elaborate, his colleagues invariably point to his common sense and implacable level-headedness. In a loving profile in the second issue of *Brill's Content*, Michael Kramer, then the editor in chief, waxed romantic about the pundit he called "the class of the field." "There are those the rest of us seek out for guidance," he sang. "They are the calm, sober voices we reference to test our own theories and check our own tendency to hyperventilate. This is particularly true in political journalism where one person stands out—David Broder." Later in the piece, Kramer explained that Broder's "influence derives from the entirety of his non-hysterical work, an oeuvre that has conferred on him an authority no journalist has enjoyed since James Reston wrote for the *New York Times*." *LA Times* Bigfoot Ronald Brownstein added, "Many of us take Broder into account, and particularly in times of crisis, like now, because he never loses his head."[1] In the winter of 2000, during the post-election crisis in Florida, Broder's beloved colleague at the *Post* (and before that, the *Washington Star*), Mary McGrory, felt compelled to write, "Dear reader: Be warned. I am about to commit heresy. The consequences could be unspeakable and any interdiction that falls on me might extend to you. It is not too late to turn back. I'm about to tell you that David Broder is wrong."[2]

Broder's meticulous dedication to the nuts and bolts of his craft, along with his disdain for the Washington social scene, are indeed "awesome." Broder's *Post* column is syndicated in more than 300 papers and he appears frequently on NBC's *Meet the Press*, PBS's *Washington Week in Review*, and CNN's *Inside Politics*. But unlike most pundits, he does not come armed with supposedly inside information from partisan political operatives. Rather he makes a conscious effort to focus on the arguments the campaigns make and the views he understands the voters to hold. He defines his technique with the modesty that is almost unique by Beltway standards. "I am not a terribly interesting or fluid writer and I don't have any deep philosophical thoughts . . . so if I didn't do the reporting, I couldn't do the column." Broder also eschews the familiar pundit/prediction game. At a speech where he was being honored at the Kennedy School at Harvard in 1999, he went so far as to issue a public mea culpa, explaining that when Tim Russert asked his guests to issue predictions about the 1998 Congressional races, "we ended up looking like a bunch of jerks because none of us knew what was going to happen in any of these elections and it wasn't a reporter's kind of a role."

Sometimes Broder is identified in the media as a "liberal," usually a centrist, but never a conservative. Like Reston before him, Broder is a man of the floating center. His deepest beliefs are process-related. Broder believes with all his heart and soul in professional politicians and in successful political parties, and is willing to subordinate virtually all matters of substance to this belief. He believes the trains should be made to run on time, almost without regard of in which direction they happen to move. And Broder also believes in taking almost all politicians at their words. He goes so far as to admit that in recent years, he has tended purposely to shy away, "maybe more than is justified, from writing stories that I know will add to the depth of an already deep public cynicism about what's going on in this country." This is the most basic belief of the insider establishment. R. W. "Johnny" Apple Jr., the *New York Times*'s most revered correspondent, joins Broder in cautioning against the kind of journalism that might upset people too much. Writing in the wake of reports that George W. Bush might have ignored specific warnings about a 9/11-type attack, he warns, positing no evidence, Americans "crave unity above everything." The problems with genuine "full-throated debate" are its "costs: to national unity, to confidence in the electoral process and to respect for leaders in general."[3] This is a deeply held belief of the ideological center and, in addition to overt discomfort with democratic debate, it is also profoundly "conservative" with regard to whose interests in the system it seeks to conserve.

During the course of four decades at or near the top of the heap of admired political pundits and reporters—and Broder is unusual for being revered in both categories—he has repeatedly demonstrated little patience with politicians who do not honor the role of the permanent establishment at the expense of democratic-inspired messiness and dissatisfaction with the status quo. Back in 1968, he felt the anti-war activities of the likes of Robert Kennedy and Gene McCarthy were "degrading . . . to those involved"—as if ending the horrific Vietnam War might not be worth a little indigestion in one's political system. Like most members of the insider establishment, Broder soured on Nixon during Watergate and treated the humble, homiletic Gerald Ford as a kind of God-sent gift to the nation following Our Long National Nightmare. Jimmy Carter's anti-Washington populism, not surprisingly, won little favor with him.

It was during the Reagan era, however, when the search for solid, centrist ground yielded an island of intellectual quicksand for Broder. As Edward Herman discovered in a study of Broder's columns during this period, when the president decided to bomb Libya in 1986 in order to try to kill Muamar Khaddafi, Broder assured readers that "Reagan has been insistent that every possible step be taken to spare the innocent."[4] Just how that tidbit of hard news was checked out, he does not say. Broder repeatedly lauded Reagan for his "presidential" qualities and "national leadership of a high order" while dismissing his dishonesty and intellectual incompetence as "overshadowed by the grace with which he functions as chief of state in moments of national tragedy and triumph."[5] Reagan's opponents, however, are dismissed as "quick-lipped liberals" who "pop off in opposition" to the Supreme Court nomination of the extremist Robert Bork.[6] During the Iran-Contra scandal, Broder frequently dressed down those who sought to hold the president to some Constitutional standard, preferring instead to plead for the efficacy of the presidency, despite the nefarious (and frequently criminal) purposes to which Ronald Reagan happened to arrogate its powers.

Following the 1988 election, Broder would prove no less indulgent to his bonding buddy, George Bush, than he had been to Reagan, as Edward Herman demonstrated. During the 1989 Panama invasion, Broder referred to the signatories of a letter to President Bush denouncing U.S. violations of the United Nations Charter and the Organization of the American States' Agreement, as "69 left-wing politicians and activists"—a description that would have been news to the longtime former chair of the Senate Foreign Relations Committee, the late J. William Fulbright. Their arguments, moreover, he insisted, were mere "nonsense" and "static on the left." Similarly, during the debate on the Gulf War, Broder mocked the Democratic opponents' "usual spectacle of disarray" as they resisted giving George H. W. Bush the authority he sought to launch a war with Iraq. In doing so, Broder credited the administration's explanation that it had actively sought a diplomatic solution before choosing war. In doing so, he was being even more generous than was his usual custom.[7]

Bill Clinton, who was greeted with hostility almost immediately by the Beltway establishment, received no such indulgence from the dean. In line with the conventional wisdom of the moment, Broder regretted in his column that that "the Democratic Congress pulled Clinton to the left in 1993–94, to the detriment of their party."[8] And while his observation was, in insider circles, so obvious as to be axiomatic, it was also false. At Alan Greenspan's request, and immediately upon taking office, Clinton dropped the stimulus package he promised in his campaign with nary a peep from Congress. He pushed the costly ban on assault weapons in the crime bill over the objections of most in the party caucus. True, he pursued health care before welfare reform, which turned out to be a political error, but on that front he was being pushed by the extremely liberal senior Democratic senator from New York, Daniel Patrick Moynihan, to do just the opposite. Clinton pursued the NAFTA and GATT accords to the delight of conservatives and establishmentarians and to the chagrin of both his base and most Americans. The debacle over gays in the military was foisted on Clinton by Sam Nunn and other conservatives (within and without the military) who sought to undermine the president's authority to carry out his campaign promise. And David Broder, of all people, should know better than to blame Congressional Democrats for the tax increase for which Clinton forced so many in his party to risk their political lives. The measure passed by a single vote and cost many Democrats their jobs. While the *Wall Street Journal* editorial pages repeatedly warned of impending economic catastrophe, the tax increase also turned out to be one of the most responsible and successful pieces of economic legislation in recent American history.

Broder also engaged in some decidedly suspect historical revisionism when blaming Bill Clinton, rather than Newt Gingrich and his minions, for the government shutdown of 1995–1996.[9] According to Broder's interpretation, noted on the Daily Howler Web site, "Clinton forced exactly that kind of government crisis. He convinced the public he was fighting to save Medicare from the new GOP majority on Capitol Hill, and saddled the Republicans with blame for the shutdown." But as Broder surely knows, when Congress and the White House can't agree on a budget, the problem is almost always addressed by a Continuing Resolution that keeps everything running at current levels, while the new budget is hammered out. This time, however, Gingrich and the Republicans refused to accept the traditional CR process. Instead they attached the entire text of their proposed new budget to it and simply invited Clinton to capitulate. Broder's history is simply the Gingrich spin.

Though famous for his calm, cool demeanor, Broder's distaste for President Clinton boiled into irrational anger during the Lewinsky affair. Much of his ire seemed to derive from a belief, implicit in a comment he made to Sally Quinn in the *Washington Post*, that Bill Clinton had no right to be in Washington as president, despite his having been elected to serve there twice by his fellow citizens. "He came in here," Broder told Quinn, "and he trashed the place, and it's not his place."[10] What right, the dean of pundits seems to be asking, does a mere president have to upset the comfortable mores of the establishment that has ruled the city virtually undisturbed for decades?

Broder was so enraged by what he learned of the president's behavior that it led him to make arguments that were genuinely offensive to common sense. At one point, for instance, he tried to argue that Clinton's consensual sex with Monica Lewinsky and resultant dishonesties were somehow "worse" than Richard Nixon's police-state tactics during Watergate. "Nixon's actions," he reasoned, "however neurotic and criminal, were motivated by and connected to the exercise of presidential power. He knew the place he occupied and he was determined not to give it up to those he regarded as 'enemies.'"[11] In other words, if a president uses state power to destroy his enemies, his behavior is ipso facto more honorable than one who indulges a personal weakness on his own time in a private manner. Broder's argument is both morally and logically indefensible. His point seems to be that personal failures in a president are inexcusable, but the use of the means of the state to carry out his purpose, no matter how evil or nefarious, well, that's what politicians do. If you replace the word "Nixon" with the words "Stalin" or "Hitler," the argument's logic remains unchanged.

Broder's coverage of the 2000 election reflected an establishment bias in favor of George W. Bush. While Broder may have had a few concerns about Bush's relative lack of experience, these vanished with the naming of a Broder hero, Dick Cheney, to the ticket. Again, Broder insisted on dismissing the substance of anything Richard (or his wife, Lynn) actually said in favor of the genial Reaganesque style in which he said it. "Democrats will have no difficulty finding rhetoric and policy stands by both Cheneys that will raise liberal hackles," he noted. "But his manner gives him immunity from the extremist label. Voters who saw his televised briefings during the Persian Gulf War remember the calm voice and thoughtful expression that are his natural style." By choosing a man whom Broder considered "a grownup" to be his vice president, Broder wrote, Bush "gave evidence of his own sense of responsibility."[12]

Repeatedly during the campaign, Broder filed as if dictating from Bush/Cheney talking points. Broder also accepted at face value Bush's claim that "in a Bush presidency, abortion would not be outlawed . . . until a lot of people change their minds."[13] But how to square that with Bush's desire to appoint justices who emulate his heroes Clarence Thomas and Antonin Scalia? Perhaps wisely, Broder ignored the question. Broder even went so far as to argue that "Bush makes no more verbal mistakes than most of us do." (Oh really? "Reading is the basics for all learning"; "It is not Reaganesque to support a tax plan that is Clinton in nature"; "I understand small business growth. I was one";[14] and so on.) Meanwhile the famously conscientious reporter repeated the fanciful story of Gore's youth in the "swank Fairfax hotel." In fact there was nothing "swank" about this extremely modestly priced residential hotel where the Gores lived, as more careful journalistic inquiries have demonstrated.[15] Broder attacked Gore's campaign for allowing "a man with a genuine history as a New Democrat to appear, at times, an old-fashioned liberal" and for "exploiting the hoariest of Democratic arguments: Don't let Republicans take your Social Security away." Again, the substance of the claim was unimportant. Bush's plan really did constitute a serious threat to the future of Social Security, owing to its double-counting arithmetic. But to point this out is considered "partisan" by the famously centrist dean.[16]

During the Florida election crisis, Broder made a few more gaffes that, again, almost perfectly reflected Washington's own house of mirrored-wisdom. An alarmed Broder wrote, "This nation has rarely appeared more divided than it does right now,"[17] going so far in another column to compare the election counting crisis to the assassination of John F. Kennedy, making this Broder's "saddest Thanksgiving week since 1963."[18] But while Broder's sadness was no doubt genuine, the rest of the country was doing just fine. Nobody seemed to care much for Bush or Gore in the first place. It was only the denizens of the inner Beltway who seemed unable to stand the suspense, and hence, demanded over and over that the man who won the popular vote and probably deserved to win Florida by any sensible counting standard concede to the establishment favorite, George Bush. Broder led the pack in creating a false sense of crisis around a fair count. Opinion poll after opinion poll at the time of Broder's writings emphasized the public's desire for an "accurate" result over a "fast" one and demonstrated no particular concern over the delay.[19]

Broder's primary complaint about Florida was that of the typical Washington fixer: "All that was needed," he wrote, "was an agreement between the rivals on how the tie would be broken. But that never happened. The necessary phone call was never made. Instead, both of them immediately began deploying the unholy trinity of contemporary American politics—lawyers, campaign consultants and media advisers—and set out to win it for themselves." Broder does not bother to explain just what that agreement might have contained should the phone call have been made. The important point is that it be left to the pros.

Broder's embrace of a host of unproven conservative assertions under the guise of anti-ideological, sensible centrism is hardly an isolated story. It is, in fact, the norm rather than the exception, and it affects "liberals" just as much as conservatives. Conservative assumptions rule the roost in key locations of the "liberal" punditocracy just as much as they do in the Broderesque middle. Consider the case of liberalism's most venerable flagship journal, the *New Republic*. While the *Nation*, which is to the left of *TNR* on just about everything, has seen its readership rise to nearly 50 percent higher than *TNR*'s—122,000 to just 85,000, at last count—the latter remains the weekly of choice for liberal Washington insiders.[20] This is in part due to its Washington base, but also because the *Nation* is considered by non-liberals to be ideologically out of the loop. The country's longest continuously published weekly magazine is also hindered by the continued appearance in its pages of a longtime Stalinist communist, Alexander Cockburn, whose unabashed hatred for both America and Israel, coupled with his ravings against such stalwart progressives as democratic socialist representative Bernie Sanders of Vermont and the late Senator Paul Wellstone of Minnesota, tarnish the reputation of its otherwise serious contributors. *TNR*, on the other hand, operates from deep within the Washington consensus, picking up the conventional wisdom from week to week and either endorsing it or dissecting it, and hence is able, together with the *Weekly Standard*, to shape that conventional wisdom with sharply written editorials and frequent first-rate reporting.

*TNR*'s political genesis is worthy of scrutiny because it so frequently provides journalistic insiders with a kind of short-hand version of liberal thinking on a weekly basis, however inaccurately. When Martin Peretz purchased the magazine with funds his wife inherited from her family's Singer Sewing Machine fortune in 1974, he swore fealty to its traditionally progressive path originally set forth by its famous founders, Herbert Croly, Willard Strait, and Walter Lippmann—among others—a half century earlier. But Peretz quickly grew impatient with his own promises and soon began firing the staff and replacing it with writers more to his liking. By the early 1980s, the *New Republic* had shaken off what its publisher was calling the "dead-weight of knee-jerk liberalism" and became, simultaneously, the best liberal and the best neoconservative magazine in America.[21] Because of the creative tension between its opposing halves, from week to week it was never entirely possible to pin the magazine down. Peretz bragged of the magazine's commitment to political schizophrenia. It made for interesting, even exciting, reading, but the fact of throwing over three-quarters of a century of history as so much "dead weight" had the effect of empowering conservative arguments merely because they appeared in its allegedly liberal pages.

Michael Kinsley once suggested the magazine might be renamed "Even the liberal *New Republic* . . . " in tribute to the epidemic of conservative writers who continually touted the magazine as a suddenly enlightened source of common sense.[22] Norman Podhoretz called it "indispensable." George Will termed it "the nation's most interesting and most important political journal." *National Review* named it "one of the most interesting magazines in the United States."[23] White House staffers could not wait for the magazine to arrive in the mail. They had twenty copies messengered every Thursday afternoon, as the magazine returned from the printer. These were the Peretz/*TNR* glory days when the policy debate seemed to hang on its editorials and its editors went forth from pundit program to pundit program to spread the Word.

The magazine began to fall to earth after Kinsley and successor-predecessor-successor, the eloquent anti-communist/social democratic Hendrik Hertzberg, finished trading the top job in 1991. Peretz, whose politics were increasingly motivated by his affection for his former student Al Gore and his commitment to vilifying those he deemed to be insufficiently sensitive and supportive of Israel, made a series of missteps in handing out the editor's chair. As a result, the magazine endured one public humiliation after another during the 1990s. First one of its star young writers, Ruth Shalit, was accused of a string of plagiaries. Next, its high-profile "gay-Catholic-Tory-editor," Andrew Sullivan, was fired, after having been derided in various articles by his colleagues for caring more about posing for Gap advertisements than editing the actual magazine. The changes he did bring to the magazine were almost uniformly awful. He put Stephen Glass, who turned out to be a serial liar, in charge of fact-checking. He featured Charles Murray's racist pseudo-science on the cover of the magazine and endorsed it himself. He solicited and published essays by nutty Camille Paglia, who wrote of "Hillary the man-woman and bitch goddess." He published a disgracefully dishonest assessment of the Clinton Administration's health care plan by a then-unknown socialite named Betsy McCaughey that, perhaps more than any other, turned the conventional wisdom against the most important proposed social reform of the past thirty years for the sake of contrarian buzz.[24] The magazine also published Michael Lewis on the topic of the "weird degradation" of being married to a beautiful model, upon whose (apparently terrific) ass men would publicly comment. (Lewis is a first-rate writer. But everybody needs an editor.) One conservative writer compared the magazine under Sullivan to "watching a middle-aged accountant try on a pair of nipple rings." The bitterness of his departure, however, was magnified by Sullivan's decision to announce his infection with the HIV virus at the same moment his firing hit the newspapers. Literary Editor Leon Wieseltier felt compelled to tell a reporter that Sullivan's problems at the magazine were "professional and personal," but decidedly not "medical."[25]

Life did not exactly improve with the hiring of Michael Kelly. In the press release announcing his hiring, Peretz compared his new editor to Thucydides. Alas it would be difficult to find a less apt role model going all the way to the ancient Assyrians. Kelly encouraged the pathologically dishonest Stephen Glass to branch out. The ex-Heritage Foundation worker bee, for instance, eviscerated Michael Jacobson of the Center for Science in the Public Interest as a left-wing zealot and a fraud. When Jacobson complained that the piece was part of an industry-backed smear campaign, Kelly wrote: "Mr. Jacobson, you lied, and you lied because lying supported your thesis, and you attempted to cover up your lie. . . . I await your apology to Stephen Glass and this magazine." An internal investigation later concluded that the Jacobson piece, along with twenty-six other stories, contained fabricated material.[26]

But Glass was hardly the magazine's only problem under Kelly. It turned out that, in Michael Kelly, Martin Peretz had managed to hire an editor for America's most important liberal magazine who hated liberals and liberalism. He termed it an "ideology of self-styled saints; a philosophy of determined perversity. Its animating impulse is to marginalize itself and then to enjoy its own company. And to make it as unattractive to as many as possible," adding for good measure, "If it were a person, it would pierce its tongue." Kelly did not interfere with Peretz's well-known hatred of Arabs. (Peretz's distaste for dark-skinned foreigners appears to extend well beyond the Palestinians. In a 1982 interview with the Israeli newspaper *Ha'aretz*, Peretz explained to a reporter that Israel needed to turn the Palestinians "into just another crushed nation, like the Kurds or the Afghans" and thereby make their problem "boring.")[27] Kelly also shared Peretz's animus toward affirmative action, which interviewers for the job had been led to understand was an a priori condition for hiring.[28] Few if any people of color worked at the magazine in editorial positions under Peretz's ownership, and *Washington Post* publisher Donald Graham quipped that an appropriate slogan for the magazine might be: "Looking for a qualified African-American for over seventy years." But the obsessive beating that Kelly felt compelled to give the Clinton/Gore administration proved so relentless and, on occasion, so frenzied and obsessive, that Peretz could no longer stand it—particularly when he was so heavily invested in Al Gore's presidential candidacy. The delicate balance of having a smart liberal edit a neoconservative magazine was destroyed, first by Sullivan and now, finally, by Kelly. By the end of Kelly's destructive reign *TNR* was a liberal magazine only in memory.

When Peretz finally pushed Kelly over the side, he replaced him with longtime contributor Charles Lane, who quieted down the clamor and restored some equanimity to the troubled weekly. He was repaid for his efforts by learning of his own firing by Peretz from a *Washington Post* reporter. Lane's replacement was Peter Beinart, then twenty-eight, a favorite of the owner's who had spent his entire working life at the magazine. Beinart was a liberal on many domestic issues but was in no position to challenge Peretz's growing animus against liberals and leftists, particularly as it pertained to foreign policy. Following 9/11, the lack of a strong personality at the helm meant that no one could reign in some of Peretz's more embarrassing racial excesses. ("I do not understand why so many people are so surprised by the radical evil emanating from the Muslim world," Peretz wrote after the attack.[29])

No less damaging to the magazine's reputation was the armchair generalizing in which its editors engaged about the war, going so far as to mock General Powell, a man who had more experience in war than the magazine's entire staff (and possibly its readership) added together. When Powell spoke of the need to find a solution so that Israelis and Palestinians could live in peace, the magazine's editors treated the former general and war hero as if he were an underprepared affirmative-action student in a cutthroat Harvard seminar. *TNR* found "the banality of Colin Powell's address on American foreign policy" to be "breathtaking."[30] As if that weren't churlish enough, the same magazine that provided a cheerleading section for that highly naturalistic and deeply inspirational orator, Al Gore, had the temerity to complain of Powell's allegedly "irksome manner of the motivational speaker for whom every trivial remark is more proof of his mettle." *TNR* went so far as to accuse Powell of providing "a kind of bizarre ratification of Osama bin Laden's view of the problem." Why? "There is bin Laden attempting to persuade the Muslim world that what he wants is justice for the Palestinians, and here is Powell attempting to persuade the Muslim world that what he wants is justice for the Palestinians." Even to appear to care about "justice for the Palestinians" is to give aid and comfort to the terrorist bin Laden. Later, in the spring of 2002, the magazine called upon President Bush to fire his generals for the crime of "military insubordination." Their offense: speaking honestly and openly to the media—or as the editors put it, "us[ing] the media to create a political environment that forecloses the president's options." Meanwhile, the editors' peevishness against the war hero Powell appeared to know no bounds. Their example of the dangers posed by an honest military opinion included "when a general named Colin Powell penned op-eds in 1992 cautioning policymakers against intervening in Bosnia."[31] It was once possible to parody *TNR*, in Frank Mankiewicz's phrase, as a "Jewish *Commentary*." But by this time, editors occupied so much territory inside the land of self-parody, they looked to be ready to build settlements.

*TNR*'s editors were not merely spectacularly wrong about the war, but frequently nonsensical. In the magazine's November 19 editorial, for instance, it complained that we were losing the war because, like President Clinton, who had "stupidly . . . ruled out the use of ground forces" in Kosovo, George Bush was now sending "the same lulling message: the United States will not put large numbers of troops on the ground." Oddly, the very same editorial noted that ethnic cleansing in Kosovo ended only when "Slobodan Milosevic was confronted with the threat of an imminent deployment of American ground forces." Since Clinton had supposedly ruled that out, one can only imagine who it was that threatened their "imminent deployment."

In the same remarkable editorial, the editors grumbled that U.S. military efforts had "gotten us exactly nowhere." The clear result: "The Taliban will rule Afghanistan through the winter, thereby handing the United States a humiliating and gratuitous defeat." Note that these examples of *TNR*'s deeply misguided defeatism come only from those articles written under the magazine's editorial voice. When editor Peter Beinart wrote a column intending to smear the *Nation* as "anti-American," he deployed as evidence a single article written by someone whose name appears nowhere on the masthead and who enjoys no institutional affiliation with the magazine.[32] (This was not only sleazy, it was also quite lazy, as some genuine *Nation* writers, particularly comrade Cockburn, would have provided inviting targets.)

The damage to the public discourse wrought by *TNR* did not even end in its pages. Over the years, it has helped launch the careers of a bevy of hawkish writers who have carried the talent for malevolent invective with them like a communicable disease. (Involuntary) Ex-Editors Andrew Sullivan and Michael Kelly did their best to revive the tactics of Joe McCarthy and Roy Cohn during this war by whipping up hysteria about "Fifth Columns" and "liars, frauds and hypocrites" when characterizing those deemed to lack sufficient enthusiasm for the endeavor. Ex-senior editor Jacob Heilbrunn also sounded very much like the armchair warriors in his former office. Writing in the *Los Angeles Times* on November 4, Heilbrunn prematurely credited the Taliban with victory, falsely declaring, "The U.S. is not losing the first round against the Taliban; it has already lost it." This analysis echoed that of former *TNR* senior editor Charles Krauthammer, who complained in the *Washington Post* on October 30, 2001: "The war is not going well. The Taliban have not yielded ground. Not a single important Taliban leader has been killed, or captured or has defected."[33] In virtually every one of these cases, the pundits' prescription was the same: Bring in the ground troops and expand the fighting or risk humiliation and defeat.

The great irony of the destruction the *New Republic* has wrought to the liberal position was the fact that beneath its loud conservative breast-beating, it remained home to any number of talented and articulate liberal writers on many domestic, legal, and economic issues. Moreover, Wieseltier's pages continued to boast some of the finest literary criticism to be found anywhere. Rarely does the magazine ever manage to publish even a single issue without containing something of value. Even today it boasts some of the most perspicacious writers on a variety of domestic issues that can be found at any publication. John Judis, Jonathan Cohn, Jonathan Chait, and Greg Esterbrook, together with the younger writers Franklin Foer, Noah Schieber, Ryan Lizza, and Sarah Wildman, among others, are always worth reading and frequently come up with both original perspectives and reporting on issues that manage to pierce the conventional wisdom in important ways. The reader will see that I have relied on these bylines with some frequency in this work.

But the liberals could not match the ferocity of the neocons, who, on many issues, were to the right even of the Rupert Murdoch-funded and William Kristol-edited *Weekly Standard*. As *TNR*'s post-Kinsley/Hertzberg decline continued apace, it became all the clearer why Peretz proved so eager to unload controlling interest in the magazine to the conservative investors Michael Steinhardt and Roger Hertog. The latter, a prominent patron of conservative organizations, is also chairman of the Manhattan Institute and a trustee of the American Enterprise Institute. Both he and Michael Steinhardt supported George Bush over Peretz's pet, Al Gore, in 2000.[34]

The trials and tribulations of the fate of American liberalism at *TNR* are important not only because of its storied history as one of its most important twentieth-century institutions, but also because even with all the above-accumulated evidence, the "even-the-liberal-*New Republic*" formulation remains a staple of our political discourse. The notion of a genuinely liberal *New Republic* is so out of date that, in the spring of 2002, the magazine carried a full-page subscription advertisement bearing the likeness of Orson Welles. The long-dead director was quoted explaining, "The democratic cause is served by the *New Republic*. It is one of the most valuable institutions of American journalism." This was a new concept in the history of sound-bite advertising—using a testimonial more than fifty years old from a man long dead. Rather amazingly, however, much of the alleged SCLM still have not gotten the news. Steinhardt himself said he was pretty sure the magazine he was buying into "was not a liberal one."[35] Yet *Washington Post* coverage questioned why a conservative would wish to place his millions at the service of this alleged "liberal bastion."[36] Part of the problem was no doubt laziness. But an equal, if not larger, part is that media conservatives have found it convenient to call the magazine liberal to tar legitimate liberalism as beyond the pale. When plugged into a late September 2002 Google search, the words "liberal New Republic" resulted in 341 recent hits.

The unconscious casting of the conservative pundit David Broder as an anti-ideological soothsayer and the neoconservative *New Republic* as a liberal voice has the predictable effect of recalibrating an entire ideological spectrum toward the right. Calling a conservative a centrist and a neoconservative a liberal means that no genuine liberals are allowed into the game. No less significant, however, is the issue of the distance the spectrum has traveled into right field.

While there are certainly some nutty leftists out there, they are for the most part confined to extremely obscure media outlets. When a conservative *Boston Globe* columnist named Jeff Jacoby chose to complain "slander is just fine when the left does it," as he titled one column, he was compelled to resort to the following examples:

> Gay activist Dan Savage boasted on Salon.com of his efforts to infect Gary Bauer with flu. In his New York Press column, Alexander Cockburn suggested "dropping a tactical nuclear weapon on the Cuban section of Miami." A sickening TV spot by the NAACP showed a pickup truck dragging a chain and accused Bush of having "killed" James Byrd "all over again" when he opposed a change in the Texas hate crimes law.
>
> For pure vitriol, nothing matched the eruption of former Clinton aide Paul Begala, who wrote on MSNBC.com about the map with color-coded election returns that showed a sea of red for Bush with small blotches of blue for Gore. "But if you look closely at that map you see a more complex picture. You see the state where James Byrd was lynched-dragged behind a pickup truck until his body came apart—it's red. You see the state where Matthew Shepard was crucified . . . for the crime of being gay—it's red. You see the state where right-wing extremists blew up a federal office building and murdered scores of federal employees: red. The state where an Army private thought to be gay was bludgeoned to death with a baseball bat . . . and the state where Bob Jones University spews its anti-Catholic bigotry: they're all red, too." Ugly, nasty stuff. A conservative who talked this way about liberals would be lacerated. When will liberals stop talking this way about conservatives?[37]

Just look who Jacoby is forced to choose as targets for his fulminations: a gay sex columnist—a self-described "pushy fag"—for the alternative press writing on a Web site; a discredited Stalinist who continues to be allowed, for reasons I do not understand, to stain the good name of the *Nation* with his presence; a television commercial by the NAACP; and the political consultant Paul Begala on the MSNBC.com Web site. Jacoby's other targets in this column, no less marginal, included the foolish ex-talk show host Bill Maher, the Naderite filmmaker Michael Moore, and a shamefully quoted-out-of-context Bill Clinton.[38] These are not exactly targets of the caliber of say George Will, Robert Novak, Pat Buchanan, or even Jacoby himself, who writes a column in one of the nation's most important dailies that is frequently accused by conservatives of demonstrating a distinct liberal bias.

One is tempted to wonder if the charges against the *Globe* might not be true, and if Jacoby was hired as a kind of Manchurian columnist, spotlighted for the purposes of discrediting all conservative pundits. He is certainly not doing the conservative cause much credit. Take, for instance, his attack on Begala quoted above. Jacoby did not mention in his column that Begala was not simply spouting off about the horrors of "blue" America in isolation. As Nick Confessore pointed out at the time, Begala was responding directly to comments made by former *Boston Globe* pundit (and plagiarist) Mike Barnicle on MSNBC, in which Barnicle looked at the same electoral map and concluded that it divided America into two camps: "Wal-Mart versus Martha Stewart . . . Family values versus a sense of entitlement." Begala wrote that neither Barnicle's view nor the one he presented put forth an accurate picture of the nation. His intended purpose was satire. When contacted about his error by reporter Dan Kennedy, Jacoby preferred to stick to his badly aimed guns, though he did not attempt to defend its substance. "He's basically full of shit," Jacoby replied. "He makes it absolutely clear to anyone who reads his piece that he considers conservative voters to be the lowest of slime." [39]

To be fair to Jacoby, his journalistic standards are not that pathetic when viewed in the context of some other conservative pundits. The *Wall Street Journal's* Peggy Noonan decried what she termed Begala's "remarkably hate-filled column." [40] Like a mini House Committee on Un-American Activities, the former *TNR* editor and British national Andrew Sullivan took to issuing a sarcastic "Begala Award" on his Web site to those whose patriotic fervor he deemed insufficient. The *Washington Post's* Michael Kelly deployed the same tactic to term Begala "a political thug," adding: "Mr. Begala can be counted on to spelunk the lowest level of the sewer. But even for him, the passage above must stand as the ultimate smear." Blasting off into journalistic outer space, Kelly—writing during the 2000 Florida election crisis—deployed his misreading of Begala's argument to warn against the danger of allowing a Gore presidency:

> This is why the Clinton-Gore selling of the White House was such a bad thing: The greedheads-in-chief didn't trash one White House; because they got away with it, they guaranteed the trashing of future White Houses. So too with the vote-rigging in Florida. There have been close presidential elections before, and there have been elections in which the loser was certain he had been robbed. But never before has any presidential candidate done what Gore has done; never before has the loser taken to the courts rather than accept the verdict rendered—at this point, twice over.
>
> Even if Gore ultimately loses in Florida, he will have come very, very close to winning. Moreover, he will have done this with his image-skin more or less intact. For Gore has already won an astonishing propaganda victory: With the help of reasonably sympathetic coverage from a largely Democratic and liberal national press corps, he has managed to spin his extraordinary, radical, unprecedented behavior as reasonable—and legitimate. This probably ensures that future close presidential

elections will produce future Gore Losers, marching off to the courts and the cameras with their armies of lawyers and thugs, demanding recounts, rewriting the rules and the laws, convincing more and more Americans that their electoral system is, like those in most of the world, just another rigged game.[41]

Of course Begala did not even remotely say that votes won by Bush were "really not legitimate." He did not say any of the things for which Kelly attempted to hold him responsible. He was merely criticizing Barnicle's slander of those parts of the nation that voted in the majority. Though the Florida example will be discussed at length in a later chapter of this work, what Kelly's ethics-free flight of fancy demonstrates is the political value to Republicans of conservative punditocracy dominance. Nowhere, for instance, does it appear relevant in Kelly's calculations that Gore actually won the popular vote and would likely have won any fair and full count of Florida.

Rather amazingly, Jacoby's slanderous misuse of Begala's column does not even appear to be a particularly lazy or inaccurate day for him. About six months earlier, on July 3, 2000, he published, under his own byline, the contents of an e-mail he received about the alleged tragedies that allegedly befell a number of signers of the Declaration of Independence. Once again, he had conservative company. Oliver North did the same thing on MSNBC.com. Jonah Goldberg published portions of it on National Review Online. Unhappily for Jacoby, the e-mail turned out to have been based on a document that had been widely circulated through the ages, as well as almost entirely fictional.

When the hoax was discovered, Jacoby's editors suspended him for four months, a rather light sentence given the fact that plagiarists on the very same page had been unceremoniously fired. Nevertheless the conservative white male victimization machine whipped itself into a full-fledged frenzy, decrying alleged liberal ideological "censorship." David Horowitz complained on his Web site that it was "self-evident that no one but a conservative would have been treated this way." (Though Horowitz seemed never to have read the column himself, as he appeared to think it referred to the authors of the Constitution, rather than the Declaration of Independence.) James Taranto of the *Wall Street Journal* editorial page's Web site ominously noted, "Jacoby happens to be the *Globe's* only conservative columnist, and some conservatives now accuse the paper of singling him out on ideological grounds." His colleague John Fund at the page informed the *Washington Post*, "It's an open secret that Jacoby was viewed at best with sneering indifference and at worst with contempt and hostility in the newsroom." Meanwhile, Jonah Goldberg, who probably should have stayed out of this one, accused the "liberal" *Globe* of, "gunning for [Jacoby] by blowing the situation out of all proportion."[42]

Jacoby circulated an excuse-laden e-mail in which he sought to minimize his transgressions. "As a columnist, I don't undertake original historical research, but I care greatly about accuracy."[43] In fact, it's hard to see that Jacoby does any research, historical or otherwise. Not only did Jacoby publish work under his own name that was not his own, he did not do even the most rudimentary check to determine its probity. He did, according to his e-mail, pull a few high-school-level history books off of his shelf, including an encyclopedia. But it apparently never occurred to him to visit the local library either. Nor did he bother to pick up a phone and try to reach a genuine colonial historian at say, Harvard, MIT, Tufts, Brandeis, Boston College, or Boston University—where he had once been employed—all of which were within a local phone call from the *Globe*'s offices. (Colonial historians are not exactly a rare breed in and around New England, after all.) Jacoby, in other words, did not do a dime's worth of fact-checking before throwing up someone else's words under his own byline in the newspaper's pages. To top it all off, even his mea culpa was factually inaccurate. Jacoby blamed the original mistake on a column "published by Rush Limbaugh." In fact, it was published by Limbaugh's father, Rush Sr. This would be a minor error were it not for the fact that he was talking about the most popular talk show host in the universe. Jacoby, it should be noted, like so many conservative pundits, was not a journalist by training before being given newsprint columns upon which to voice his opinions. A lawyer by training, he began his career working on a congressional campaign, as an assistant to Boston University president John Silber, and as a founding director of the far-right Pioneer Institute. In 1987, he was hired by the *Boston Herald*, a right-wing tabloid, as an editorial writer, and seven years later by the *Globe*. Rather than a victim of alleged liberal media prejudice, Jacoby was actually an affirmative-action baby, albeit one issued from a program designed for incompetent conservative pundits.

---

A final measure of just how effective far-right voices have become in driving debate into its ideological corner is the incredibly tender fashion in which they are treated by Howard Kurtz. By virtue of his responsibilities at CNN as host of *Reliable Sources* and in the *Washington Post* as its media reporter and columnist—the *New York Times* does not have a comparable position—Kurtz is widely recognized as the most influential media reporter in America, akin to the top cop on the beat. There is no question that Kurtz is a terrifically energetic reporter, and readers will see that I have relied on his work frequently in this book. I have no concerns whatsoever about the truthfulness of what he publishes. But all media writers, including myself, walk a difficult line with regard to conflicts of interest.

As a reporter and a wide-ranging talk-show host, Kurtz, unlike a columnist, cannot choose simply to ignore news. What's more, the newspaper for which he writes cannot help but cover CNN, the network on which he appears, and vice versa, as they both constitute veritable 800-pound gorillas in the media jungle. Nor, for that matter, can Kurtz avoid covering their respective competitors, which is another form of conflict of interest, however unspoken. In addition, Kurtz is a prolific author of books, which implies that he has an interest in being well reviewed and booked as a guest on television shows that might promote his books. Finally, he also writes free-lance articles for other publications. Because neither the *Washington Post* nor CNN is willing (or able) to say to Kurtz, "You will work for us and only us"—and pay him enough to do so, as say, *New York* magazine does with the brilliantly acerbic Michael Wolff—Kurtz is in the extremely difficult position of facing a conflict of interest whether he writes or discusses a media issue or whether he ignores it.

But Kurtz's conflicts are rarely raised in the media, owing to the power of the real estate he controls. In one rare examination, however, prompted by the complaints of MSNBC's Jerry Nachman, the *Los Angeles Times* quoted William Serrin, the former head of the New York University journalism department, calling Kurtz's competing loyalties "dangerous" and "outrageous. . . . Do we really think he'll go on CNN and do a provocative attack on the Post?" James Fallows, author of *Breaking the News: How the Media Undermine Democracy*, was also critical. "Since Howie Kurtz has been so vigi-lant over the years about financial conflicts of interest, you have to ask how he would cover this situation if it involved someone else," Fallows insisted. He continued, "My guess is that he'd take Jerry Nachman's side of the argument. After all, you have a very influential media critic receiving a regular salary—and getting valuable broadcast exposure—from one of the networks he covers."

Kurtz responded to the criticism in anger. He termed it a "partisan" attack, and insisted, "Everyone knows I work for CNN and the *Post* and that I regularly criticize both on TV and in print, in ways that few journalists do when reporting on their employer. We're totally out front and in the open about my affiliations, and readers and viewers can make up their own minds as to whether I'm reporting fairly on these organizations. Just a few days ago, I wrote an article for the *Post* about dumb com-ments made by Ted Turner [CNN founder]. . . . People who know me, know that I'm fair."[44] It is an ironic defense to say the least. In the first place, Nachman's question is not about Kurtz per se, but about the structural institutional conflict his various roles inevitably create. Kurtz could be Mother Teresa and the conflict would still not dis-appear. Moreover, the case with which he chooses to defend himself actually works to indict him. As Kurtz must surely know, there is criticism and then there is *criticism*. Ted Turner has been powerless at CNN for many years and regularly condemns the direction it has taken under AOL Time Warner. The *New York Times* terms him "the company's biggest inside critic."[45] It's hard to imagine that anything would please the current brass there more than beating up on Crazy Old Ted, particularly when his recent comments equating Israeli and Palestinian "terrorism" were attacked by virtu-ally every respectable commentator who addressed them. Any criticism of Turner that appeared to be coming from a person connected to CNN would have been most welcome at that difficult moment.[46]

Because he juggles so many balls simultaneously, Kurtz is a particularly useful weathervane to determine the relative power of his various affiliations. It is no secret to anyone in the industry that CNN has sought to ingratiate itself with conservatives in recent years as it has lost viewers to Fox. Shortly after taking the reins, in the summer of 2001, CNN's chief, former *Time* magazine managing editor Walter Isaacson, initiated a number of moves designed to enhance the station's appeal to conservatives, including a high-profile meeting with Congressional Republican leaders to listen to their concerns. The bias inherent in Kurtz's work at the *Post* and CNN would be consistent with that of a media critic who had read the proverbial writing on the wall.

Whatever his personal ideology may be, it is hard to avoid the conclusion, based on an examination of his work, that Howard Kurtz loves conservatives but has little time for liberals. Kurtz's overt sympathy for conservatives and their critique of the media is, given the power and influence of his position, not unlike having the police chief in the hands of one faction of the mob. Here, for instance, are just a few of Kurtz's interventions on behalf of George W. Bush during the summer of 2002, when the president appeared to be, however briefly, on the ropes against any and all charges related to his dealings with Harken Oil, corporate responsibility, and the state of the economy:

"Why is the press resurrecting, like that seven-million-year-old human skull, this 13-year old incident, in which Bush sold some stock in his company Harken Energy?"

"Laura Ingraham, is this the liberal press, in your view, trying to prove that Bush is soft on corporate crime because he once cut corners himself?"[47]

"Regulators concluded he did nothing improper. Now, there may be some new details, granted, but this is—is this important enough to suggest, imply or otherwise infer, as the press might be doing, Molly Ivins, that this is somehow in a league with Tyco or Worldcom or Enron?"[48]

"Is there a media stereotype, Bush and Cheney, ex-oilmen, ex-CEOs in bed with big business that they can't shake?"[49]

"Are the media unfairly blaming President Bush for sinking stock prices? Are journalists obsessed with Bush and Cheney's business dealings in the oil industry, and is the press turning CEOs into black-hatted villains?"[50]

"If you look at all the negative media coverage, Rich Lowry, you'd think that Bush's stock has crashed along with the market. Is he hurting, or is this some kind of nefarious media creation?"[51]

"And why is that the president's fault? Is it his job to keep stock prices up?"[52]

"But it seems to me the media have kind of created a Catch-22 situation here. If Bush doesn't talk about the economy, you see a lot of stories saying he's out of touch. On the other hand if he does have a conference devoted to raising public awareness of the, of the economic situation, the media say, well, this is just a political effort designed to give the appearance of concern by the president. Is that unfair?"[53]

Kurtz even gave credence to the ludicrous Limbaugh-like insistence that somehow Bill Clinton caused the corporate meltdown of the summer of 2002. Kurtz quoted these arguments, noting, "They say well he set a bad example for the country. He showed he could lie and get away with it, so is that a reverse kind of 'let's drag in the political figure we don't like and pin the tail on him?'" It was, as his guest Martha Brant had to inform him, "a ridiculous argument," surprising Kurtz, who asked again, "You're saying there's no parallel?"[54] Recall that this is the premier program of media criticism, hosted by the most influential media reporter in America. It did not occur to Kurtz to note, for instance, as Peter Beinart did, that Bill Clinton vetoed the 1995 bill that shielded corporate executives from shareholder lawsuits or that Clinton's Securities and Exchange Commission chief wanted to ban accounting firms from consulting contracts with the firms they were also auditing. That override occurred with the vote of every single Republican. Thirty-three of thirty-seven members of Congress who signed their names to protests against the Clinton S.E.C. were also Republican. The man who led the effort was Harvey Pitt, then a lobbyist, whom George W. Bush chose to head the SEC and who was later forced to resign.[55] But to Kurtz, it is somehow a legitimate, intelligent question to debate on a media criticism program whether Clinton's lying about getting blow jobs in the Oval Office was somehow responsible for the multibillion-dollar corporate accounting scandal his administration sought to prevent.

In addition to flacking for Bush, Kurtz also flacks for Bush's flack, Ari Fleischer. This press secretary, as many have noted, is remarkable for his unwillingness to answer the simplest question with a straight answer. Dubbed the "flack out of hell" by *GQ* magazine when he was still a Congressional staffer, Fleischer does not merely spin reporters, as is customary in the job he holds, but rather, he treats them with unmasked contempt, answering their specific queries with condescending civics lectures. Michael Kinsley described his technique as the employment of "a sort of Imperial Court English, in which any question, no matter how specific, is parried with general assurances that the emperor is keenly aware and deeply concerned and firmly resolved and infallibly right and the people are fully supportive and further information should be sought elsewhere."

Fleischer, of course, serves at the pleasure of the president and in stiffing and insulting the press, he can honestly be said to just be doing his job. As Bob Schieffer, host of CBS's *Face the Nation*, noted, "This is not an administration that's interested in a happy press. What they're interested in is getting their message across."[56] His colleague Bill Plant adds, "In this administration, the controls on information are tighter than in any other one I have covered." Plant has been around since 1980.[57] Sometimes it works to its advantage, sometimes not. In September 2002, ABC's nonpartisan guide to inside politics, *The Note*, noticed, on the occasion of one of Fleischer's routine denials of something virtually everyone who paid attention knew to be true: that is, that some disagreement existed within the administration over the course to take with Iraq. "Indeed, Fleischer said this fewer than forty-eight hours before Secretary of State Colin Powell admitted 'I think there are lots of differences—some are real, some are perceived, some are over-hyped' and Republican Senate Majority Leader Trent Lott told reporters 'I do think that we're going to have to get a more coherent message together.'"[58] *The Note* noted that the Bush team has always had a credibility problem with some reporters because of their insistence on saying "up is down" and "black is white." The authors added, while "the public doesn't necessarily see or pay attention to all of this, there has been a corrosive effect on the filter through which media and political elites view Administration statements and actions."[59]

All this makes it more unusual for a journalist to celebrate the man responsible for shutting down the avenues of communication to journalists by any means necessary and deliberately misleading them about the truth. But with what appears to be the journalistic equivalent of the Stockholm Syndrome, to Kurtz everything about Ari Fleischer comes up smelling roses. During the 2000 campaign, he was "well liked by journalists."[60] Even after Fleischer had deliberately misled a gullible press corps about the level of alleged "vandalism" undertaken by departing Clinton administration staffers, Kurtz judged him "by most accounts, [to have] nearly played error-free ball as Bush's spokesman."[61] Kurtz also marveled at Fleischer as "a star . . . accustomed to the pressure-cooker life of White House flackery" who "isn't shy about elbowing those who got out of line." (This was Kurtz's way of describing Fleischer's attempts to threaten a reporter who asked Fleischer an uncomfortable question and was informed that he had been "noted in the building," along with Fleischer's censorious comments about the comedian Bill Maher.)[62]

Despite his affection for Fleischer, what Kurtz does best is puff up right-wing pundits, helping them to build credibility in the mainstream by treating them as brave-hearted warriors in a hostile leftist media world. Many months after Bernard Goldberg's central accusation regarding the allegedly unfair labeling of "conservatives" by liberals had been revealed to be pure ignorant hokum by Geoffrey Nunberg in the *American Prospect* (twice), Kurtz was still repeating the accusation.[63] He repeatedly celebrates the work of the *National Review* and its online component, which together, in Kurtz's words, "take a special pleasure in castigating the liberal media."[64] Kurtz even accused Tom Daschle of "having lost a couple of screws" for taking on Rush Limbaugh's hysterical attacks. (See chapter 5 for an example.)

The most popular guests on Kurtz's program are conservatives. His favorite of all, judged by the number of appearances as well as the sheer number of valentines regularly sent in his column, would have to be Rich Lowry, editor of William F. Buckley Jr.'s *National Review*. According to Kurtz, Rich Lowry "oozes niceness." He boasts an "aw-shucks charm and boyish grin" with a "sting [that] is usually softened by a soothing wit" and "enjoy(s) going against the grain." He has, moreover, "given the magazine something of a hipness injection" by writing "such in-your-face cover headlines about Al Gore and Bill Clinton as 'Thou Shalt Not Steal' and 'Farewell to the Big Creep.'"[65] (Kurtz means this to be a compliment.) When Lowry is otherwise indisposed, Kurtz is eager to book virtually anyone else on the *National Review*'s editorial staff onto the program, including online editor Jonah Goldberg, managing editor Jay Nordlinger, senior editor Ramesh Ponnuru, or White House correspondent Byron York to offer up the hard-right perspective on the news, with only the most tepid of response from the center-left.

Kurtz celebrates conservatives, as he did Rich Lowry, for "going against the grain." According to Kurtz, these lovable conservatives are always rooting for the wrong team, even when they don't. In what is surely one of the silliest suck-up sentences ever published outside the confines of *Tiger Beat*, Kurtz praised Kristol, who, "by his own admission . . . is a contrarian," for being "that rarity in Manhattan, a Mets fan."[66] In fact, when Bill Kristol (and I) were growing up, Mets fans were far more populous than Yankees fans. For instance in 1970, when I was ten and Bill Kristol was seventeen, the Mets outdrew the Yankees in home attendance by nearly 250 percent, slightly more than they had the previous year. The Yankees, beginning in 1965, were a lousy team with no personality, while the Mets were the cities' beloved bums who rose to greatness in one of the most inspiring sports stories of the centuries. The Mets captured the city's romantic imagination from the first pathetic moments of their first season. As the *New Yorker*'s Roger Angell put it in the spring of 1962, "The only early amazement generated by the Mets had been their terrifying departure from the runway in a full nose dive."[67] For the entire existence of their franchise—save perhaps the horrible summer of 2002—the Mets have been "New York's Most Beloved Baseball Team," as they were named in the subtitle of a recent history of the club.[68] There was nothing remotely contrarian ever about being a Mets fan, save for Kurtz's desire to paint Kristol as a hero on such flimsy ground.

But brave Bill Kristol is hardly alone. In language that would not be out of place in a mid-sixties Beach Boy fanzine, Kurtz writes of Tucker Carlson that he "exudes an unmistakable sense of California cool. . . . He is by all accounts devoted to his wife, Susie, a former religion teacher, and their three children. He goes to church every Sunday. He's an amateur carpenter who is trying to fix up their century-old house in Alexandria. He gardens. He unloads groceries from the boat at their summer place on a Maine island. His main vices are booze and cigarettes." Sean Hannity, the conservative talk-show host on Fox, is also quite a guy. "What's the 40-year-old conservative talker's secret?" Kurtz asks, once again, taking on the voice of a writer for *Seventeen*. "Hannity says he's still the same blue-collar guy who grew up as the son of a Long Island probation officer, delivered newspapers at age 8, later tended bar and flipped hamburgers, dropped out of college and became a building contractor and father of four children."[69] (Try imagining an alternative to this sentence: "Hannity says he has become a total jerk, whose millionaire lifestyle has allowed him to live a life of endless champagne, caviar and call girls. . . .") Kurtz also lends his columns to conservatives to trade compliments. Marshall Wittmann of the Heritage Foundation calls Bill Kristol "the Bill Buckley of the next generation."[70] But Wittmann is a great guy too, and look here, a non-conformer. "He has more to say than most people," says *Weekly Standard* editor Bill Kristol, an old pal. "He does think ahead and tries to figure out how the ball's going to bounce down the road. It's not just the same conventional wisdom."[71]

With the possible exception of Rich Lowry, whom he has quoted more than forty times in two years, Kurtz's heart beats perhaps truest for Andrew Sullivan. Kurtz has quoted Sullivan more than seventy-five times in the past decade, according to Nexis, but this is partially a tribute to Sullivan's unmatched ability to make himself a news story.[72] In Kurtz's view, Sullivan is always good news: "a pugnacious writer with a superhero's capacity for multiple identities . . . , a brainy Brit immersed in lowbrow American culture . . . caustic conservative in the liberal magazine universe . . . [possessing] a college debater's tenacity and a showman's flair, the Adams-Morgan resident has a grand old time surprising and infuriating his friends, his enemies and, for added spice, his employers." Kurtz marvels at Sullivan's ability to hang with celebrities, noting that he has "hobnobbed with the Kennedys at Hyannis Port, lunched with John McCain in the Senate dining room, sailed on Barry Diller's yacht. But despite his cocky persona, Sullivan sticks with his decidedly un-famous friends and spends the summers at his waterfront condo in Provincetown, Mass." (No doubt the Provincetown proletariat (including for instance, Norman Mailer, the country's most famous writer), is grateful for the little bit of celebrity light Sullivan shines in its dreary mill-town midst.) Meanwhile, back in Washington, Kurtz's next stop on this whirlwind afternoon is Sullivan's apartment, "which can only be described as a fabulous space."[73]

Kurtz goes further than just writing uncritical puff pieces about the right-wing media in the *Washington Post* and ensuring that their views are represented—often with no liberal counterpart—on his CNN program. He flacks for them as well, debasing the newspaper's standards if necessary. He certainly did so for Sullivan in the case of the *New Republic* and the *New York Times*, in the spring of 2002. With no evidence except quotes from the likes of Lowry, Kurtz attributed the move on the part of both magazines to a kind of retaliation for Sullivan's criticism. As if working out of

Sullivan's own PR office, Kurtz wrote, "Andrew Sullivan, the confrontational conservative columnist, has been attempting the high-wire act of writing for the *New York Times* while frequently whacking the *Times* for liberal bias on his Web site. Now the tightrope has snapped." Kurtz also noted, "Sullivan's opinions also cost him his weekly 'TRB' column in the *New Republic*, where he is still listed as a contributor. During the 2000 campaign he assailed Al Gore, a longtime friend of owner Martin Peretz, who at one point complained about Sullivan's 'fevered' and 'absurd attacks.' Sullivan also wrote on his Web site that the *New Republic* 'has now sadly all but surrendered to the left of the party.' Editor Peter Beinart began writing the TRB column last fall." Strangely, in writing this piece entirely from the perspective of Sullivan's hurt feelings, Kurtz quoted no one from the *New York Times* or the *New Republic*.[74]

Again the question of a potential personal conflict raises its head. Was Kurtz repaying the *New Republic* for the unflattering cover story it published on his work—just about the only one to appear anywhere in the media where his presence looms so large?[75] To say that *TNR*'s story affected Kurtz in any way is to engage in a bit of indefensible dimestore psychoanalysis. We cannot know his motivations—just as Kurtz cannot know why the *New Republic* or *New York Times* decided to dump Sullivan. And what of the journalistically questionable attack on the *Times*? Of course, it is no secret that the attendant standards for a *Washington Post* reporter tweaking the *New York Times* are not necessarily those of say, Robert Caro on Robert Moses. But Kurtz did not even entertain any view save that of Sullivan and his conservative comrades. He did not mention, for instance, the discomfort that Sullivan caused the *Times* in initially accepting for his Web site—and then returning—thousands of dollars from the pharmaceutical industry shortly after he praised the industry to the skies in the pages of the magazine. (Of course a man who works for the *Washington Post* and CNN, while covering both, may not view this as a significant problem—or one that he can, in good conscience, address.) And while Sullivan's work for the *Times* may have been better disciplined than his Web site, in which he frequently recounts stories about his car, dinner dates, his "stomach evacuations," and his thirty-two inch waistline, in between dishonest McCarthyite missives against liberals such as myself, Susan Sontag, and Paul Krugman, his work there certainly must have embarrassed the Newspaper of Record. As Judith Shulevitz pointed out in a critique of Sullivan's "dangerously misleading" paean to testosterone, he was permitted to "mix up his subjective reactions with laboratory work." Stanford neurobiologist Robert Sapolsky told Shulevitz at the time, Sullivan "is entitled to his fairly nonscientific opinion, but I'm astonished at the *New York Times*." The Sullivan Principles of Pre-emptive Sexual Disclosure also must have embarrassed the *Times* magazine when he used its pages to out as gay two Clinton Cabinet members and liberal Democrats like Rosie O'Donnell, something he no doubt came to regret when his own sex life became tabloid fare.[76]

Because Kurtz is not interested in the ideas of the conservatives he profiles, merely in their charming and non-conformist personalities, he is able to act as a kind of PR agent for them without addressing the question of whether the work of those he so enthusiastically champions has any genuine merit. Meanwhile, it would be hard to find a single liberal who has enjoyed the love bombs from Kurtz to which so many conservatives appear entitled in both of his high-profile outlets.

Because Kurtz shares the view of the media as a bastion of leftist thought control, he has said that anyone who does not share this view "is just in denial."[77] He even asked his fellow CNN anchor Aaron Brown on the air whether Brown worried "that a lot of people out there may believe that CNN and other news organizations tilt to the left?"[78] His views, as manifested not only in these statements but also in his coverage as well as in the direction of his talk show, go a long way toward proving the adage, "It is better to know the judge than to know the law." When it comes to mainstream media criticism, Howard Kurtz is "the judge." For journalists charged with liberal bias, that means a "guilty" verdict nearly every time. Case closed; evidence unnecessary.

# 5

# The Punditocracy Three

*Radio and the Internet*

TALK RADIO IS A GREAT DEAL MORE POPULAR—and powerful—than most of us realize. Twenty-two percent of all Americans surveyed say they listen. In some major cities, the number is as high as 40 percent.[1] Conservative domination of the talk-radio airwaves is so extensive as to be undisputed, even by the usual suspects. There's not a single well-known liberal talk-show host in the nation and barely a host who does not at least lean well in the direction of the extreme right. The most popular shows are hosted by Rush Limbaugh, G. Gordon Liddy, Oliver North, Sean Hannity, Armstrong Williams, Blanquita Collum, Michael Savage, Neil Boortz, Bob Grant, Bob Dornan, Michael Medved, Michael Reagan, Dr. Laura Schlesinger, Howard Stern, Don Imus, Michael Graham, Ken Hamblin, and Laura Ingraham. Every single one is a movement conservative with politics located at the extreme far-right end of the political spectrum. So far to the right is the general pack of talk-show hosts that, early in the Clinton Administration, G. Gordon Liddy felt empowered to instruct listeners on the best way to assassinate U.S. government officials from the Bureau of Alcohol, Tobacco, and Firearms without receiving much in the way of censure from this community. (His exact words were "Head shots. Head shots.") Once, during a joint C-Span appearance with a right-wing talk-show host and activist, Paul Weyrich, I challenged him to condemn Liddy's statement and he refused, as he put it, to "criticize a brother talk-show host," even for advocating the murder of U.S. government officials. When Bill O'Reilly joined the ranks of radio talk-show hosts in the spring of 2002, he could legitimately claim to be a relative liberal in their midst. Even the Internet gossip Matt Drudge, no stranger to irresponsible right-wing rumor-mongering, says that when he has a story that is "playing among the wing nuts, this tells me it's going to be a huge talk-radio thing."[2]

Indeed, because the radio business has become so centralized in recent years, it is easy for talk-show hosts to spread themselves across the dial with incredible speed. O'Reilly's show debuted in the spring of 2002 with 205 stations, ahead of Michael

Medved's 130, Sean Hannity's 150 or so, and Laura Ingraham's nearly 200 markets. But O'Reilly was still way behind Limbaugh's market share, which has gone as high as 650 stations and anywhere from fifteen to twenty million listeners, depending on whose statistics you prefer.³ Few progressives are ever given shows, and efforts such as Gary Hart's and Mario Cuomo's haven't amounted to much. The left-wing Texas populist Jim Hightower appeared to be building a strong regional audience back in the mid-1990s, but he was highly critical of Disney and its owner, Michael Eisner. Not long after Disney bought the station, Hightower's show was abruptly canceled. KGO in San Francisco, perhaps alone in the country, boasts two liberal hosts, Bernie Ward and Ray Taliafero, whose shows appear at 10 P.M. to 1 A.M. and 1 A.M. to 5 A.M.— not exactly primetime. The *Washington Post*'s Paul Farhi notes, "The drought has gotten so bad that the talk industry is starting to manufacture its own outrage." A few months ago, *Talkers* magazine reported on the existence of an anonymous creature it termed the 'Lone Liberal,' who was eager to appear on radio talk shows to do battle with its legions of conservative hosts. Its publisher, Michael Harrison, reported that this exotic animal was "hot as a firecracker" on the circuit, averaging eight to nine talk-show bookings a week. In fact, the Lone Liberal was always a ruse, played by Harrison himself. "I'm far more conservative than the Lone Liberal," he explained. "I live in the real world."⁴

Edward Monks, a Eugene, Oregon, attorney, calculates that in his city, conservatives enjoy a 4,000-to-zero hour advantage over liberals on the radio. He wrote in *The Register-Guard*: "Political opinions expressed on talk radio are approaching the level of uniformity that would normally be achieved only in a totalitarian society. . . . There is nothing fair, balanced or democratic about it."⁵ Monks noted that as recently as 1974, such domination would have been not only inconceivable, but illegal. Back then, the Federal Communications Commission was still demanding "strict adherence to the [1949] Fairness Doctrine as the single most important requirement of operation in the public interest—the sine qua non for grant for renewal of license." This view was ratified by the U.S. Supreme Court in 1969 when it reaffirmed the people's right to a free exchange of opposing views, with roughly equal time given to all sides, if demanded, on the public airwaves. The doctrine was overturned by the Reagan-appointed FCC in 1987. The chairman then, Mark Fowler, made clear his view that "the perception of broadcasters as community trustees should be replaced by a view of broadcasters as marketplace participants."⁶ Meanwhile, media companies, together with cigarette and beer companies, working with Republican Senator Bob Packwood, set up the Freedom of Expression Foundation to fight the fairness doctrine in the U.S. Court of Appeals for Washington, D.C. The companies won in a 2-to-1 decision in which the two judges ruling in their favor happened to be Robert Bork and Antonin Scalia. President Reagan vetoed attempts by Congress to reinstate the doctrine, and the net result has been the complete far-right domination of the nation's airwaves, owing entirely to what analysts call "marketplace realities."

The amazing career of Rush Limbaugh owes a great deal to that moment in history. It is testament to just how well success succeeds in the U.S. media, regardless of accuracy, fairness, or even common sense. Limbaugh's legendary lies and mythological meanderings have been rewarded not only with legions of listeners, but also with incredible riches—a contract said to be worth $250 million over seven years. It has also won him the respect of the media establishment. Limbaugh, for instance, has been treated to laudatory coverage in *Time* and *Newsweek* and was invited by host Tim Russert of *Meet the Press* to be a guest commentator on what is certainly the most influential political program on television. And yet Limbaugh is, to put it bluntly, deranged. Fairness and Accuracy in Reporting has published an entire book of Rushisms that have turned out to be false, unsubstantiated, or just plain wacko. It is not just, as Maureen Dowd put it, his obsession with "feminazis," "environmental wackos," Anita Hill, Jesse Jackson, Hillary Clinton, Teddy Kennedy, Mario Cuomo, homeless advocates, dolphins, spotted owls, trees, "commie libs," and "the arts and croissant crowd."[7] Limbaugh pushes the bounds of good taste in any medium, not to mention simple human decency, such as the time on his now-defunct TV show, he asked, "Did you know there's a White House dog?" and held up a photo of then-thirteen-year-old Chelsea Clinton. Another time, he showed a picture of Secretary of Labor Robert Reich that showed him from the forehead up, as though that were all of his frame that the camera could capture.[8] (The diminutive Reich had a bone disease as a child.) Even when Limbaugh is not insulting the looks of young girls or making fun of childhood diseases, his ideological flights of fancy should leave any even remotely discerning listeners shaking their heads in disbelief.

Still, Limbaugh can have a real impact on issues, irrespective of the crackpot notions that inform his views. When, in June 2002, the Bush Administration gave up its Sisyphean battle to deny the reality of global warming—a fact of life accepted by the entire panoply of world governments as well as virtually every climatologist of note in all of these nations, Rush was aghast. He knew better.

> When I first became aware of this story Sunday night, I thought about what I would say on Monday's program: "Well, folks, guess what? I have been wrong about global warming. The president says it is happening and that human beings are causing it, so I've been wrong." I couldn't say that because I don't think I am wrong. There are too many scientists out there whom I implicitly trust who have proven to me these predictions are basically apocalyptic doom and gloom based on raw emotion. Even the global warming advocates, to this day, will not tell you it is definitively happening.[9]

Recall that the Bush Administration was not actually proposing to do anything about global warming. It had, in fact, put itself in the absurd position of predicting horrific consequences of global warming and yet remaining politically unwilling or unable to avert them. One might therefore draw the conclusion that Bush's cabinet reluctantly came to their long-averted conclusion, particularly given the criticism the administration received for refusing to go along with the Kyoto Protocol, a treaty that all the other civilized nations of the world had signed. But Rush was not fooled. Bush and company had, for reasons he did not explain, caved into "the environmentalist wacko coalition." The president had morphed into "George W. Algore."[10] (Within twenty-four hours the White House retreated, retracting the president's admission that global warming was, in fact, real.[11] In related news, the White House also announced that gravity was just a theory, too.)

Limbaugh is also, surprise, surprise, not a terribly competent student of history. In July 2002, a liberal caller sneaked onto his phone lines, initially pretending to be a dittohead, and chastised Rush for what the caller believed was the hypocrisy in the disparity between his treatment of Whitewater and Bush's Harken Oil stock sale. Rush became furious and explained himself thusly: "Everybody knows that Bill Clinton was corrupt, everybody knows that Bill Clinton was a lying, scheming SOB, everybody knows that Bill Clinton violated the law, he was held in contempt of court. Everybody knows that he was having BJs given to him in the oval office by an intern while 19 rangers and Delta Force members were dying in Somalia. Now if you want to compare him to Bush, you go right ahead. . . ."[12] The U.S. intervention in Somalia ended in 1993. The blow jobs began in 1995. But that's close enough for Rush.

Even more bizarre than these fusillades is the following transcript, taken from Limbaugh's program on July 20, 2001, in which he actually seemed to make a serious argument that Tom Daschle, leader of the Democratic majority in the Senate, was none other than the Fallen One, the Duke of Darkness, Satan himself. I quote from an extended transcript as published on the Web site, Spinsanity.com:

I have a question for you, folks, and I know that this is going . . . you have to listen very carefully here, this is going to push the envelope. . . . How many different versions of Satan, the devil, have you seen in your life? I mean, the comic book devil with the red face and the horns, seen that one. We've seen the Satanic devil of the horror films. We've seen the devil portrayed as just an average man, a human being, in the movie *Rosemary's Baby.* We've seen the comic devil of TV shows. We've even seen the smooth, tempting devil in Hollywood movies. Is Tom Daschle simply another way to portray a devil?

. . . There is no desire on Daschle's part to bring people together. There certainly is no bipartisanship flowing through his veins, nor is he leading any bipartisan effort. There is no working with the president on any of this. He's criticizing Bush, he's attempting to further the notion that Bush is illegitimate, incompetent, unintelligent. . . . Just yesterday, as Bush winged his way to Europe on a crucial mission to lead our allies into the twenty-first century, with Europe's flagging economy, talking about mutual defense in the twenty-first century, realistic environmental solutions, solutions for world poverty, not this stupid Kyoto stuff and not allowing the United States to be robbed blind by the U.N. and the poor nations of the world, up pops "El Diablo," Tom Daschle, and his devilish deviltry, claiming that George Bush is incompetent, criticizing Bush at the very moment he is engaging in these efforts to improve our relationship with these world leaders. . . . Hang in there, folks. Now don't go bonkers—the devil comes in many disguises as we all know. . . . Let me stretch this analogy just a little bit farther. What would your reaction be if I were to say that I think Daschle has cast a spell on the media?[13]

Listening to Limbaugh, the idea that he enjoys genuine power in the political life of the nation leaves you shaking your head in awe and amazement. But it is impossible to ignore. Limbaugh's radio audience is the largest any program on the medium has enjoyed since the advent of television. President George H. W. Bush invited him for a White House sleepover, as well as to be his honored guest at his State of the Union address, seated next to Barbara Bush, in a demonstration of fealty and respect. Shortly thereafter, in 1993, *National Review* termed him "the leader of the opposition." William Bennett averred that Limbaugh "may be the most consequential person in political life at the moment."[14] When the Republicans took the House back in 1994 in a profound and humiliating rebuke to President Clinton, Limbaugh's broadcast received a lion's share of the credit. *Washington Post* media reporter Howard Kurtz even defended nonsense like the above as "policy oriented." As Newt Gingrich's former press secretary Tony Blankley noted,

After Newt, Rush was the single most important person in securing a Republican majority in the House of Representatives after 40 years of Democratic Party rule. Rush's powerful voice was the indispensable factor, not only in winning in 1994, but in holding the House for the next three election cycles. At a time when almost the entire establishment media ignored or distorted our message of renewal, Rush carried (and often improved) the message to the heartland. And where Rush led, the other voices of talk radio followed.[16]

This influence cannot be said to have diminished markedly during the past decade, even after Limbaugh lost his most-favored targets when the Clintons left the White House. Much to his chagrin as a McCain supporter, William Kristol credits Limbaugh with rallying conservatives behind Bush during the 2000 presidential primaries. "He

helped make it the orthodox conservative position that McCain was utterly unacceptable and also that Bush was fine, neither of which were intuitively obvious if you're a
conservative," Kristol said. McCain's South Carolina political adviser, Richard M.
Quinn, concurred, adding that the Arizona senator never recovered, in his opinion,
from Limbaugh's repeated descriptions of the conservative Republican as a "liberal" in
an extremely conservative state. "I never polled on the impact of Limbaugh," Quinn
told the *New York Times*. "But anecdotally, I heard it all the time. You would hear on
the street repetition of what Rush was saying about McCain. There was a general sense
in the campaign that Limbaugh was definitely hurting us."[17] Blankley put it bluntly:
"Given the closeness of the election, but for Rush Limbaugh's broadcasts, we would
now be led by President Al Gore."[18] In the 2002 midterm elections, NBC used him as
one of its analysts. And on September 11, 2002, Vice President Cheney had just one
planned interview on his schedule to mark the hallowed anniversary of the tragedy of
a year before: a phone interview with Rush Limbaugh. Cheney canceled his appearance at the last minute, citing his removal from public view to a "secure location,"
under the raised state of alert declared by federal officials as the reason for his no-show.
Apparently his "secure location" did not contain a telephone.

It is particularly impressive that Limbaugh has managed to maintain his popularity following the loss of his biggest target, Bill Clinton, and the eclipse of radio beginning in the mid-1990's explosion of the Internet. The explosion of the use of the Web
may prove to be one of the great technological transformations in the history of
human communications. By the end of 2001, a single site, www.yahoo.com, boasted
more than 70 million users, with an annual increase rate of 18 percent.[19] While the
Internet has enormous value for more reasons and purposes than can be profitably
counted, for scholars, for communities, for journalists, and for just goofing off, for
political purposes it turns out to have a great deal in common with radio. Not unlike
the way in which the irresponsible right-wing talk-show network forms its own self-
referential information circuit, "news" on the Net is passed along from one site to
another with little concern for its credibility. Also like radio, this tactic of combining
the unverifiable with a metaphorical microphone has been perfected by the far right
to create a doubly deceitful dynamic of ideological extremism, false information, and
accusation against which truth—and liberalism—have little chance to compete. Rush
Limbaugh, meet Matt Drudge.

While the Net is economically dominated by a tiny number of large corporations,
just like television and radio, the information that appears on it is not. Standards for
established news services with a net presence have by and large been maintained;
however, the true story of political news on the Net is with the small, right-wing sites
that use the Web almost as effectively as they use talk radio. Web sites like the Drudge
Report, NewsMax.com, WorldNetDaily.com, FreeRepublic.com, Townhall.com,
Lucianne.com, JewishWorldReview.com, and National Review Online boast regular

readers in the millions. What's more, they are dedicated readers and in many cases, like the Limbaugh audience, so far to the right as to tend toward outer space. For instance, Joseph Farah, a columnist for Worldnet, warned his readers in October 2002, "The Democrats—far too many of them—are evil, pure and simple. They have no redeeming social value. They are outright traitors themselves or apologists for treasonous behavior. They are enemies of the American people and the American way of life."[20] On Lucianne.com, a number of posters celebrated the plane crash that killed Paul Wellstone, his wife, and daughter, in late October 2002 and expressed the hope that Ted Kennedy would meet a similar fate.[21] Even further out in the right wing ozonosphere, is the site FreeRepublic.com. While posts terming Gore a "traitor" are commonplace, alongside the addresses and phone numbers of allegedly liberal politicians and judges, a UPI story unearthed one user who sympathized with Timothy McVeigh and another who called him a "modern-day Paul Revere." According to figures published in the *New York Times*, the average "Freeper" Web visit lasts an amazing five hours and fourteen minutes.[22] It's not a hobby for these people, it's a life.

During the election crisis in Florida, these sites demonstrated their political value to the Republican side. As the Web site funded by Richard Mellon Scaife, frontpage.com, reported, conservative "community news sites like FreeRepublic.com and conservative news sites like NewsMax.com and WorldNetDaily.com, which earned their chops during the impeachment imbroglio" were, during the Florida crisis, "once again galvanizing the political right in support of George W. Bush's claim that he won the election." Weeks before President Clinton's impeachment by the House, FreeRepublic sponsored a rally that drew an estimated 5,000 to 6,000 pro-impeachment protestors to the Washington Monument. One user posted the e-mail addresses and work phone numbers of the seven justices of the Florida Supreme Court.[23] If it is possible, as I'll discuss, to trace the ultimate determination of the 2000 Florida fracas to what the conservative pundit Paul Gigot approvingly termed a "bourgeois riot" outside the Miami-Dade County board of elections office, then the activists inspired by these sites and organized within them can take credit for helping Republican Party officials make history—and undermine democracy.[24]

Liberals, of course, have their own sites, and some generate a great deal of traffic. But the best known, Salon.com and Slate.com, are run by journalists, not activists. And both make it a point of regularly publishing the views of the other side, including even the right's most extreme expressions, including Andrew Sullivan and David Horowitz in Salon's case, and Sullivan, Christopher Caldwell, and even Charles Murray in Slate's. (Many liberals also believe that Slate's official Weblogger, Mickey Kaus, is playing for the conservative team as well. Though he terms himself a "neoliberal," Kaus happily admits to being "a Dem who likes trashing Dems.")[25] Those liberal sites that are devoted to activism, such as Media Whores Online, BartCop, and Buzzflash, process a miniscule amount of traffic (and vitriol, for that matter) compared to, say, the folks at FreeRepublic.com and Lucianne.com. In the relatively new phenomenon of Weblogging—or "blogging"—the biggest names are also conservatives. Perhaps the best known of all non-professional Webloggers is Glenn Reynolds of "Instapundit," whose open-minded politics lean libertarian, but who is definitely in the conservative camp. The rest of the "Blogosphere" is also more conservative than liberal, but when speaking exclusively of the elite media, does not have much relevance beyond the Web sites of those journalists who have established their names elsewhere, such as Mickey Kaus or Josh Marshall.*

Undoubtedly the biggest star of Net journalism—its Rush Limbaugh if you will—is the self-styled Walter Winchell-in-a-fedora, Matt Drudge, who claims more than 100 million visits a month to his bare-bones, next-to-no-graphics site. Like Limbaugh, Drudge professes nothing but contempt for the mainstream news establishment. Viewed, he crows, "daily not only by presidents and world leaders, CEOs, anchormen and top media editors," Drudge claims to be "powered" only by endless curiosity and a love of freedom.[26] Of course with numbers like his, the media he disdains cannot help but celebrate him. Drudge was named one of *Newsweek*'s new media stars and *People*'s Twenty-Five Most Intriguing People. The *American Journalism Review* ran a cover story entitled, "Journalism in the Era of Drudge and Flynt," and the *Columbia Journalism Review* cited his outing of the Monica Lewinsky affair in 1998 as one of the ten key dates in the media history of the twentieth century.[27]

Originally an amateur Hollywood gossip who picked through garbage cans to get his goods, Drudge became an overnight phenomenon as a kind of bulletin board for unsubstantiated political rumor and right-wing character attacks. Drudge describes his work habit as sitting in his apartment "petting the cat and watching the wires—that's all I do."[28] But he also receives a great deal of e-mail. One of his favorite tactics is to steal a working journalist's story—leaked to him internally—and post its still-in-the-works details on his Web site before the author can publish them. His big moment in media history consisted of little more than posting the purloined work of *Newsweek*'s Michael Isikoff, while the magazine's editors sought further confirmation before publishing it. Drudge did it again when NBC News was trying to decide how to handle an unsubstantiated twenty-one-year-old accusation of sexual assault against President Clinton. Drudge rarely bothers to independently verify his stories, so he often appears prescient—when, in fact, he is simply overlooking what is widely understood to be the essence of journalism. Tim Russert learned this to his chagrin when Drudge posted three stories on his site about the Buffalo-born newsman's considering a run for governor of New York. "All three stories—they are just plain dead

---

*I suppose I am one of these, as I write a daily Weblog at www.altercation.msnbc.com. Check it out.

wrong," Russert complained. "And he never called me about them, never."[29] The only surprising thing here is Russert's surprise.

Drudge is a self-described misfit with few social graces, and modesty is certainly not one of them. Drudge calls his apartment "the most dangerous newsroom in America."[30] "If I'm not interesting, the world's not interesting," he writes. "And if I'm boring, you're boring."[31] Despite his disdain for traditional news ethics, and a lack of any discernible effort in the areas of reporting or punditry, Drudge's impact is huge. He counts his hits in the millions and can single-handedly drive hundreds of thousands—sometimes millions—of readers to any story he posts on the Web. When he purloined and posted Isikoff's Lewinsky scoop, he jump-started a political meltdown that led to the only impeachment of an elected president in American history. When he then went on to post the story of Clinton's alleged mulatto "love child," he made a national fool of himself, but hurt no one, save those gullible and irresponsible media outlets—most notably Rupert Murdoch's *New York Post* and Sun Myung Moon's *Washington Times*—who trusted him and reprinted it. But when he posted a malicious lie about Clinton adviser and ex-journalist Sidney Blumenthal having "a spousal abuse past that has been effectively covered up," replete with "court records of Blumenthal's violence against his wife," Drudge attacked an innocent man. But even this did not seem to hurt Drudge's reputation. Much of the media preferred Drudge to Blumenthal, whom many reporters resented for personal and professional reasons. In none of these cases did Drudge profess regret, though he did retract his false accusation against Blumenthal before the latter launched a libel suit against him.[32] As for the Clinton "love child" concoction, Drudge bragged, "I'd do it again."[33]

During the Lewinsky crisis, Drudge became so big the Internet could no longer contain him. He was given his own television program on Fox, where he was free to spout unconfirmed rumors with fellow conservative conspiracy nuts until he was informed by management that he would not be allowed to show a *National Enquirer* photo of a tiny hand emerging from the womb during a spina bifida operation on the fetus. Drudge wanted to use the photo as part of his campaign against legal abortion. When even the Fox executives found this idea not only repulsive but misleading, Drudge quit the show. Roger Ailes, whose brilliant idea it had been to hire Drudge after watching him spout baseless conspiracy theories on Russert's program, complained, "He wants to apply Internet standards, which are nonexistent, to journalism, and journalism has real standards. It can't work that way."[34] It should come as no surprise to anyone that Drudge is also a successful force in radio, with a two-hour Sunday evening show hosted by ABC that is heard in all fifty states and literally hundreds of major markets.[35]

Drudge also published a book—well, sort of a book. The tome was "written" with the assistance of the late Julia Phillips. Of the 247 pages contained in *The Drudge Manifesto,* the reader is treated to forty blank pages; thirty-one pages filled with fan mail; twenty-four pages of old Drudge Reports; a thirteen-page Q & A from Drudge's National Press Club speech; ten pages of titles and the like; six pages of quotes from various personalities like Ms. Lewinsky and Madonna; four pages of a chat transcript; and, well, a great deal more filler. That leaves the reader with just 112 pages or bare-ly 45 percent of actual book. (And even nine of these are Drudge poetry.)[36]

But even with all the strikes any journalist could imagine and then some against him, Drudge still gets results for his combination of nasty innuendo and right-wing politics, often by planting items that would be picked up by allegedly respectable journalists in national newspapers. In the Arkansas Senate race of 2002, the Associ-ated Press reported that Democrat Mark Pryor found himself forced to respond "to an item on the Drudge Report Web site of Internet gossip Matt Drudge" in a lightly sourced story that alleged the hiring of an illegal immigrant for housekeeping duties. (In fact the woman in question later signed a sworn affidavit testifying to the fact that she was a legal U.S. resident and had been paid to lie.)[37] In May of the same year, for example, Drudge carried a report that ex-conservative journalist David Brock, whose *Blinded by the Right* embarrassed virtually the entire movement, had suffered a "breakdown" while writing the book and had to be hospitalized—something Brock reluctantly confirmed when contacted. Drudge did not mention on his site that he had considerable reason to hold a grudge against Brock, who had published in his book that he received an e-mail from the Internet snoop that said he wished the two could be "fuck buddies." (Brock is an open homosexual. Drudge is not.) As the gay journalist Michelangelo Signorile wrote, "You'd think that no respectable journalist would further the new Drudge sludge on Brock, at least not without a fuller expla-nation that included Drudge's possible motives." But in fact the *Washington Post* did publish it—or at least the parts Drudge wanted published, leaving out any discussion of his motives—and adding quotes from three conservatives who continued the char-acter assassination of Brock that Drudge initiated. Nowhere in the *Post* item did the newspaper attempt to establish any journalistic relevance to the item, which is rather amazing when you consider the fact that its former publisher, the late Philip Graham, father of the current head of the Post Company, Donald Graham, was himself hos-pitalized for mental illness, before taking his own life.[38] (Making this story even stranger, the *Post*'s Howard Kurtz reported in 1999 that Drudge's own mother had been hospitalized for schizophrenia.)[39]

Just before Election Day 2002, Drudge and Limbaugh combined, together with Brit Hume of Fox News and the *Wall Street Journal* editorial page, to effect a smear against the Democratic Socialists of America (DSA) and, by extension, the late Senator Wellstone's re-election campaign. This episode too had all the trademarks of the con-servative echo-chamber effect, including unproven innuendo, inaccuracy, repeated cavalier use of unchecked facts, all in the service of a clear political/ideological goal. As reported by Bryan Keefer of Spinsanity, DSA posted a pop-up advertisement on its site on October 9 seeking contributions to pay the cost of bringing young people to Minnesota, where same-day registration is legal, to help register Wellstone voters in what was certain to be a close race. Shortly after the advertisement appeared, however, a local conservative organization sent out a press release in which it manipulated the original text to make it appear that DSA was planning to transport people not to register Minnesotans to vote, but to vote themselves, with the hopes of stealing the election.

Drudge saw the story in a local paper and headlined his site's line: "Socialists Sending People to MN to Illegally Vote for Wellstone." This apparently sent Limbaugh into action, as the radio host melodramatically informed his listeners, "DSA has been caught." With his typical respect for accuracy, Rush added, "You can go in there and register and vote and split the same day, you can go home, you don't even have to spend the night in Minnesota and freeze if you don't want to, you can go in there and vote and leave." Next up was Fox News's Brit Hume, who announced to that network's viewers, "The Democratic Socialists of America, which bill themselves as the largest socialist organization in the country, is raising tax-deductible money to send people to the state of Minnesota, where they can take advantage of same-day registration to vote for the liberal incumbent Paul Wellstone." These reports apparently inspired the *Journal* editors who—again, contrary to all available evidence—insisted, "The Democratic Socialists of America recently posted an ad on their Web site inviting tax-deductible contributions to 'bring young people to Minnesota' to vote in the close U.S. Senate race there." As Keefer noted, while the loosely worded ad did originally raise questions about whether tax-deductible funds were being properly used for issue advocacy—and hence was rewritten for clarifying purposes—never in any of its texts did it even imply, much less encourage, anyone but Minnesotans to pick their own senator. It is perfectly legal in that state to encourage people to vote and even to take them to the polls.[40]

Of course, Wellstone's death made the effects of this story moot, but cases like the above demonstrate just how profoundly journalistic times are a-changing. And the result of these changes is yet another victory for conservatives and scandal-mongers—and in Drudge and Limbaugh's cases, both at once—who seek to poison our political discourse with a combination of character assassination, ideological invective, and unverified misinformation. The resulting loss of credibility for phantom SCLM bespeaks not only the profession's misfortune, but democracy's as well.

# 6

## The Punditocracy Four

### Experts and the World of Ideas

THE FINAL CIRCLE of the punditocracy is made up of the so-called "experts," who come in a few varieties. The most common are those who are called upon to debate a policy on television or to shore up a reporter's story with the proper soundbite, often asked for and offered with an implicit understanding of what is required on both sides. For many years, most of the experts solicited by reporters were members of the Establishment, either from academia or research institutes such as the Brookings Institute, the Carnegie Endowment for International Peace, or the Council on Foreign Relations, where many ex-officials came to rest after serving their time in office. These scholars and ex-officials tended to lean toward the center-left of the American consensus on social and economic matters, but shilly-shallied back and forth between hawkish Cold War ideology and dovish developmental arguments about foreign policy.

The center of political gravity began to change, however, in the mid-1970s, with a financially driven political transformation of the world of policy expertise. Inspired by writings of Irving Kristol, conservatives had come to believe that the Establishment had lost its collective nerve and joined the counter cultural Jacobins of the antiwar and civil rights movements, thereby creating a new class dedicated above all to its own perpetuation. This New Class, with its ready access to the media, academia, and the world of foundations, enjoyed manipulating Americans into believing that they were an evil people who rained death and destruction on Vietnam in order to satisfy their own sick compulsions. Watergate, during which the media carried out a successful coup d'état (in Norman Podhoretz's judgment), only increased the appetite of the New Class for cultural supremacy, masked as consensus. New Class radicals had swallowed the entire political and academic establishment and annexed the Supreme Court. Working with Robert Bartley of the *Wall Street Journal* editorial page and a few like-minded intellectuals, Kristol set about wresting control from the New Class. Armed with corporate and conservative fortunes, Kristol and others organized to create an alternative or Counter-Establishment.

The plan worked magnificently. With billions made available by billionaires like Nelson and Bunker Hunt of Texas, Richard Mellon Scaife of Pennsylvania, Joseph Coors of Colorado, and the Reverend Sun Myung Moon of Seoul, the right set about changing the terms of the debate. Unable to transform (or blow up) the Brookings Institution, the conservatives created the American Enterprise Institute (AEI), the Center for Strategic and International Studies (CSIS), the Heritage Foundation, and a host of smaller ideological shops to drown out the liberals and moderates with their own analyses. According to a 1997 report by the National Committee for Responsive Philanthropy, between 1992 and 1994 alone, just twelve conservative foundations awarded $210 million to various right-wing agenda-building institutions. The comparable figure raised for liberal groups—such as the extremely cost-effective Center for Budget and Policy Priorities—was just $18.6 million.[1] What's more, the larger conservative foundations and think tanks are just the visible tip of a mighty iceberg. The 2000 edition of the Heritage Foundation's guide to conservative research and pressure groups in Washington listed 300 like-minded groups in the Washington area alone.

Superior resources tell only part of the story; superior marketing abilities tell one just as significant. William Baroody, the former president of the American Enterprise Institute, explained: "I make no bones about marketing. . . . We pay as much attention to the dissemination of the product as we do the content. We're probably the first major think tank to get into the electronic media. We hire ghost writers for scholars to produce op-ed articles that are sent to the one hundred and one cooperating newspapers—three pieces every two weeks."[2] AEI is hardly alone in that emphasis. The Hoover Institution maintains an active public affairs office that links it to 900 media centers across the United States and 450 media centers abroad. The Manhattan Institute in New York runs hundreds of journalists' forums and briefings on issues from tort reform to debates over the appropriate manner of dealing with young women's sexuality.[3]

Of the groups listed in the Heritage Foundation directory, the most important and influential is almost undoubtedly Heritage itself. With an operating budget of just over $32.5 million in 2000, it tends to overshadow all other right-wing research institutes while also setting the agenda for those that follow in its wake.[4] With the virtually unprecedented generosity of its conservative donor base, Heritage created a new type of research organization that paid considerably less attention to "research" than traditional think tanks on the model of the Brookings Institute, and far more to political activism, coupled with self-conscious construction of conservative cadres in every branch of government and the media.

The result of these differences is that Heritage is equipped to be much more of a "player" in the daily rough-and-tumble of political decisionmaking than are its competitors. Its scholars are not "scholars" in the traditional sense, but more like political operatives. They are expected to spend at least as much time networking with reporters and government staffers as on research, which must be up to date and on time. Heritage expends a great deal of effort on tracking legislation and, frequently, shaping the hearings as well as press coverage of those hearings. For these reasons, among many others, the right's "research" is not constricted by academic standards of scholarship and evidence, and most of it would not stand up to such scrutiny. As Heritage President Edwin Feulner explained in 1995, "We don't just stress credibility. We stress timeliness. We stress an efficient, effective delivery system. Production is one side; marketing is equally important." Burton Pines, a Heritage vice president, has added, "We're not here to be some kind of Ph.D. committee giving equal time. Our role is to provide conservative public-policymakers with arguments to bolster our side."[5]

Heritage computers are stocked with the names of over 3,500 journalists, organized by specialty. Every Heritage study goes out with a synopsis to those who might be interested; every study is turned into an op-ed piece, distributed by the Heritage Features Syndicate, to newspapers that wish to publish them. Heritage has two state-of-the-art television studios in its offices. Its Lehrman Auditorium is equipped with an advanced communications system for live feeds to TV and radio networks. "Our targets are the policymakers and the opinion-making elite," said Pines. "Not the public. The public gets it from them."[6] Heritage provides lawmakers and talk-show guests with colored index cards stating conservative positions in pithy phrases on every imaginable issue. According to Heritage's "vice president for information marketing," these cards have been "wildly successful" with Republicans in Congress for media appearances. They are also a big help for conservative pundits on television, who otherwise would risk embarrassment due to how ill-informed they are on a variety of issues about which they are called upon to argue.[7]

While the foundation's burgeoning influence only became visible to mainstream observers with Ronald Reagan's 1980 election to the presidency, it had been building slowly for years. On October 3, 1983, at Heritage's black-tie tenth-anniversary banquet, Reagan himself declared: "Historians who seek the real meaning of events in the latter part of the twentieth century must look back on gatherings such as this."[8] Indeed, the foundation's *Mandate for Leadership* became a blueprint in the Reagan White House. The mandate advocated greater freedom for the Pentagon and intelligence agencies, coupled with reductions in spending for education, welfare, health services, and other social programs. Perhaps as many as two-thirds of these recommendations were adopted within Reagan's first year in office. *Mandate for Leadership II*, written when Reagan won reelection in 1984, recommended massive cutbacks in food stamps, Medicare, child nutrition, farm assistance, and legal services for the poor, along with the vast expansion of U.S. missile defense research and support for right-wing dictatorships. These, too, would become a staple of political discussion during the next few years. In spite of even these stunning successes, the foundation's influence reached its zenith with the administration of George W. Bush. Times were certainly flush. In April 2001, three months after the inauguration, the foundation unveiled plans for a second building housing an additional 63,000 square feet of space, next door to its already spacious headquarters. During the Bush transition, Heritage staffers passed on 1,200 to 1,300 names and resumes to the White House and were said to emerge quite pleased with the number who were eventually hired, including the current Secretary of Labor, Elaine Chao, a former Heritage Distinguished Fellow.[9]

Just how much of the foundation's achievements are attributable to its burgeoning media presence is hard to quantify. Heritage's mission statement, written in 1973, calls for the foundation to "formulate and promote conservative public policies based on the principles of free enterprise, limited government, individual freedom, traditional American values, and a strong national defense."[10] But it does this by insinuating its ideology into the national conversation, misidentified as neutral information. For instance, "Dean" Broder lauded both Heritage and the Cato Institute for what he called "their intellectual honesty and their willingness to question conventional wisdom, even when their friends are in power." He praised both institutes as "models of healthy democratic discourse at a time when too much of the policy debate here takes the form of 'Crossfire'-style exchanges of insults."[11] This is, to say the least, an extremely generous view.

Broder's high opinion of both Heritage and Cato is unsurprisingly reflected in the rest of the media. According to the results of a study undertaken by Fairness and Accuracy in Reporting, Cato and Heritage finished numbers two and three in providing "expert" quotes during 2001, just behind the Brookings Institution.[12] These numbers were consistent with previous years and representative of a universe—created by the right's heavy investment in counter-Establishment institutions—in which conservatives have been able to shift the center of discourse in the media well in its own direction. According to FAIR's study of over 25,823 citations for the twenty-five leading think tanks, as quoted in the Nexis database files for major papers and broadcast transcripts, the top think tanks were ranked as follows (pre-9/11 rankings appear first, post-9/11 rankings appear in parentheses).

1 (2): Brookings Institution
2 (6): Cato Institute
3 (5): Heritage Foundation
4 (1): National Bureau of Economic Research
5 (8): American Enterprise Institute
6 (4): Council on Foreign Relations

7 (3): Center for Strategic and International Studies
8 (7): RAND Corporation
9 (22): Family Research Council

Although Brookings, Carnegie, and others are often called "liberal" by conservatives, this is clearly done for strategic reasons. The head of Brookings during the Clinton years was a Republican. So too are many of its fellows. Much the same can be said of Carnegie and the Council on Foreign Relations, both of which boast a healthy percentage of ex-denizens of the Reagan and Bush administrations in their most influential positions. Genuinely liberal think tanks of the type where mainstream Republicans and conservatives would honestly feel out of place do not really enter the picture until we get to numbers eleven (the Urban Institute) and twelve (Economic Policy Institute). Adding them all together, conservatives enjoy about 48 percent of all mentions, centrists 36 percent, and progressives just 16 percent.[13]

While many of the most promising intellectual talents on the left have eschewed the "real" world of public discourse for the cloistered confines of narrow academic debates, the right has been taking its message to "the people" in the form of best-selling book after best-selling book. It is a painfully ironic fact that in a society as culturally debased as ours, books can have a significant political and ideological impact precisely because they are rarely read. Book reviews and op-eds based on the reviews become the currency through which big ideas are traded in the ideological marketplace. Reviews, recall, are frequently written by people with considerably fewer qualifications than the writers themselves; often a journalist or general interest writer with only a passing knowledge of a topic will be asked to review the contribution of a scholar who devoted his or her entire professional life to its study. But because so many more people will see a review than the book itself, the former provides a vehicle to make what passes for an extended argument in the media. This is not always a bad thing. Few people tend to read serious books, and reviews publicize the ideas contained in them. Dwight Macdonald helped launch the nation's War on Poverty with his *New Yorker* review of Michael Harrington's *The Other America: Poverty in the United States* in 1962, in part by helping to convince the president of the United States that we had a problem.[14] But the world of book reviewing is not exactly overflowing with writers of the caliber of Dwight Macdonald; nor are the nation's cultural—or elected—leaders particularly receptive at this moment to arguments that appeal to our most generous impulses.

Michael Joyce, the former president of the Lynde and Harry Bradley Foundation in Milwaukee, understood the selling of ideas as well as anyone. In the late 1990s he compiled a list of more than 400 books the foundation helped support. Joyce explained, "We have the conviction that most of the other media are derivative from books. Books are the way that authors put forth more substantial, more coherent arguments. It follows that if you want to have an influence on the world of ideas, books are where you want to put your money. It is what we are most proud of, of all the things we've done here." Bradley also invested $3.5 million to start up Encounter Books, named after the defunct journal of neoconservative ideas, for exactly these purposes.

For instance, to understand how liberals grew so defensive on affirmative action, look to Terry Eastland's *Ending Affirmative Action: The Case for Colorblind Justice* (1994), funded by Olin and Bradley; Frederick Lynch's *The Diversity Machine: The Drive to Change the "White Male Workplace"* (1997), also funded by Olin, and *Invisible Victims: White Males and the Crisis of Affirmative Action* (1989); and Abigail and Stephan Thernstrom's *America in Black and White* (1997). At the Manhattan Institute, Peter Huber's *Liability* (1988) and *Galileo's Revenge* (1993) and Walter Olson's *The Litigation Explosion* (1991) helped spark the national debate on civil justice, the use of social science in the courts, and the nationwide attack on trial lawyers commonly known as "tort reform."

The right continues to fund far more than attacks on traditional liberal policies. Liberalism itself is attacked as illegitimate. To understand how alien leftist beings have kidnapped your college-age children, see Roger Kimball's *Tenured Radicals: How Politics Has Corrupted Our Higher Education* (1988) and Charles J. Sykes's *Profscam: Professors and the Demise of Higher Education* (1988). Also quite popular among conservative funders has been a full-frontal attack on the "culture of the Sixties." With that in mind, we have the Manhattan Institute's Myron Magnet, whose *The Dream and the Nightmare* (1993) blamed the Sixties counterculture for the creation of the urban underclass; John DiIulio's Olin-funded jihad, an endless series of journal articles, against a "permissive" penal code; Allan Bloom's best-selling jeremiad against modernity, *The Closing of the American Mind* (1987); and a seemingly endless series of scoldings about our moral failings by the likes of Robert Bork, William Bennett, and Michael Novak. Each one of these books was generously supported by one or more of the foundations mentioned above, and each has played a significant role in moving the political discourse to the right. During the House impeachment vote, for instance, ABC News chose Bennett and NBC chose Bork as guest commentators, despite the fact that their positions were deeply outside the mainstream of popular opinion on the subject. No liberals were similarly deployed.

What's more, these funders have set up an entire echo-chamber network of publications to support the works of their writers, the better to inject them into the bloodstream of mainstream media debate.

Bradley's list of subsidized authors, for instance, includes Charles Murray, Terry Eastland, Norman Podhoretz, David Horowitz, John DiIulio, and Amitay Schlaes. Their books are almost always favorably and prominently praised in widely disseminated reviews in such organs funded by Bradley (together with Scaife and the Olin Foundation) as the *National Interest* and the *Public Interest* (both overseen by Irving Kristol), *Commentary* (funded by Rupert Murdoch and the Bradley, Olin, and Scaife foundations among others), the *New Criterion* (funded by Scaife and Olin), *Reason* (funded by Scaife, among others), *American Spectator* (funded with Scaife, Olin, and Bradley money), the Manhattan Institute's *City Journal*, the Heritage Foundation's *Policy Review*, and AEI's *American Enterprise*—along with William Buckley's *National Review*, Steve Forbes's *Forbes*, Robert Bartley's *Wall Street Journal* editorial page, and Rupert Murdoch's *Weekly Standard*, *New York Post*, and Fox News Channel and network. On PBS these ideas are often taken up on the program, *Think Tank*, hosted by AEI's neoconservative political scientist Ben Wattenberg and funded in large measure by the Bradley, Olin, and Smith Richardson foundations. Taken together, these publications and outlets pack a powerful cultural wallop. Add them to the numerous and well-respected right-wing pundits working in mainstream newspapers and television stations and you have the makings of a media tsunami.

But even without their own counter cultural network, conservative books do quite well with SCLM reviewers. Per usual, conservatives like to imagine a liberal conspiracy. Michael Barone, speaking to the *Washington Post*, whined, "The New York-based publishing industry has a monopartisan, liberal point of view. Many editors don't want to publish certain books. Bookstores won't stock them. You've got a kind of left-wing industry."[15] But the likes of Bloom, D'Souza, Fukuyama, and Huntington often receive celebratory reviews from the very places that conservatives attack as the liberal media's ground zero: the culturally elitist book reviewers on the east and west coasts. The (genuinely) liberal *Los Angeles Times Book Review* even managed to find a reviewer who would admire Ann Coulter's frantic screed, *Slander*, something even few conservative publications could bring themselves to do.[16] Perhaps most significantly, David Brock's vicious and deceitful attack on Anita Hill, which he has since disowned as a pack of pathological lies, was launched on its path to respectability and best-sellerdom by the "liberal" reviewers of the *New York Times*. Brock admits that when he first heard that *Times* reviewer Christopher Lehmann-Haupt had described his book as "well written, carefully reasoned, and powerful in its logic," he first wondered whether this praise from the *Times* was a practical joke.[17] The book was also well-received in the *Washington Post* and by David Garrow, the author of a biography of Martin Luther King, writing in *Newsday*. Since none of the reviewers who praised Brock were competent to judge the quality of his research, they must have been predisposed to swallow his lies, though why this was, we can only speculate. Some may have wished to embrace a "contrarian" voice, no matter how shoddily sourced. Some might have been hoping to build a bit of "street cred" in an increasingly conservative political culture. Meanwhile, if indeed a liberal media conspiracy exists in the culture industry, it is playing one very strange game.

Brock credits his publisher at Free Press, Erwin Glikes (now deceased), with coaching him and teaching him that "the price of media credibility, of being taken seriously as a journalist, was to call black 'white,' to deny that I had a political agenda."[18] Brock noted that Glikes helped jump-start the media's reaction by hand-delivering a pre-publication copy of the book to another author he edited, the pundit George F. Will, who "took the bait" in *Newsweek* by trumpeting Brock's lies and naked character assassination as "an avalanche of evidence that Hill lied" in her testimony at the hearings.[19] Using this technique, Glikes had already successfully published the work of Allan Bloom, Robert Bork, and Dinesh D'Souza. Their books helped to define the debate about the topics about which they wrote, even inspiring entirely new debates where none existed before.[20] Eventually, should they strike the proper chord, a transformed debate can pave the way for new laws that serve the author's agenda, or perhaps more importantly, that of his funders.

The transformation of the public discourse is categorically a different undertaking than merely publishing a best-selling right-wing hatchet job—particularly one that is purchased in bulk by conservative organizations. The latter is often the case with those published by the conservatives at Regnery. According to Barone, Regnery publishes "what American people want and what the publishing industry is inclined not to provide."[21] This is nonsense. Tiny numbers of people buy Regnery books, just as tiny numbers of people buy just about any book. (It is possible to make the *New York Times* best-seller list with as few as 30,000 copies sold.) But Regnery books do make money, and this confuses journalists into thinking that they enjoy an influence beyond the media. As part of a larger conglomerate tied in with movement newsletters, magazines, book clubs, mailing lists, and various fund-raising arms for conservative causes—among them, *Human Events* magazine, the 75,000-member Conservative Book Club, the *Evans and Novak Political Report*—Regnery can create a best-seller from its various constituent elements almost without a bookstore customer ever even noticing a given publication. Regnery Publishing, named after its founder, Henry Regnery Sr., began its tenure as a publisher with a distinguished list of conservative thinkers and philosophers that included Russell Kirk's *The Conservative Mind*, William F. Buckley Jr.'s *God and Man at Yale*, Whittaker Chambers's *Witness*, and Barry Goldwater's *Conscience of a Conservative*. Under its current guise, run by Henry's son, Alfred Regnery, the company's list tends toward conservative arguments designed to appeal to the faithful on almost any imaginable issue, from family values, to Ivy League Communists, to corrupt teacher unions and the dangers of gun confiscation and the like. Such books help feed and expand the conservative movement, but only rarely affect mainstream discourse, except indirectly, because of the company's relaxed attitude regarding editorial quality control. Regnery's biggest sellers for the past decade have focused on fantastical accusations and near-science-fiction-level plots involving Bill Clinton and a host of his allegedly murderous associates. Among these, published between 1996 and the end of the Clinton presidency, were: Roger Morris's *Partners in Power: The Clintons and Their America*, Bill Gertz's *Betrayal: How the Clinton Administration Undermined American Security*, Edward Timperlake and William C. Triplett's *Year of the Rat: How Bill Clinton Compromised U.S. Security for Chinese Cash*, Ann Coulter's *High Crimes and Misdemeanors: The Case Against Bill Clinton*, Ambrose Evans-Pritchard's *The Secret Life of Bill Clinton: The Unreported Stories*, Gary Aldrich's *Unlimited Access: An FBI Agent Inside the Clinton White House*, and R. Emmett Tyrrell's *The Impeachment of William Jefferson Clinton: A Political Docu-Drama* and *Boy Clinton: The Political Biography*. To date, five of these books have made various best-seller lists, and *Unlimited Access* has sold 750,000 copies, and "it's still selling," according to Alfred Regnery.[22] A Regnery book can, on occasion, jump-start a political conversation, as Bernard Goldberg's *Bias* did in 2001–2002. But these are relatively rare. Most often, the books are easily ignored by the mainstream media and must make their way into the mainstream political discourse through reviews or repeated rumor-mongering in places like the *American Spectator* or the *Wall Street Journal* editorial pages. (We will hear more about this in Chapter 13.)

Conservative investment in ideas has achieved a great deal toward making the lifestyle of the conservative intellectual an extremely attractive one, particularly when compared with those of a workaday journalist or college professor. In addition to all-expenses-paid invitations to fancy conferences, cushy offices, and regular consulting calls from top GOP politicians, including presidential advisers, the money can be pretty good too. Between 1992 and 1994, Dinesh D'Souza enjoyed $483,023 at AEI; Irving Kristol, $380,600, also at AEI; Robert Bork managed to scare up $459,777 for his office at Heritage; and William Bennett, also at Heritage, garnered $275,000 in addition to his considerable book and lecture earnings. Fellowships at the left's much smaller institutes do not, to put it mildly, compare. Small progressive funders like the Schumann Foundation, which generously supported this book, for instance, are in no position to make the researching of a book quite so comfortable or profitable. AEI noted in its 1998 report that "the most significant areas of expense growth were in the economics studies area and in efforts toward broader dissemination of our research." Thirteen percent of its more than $14 million 1997 budget went to publications and another 14 percent to "marketing and management." Those two figures together are more than most liberal foundations spend on their entire operations.

Perhaps the most successful publishing foray into the world of ideas by a combination of right-wing funders and their compatriot intellectuals is the amazing public relations achievement undertaken on behalf of the work of the formerly obscure Charles Murray. How many 800-plus page nonfiction books featuring over a hundred pages of graphs and source materials have managed to sell upward of 300,000 copies in hardcover in recent years? How many have inspired *Vanity Fair*-type celebrity coverage in virtually all major news magazines, as well as a special issue of the *New Republic*, which featured no fewer than seventeen responses? How many authors of such books have been featured in major Hollywood films, carried by characters wishing to demonstrate intellectual toughness?[23] The answer to all of the above is precisely one: Murray's *The Bell Curve*.[24]

Back in 1982, however, Charles Murray was still a "nobody," in the words of William Hammett, president of the Manhattan Institute and about to become Murray's chief patron. Murray's ascendancy would never have been possible without the patient, farsighted investments in his work by a conservative network of funders and foundations, including the reclusive billionaire Richard Mellon Scaife, the Olin Foundation, the Manhattan Institute, the American Enterprise Institute, and, perhaps most significantly, Milwaukee's Lynde and Harry Bradley Foundation. They not only supported Murray when he needed time to research and write his books, they funded elaborate publicity campaigns to ensure that Murray's argument would dominate media discourse.

The story of Murray's rise in just one decade from being a public nobody to being America's best-known and perhaps most influential public intellectual is an odd but instructive tale with regard to just how easily conservatives can manipulate the SCLM and legitimate views once considered unspeakable in polite society. As a writer, Murray displayed an uncanny ability to offer what appeared to be a reasonable and scholarly sounding voice to opinions and arguments that had hitherto been considered beyond the pale of respectability. Indeed, he has been quite self-conscious regarding this purpose, as evidenced by the fact that in his proposal for his first book, *Losing Ground*, he explained to potential publishers that his work would be welcomed by people who secretly believed themselves to be racists. "Why can a publisher sell it?" he asked. "Because a huge number of well-meaning whites fear that they are closet racists, and this book tells them they are not. It's going to make them feel better about things they already think but do not know how to say."[25]

Trained as a Ph.D. in political science but without any formal credentials in economics or psychometrics, the design of research and measurement of human characteristics—the two fields in which his work managed to incite national debates—Murray's work has met with little but vituperation and disgust among those experts competent to judge its scientific merits. Yet owing to a series of brilliant and extremely well-funded marketing strategies, and an unarguable genius for locating the g-spot of the political/intellectual marketplace, Murray somehow managed to transform public debate on issues where he lacked what most in the field would consider basic professional competence.

Back when Murray was still laboring in obscurity, he managed to get on the radar screen of William Hammett, and secure an invitation to speak at a lunch sponsored by the Manhattan Institute. Meanwhile, Murray sent a copy of an article he wrote for the Olin Foundation-funded neoconservative journal *Public Interest*, co-founded and edited by Irving Kristol. Kristol called Michael Joyce, whom he had helped hire to run the Olin Foundation, and explained that Murray wanted to turn his article into a book but needed money to do so, as no commercial publisher would pay a living wage for a wonky right-wing study of welfare policy by a nobody from Iowa. A series of quick phone calls resulted in a generous series of grants from conservative foundations.[26] Viewing Murray's work as a potential antidote to Michael Harrington's *The Other America*, which helped inspire the War on Poverty, Hammett wrote in a private memo at the time, "Every generation produces a handful of books whose impact is lasting; books that change basic assumptions about the way the world works. Charles Murray's *Losing Ground* could become such a book. And if it does it will alter the terms of debate over what is perhaps the most compelling political issue of our time: the modern welfare state."[27] Right again.[28]

According to Murray's formulation, welfare did not ameliorate or attenuate the ravages of poverty; it perpetuated and entrenched them. Instead of empowering poor people, it created a dangerous dependency on federal handouts that sapped their energy and destroyed their initiative, thereby preventing them from acquiring the productive skills they need to achieve success in America's market economy. "We tried to provide more for the poor and produced more poor instead," Murray lamented. It was time to scrap the entire system and let the poor fend for themselves.

Unfortunately, Murray's assertions were based on a series of internal contradictions, specious arguments, and outright phony claims unsupported by his data. For instance, his assertion that the hope for welfare payments was the main source of illegitimacy among black teenagers posited no evidence for this claim and failed to explain why the rate of illegitimacy rose for everyone—and not just welfare recipients—after 1972, while the constant-dollar value of those welfare benefits declined by 20 percent. While continually insisting on the impotence of the Great Society programs of the Johnson administration, Murray never once explained the development of the black middle class during this period. Moreover, why blame the welfare policies of the late Sixties and early Seventies for the decline in participation of black males in the labor market when the decline actually dates back to the late Fifties? It turned out that Murray's calculations relied on the highly disputed figures of an obscure economist named Timothy Smedding. Using more traditional and widely accepted measurements, Christopher Jencks calculated that, contrary to Murray's central claims, the percentage of the population defined as poor in 1980 was only half the size it was in 1965 and one third the size it was in 1950.

Much of Murray's argument was taken up by a "thought experiment" based on a fictional unmarried couple he named Harold and Phyllis, who lived in Pennsylvania, who made what Murray argued was an entirely rational economic decision to remain on welfare. But Murray screwed up his math. While Pennsylvania was indeed atypically generous to welfare recipients in 1980, the couple's income would still have been over 30 percent higher if Harold had worked at a minimum wage job rather than Phyllis collecting welfare as the sole means of support for the family.[29]

Despite these weaknesses, Hammett's prediction proved prophetic. Nothing so trivial as fundamental flaws in both reasoning and calculations managed to interfere with the Manhattan Institute's plans to turn Murray's blame-the-victim argument into the nation's new conventional wisdom on welfare. The publicity campaign for *Losing Ground* was planned and executed with impressive discipline and imagination. Surely it had no precedent in the world of welfare wonkdom. Before it began, Hammett informed his colleagues "any discretionary funds at our disposal for the next few months will go toward financing Murray's outreach activities." He then mailed out a massive number of copies to academics, journalists, and public officials, sent Murray on a national speaking tour, and raised another $10,000 to "gather twenty of the nation's leading scholars from both the conservative and liberal camps, along with some of the best writers on the subject, for a two-day discussion," according to an internal memorandum. Well-known columnists and other members of the media were paid between $300 and $1,000 apiece to participate. Taking advantage of the economic illiteracy of the punditocracy, Murray was able to sell his idea to these opinion-makers without having to respond to difficult queries that might have been posed by a competent economist. (No one, for instance, suggested submitting any part of *Losing Ground* to a peer-reviewed professional journal.) The pundits who liked it did so because it reinforced their own respective worldviews—along with the arguments necessary to support the Reagan Administration's assault on the welfare state. Reagan liked to tell stories about "welfare queens" buying vodka with their food stamps. Most people understood these stories to be apocryphal, but conservatives repeated them in the belief that they contained within them a "larger truth." Now here was Charles Murray with a book full of graphs and economic data that appeared to "prove" the larger story that Reagan's imagined anecdotes hoped to impart. For conservatives seeking to weaken the welfare state, and for liberals and moderates seeking to make themselves appear more "relevant" in a period of conservative ascendancy, there was no sense in looking this gift horse too closely down the mouth.

In spite of the book's errors, or because his readers were oblivious to them, *Losing Ground* quickly became a cause celebre for pundits and politicians alike. "This year's budget-cutters' bible seems to be '*Losing Ground*,'" noted a *New York Times* editorial early in 1985. "Among movers and shakers in the federal executive branch," the newspaper reported, *Losing Ground* had quickly become holy writ: "In agency after agency, officials cite the Murray book as a philosophical base for proposals to slash social expenditure."[30] The book was the subject of dozens of major editorials, columns, and reviews in publications such as the *New York Times*, *Newsweek*, the *Dallas Morning News*, and the *New Republic*. As Charles Lane observed in the *New Republic*, its success could be viewed as "a case study in how conservative intellectuals have come to dominate the policy debates of recent years."[31] Even once the book's obvious weaknesses had been identified, as experts began to weigh in from professional journals, they barely made a dent in its effectiveness as a weapon in the ideological wars. A decade or more later, conservatives were still wielding *Losing Ground* like a sword against the scourge of more money for the poor. When Murray was invited to be a guest on ABC's *This Week* during this same period, host David Brinkley lavishly praised him as "the author of a much-admired, much-discussed book called *Losing Ground*, which is a study of our social problems." Minutes later, Murray was explaining his solution: "I want to get rid of the whole welfare system, period, lock, stock and barrel—if you don't have any more welfare, you enlist a lot more people in the community to help take care of the children that are born. And the final thing that you can do, if all else fails, is orphanages."[32] More than a dozen years after publication, the *Philadelphia Inquirer* accurately recalled that *Losing Ground* "provided much of the intellectual groundwork for welfare reform," just as the new House Speaker Newt Gingrich was suggesting that children in poverty be put in orphanages.[33]

Despite the success and continuing influence of *Losing Ground*, Murray soon shifted gears. Race is largely absent from *Losing Ground*. But Murray had a chance meeting with Harvard professor Richard Herrnstein, who had been arguing in various places—including the "liberal" *Atlantic Monthly*, that, "In times to come, the tendency to be unemployed may run in the genes of a family about as certainly as bad teeth do now."[34] Murray was clearly excited by arguments like these and decided to redirect his own research toward it. In 1990, the Manhattan Institute decided that it did not want to associate itself with this kind of research and informed Murray to find another home for his work on what he termed "the genetic inferiority stuff."[35]

Fortunately for Murray, Michael Joyce, who had been so instrumental in supporting him at the Olin Foundation, had now taken over the Bradley Foundation. Murray's $100,000 grant was moved from the Manhattan Institute to the American Enterprise Institute, after a brief—and failed—attempt to place him in the more centrist and Establishment-oriented Brookings Institute. Murray was, once again, extremely fortunate in his choice of sponsors. By the time he completed his second book, he had received more than $750,000 since the Bradley Foundation had begun its support, with more than $500,000 coming during the four years he worked on *The Bell Curve*.[36]

The publicity campaign for *The Bell Curve* mimicked that of *Losing Ground*. It is safe to say that most scholarly books containing hundreds of pages of regression analyses and primary source-based historical, economic, and sociological claims would first be published, at least in part, in academic quarterlies that vet submissions by scholarly peer review on the part of an editorial board. But Simon and Schuster did not even send *The Bell Curve* to reviewers in galleys, and neither did its authors. A *Wall Street Journal* news story reported that the book had been "swept forward by a strategy that provided book galleys to likely supporters while withholding them from likely critics." The *Journal* suggested that AEI "tried to fix the fight when it released review copies selectively, contrary to usual publishing protocol." Murray and AEI also hand-picked a group of pundits to be flown to Washington at the think tank's expense for a weekend of briefings by Murray and discussion of the book's arguments.[37] This strategy paid off when the book was released and the publicity machine put into action, long before the scientific establishment could garner a look and form any coherent judgments.

Couched between an endless array of tables, charts, and ten-dollar words, the Murray/Herrnstein thesis, at its core, was disarmingly simple. The book's first sentence is: "This book is about differences in intellectual capacity among people, and groups, and what these differences mean for America's future." The authors blame many of the nation's social problems, including the persistence of an "underclass" characterized by high levels of crime, welfare, and illegitimacy, on the fact that black people are just not as smart as white people. After all, they argue, all racial barriers to advancement have been removed from American society; hence, we have arrived at a near-perfect consequential relationship between IQ and socioeconomic achievement. And because the authors believe IQ to be largely the product of one's genetic inheritance, it is futile for society to try to boost those doomed to failure beyond their natural stations in life. In addition, high-IQ women are now entering the workforce at record rates and refusing to reproduce at rates comparable to that of poor and stupid women, who rarely work and collect lots of welfare money. These trends are "exerting downward pressure on the distribution of cognitive ability in the United States," and doing more than their fair share to increase crime, welfare dependency, and illegitimacy. Because the rest of us cannot be expected to simply sit tight and let our society slip inexorably into anarchy, the authors predict a future semi-fascist "custodial state" for America, not unlike "a high-tech and more lavish version of an Indian reservation." Unfortunately, the dumb ones among us will lose such cherished rights as "individualism, equal rights before the law, free people running their own lives," according to the authors, but such measures will become unavoidable lest steps are taken to address the coming crisis of a national dysgenic downturn.

Interestingly, while *The Bell Curve* sets out to achieve the same aims as *Losing Ground*—the reduction and eventual elimination of all transfer payments to the poor and indigent—it does so by directly contradicting *Losing Ground*'s central argument. In *Losing Ground*, Murray placed the lion's share of responsibility for the creation of the American underclass at the feet of government anti-poverty programs, primarily welfare. "Focusing on blacks cripples progress," he declared in a 1986 op-ed piece (titled "Not a Matter of Race"). But in *The Bell Curve*, as Mickey Kaus noted, Murray attributed the existence of an underclass to the "true" difference between blacks and whites—the intellectual deficiency of blacks (among others), whose IQ scores averaged fifteen points below those of whites. Moreover, in *The Bell Curve*, Murray argued that entry to the welfare rolls almost qualified as prima facie evidence of a low IQ, while in *Losing Ground*, he purported—albeit using cooked statistics—to demonstrate that in many instances, it was a perfectly rational choice over certain job choices and even sometimes marriage.

Though he contradicted his earlier argument, Murray marketed *The Bell Curve* by relying on the same psychological insight he made in his proposal for the first one: namely that many people worried that, privately, they were racists, and yearned for expert reassurance that the rest of the nation shared their prejudice. "The private dialogue about race in America is far different from the public one,"[38] he wrote in the *New Republic*. *The Bell Curve* aimed to replace the public dialogue—the one in which all peoples were deemed created equal, their genetic makeup considered to be only a portion of their destiny—and replace it with the private one in which blacks and Latinos were understood to be inferior to whites and Asians.

Aided by another brilliant marketing campaign, *The Bell Curve* inspired a media firestorm. The book entered the public discourse, as one writer commented, "like a noseful of cocaine." It spent fifteen weeks on the *New York Times* bestseller list, outselling *Losing Ground* by a factor of ten to one, and even this was only a tiny measure of its spectacular success. Magazines published special issues; talk shows offered up two-part editions; and four separate collections of essays were published, devoted entirely to arguments about the book. As Chester Finn asked in January 1995, "Is there anyone left with access to a microphone, television camera, or printing press who has not unburdened himself of an opinion of *The Bell Curve*?"[39]

Much as Blanche DuBois depended of the kindness of strangers, Charles Murray depended on the ignorance of pundits. The initial debate on *The Bell Curve* was conducted almost entirely by people who had no professional capacity to assess its science. "I am not a scientist. I know nothing about psychometrics," wrote Leon Wieseltier, one of the most learned and least retiring members of the elite media, in the *New Republic*.[40] Even the *New York Times Book Review*, unchallenged as the most influential book review on earth, assigned the book to a science reporter, rather than a practicing scientist, much less a biogeneticist. As a result, the early reactions to the book proved to be a kind of Rorschach test for pundits on what innocent reviewers assumed to be the scientifically proven conclusions relating to the genetic intellectual inferiority of blacks and what might be done about it, rather than the more fundamental question of whether Murray and Hernstein had, in fact, proven anything. For instance *Time* called the book "845 pages of provocation with footnotes," while *Newsweek* defended its sourcing as "overwhelmingly mainstream."[41] Not surprisingly, Murray's oddest claims about *The Bell Curve* and the controversy it provoked related to race. Over and over he insisted that the claims he made about black genetic inferiority were both unimportant to the book's central thesis and generally uninteresting. He wrote in his 10,000-word essay in the *New Republic*:

> Here is what we hope will be our contribution to the discussion. We put it in italics; if we could, we would put it in neon lights: The answer doesn't much matter. Whether the black-white difference in test scores is produced by genes or the environment has no bearing on any of the reasons why the black-white difference is worth worrying about. If tomorrow we knew beyond a shadow of a doubt what role, if any, were played by genes, the news would be neither good if ethnic differences were predominantly environmental, nor awful if they were predominantly genetic.[42]

Yet Murray could hardly claim to be unaware of the explosive potential of his work and the likelihood that it would anger many people of good will. After all, he had been asked to leave his professional home at the Manhattan Institute over its subject matter. Murray noted in the *New Republic* that the subject upon which he was writing tended to leave people "scared stiff about the answer." He told a reporter that his investigation for *The Bell Curve* "was a case of stumbling onto a subject that had all the allure of the forbidden. Some of the things we read to do this work, we literally hide when we're on planes and trains. We're furtively peering at this stuff."[43] One wonders whether this is one place where Murray took Glikes's advice, as David Brock described it, to call black "white" and "deny a political agenda" as "the price of media credibility."[44]

Whatever Murray's reasoning, it worked. The *New York Times Magazine* made him its cover story. In a deeply sympathetic review in *Forbes*, Peter Brimlow, who had attended AEI's pre-publication conference, hailed the book's "Jeffersonian vision." (Brimlow was apparently innocent of any knowledge of Jefferson's views of the allegedly physiological basis of what he deemed to be black intellectual inferiority in his famous 1787 essay "Notes on the State of Virginia.")[45] Ben Wattenberg gave Murray an extremely generous hearing on a special two-part version of *Think Tank*. The *American Spectator* assigned the book to the extremely conservative African-American sociologist Thomas Sowell, who also proved notably sympathetic with the authors' goals as well as their motives. The review published in *Commentary* was authored by Chester Finn, a writer funded by Olin and housed at the Manhattan Institute, who also proved quite sympathetic, though disappointed that the authors did not go even further in their conservative prescriptions to solve the dysgenic crisis they diagnosed. *Commentary* also offered Murray the opportunity to speak directly to his critics in a lengthy riposte to the reviews elsewhere.

Undoubtedly the biggest political boost *The Bell Curve* received was from the *New Republic*. The editors of this once-liberal magazine's decision to carry Murray's arguments at such length was symbolic to say the least. At more than 10,000 words, it proved to be one of the longest articles ever published in the magazine's nine-decade life. When added to the seventeen responses published with it, it's safe to say that no topic had ever galvanized the editors of what was once America's liberal flagship quite to this degree, save perhaps the evil doings of Yasir Arafat, among other Arabs since time immemorial. Then-editor Andrew Sullivan argued in his unsigned editorial, "the notion that there might be resilient ethnic differences in intelligence is not, we believe, an inherently racist belief. It's an empirical hypothesis, which can be examined." This defense of Murray and Herrnstein's right to free speech rather than the validity of their argument sounds plausible until one remembers that Holocaust denial is also an empirical hypothesis that can be examined. Clearly the magazine's editor and owner sought to give Murray's arguments that magazine's imprimatur. (Today Sullivan says he believes the book to be "one of the bravest, smartest books of the decade.")[46] Aside from Sullivan's editorial, the only essay resembling an outright endorsement of Murray's arguments came from Peretz himself. He devoted his essay to the alleged injustices perpetrated in the name of group-admissions to universities and (somehow) compared the United States unfavorably to Israel's "ingathering of the exiles" on this point. A few *New Republic* editors have been known to play a game with one another in private whereby they try to insert favorable references to Israel in places where they clearly do not belong. Here Peretz seemed to be playing too.

The criticism came in two waves. The first, largely from journalists and published in mass-market publications, focused largely on the book's political implications. All they could do, really, was invite readers to accept their worldview as superior to that of Murray and Herrnstein's. But because the authors were presumed by most to be far more expert in their chosen field than their journalistic critics, these criticisms enjoyed precious little authority to dent *The Bell Curve*'s argument's impact and almost none in damaging the book's popularity. But the second wave of reviews, which did not arrive until much later, comprised expert opinion in the relevant field and provided a belated substitute for the peer-review process to which Murray and Herrnstein were originally unwilling to submit.

Once experts in the fields of psychometrics, dysgenics, and genetics began to weigh in on the book, not much of it was left. Scholarly examination repeatedly demonstrated that the statements that form the very core of *The Bell Curve*'s arguments were either highly questionable or demonstrably false. For instance, Hernstein and Murray insisted, "it is beyond significant technical dispute that cognitive ability is substantially heritable." But as a group of British geneticists and psychometricans pointed in response, "Research in this field is still evolving, studies cited by Herrnstein and Murray face significant methodological difficulties, and the validity of results quoted are disputed."[47]

The mistakes grow even graver. Murray and Herrnstein actually seek to quantify the degree to which such intelligence is heritable. "Half a century of work, now amounting to hundreds of empirical and theoretical studies," they write, "permits a broad conclusion that the genetic component of IQ is unlikely to be smaller than 40 per cent or higher than 80 per cent. . . . For purposes of this discussion, we will adopt a middling estimate of 60 per cent heritability." The authors appear to the unsuspecting reader to be the soul of caution in this regard. Alas, as Nicholas Lemann reported in Slate, another study by three scientists at Carnegie Mellon University, employing exactly the same data base, suggested "a narrow-sense heritability of 34 per cent and a broad-sense heritability of 46 per cent," a far cry from the figures employed by Murray and Herrnstein.

In perhaps the key test of the honesty of the underlying science of the book, trained experts in the field found they could not reproduce its results. For instance, one chart in *The Bell Curve* purports to show that people with IQs above 120 have become "rapidly more concentrated" in high-IQ occupations since 1940. But Robert Hauser and his colleague Min-Hsiung Huang retested the data and came up with estimates that fell "well below those of Herrnstein and Murray." They add that the data, properly used, "do not tell us anything except that selected, highly educated occupation groups have grown rapidly since 1940." In another example of same, also unearthed by Lemann, Herrnstein and Murray attempted to measure socioeconomic status by averaging four factors of equal weight: mother's education, father's education, father's occupation, and family income. Since the last two were missing from their data sample, however, they simply substituted an average for the entire sample. But six scientists at the University of California at Berkeley recalculated the effect of socioeconomic status, using the same variables but weighting them differently. They found the book's estimates of the ability of IQ to predict poverty suddenly to appear profoundly exaggerated—by 61 percent for whites and 74 percent for blacks.[48] Robert Hauser noted, "To begin with, several of the numbers in [*The Bell Curve*] are simply wrong. There are no fewer than five copying or multiplication errors in age- and test-specific entries in the body of" a single table. These mistakes, he noted, led the authors to "understate both the initial black-white differences and the changes in test scores across time." Rerunning the data with a more accurate standard deviation, Hauser came up with a significantly higher black-white IQ convergence.[49]

In fact, the entire study is built on a faulty edifice. In his final summary statement of his *TNR* essay, Murray wrote, "In study after study of the leading tests, the idea that the black-white difference is caused by questions with cultural content [i.e., that the tests are "biased" against the culturally deprived] has been contradicted by the facts."[50] If this statement by Murray is false, then virtually everything else in the book must also be false. Jared Diamond, the celebrated professor of physiology at the UCLA School of Medicine and an extremely highly regarded expert in evolutionary biology and biogeography, is one of many experts who insists that this statement—at least in its descriptive sense regarding "study after study" cannot be justified. In his Pulitzer Prize-winning book, *Guns, Germs and Steel*, Diamond explained:

> Even our cognitive abilities as adults are heavily influenced by the social environment that we experienced during childhood, making it hard to discern any influence of preexisting genetic differences. Second, tests of cognitive ability (like IQ tests) tend to measure cultural learning and not pure innate intelligence, whatever that is. Because of those undoubted effects of childhood environment and learned knowledge on IQ test results, the psychologists' efforts to date have not succeeded in convincingly establishing the postulated genetic deficiency in IQs of nonwhite peoples.[51]

Diamond's observation seems particularly relevant given the apparent carelessness with which Murray and Herrnstein applied their false assumptions to the scientific studies they professed to assess. For instance, to take just one small example, Murray and Herrnstein note that South African "coloureds" have about the same IQ as American blacks. This helps to prove their case, they argue, because, "the African black population has not been subjected to the historical legacy of American black slavery and discrimination and might therefore have higher scores."[52]

But their claim of extremely low IQs for black Africans—"very dull" in the authors' words—derives from tests conducted in South Africa before the end of apartheid, a circumstance that could hardly be more relevant. Yet this qualification is nowhere to be found in *The Bell Curve*.[53] Nor do the authors find space to mention the racist assumptions of the scientist who conducted the research. To top it all off, they misread the data upon which they were relying, and thereby screw up their own calculations.[54] Other scientists found countless other incidents of the authors either ignoring data that conflicted with that which they cited or unaccountably failing to include or address important studies that would throw a monkey wrench into their reasoning.[55]

As a result of the above, more than a few members of the expert community denounced the book as a kind of scholarly swindle. Writing in a special September 1995 issue of the *American Behavioral Scientist*—exactly the kind of journal that would have offered a peer review-reading of *The Bell Curve* had the authors been willing to submit to one—Michael Nunley, a professor of anthropology at the University of Oklahoma, charged:

> I believe this book is a fraud, that its authors must have known it was a fraud when they were writing it, and that Charles Murray must still know it's a fraud as he goes around defending it. By "fraud," I mean a deliberate, self-conscious misrepresentation of the evidence. After careful reading, I cannot believe its authors were not acutely aware of what they were including and what they were leaving out, and of how they were distorting the material they did include.[56]

*The Bell Curve* "would not be accepted by an academic journal. It's that bad," added Richard Nisbett, a professor of psychology at the University of Michigan.[57] These critics were joined by many scholars, perhaps most notable among them Leon J. Kamin, a professor of psychology at Northeastern University and author of *The Science and Politics of IQ*, who had been pointedly excluded from the AEI press-release gathering, lest his expertise get in the way of the book's publicity campaign. Kamin warned, "To pretend, as Herrnstein and Murray do, that the 1,000-odd items in their bibliography provide a 'scientific' basis for their reactionary politics may be a clever political tactic, but it is a disservice to and abuse of science."[58]

But Murray and Herrnstein's research raised even more troubling questions about the authors' agenda than mere incompetence or even ideological fervor. Charles Lane discovered that seventeen researchers cited in the book's bibliography were contributors to the racist journal *Mankind Quarterly*. Murray and Herrnstein also relied on at least thirteen scholars who had received grants from the Pioneer Fund, established and run by men who were Nazi sympathizers, eugenicists, and advocates of white racial superiority.[59]

The racial problems with *The Bell Curve*'s sources went way beyond mere guilt by association. Many of the book's most important assertions rested on the work of the Pioneer Fund/*Mankind Quarterly* group of "scholars." J. Philippe Rushton of Canada's University of Western Ontario, for instance, is cited eleven times in the book's bibliography and receives a two-page mention in its appendix (pp. 642–643). Rushton professes to believe in the existence of a hierarchy of "races" in which "Mongoloid" and "Caucasoid" are at the top, and "Negroid" at the bottom. "Negroids," he argued, are younger when they first have intercourse, have larger penises and vaginas, increased sex hormonal activity, and larger breasts and buttocks. He judges that these factors, combined with the fact that black women produce more eggs and black men more sperm, lead to increased fertility, poorer parenting, and sexually transmitted diseases, including the AIDS virus. Rushton once summarized his views on black/white difference as follows: "It's a tradeoff, more brains or more penis. You can't have everything."[60]

Also, the acknowledgments in *The Bell Curve* include an authors' note indicating that they have "benefited especially" from the "advice" of one Richard Lynn, whom they identify as "a leading scholar of racial and ethnic differences." A professor of psychology at the University of Ulster in Coleraine, Lynn is also associate editor of *Mankind Quarterly* and has received $325,000 from the Pioneer Fund. He has expressed the scholarly view that "the poor and the ill" are "weak specimens whose proliferation needs to be discouraged in the interests of the improvement of the genetic quality of the group, and ultimately of group survival." Leon J. Kamin described Lynn's work as riddled with "distortions and misrepresentations of the data which constitute a truly venomous racism, combined with scandalous disregard for scientific objectivity."[61]

If *The Bell Curve* were actually a respectable scholarly contribution to the debate over the place of race and genetics in our society, then closing one's eyes to its conclusions would have been a cowardly and ultimately self-defeating response. But as Mickey Kaus pointed out, "The question isn't whether it is possible that some ethnic groups have, on average, higher mental abilities than others, it's whether Murray is a reliable guide when it comes to exploring this possibility."[62] The question of whether Murray and his late co-author Richard Herrnstein are themselves racists is a pointless and ultimately insoluble debate. What is unarguable, however, is the fact that they were willing to employ sources infected with racist underpinnings in pursuit of arguments custom-designed to appeal to racist inclinations on the part of their readers and reviewers.

The reception for *The Bell Curve* undoubtedly opened the door for yet another AEI-sponsored assault on the conventions of race relations and politely speakable racism. That book was Dinesh D'Souza's *The End of Racism*, published a year after the Murray/Herrnstein tome.[63] As Glenn C. Loury, a black neoconservative scholar who resigned his affiliation with AEI over its sponsorship of D'Souza, noted, *The Bell Curve*

> broke the taboo against open discussion of black inferiority, and many readers just could not wait to get their hands on the "proof." Now, with a slightly different line of attack, comes Dinesh D'Souza, a thirtysomething journalist with no formal research training and a well deserved reputation as a polemicist. Based at the same conservative think tank (the American Enterprise Institute) and using the same

publisher (The Free Press) as Murray, D'Souza has written what is being billed as a "bold" and "sweeping" study that "challenges the last taboo" about racism. The book has a hopeful title, "The End of Racism: Principles for a Multiracial Society." But, in fact, it is merely this year's entry in the black inferiority publishing sweepstakes, ascribing "black failure" to "the pathologies of black culture," rather than "the content of our chromosomes."[64]

D'Souza too was funded by the Olin Foundation. According to Loury, he too enjoyed that "luncheon meetings to promote the book have been arranged at exclusive business clubs in New York and Chicago, sponsored by the American Enterprise Institute and some of its wealthy patrons." The book also enjoyed a 100,000-copy initial print run and an exceptional number of galley copies sent to journalists. For his most vicious anti-black attacks, D'Souza, unsurprisingly, relied on the discredited data put forth in *The Bell Curve* and its misreading of genetic intelligence data. In a chapter entitled, "Uncle Tom's Dilemma: Pathologies of Black Culture," D'Souza argued that black culture "has a vicious, self-defeating and repellent underside that is no longer possible to ignore or euphemize." Among its main characteristics: (1) racial paranoia ("Many blacks seem to live in the haunted house of the past, apparently patrolled by the ghosts of white racism"); (2) middle-class rage ("We have to conclude that we are dealing with cases of people who live in a world of make-believe, in mental prisons of their own construction"); (3) dependence on government; (4) the cult of the "bad nigger" lionized in rap music; and (5) illegitimacy.[65] D'Souza's racial politics are, by most standards, poisonous: "If America as a nation owes blacks as a group reparations for slavery," he asks, "what do blacks as a group owe America for the abolition of slavery?" His history is no less suspect. And after slavery was ended, he writes, the white South imposed segregation "to protect blacks."[66]

What Murray, Herrnstein, and later D'Souza helped accomplish was to offer permission to well-educated and sophisticated people—the kind of people Murray congratulated for having the high intelligence and good taste to read his book—to say the kinds of things that had previously been placed off limits. There can be no doubt that in the past several years, conservatives by their own statements have eroded the taboo against public racism. The net result has been what Anthony Lewis termed a kind of "racist chic" in which Murray and D'Souza argued "that white Americans have nothing to be ashamed of: If blacks have problems, it is their fault. Read this book, and stop worrying about your feelings toward blacks."[67]

Following on Murray and D'Souza, on a more popular level, conservative provocateur David Horowitz felt free to instruct young blacks attending college in their college newspapers that "trillions of dollars in transfer payments have been made to African-Americans in the form of welfare benefits." He was ignorant, apparently, of the fact that most welfare recipients are white, and that the primary welfare program,

Aid to Families with Dependent Children, was denied to blacks for decades on the grounds that they lacked "suitable homes."[68] Despite the clear racist intent of this purposeful misinformation, Horowitz, like Murray and D'Souza before him, was invited on many television and radio talk shows as a result. The one-time apologist for the Black Panther Party and champion of left-wing terrorism as editor of *Ramparts* during the Sixties underwent a conversion to a similarly considered form of right-wing extremism. Termed "A Real, Live Bigot," in *Time* magazine, Horowitz nevertheless found himself lovingly profiled in the *Washington Post* style section, given his own column in liberal Salon, and celebrated by many mainstream personalities. This would not be possible without the efforts of Murray and D'Souza.[69]

Moreover, listen to Rush Limbaugh, who told a black caller, "Take that bone out of your nose and call me back." "The NAACP should have riot rehearsals," he announced on another occasion. "They should get a liquor store and practice robberies." When Senator Carol Moseley-Braun's name was mentioned on his program, Limbaugh played the theme song *Movin' On Up* from the Seventies black sitcom *The Jeffersons*. "Have you ever noticed how all newspaper composite pictures of wanted criminals resemble Jesse Jackson?" he asked listeners.[70] It is fair to ask whether conservatives feel as emboldened to trespass on what were once clear societal conventions against this kind of publicly expressed racial hatred. If not, then this is yet another accomplishment for which the New Right might credibly claim credit—aided and abetted, once again, by the so-called "liberal media."

# 7

# What Social Bias?

IT IS AXIOMATIC that if you look hard enough, you can find, without trying very hard, what most people would term a "liberal" bias all over the mainstream media. Journalism, lest we forget, is a nearly perfectly inexact science, the first draft of history and all that. Any number of biases—liberal, conservative, religious, ethnocentric, humanist, heterosexist, age-ist, class-ist, racist, able-ist, weight-ist, to name just a few—can creep into a story despite the best efforts of reporters, editors, and producers to keep them at bay. The key question to ask is not whether examples of bias can be found, but exactly where is bias pervasive and what is its effect on the news and American public life?

Though the evidence is sketchy, I tend to believe that on many social issues, conservatives have a case. Elite media journalists, like most people in their education brackets and geographical locations, rarely come into contact with religious fundamentalists. So it can be difficult for them to know what people who live, culturally and sociologically, in a far-off land might perceive as biased.

If religion were the only measure of bias then conservatives would have a strong case. Politically speaking, the Republicans are the party of evangelical and fundamentalist Christians, and the Democrats are the party of secularists. Journalists are far more comfortable with the latter; indeed, they consider their position to be the "normal" one. Indeed, it is so normal, it does not occur to anyone to point it out. Thus the *New York Times* ran twice as many stories on the power of fundamentalists and evangelicals in the Republican party in 1992 alone than both the *Times* and the *Washington Post* together ran on secularists in the Democratic Party during the entire decade of the 1990s.[1] Ipso facto, religious conservatives might wish to argue, if the media is secular and the Democrats are secular, the two are quite naturally allies against the faithful on those issues where religion plays a role in the public sphere.

Moreover, even with the best of intentions, religion is hard to cover as "news" because it is, by definition, a matter of faith. How is a reporter trained in "who, what, when, where, and why" to treat reports of, say, a miracle or a visitation? Few reporters have much experience with fundamentalist Christians and most, I would venture, are clueless about what it is they believe. Stephen Carter, a Yale Law School professor, noted that during a 2000 presidential debate, reporters would use the terms "fundamentalist" and "evangelical" as if they were synonymous. Media who are unable to understand these distinctions, he wrote, "will be equally unable to understand why, in his presidential campaign, the Reverend Pat Robertson ran worse among fundamentalists than among white voters generally."[2] Garry Wills, whose lifelong interest in religion and politics is almost unique among liberal public intellectuals, mused on this problem in the *Washington Post Book World*, recalling that David Broder once admitted that his Rolodex contained sources for law, economics, or history, but not a single person to call up about Mormonism. Wills noted the religion writer Martin Marty's observation that more Americans go to church on a weekend than attend sports events, "but look at the difference in newspaper space given to religion and to sports."[3]

But most reporters are ignorant about most things, which is rarely seen as a barrier to coverage. Ignorance is not the same thing as bias. Most reporters can't tell a flintlock from a firing pin and know little about auto racing, evangelicalism, farming, hunting, and many other pastimes of crucial importance to many Americans. But one hears much the same complaint from astronomers, physicists, historians, jazz musicians, marine geologists, cops, firemen, Springsteen fans, Grateful Deadheads, and just about everybody else who sees a complex area of their professional or personal lives oversimplified or misunderstood by a reporter who covers it. Reporters cannot know what the experts, or even enthusiasts, do, much less those who have lived with a particular phenomenon their entire lives. The conservative activist and organizer, Grover Norquist, attributes most of his dissatisfaction with the media's biases to what he terms reporters' "lazy self-centeredness." Journalists, he complained, "simply assume the rest of the country is interested in the same things they are. They project out from their own personal lives."

According to Norquist, media-types "worry about gay rights, abortion, gun control, but those are not issues that are important to most people"[4]—and he has a point. When, in June 2002, Katie Couric interviewed former anchor Linda Ellerbee about the evening *Nick News* show (featuring Rosie O'Donnell and called "My Dad Is Different") that Ellerbee was hosting for children about gay families, it was clear to all on whose side the angels rested. Tom Shales made the point explicitly in the *Washington Post*, writing, "Only the most alarmist and paranoid could find anything insidious or threatening here."[5] The show allegedly produced 100,000 e-mails of pre-program protest, organized by the right-wing Traditional Values Campaign. Their spokespeople complained that the program was "a cover for promoting homosexuality for kids" and went so far as to explain, "Sodomy is not a family value."[6] (The program did not really mention sex.) Rhetoric aside, it is not hard to understand why these conservatives see their way of life as under siege by such programs and do not appreciate being labeled as "alarmist and paranoid" for doing so.

But the "tolerance" question, just like that of ignorance, can cut both ways. The mere fact that three of the top political reporters for the *New York Times* in recent years have been openly gay men is mistaken as evidence of bias by some in the conservative media establishment—and no doubt by some Americans as well. Not long ago, Brent Bozell III attacked the *New York Times* for appointing a gay man to a top position, suggesting that this "signals that [*Times* editors are] promoting their newspaper as an aggressive liberal lobbying tool not only to prevent Republican campaign victories, but to pave a smooth and silky path for cultural relativism as well."[7] In fact, one of the *Times*'s openly gay reporters, Frank Bruni, became something of a joke to his colleagues owing to his enormously sympathetic coverage of George W. Bush. A quick perusal of his book on the 2000 campaign, *Ambling into History*, provides ample evidence that Bush could not have asked for a more generous Boswell from the Newspaper of Record.[8] Bozell apparently, like President Bush, does not know many openly gay individuals, hence he has trouble believing that one might be able to separate sexuality from professional commitment. (The president is quoted in Bruni's book announcing "An openly known homosexual is somebody who probably wouldn't share my philosophy.")[9]

The utility of the conservative conspiracy theory, regardless of its basis in fact, is that it presents the bare bones of a coherent notion of liberal media domination. After all, if the *New York Times* is crusading on behalf of gay rights, or special treatment for African-Americans, this implies a great deal more than just the avowed sympathies of one newspaper. It is a given in the media business that television news producers take their cues from that morning's *Times*, with an assist from the *Washington Post* for political stories. So too do many other newspaper and television editors nationwide. If the *Times*, and to a lesser degree the *Post*, are genuinely biased in a liberal direction, then by extension, so will be much of the media. This explains why critics focus so much of their ire on these two newspapers, though their combined reach is fewer than one in a hundred Americans.

As I write this, a mini-consensus has developed among conservatives and others, stoked by the Web sites of Andrew Sullivan and Mickey Kaus, arguing that *Times* executive editor Howell Raines has decided to convert the newspaper into a crusading liberal organ—and I am excluding the heated debate over whether reporting dissension about beginning an aggressive war constitutes opposition to it, as so many conservatives argue, though I will discuss it later. (However, Sullivan's criticism must be viewed through the prism of his belief, presented sans evidence, that Raines personally ended his career as a contract writer for the *Times Magazine* for reasons of pique.) Perhaps it is a function of my own liberal biases—to which I readily admit—

but I am at a loss to find much evidence for this view. On any given day one can find reports in the *Times* that gladden a liberal's heart alongside those that infuriate it. There is bias evident in the paper every day, but it's hard to determine a pattern in it. Despite being one of Bill Clinton's most vociferous critics and Ken Starr's biggest boosters as the paper's editorial page editor, Raines was viewed by many to be a flaming liberal during his years there, largely owing to the page's passion for campaign finance reform. Robert Samuelson, the conservative economics columnist for *Newsweek* and the *Washington Post*, went so far as to argue that Raines should be denied the executive editor's job on the basis of his alleged liberalism.[10] But in a 17,000-plus-word *New Yorker* profile, the only evidence that reporter Ken Auletta could uncover for this view was a single story—during a period of nine months—in which Raines decided that a study revealing that blacks in New Jersey tended to speed more than whites, hence complicating the issue of racial profiling, should be run on the front page of the metro section rather than on page one. Raines noted in Auletta's story that the newspaper did not even possess a copy of the study and that the editor had concerns about its methodology. An anonymous editor sought to blame the decision on the fact that "Raines was being politically correct," but he would not even say these words himself.[11] Overall, it was pretty thin gruel.

Meanwhile, Jack Shafer, Slate's libertarian media critic, has also critiqued what he terms to be pro-environmental biases in *Times* news reports.[12] He faulted the *Times* for overplaying a story in early July 2002, when the Bush administration allegedly decided to "roll back" pollution regulations that had required utilities to install additional pollution controls when they modernized or expanded their power plants. In fact, the *Times* story—as opposed to its headline—was quite sympathetic to the administration's move that did, indeed, relax Clinton-administration regulations on polluters. But on most days, environmentalists are just as furious at the *Times*—and the rest of the media—as the Bush Administration is. As the neoliberal environmental critic Greg Easterbrook told Howard Kurtz, "The media have done a shockingly poor job of not challenging either the left or the right on [the environment]."[13]

Of course in all but the most egregious cases, media bias is largely a subjective matter. From my own perspective as an urban, East Coast liberal who is surrounded by others who hold views not unlike my own, I am certainly prepared to believe that members of the elite media transmit liberal views in the guise of objective reporting on occasion. On some issues this bias might be called pervasive, as David Shaw has consistently argued, for instance, in a multi-part examination of the elite media's treatment of abortion during an eighteen-month period. The *Los Angeles Times* published it during the summer of 1990. "Responsible journalists do try to be fair, and many charges of bias in abortion coverage are not valid," Shaw wrote. "But careful examination of stories published and broadcast reveals scores of examples, large and small, that can only be characterized as unfair to the opponents of abortion, either in content, tone, choice of language or prominence of play."[14] Shaw then goes on to give dozens if not hundreds of examples that any fair-minded person who is not a partisan of one side or the other would have to agree are slanted in the direction of the side that favors legal abortions. Among these, and I quote at length again, are:

- When the *Washington Post* wrote about proposed anti-abortion legislation in Louisiana last month, it spoke of the state House of Representatives' making a decision on "a woman's reproductive rights." As Douglas Johnson, legislative director for the National Right to Life Committee, pointed out, "In discussing abortion as a matter of 'a woman's reproductive rights,' the *Post* adopts both the paradigm and the polemic of the abortion-rights lobby."

- When the *Los Angeles Times* covered the same story, it referred to the proposed legislation as "the nation's harshest." That's the view of abortion-rights advocates; it's "harsh" toward women's rights. But abortion opponents regard the legislation as benevolent—toward the fetus.

  The language used in coverage of the Louisiana legislation is not an anomaly. Virtually all the media refer to anti-abortion legislation as "restrictive." What is it "restricting"? The right of a woman to have an abortion. But abortion opponents would describe the legislation as "protective"—"protective" of the fetus.

- The Associated Press, *Washington Post*, *Boston Globe*, and *Time* magazine, among others, have referred to those who oppose abortion "even in cases of rape and incest" (circumstances under which most people approve of abortion). But the media almost never refer to those who favor abortion rights "even in the final weeks of pregnancy" (circumstances under which most people oppose abortion).

One could go on, and Shaw does, but the point ends up being undeniable. The story does not exactly make the "liberal media" case, however. In the first place, what was it doing in the "liberal media" at all? Second, critics need to take note of its profound influence on how the issue was covered after the story appeared. Shaw won a Pulitzer Prize. His findings were accepted and editors, reporters, and producers alike did their best to implement changes in their coverage. Today journalists are constantly on alert for bias in the pro-choice direction. In fact, during the great anthrax scare of 2001, abortion clinics had a legitimate complaint that they could not interest the media in the anthrax threats and attacks that they were receiving. It was possible, by the summer of 2002, to wonder if the balance on abortion coverage had not tipped entirely in the opposite direction. For instance in July of that year, the allegedly liberal *Washington Post* endorsed for confirmation to a key federal appeals court a judge whose record, the newspaper reported, led Senate Democrats to suggest "repeatedly that she has interpreted the law to suit her own conservative views on abortion."[15]

Abortion is not the only issue where a fair-minded observer might point to a pervasive liberal bias. Michael Massing, a liberal contributor to the *Nation* and former executive editor of the *Columbia Journalism Review,* testified in the latter to finding credible evidence of liberal bias on issues related to the death penalty and gun control. Massing observed:

> In recent months, national news organizations have produced a flood of stories questioning how the death penalty is administered in this country. These accounts have documented the poor legal representation available to death-row inmates, the extra-harsh treatment minorities generally receive, and, most dramatically, the growing number of innocent people who have been condemned to death. As an opponent of capital punishment, I applaud such stories. Yet I also believe that they lean toward one side of the issue, and that the coverage would be enhanced if more attention were paid to, say, the families of murder victims and the ordeal they must endure. Similarly, in the case of gun control, the press has run countless stories on the lax regulation of gun shows, the ease with which criminals can get firearms, and the political clout of the National Rifle Association. Comparatively few articles have probed the tactics of Handgun Control or explored the argument that allowing citizens to carry concealed weapons can deter crime. Does every member of the media think this way? Of course not. But there is a prevalent mindset that reinforces itself through peer and social pressure. This would be true anywhere, but it is magnified by the concentration and intensity of media life in New York. A similar elite slant can be detected, I think, in the coverage of abortion, gay rights, the environment, affirmative action, school prayer, and the other hot-button issues of the culture wars.[16]

Michael Waldman, former chief speechwriter for President Clinton and an alumnus of Ralph Nader's Congress Watch, also noted, "There were certain issues where the press really did move in lockstep. They weren't always the ones you would expect. The press was predictably for campaign finance reform, for example, though they were far more interested in exposing hypocrisy than in covering flagrant and legal campaign finance abuses."[17] I concur that the overall flavor of the elite media reporting favors gun control, campaign finance reform, gay rights, and the environmental movement, but I do not find this bias as overwhelming as some conservative critics do, or even as Massing does. The mere fact of paying more attention to a story than an audience would likely choose—as clearly seems to be the case with both campaign finance reform and the death penalty—is hardly evidence of a bias on one side of the issue or the other. It is merely evidence of editorial judgment—something a democracy depends on journalists to do in spite of, rather than in accord with, market pressures. Moreover, as often as not, the impulse of the journalists and editors/producers is to over-compensate in advance to appease predictable criticism—and thus to end up with a story that is in fact weighted more against, rather than in favor of, their own beliefs.

The one social issue of alleged media bias that has received undoubtedly the lion's share of attention from conservatives is race. The (mainly) liberal sensitivities of journalists, coupled with a corporate-driven PC-sensitivity to offending anyone who might start a boycott or cause some other kind of trouble, has vastly complicated the profession's ability to cover any issue perceived to touch uncomfortably on race. Media corporations were directed almost exclusively by well-educated white men through the mid-1970s. These men came to understand that they could neither accurately report nor represent America if they excluded the views and interests of those unlike themselves. They had many motivations—commercial, journalistic, moral, even religious. The 1968 Kerner Commission Report, which blamed the 1960s riots on white racism, termed the national media to be "shockingly backward" in their coverage and employment of people of color. It criticized them for viewing the world almost exclusively through "white men's eyes." As a result of such impetuses, the media embraced the concept of "diversity" wholeheartedly, without knowing exactly how to go about fulfilling that mandate. News organizations hastened to transform "the way we view each other and the way we view the news" as articulated by *New York Times* publisher Arthur Sulzberger Jr.[18] Along the way, they made a few mistakes.

Critics have a smorgasbord of choices if they want to mock the hypersensitivity to various minorities on the part of these men—and now women—in the elite media structure. There is the undeniable presence of informal quotas in hiring practices, along with bonus payments and promotional structures designed to increase the percentage of minority reporters, editors, and producers. Many news executives have also demonstrated an occasionally laughable hypersensitivity to complaints of racial "insult" at the slightest provocation. One famous incident involved a list issued by editors of the *LA Times* of forbidden phrases. The list included: "gyp," "WASP" "illegal alien," even "Dutch treat." Another object of deserved mockery was the policy of alleged "mainstreaming" instituted by the Gannett organization (and since scaled back), demanding that news stories reflect "the face of the country." Some news organizations instated racial quotas for quotes as well as for "positive" stories and flattering minority photos.[19] The evident paternalism of such efforts was clear when then-*LA Times* publisher, Mark Willes—who, to be fair, was a business executive and never a journalist—proposed the creation of a new news section designed to attract more Latino readers. He also suggested in an interview that the paper needed to be made more alluring to women and minorities by publishing stories that were "more emotional, more personal, and less analytic."[20]

But the nitty-gritty problem of how to handle race in the media remains one that can make even the smartest of people look stupid. When twenty-four-year-old *New Republic* writer Ruth Shalit did an extremely long article on the *Washington Post*'s difficulties in dealing with race-related issues in October 1995, entitled "Race in the Newsroom," both her piece, and the reaction to it, evinced many of the problems it sought to examine.[21] Yet despite a number of mistakes, including at least one serious one, her article turned out to be enormously instructive.

"Twenty-five years ago, the Post—like most newspapers—was a largely white, middle-class bastion," Shalit began by noting. "There were no black assignment editors, no black foreign correspondents, no black reporters on the National staff. And its paternalism toward the black community was legendary." She then examined some of the attempts to make amends for that history. She cited, for instance, examples of African-American reporters receiving a degree of indulgence from the paper's editors that would be unthinkable for a white reporter. Describing his own work in terms that would clearly be tagged as racist if spoken by a white person, African-American reporter Kevin Merida explained, "the black experience is part of who I am" and so he tried "to incorporate that in my coverage." Merida gave her examples of three stories: an admiring profile of ex-Senator Carol Moseley-Braun; an attack on art in the Capitol as "colonialist and lacking in racial diversity"; and a complaint about the Senate for its condemnation of Khalid Muhammad's racist attacks on Jews while the body stood silently for Senator Ernest Hollings's jokes about cannibalistic "African potentates." Suffice to say that not one of these stories held to traditional standards of journalistic objectivity. The obvious impression one draws is that the newspaper's editors sought to indulge their African-American writer and to privilege his arguments on the basis of the race of their author.

As Shalit's story demonstrated, this phenomenon took place repeatedly at the *Post*. Its editors allowed one writer, Nathan McCall, who had converted to Islam while in prison, to write an extremely gentle and approving story about a visit to the *Post* editorial board by the Jew-hating, UFO-imagining Black Muslim leader, Louis Farrakhan. Shalit noted, "Although the front-page story acknowledged that 'many of the questions and much of Farrakhan's talk dealt with his reportedly disparaging references to Jews and Judaism,' the *Post*'s story focused on what McCall termed Farrakhan's express 'desire for the media to print the truth' about him and his message. . . . He said that as a spiritual leader, he is concerned about the welfare of the entire nation." In another incident, Shalit reported that one *Post* editor would not even allow the newspaper to term Farrakhan, a self-professed admirer of Hitler, "controversial."[22]

The *Post* management reacted furiously to Shalit's story, and it had a point. Just who was this novice upstart *New Republic* reporter to judge their sincere and painful efforts to address this most complex and gut-wrenching of topics? The *New Republic*, *Post* publisher Donald Graham was no doubt pleased to point out, had never employed a senior-level black writer or editor since its founding in 1914. ("Since she works at the *New Republic*," Graham's letter stated, "the last practitioner of de facto segregation since Mississippi changed, Ms. Shalit has little or no experience in working with black colleagues."[23]) Shalit herself turned out to have a history of serial plagiarism, and this made it easy to brush her off. But the basic thrust of the story held up quite well under the attack. Even with the best of intentions, race is a problem that journalism just does not know how to fix.

In 2001, William McGowan, a fellow of the conservative Manhattan Institute, published a book entitled *Coloring the News*, in which he complained of "an invisible liberal consensus" rather than "an active liberal conspiracy" within the media to hide the truth about "diversity"-related issues—meaning primarily race—from the American public.[24] Attempting to give the book the whiff of *Bell Curve*-like forbidden fruit and thereby create a media scandal, its publisher, the Bradley Foundation-funded Encounter Books, originally claimed that the book had been rejected by the Free Press owing to "fear of publishing such a controversial issue." As the saying goes, interesting if true. The reality turned out to be more mundane. McGowan had signed with Free Press, an imprint of Simon and Schuster, in the days when it was an outpost of the conservative movement, specializing in racist and dishonest works like *The Bell Curve* and *The Real Anita Hill*, and Adam Bellow was its editor in chief. After its guiding spirit Erwin Glikes died and his successor, Bellow, faltered, the company was taken over by new management. The new editorial team was, in fact, eager to publish McGowan's book when he delivered it in 1999, but he was no longer so eager to have it published by an imprint that did not share his own ideological proclivities. As McGowan later admitted, the only problem was that he feared they "wouldn't have supported it the way I wanted them to."[25]

While *Coloring the News* is nowhere near as badly written or shoddily constructed as Bernard Goldberg's *Bias* or Ann Coulter's *Slander*, neither is its argument convincing, nor its reportage entirely reliable. In his eagerness to accuse the media of attacking racism where it does not exist, McGowan took refuge in a *New Yorker* report by Michael Kelly that argued that the church burnings in the U.S. South in early 1996 were not racially motivated. In fact, a *Columbia Journalism Review* editor dissected and discredited this report of Kelly's, which McGowan ignored. (Kelly was, once again, overeager to discredit everything Bill Clinton had ever said or done.)[26] Many of McGowan's sources were authors and studies who had received funding from the same network of conservative ideological "scholarship" that underwrote his own work and have also proven themselves unreliable. Moreover, as Seth Mnookin noted in a review in the *Washington Monthly*, a publication where McGowan had once worked, "McGowan's analyses are so misleading one has to wonder if the deception is purposeful." In the case of his treatment of a December 1995 murder in Harlem, where a black man named Roland Smith set fire to a Jewish-owned store called Freddy's Fashion Mart, shooting seven people to death, McGowan blamed the *New York Times* for allegedly "depict[ing] Smith as a man of 'principle,' explaining that he lived 'an ardent credo' of black 'self-sufficiency' and 'resistance,' and that his actions inside Freddy's were not criminal per se, but a strange act of suicide in protest against the 'institutional force' of white racism." In fact, the very article McGowan discussed terms the killer to be mentally deranged and quoted a former friend of his observing, "It was an act of insanity for all of us looking in on it." The same day's newspaper, as Mnookin noted, carried an editorial that explained, "Roland Smith was driven by a sick hatred of whites and Jews and by the criminally irresponsible anti-white and anti-Semitic ravings of protesters who had been picketing Freddy's."[27]

While McGowan devoted page after page to picking apart the *Times*'s coverage in cases like this one, he managed to devote only one page to its historic fifteen-part, Pulitzer Prize-winning series, "How Race is Lived in America," published in 2000. McGowan admitted that the series was an "exception" to the norm of *Times* race reporting in that it "managed to catch many of the subtleties and the sense of historical progress often lacking in most of the paper's daily coverage."[28] But if the series was an "exception"—and a rather large exception at that—McGowan does not appear remotely interested in just how or why so culturally debased an institution might have managed to produce it. It is perhaps a measure of the power of the critique of the so-called "liberal media"—along with journalists' penchant for self-flagellation in tribute to their ideology-minded critics—that this deeply flawed, ideologically driven diatribe received an award from the National Press Club in 2002.[29]

In decided contrast to the book that chose to ignore it, the *Times* series was among the most ambitious reporting projects in recent media history. Based on the work of sixteen reporters in twelve cities, it eventually filled up enough newspaper to equal a 416-page book. Part of the reason that professional journalists might have expressed disappointment with the series was intentional on the part of the *Times* editors. Beginning with a look at a racially integrated church in Decatur, Georgia, the series focused on the day-to-day experiences of various Americans, with the question of race relations defined less by political action—as it is typically in the media—than by daily experience, "in schools, in sports arenas, in pop culture and at worship, and especially in the workplace." The kinds of questions asked were decidedly non-political: "Is integration a blessing or a sellout, blacks wonder. Is it ever acceptable—or even help-ful—to make race the issue, or must a preacher and his congregation always feign col-orblindness? What are the burdens of blending in, and are they worth it? And will this last, or is the church just like so many neighborhoods—enjoying a fleeting moment of integration on the way to becoming predominantly black?" The series sought to explicate the complicated, often contradictory feelings that racial conflict and cooperation can engender in everyday life. In this regard, it was less news than extremely energetically reported sociology or social psychology, and hence a bold experiment for a daily newspaper.

Of course the articles themselves were far from perfect. They could be self-indulgent, simplistic on occasion, and they sure did, as the saying goes, slay trees. Keith Woods, who helped report the project, told the PBS *NewsHour* that he thought his piece reflect-ed all of the shortcomings of the problems upon which it reported, observing, "One of the things that staffs have learned whenever they try and tackle this issue is that, in fact, they are just like the people that they're reporting on. . . . We are in fact just as ret-icent, we are just as fearful, we have all the same hang-ups talking both within our groups and across race as anyone else does. One of the values then of this series is that for the reader, you get the opportunity to see what it sounds like to try out some ideas out loud in public."[30]

Given the size and scope of the *Times*'s undertaking, it was natural that it would also receive pointed criticism, much of it valid. Writing in Salon, memoirist Richard Rodriguez noted how odd it was that, given our multicultural society, the only two races to appear in the series were black and white. Asians and Hispanics made only rare appearances in it, and only then to illustrate a point about blacks or whites. This was rather odd, given the fact that the bifurcated manner of looking at race is viewed as passé in the hyper-multikulti-sensitive media, as well as in New York City, where the editors all work. Rodriguez thought this outdated emphasis had the effect of reas-suring the paper's white readers "that they remain at the center of our national life—which is exactly where they expect to be."[31]

This is hardly an isolated phenomenon. Despite the enormous efforts that news organizations have undertaken to achieve diverse newsrooms and management teams, whites remain the norm in the media, both behind the scenes and in the public view. For all the complaints about political correctness and an alleged multicultural reign of terror, as it is sometimes described, as recently as 2001 a study of the nightly news found that among U.S. sources for whom race was determinable, whites made up 92 percent of the total, blacks 7 percent, Latinos and Arab-Americans 0.6 percent each, and Asian-Americans 0.2 percent. (According to the 2000 census, the U.S. popula-tion is 69 percent non-Hispanic white, 13 percent Hispanic [who can be of any race], 12 percent black, and 4 percent Asian.) A single source who appeared on NBC (July 26, 2001) was the only Native American identified as having appeared on the nightly news in 2001—for 0.008 percent of total sources.³² This was no isolated case. Between January 1996 and September 1999, *Time* ran thirty cover stories, on topics ranging from homework to parental care, in which millions of Americans were symbolized by a single image: a white person. A study of *Newsweek* during the period between September 1998 and September 1999 found ten such covers, with every one featuring a white person. To be black and make the cover of one of the main newsweeklies, being "ordinary" was never enough; it required a Michael Jordan, an Oprah Winfrey . . . or an O. J. Simpson.³³

Another example of the social bias that can spill into allegedly objective news stories can be found in the disparity of coverage of crime victims, particularly when a single individual becomes the focus of intense media attention. Crime statistics do not begin to match media portrayals, with their vast over-representation of black criminals and white victims and a corresponding under-representation of white criminals and black victims.³⁴ When a white, upper-middle-class woman was raped and attacked while jogging in Central Park, it became a worldwide media story and the hysteria it inspired may have inspired false convictions of a group of young black men. But when a black woman met the same fate in the same park, at approximately the same time, nothing; next to no coverage and certainly no media-induced hysteria.³⁵ From the birth of cable news, a missing white girl who appears to have met an untimely death owing to possible foul play has always been a staple of the news, from Nicole Brown to Jon-Benet Ramsey, to Chandra Levy to Elizabeth Smart, the beautiful blond girl who graces both the cover of *Newsweek* and the pop-up screen of my AOL account as I write these words. One girl who is not on the cover of *Newsweek* or popping up on AOL, however, is a seven-year-old African American named Alexis Patterson who disappeared on her way to school one month before Smart's alleged abduction. In the latter case, the *New York Times* and *Washington Post* filed reports from her hometown of Salt Lake City. So too did the *Boston Globe*, *Miami Herald*, and countless other news outlets. Cable viewers were treated to updates on MSNBC and alleged experts scrutinized the case on CNN's *Larry King Live* and *Hardball with Chris Matthews*. But a Nexis search of Patterson's name done before people started comparing the two cases turned up only AP and local reports. After people began to notice this discrepancy, the *New York Times* sent a reporter to the Patterson home where, in their living room, the girl's parents saw MSNBC carry two reports on the Smart case, as the ticker beneath them carried the message, "Elizabeth Smart has been missing for three weeks."³⁶

Even with the best of intentions, the largely white-dominated mass media does not seem to be able to help but depict blacks in a fashion that inspires racist conclusions on the part of the audience. As Robert M. Entman and Andrew Rojecki demonstrate at length in their important study, *The Black Image in the White Mind*, a sampling of the network news drawn from 1997 shows blacks in basically three ways: "entertainer, sports figure or object of discrimination." A more detailed study of just ABC News found that the network "mainly discusses blacks as such when they suffer or commit crime, or otherwise fall victim and require attention from government." As a result, "the news constructs African-Americans as a distinct source of disruption." The authors note that since Caucasians are rarely featured in this way—relative to the number of times they are shown, "the news can easily imply a baseline or ideal social condition in which far fewer serious problems would plague the society if only everyone in the United States were native-born whites."[37]

This point is actually supported by Bernard Goldberg in his rant against liberal "bias," though it remains a mystery as to whether he is aware of this. Goldberg quoted a producer for *48 Hours*, who admitted, "All we do around here is murder, murder, murder, sex. And only about white people." Goldberg recounted the tale of a *48 Hours* producer who preemptively edited Hispanics out of stories because, he explained, his bosses "don't think our audience cares about Hispanics." Another producer, this one for NBC, explained, "Let's not kid ourselves. . . . There is no profit in people of color."[38] Av Westin, former ABC News chief, compiled a handbook for journalists covering racial issues. It is filled with the anonymous comments of some of the most influential reporters and producers in the business. Each told a similar story: "My bosses have essentially made it clear. We do not feature black people."[39]

These tendencies must be added to those of local news, which—with an "if it bleeds, it leads" mentality—vastly overemphasizes crime stories at the expense of all others. Within this context, local stations also exaggerate the degree to which criminals are alleged to be black and the victims, white. At the same time, the stations ignore virtually every conceivable contextual element of life that might induce crime, such as lack of economic or educational opportunity, wide availability of drugs, lack of local role models, and so on. It hardly requires a doctorate in sociology to understand that the news media actually contribute to ignorance-based racism rather than ameliorate it. Whatever the intent of those responsible may be—whether it is unconscious racism or merely a drive for better ratings and more money—the overall results appear incontrovertible and they do not support an argument for liberal bias.

Another way to measure the overall message the media communicates on racial issues is to examine the attitudes of the people who watch it. As most white Americans receive their information about black America from television, we can judge the question of whether the media is falsely catering to an overly liberal and generous portrayal of minorities based on the degree to which those attitudes correspond to reality—and in the manner in which they diverge. Whatever its specific source, in examining white attitudes toward black America, we find considerable ignorance and confusion. According to an extensive poll by the Kaiser Foundation, between 40 percent and 60 percent of all whites feel reassured that the average black American appears to be faring about as well and perhaps even better than the average white in employment, income, education, and access to health care. Unfortunately, this reassurance is false. While progress has been made in these areas in recent years, black America lags far behind white America by every measurable statistic. Sixty-one percent of whites questioned believe that the average black person has equal or better access to health care than the average white. The truth is that, in 2000, the U.S. Census Bureau's Current Population Survey found that blacks were nearly twice as likely as whites to be without health insurance. About half of whites believe blacks and whites enjoy roughly equivalent levels of education. Actually, the percentage of college graduates among blacks is about 17 percent; for whites it is 28 percent. "The results suggest there is the overwhelming sense among most whites that this is 2001— we could not possibly be saddled with segregation and discrimination and therefore things can't possibly be as bad as black Americans say they are," Swarthmore College political scientist Keith Reeves, who consulted on the survey, explained to a reporter.

The poll results imply ignorance on the part of most whites, rather than racism. The net results would seem to argue for an aggressive attempt by the news media to enlighten whites as to the true circumstances of black America, as the knowledge would seem to empower a change in attitudes. Whites with accurate views of black circumstances prove more sympathetic to federal intervention to ensure racial equality in education as well as fair treatment by the courts and law-enforcement authorities.[40] So if editors and producers pay more attention to black life than whites would prefer—which does not appear to be the case—would that really prove to be ipso facto evidence of bias, or merely a healthy sense of social responsibility? It's a complicated question and, as the pundits like to say, does not yield itself to "easy answers." Nevertheless, to say simply that race as portrayed in the media is governed by a combination of liberal media bias and politically correct condescension is to simplify— and ultimately falsify—an extremely complex and difficult problem. However difficult it may be, it remains a problem of which a society striving for "liberty and justice for all" cannot easily wash its hands.

# 8

## What Economic Bias?

PERHAPS THE EASIEST BIAS to identify in the media is that of business journalism. When it comes to money, journalists are easily impressed, and here it is conservatives who benefit by the fact that virtually no one questions their assumptions. "The chief business of the American people is business,"[1] President Calvin Coolidge famously observed, and so is the business of business journalism. What economists call "externalities"—the condition of workers' lives, the treatment of shareholders, sweetheart deals for favored investors, exorbitant executive compensation, special-interest lobbying in the federal agencies or on Capitol Hill—were, until recently, no more welcome on the business pages or cable chat shows than they had been in most corporations' reports to their stockholders. In fact, in most of the above cases, the topics begin to intrude on the media's storyline only when one of them reaches such mammoth proportions—say, an Enron accounting scandal or an Exxon oil spill—that it actually becomes the story.

In addition to the social issues discussed in chapter 7, a former top Clinton aide, Michael Waldman, identified "free trade" as perhaps the single issue where administration members could be most assured of friendly coverage. As the staffer charged with leading the administration's communications operation to win the fight over the NAFTA treaty in 1993, he recalled:

> I got a lot of kudos inside the White House for stories on NAFTA that I didn't even have any idea would be appearing. Without even much prompting, the press drummed away at the benefits of the agreement, and criticized the opponents. I always thought this was a combination of reporters and editors believing that the economic arguments were strong, which dovetailed with the overall posture of the owners of the news outlets. In any case, the coverage was pretty lopsided.[2]

Waldman gets no argument from the Clinton administration's arch-opponent, Grover Norquist. Free trade is, he explained, "the one issue that the establishment gets." Norquist finds this odd, because "They don't understand the minimum wage, which is simple, but they do get free trade, which is more complicated."[3] As is often the case, this left-right unholy alliance is on to something. No longer the working-class heroes of the *Front Page/His Gal Friday* lore, elite journalists in Washington and New York are rock-solid members of the political and financial Establishment about whom they write. They dine at the same restaurants and take their vacations on the same Caribbean islands. Even if one does not object to a journalist lobbying President Clinton to send Chelsea to the elite private school to which the journalist's daughter goes while trading pleasantries at a Renaissance Weekend, the very fact that such a thing takes place is at least indicative of a social order that would have been all but unimaginable a few decades earlier.[4] What's more, like the politicians, their jobs are not subject to export to China or Bangladesh. It is therefore not at all surprising to see that the Establishment ideology of "free trade at all costs" is received and transmitted no less passionately and unanimously than anti-Communism and "containment" were during the Cold War.[5]

While the 1993 NAFTA debate raged in Congress, for instance, the argument that the accord would undermine the jobs of America's lowest-paid workers by forcing them to bargain in the shadow of even worse-paid Mexican laborers garnered little sympathy among journalists. The only issue that mattered, *New York Times* editors insisted, was "America's appetite for global leadership after the Cold War."[6] The *Los Angeles Times* declared a pro-NAFTA vote to be "a vote for American foreign policy continuity."[7] The *Washington Post* called the vote "a historic test of American intentions toward the rest of the world." Senator Byron Dorgan, a Democrat from North Dakota, calculated that the *Washington Post* had published sixty-three feet worth of pro-NAFTA editorials and columns, compared to only eleven feet of anti-NAFTA commentary on its op-ed page during the same period. Another labor organization tallied up forty-eight op-ed articles in favor of NAFTA in the *Post* and just eight against. Straight news coverage was hardly any more balanced: 71 percent of expert sources quoted in the *Post* were pro-NAFTA, and only 17 percent opposed. The *New York Times* followed with 66 percent pro-treaty quotes and only 24 percent for opponents.[8]

The following year, the free-trade side—which could more accurately be termed the "free-investment" side—had so wrapped up the argument that the only real drama offered by 1994's GATT/WTO Treaty debate derived from the *Washington Post*'s failure to disclose to its readers that its owners stood to make hundreds of millions in forgiven licensing fees from a rider attached to the treaty. (To the paper's credit, it was willing to publish a full-page advertisement that pointed this out to readers.) Those treaties did not turn out as promised for many of the constituencies who supported them and by 1997 "free trade"—which had always been far more popular in elite surveys than in those of the public—had, in the eyes of voters, become a millstone around the necks of its congressional supporters. This outrage was palpable in

1997 when the House of Representatives decided to deny the president special "fast-track" authority to negotiate treaties that could not be legislatively amended. Media pundits were furious. From the right, *Post* columnist James Glassman suggested that the House of Representatives rename itself "the Washington Chapter of the Flat Earth Society," adding, "It's hard to find a respectable economist who opposes free trade, the value of which is glaringly obvious."[9] (Glassman might be termed the charter member of "the Washington Chapter of the Dow 36,000 Society," as he authored a book that predicted a rise in the stock market just before its attendant collapse.) From the left, *Times* columnist Anthony Lewis excoriated "Richard Gephardt's Democrats and their union allies [who] want to stop the world and get off."[10] From deep center, "Dean" David Broder condemned the victorious side for "pandering to the ideological extremes,"[11] despite its majority opposition in the nation at large. To oppose these pacts, regardless of reason, was by definition to be part of the "ideological extreme" in the mainstream media view, to be "scared," "pessimistic," and "unpatriotic" according to the received wisdom of the media's coverage of the issue.[12] Merely to point out that "free trade" is not really the issue in the non-rhetorical "real world," given the U.S. and other governments' willingness to attach massive subsidies to agricultural or steel industries whenever it happens to suit a politician's political needs, is somehow considered beside the point as well.[13]

Indeed, at least before the days of Osama bin Laden, it was difficult to find a topic that so inspired the media's universal anger and disgust as the individual anti-free-trade/unfettered globalization protester. Three-time Pulitzer winner Tom Friedman of the *New York Times* is a brilliant foreign affairs columnist whose views cannot easily be pigeonholed as "liberal" or "conservative." But when writing about trade, Friedman morphs into the equivalent of a Howard Stern for the Council on Foreign Relations set, terming opponents to the World Trade Organization to be "a Noah's ark of flat-earth advocates, protectionist trade unions and yuppies looking for their 1960's fix," who had somehow been "duped by knaves like Pat Buchanan."[14] Here, Friedman could barely outdo the editors of the *Wall Street Journal*, who preferred the appellation, "Luddite wackos."[15] Like many who write about the topic, *New Republic* senior editor Franklin Foer lumped together those who question free trade with garden-variety xenophobia on the traditionally anti-Semitic right, as he described the "one group that shares the Buchananite docket of suspicions—of Wall Street, capitalism, Zionism, American power: the anti-globalization left."[16]

Now, most intelligent people view globalization as a complicated process tying together nations, corporations, science, technology, disease, governance, problems, and solutions. In many contexts, the process is simply irresistible, no matter what anybody thinks about it. Hence, there can be no sensible "anti-globalization" position. But this does not imply that the current path mapped out by U.S. elites to manage the transition to a globalized world is the only conceivable one or even the best one for America and the world.

Sticking to mainstream coverage, readers would be hard-pressed to learn that any intelligent person anywhere had any questions on this point. Hence, one would also have trouble making sense of so many world developments that, according to the gospel of the Washington "free trade/free investment" consensus, should not be happening. Yet they are. For instance, free-trade globalization is no way out of poverty for workers in, say, Bangladesh—the world's fourth-largest garment producer for the United States market—who earn, on average, one and six-tenths cents for each "Harvard" baseball cap they sew. (At the Harvard Co-op in Cambridge, the caps sell for $17.) Each year Americans buy 924 million garments and other textile items made in Bangladesh. But the workers there still do not earn the thirty-four cents an hour they say they need to care for their own children.[17]

Such problems are hardly unique. While free trade has obviously been extremely beneficial to many groups in many countries, statistics indicate that during the past two decades both Africa and much of southern Asia are poorer today than they were forty years ago, particularly when one factors in the destruction of natural resources, as Cambridge University economics professor Partha Dasgupta has demonstrated.[18] A collection of economists at Washington's Center for Economic and Policy Research came up with a "Scorecard on Globalization 1980–2000," comparing those decades to the previous two decades. The news was not good. Growth was slowing down, particularly in the poorest countries, and progress in the crucial areas of life expectancy and infant mortality was shrinking, compared with earlier gains. So too, in most places, had the rate of growth in school enrollment slowed.[19] These are the keys to self-sufficiency and long-term growth.

Columbia University Professor Joseph Stiglitz was the chair of Bill Clinton's Council of Economic Advisers, chief economist at the World Bank, and winner of the 2001 Nobel Prize in economics. With the possible and only partial exception of the *New York Times*' pundit Paul Krugman, there is not a journalist alive who comes close to matching Stiglitz's credentials. Yet, Stiglitz wrote, "If globalization continues to be conducted in the way that it has been in the past, if we continue to fail to learn from our mistakes, globalization will not only not succeed in promoting development but will continue to create poverty and instability." For decades, he noted, endorsing the same protests that journalists so roundly condemn, "The cries of the poor in Africa and in developing countries in other parts of the world have been largely unheard in the West," and it was only the street protesters "who have put the need for reform on the agenda of the developed world."[20] And yet while these views are apparently sufficiently sensible for a man like Stiglitz to espouse, they meet with nothing but undisguised contempt from those who report and comment on this subject in America's elite media. In its July 7, 2002, edition, for instance, the *Washington Post Book Review* relegated Stiglitz's book to an "in-brief" review by a non-economist. Next to it, written by another non-economist, was offered up a contemptuous review of a critical study of globalization by a young Cambridge University professor. The review described the book as "both facile and sensationalist—no matter how one dresses it up," and the opening of the review actually focused on the author's clothes. [21]

Contempt for the questioning of the fundamentals of globalization and free investment is of a piece with the media's total embrace of corporate values in virtually all matters of political economy. Conservative journalists like William Powers of the *National Journal* profess to believe that the media "subscribe to the biblical view that money is the root of all evil, and [their] job is to expose that evil through news stories about bad companies." [22] He must have slept through the past decade. Journalists have always tried to "follow the money," but until recently, never have they done so with quite such visible longing. During the great boom of the 1990s, journalists embraced the zeitgeist of capitalist heroism with a zest that must have shocked and surprised many CEOs, who suddenly found themselves receiving the kind of coverage usually reserved for sluggers and young award winners. To say that the media suspended disbelief in the face of the claims of corporate America in order to embrace the larger story of an apparently never-ending stock-market-and-economic boom would be to badly understate the case.

New-economy journalism celebrated the geek entrepreneur and the hip new CEO without asking too many questions about just how long this odd, apparently profitless form of economic activity could sustain itself. Even the old magazine stalwarts could not resist the new economy's siren song. Editors and reporters portrayed executives on their covers literally in the costumes of comic-book superheroes. Scott McNealy of Sun Microsystems was portrayed as "JAVAMAN," cape and all, on the cover of *Fortune*. Apple's Steve Jobs was termed "STEVIE WONDER!" for his star turn in the same publication. Andrew S. Grove of Intel and Jeffrey P. Bezos of Amazon.com became only the fourth and fifth business executives to be named *Time* magazine's Person of the Year. [23] Martha Stewart, meanwhile, seemed ready for beatification—that is, in the days before she became a poster girl for corporate greed. [24]

An entire money-loving journalistic structure grew up around the prosperity of the Nineties and the market boom that inspired it. The boom itself, as we all know, would prove to be heavily skewed toward the wealthiest Americans. As Kevin Phillips noted in his 2002 book, *Wealth and Democracy*, "While more and more people owned stock during the period, most of these had tiny stakes; with fewer than half owning more in their portfolios than in their cars." Meanwhile, "the top 1% pocketed 42% of the stockmarket gains between 1989 and 1997, while the top 10% of the population took 86%." [25] The audience with a significant stake in the stock market was therefore by definition a wealthy one—the kind after whom advertisers naturally lust.

News organizations were particularly eager to cultivate it, shifting programming to the kind of fare that would be likely to attract them and flatter their worldview.

This shift is evident in a comparison of the television environment that surrounded PBS's launch of *Wall Street Week with Louis Rukeyser* in 1970 compared with the moment it tried to revamp the show, thirty-two years later. Back then, the network had the audience pretty much to itself and the show became a smashing success, averaging 1.74 million viewers and earning a reported $4 million postproduction profit based on underwriting grants alone. (Rukeyser also made a bundle by selling investment cruises, books, and other related paraphernalia.) The show was the typically clubby Wall Street gabfest, polite and dignified, but with no room for discussion about companies and capitalism beyond future profits and losses. In the meantime, the media's love affair with the stock market was evident everywhere, as the networks doubled the hours of airtime they devoted to the stock market in just one decade, while they simultaneously shrank the time and resources devoted to old-fashioned "news."

When PBS finally (and foolishly) forced Rukeyser to relinquish the show's reins in 2002 to make way for a show featuring the editors of *Fortune* magazine, viewers had become inundated with such programs. Significantly, even on public television, profits were at a premium. Rukeyser effortlessly moved his program to the presumably less socially responsible CNBC with no apparent changes in its format. Indeed, despite the vociferous objections of PBS president Pat Mitchell, more than 45 percent of PBS stations continued to broadcast the now for-profit program in what *Newsday* termed a "rebellion" against the Mother Ship.[26] Meanwhile, PBS turned over much of the new show's editorial control to the editors of *Fortune*, an extremely conservative publication with little but contempt for unions, environmentalists, or other opponents of big business.

Evidently, the media's market-centricity carried with it important ideological implications for the spin they put on the news. The single-minded emphasis on "wealth creation" crowded out concerns for virtually everything that might be perceived to interfere with it, such as workers' pay, environmental destruction, equity issues, and, as investors found to their deep chagrin, honest accounting. On April 30, 1997, the *New York Times* published a front-page cheerleading article headlined "Markets Surge as Labor Costs Stay in Check." The market had "rocketed" the previous day "to its greatest gain in more than five years," owing to the fact that wages had failed to rise with profits and employers had managed to hold the line as well for "benefits like health insurance and pensions." The writer did not see fit to raise the issue of restrictions on organizing that Reagan/Bush-era judges had placed on unions, effectively eviscerating their ability to band together to improve their collective lot. After all, improvement in the workers' earning power would have cast a pale on the good news, by eating into profits and hence, stock prices. Instead the *Times* chose to highlight the sentiments of a Goldman Sachs senior economist, who merrily explained, "There is no question this is a better labor cost report than we had anticipated." Yes, but better for whom? As Norman Solomon noted in an article in Harvard's *Nieman Reports*, the eighteeen-paragraph *Times* article quoted a few current and former government economists without a word from workers, their representatives, or labor advocates.[27]

Recall this was a front-page *Times* story, not one in the business pages. And yet the implications for the vast majority of the people whom the story likely affected were considered unworthy of mention. This was hardly unusual. By 2002 pay for the top CEO averaged $10 million a year while employee pay averaged a mere $25,466. The result was a relative rise in the top guy's pay, from an average of seventy times worker wages in 1985 to 410 times worker wages in 2002.[28] Rarely in our nation's history had issues of equity fallen quite so far off the table. Levels of wealth concentration during this period came to mirror those that preceded the 1929 stock market crash. What's more, the United States is nearly unique among industrial democracies in this regard. The top fifth of Americans make 11 times more than the bottom fifth, compared to ratios of 4.3 in Japan, 7.1 in Canada and France, and 9.6 in the United Kingdom.[29] It would be unfair to say these trends went entirely ignored by all major media during the 1990s, but I doubt if even the most enthusiastic media defenders would wish to argue that they received any more than a minute fraction of the attention paid to millionaires, wealth-creators, and the personalities behind the rise of the now deflated Internet bubble. How could it be otherwise in a media in which, on the network news in 2001 alone, the ratio of corporate executive appearances to those of organized labor was more than thirty to one?[30]

This bias is evident virtually everywhere, even in alleged bastions of left-liberalism like NPR, which prefers to offer its listeners regular "NPR business updates" frequently during the day along with the daily program *Marketplace*, augmented by the weekly *Sound Money*. Matt Smith of the *San Francisco Weekly* attended a conference of investigative reporters in the spring of 2002 that he accurately described as "an assemblage of the journalism profession's most idealistic members." Yet even here, among journalists who come as close to the liberal—or even leftist—cliché as you will find anywhere, Smith could find only two panels that dealt with the lives of workers, though many of the rest were dedicated to covering business. Smith inquired of an economist sent by the U.S. Bureau of Labor Statistics about whether he had been contacted by any reporters assigned specifically to covering workers' issues. The reply: "There was one intern with the *Wall Street Journal*."[31]

Reporters' obsession with corporate wealth creation, or the appearance thereof, had the effect of turning them into CEO shills at the expense of even the most fundamental laws of good journalism. For instance, when, in May 2000, United Airlines and US Airways cut a deal to merge, their executives offered a deal to the *Washington*

*Post, New York Times,* and *Wall Street Journal:* You can have the announcement story but only so long as you promise not to call any "critics" for comment. All accepted.[32]

Perhaps the most visible development in increasing the momentum of CEO-friendly coverage during the past decade was the rise to prominence of CNBC. Begun in 1989 in a low-tech studio in Fort Lee, New Jersey, CNBC began as a combination consumer news and business station. But when GE/NBC purchased the bankrupt Financial News Network (FNN) in 1991, and combined it with CNBC, management decided to ax its consumer focus and stick to stocks. As author John Cassidy would observe, "Chief executives loved to go on CNBC. When they had good news to impart, they could deliver it directly; when they had bad news, they could sugar-coat it for investors. Either way, they were assured of a respectful hearing. To the town-car passengers, who were mostly analysts and fund managers, CNBC was a platform from which they could 'talk their book'—pump the stocks that their firms owned."[33] CNBC reporters were more than content to let them do so.

The station's journalistic standards were pretty loose. Management had no problem with journalists reporting on stocks they also traded. Analysts were invited to pump their own portfolios to the gullible viewer without being asked a single skeptical question. CNBC's hosts were quite comfortable in their role as cheerleaders for the markets. "A lot of financial journalists seem to hate capitalism," explained ex-stock broker Joe Kernen, CNBC's stocks editor. "I love capitalism."[34]

Indeed, everybody at CNBC understood that market optimism was a necessary component of their viewer numbers and all did their best to stoke it. This was particularly evident in an advertising campaign launched long after the boom that made it so popular had come to an end. During the first six months of 2001, CNBC's average viewership was just 232,000, or 23 percent lower than it had been the previous year. (This number had peaked with the market in March 2000 with 418,000 average viewers, during which time the network surpassed CNN.)[35] The response was an ad campaign that featured the affable anchor Ron Insana assuring viewers, "Most people don't realize that by the time you figure out you're in a recession, it's almost over." Cashing in on the patriotic fervor that followed the 9/11 attack, host David Faber explained, "We know who our enemies are. We've identified them, and we're going after them." Therefore he rather counter-intuitively asserted that the market world was "less risky" in the aftermath of Sept. 11, not more. The campaign also featured anchor Carl Quintanilla, who is also a *Wall Street Journal* reporter, warning viewers, "I think the biggest mistake anyone could make would be to count out the American investor."[36] (In fact, the market continued to plunge.)

While the number of people watching CNBC increased markedly during market rallies, the network had the typical audience for a cable station in terms of numbers, no more than a few hundred thousand viewers at any one time. (And many of these,

I imagine, were—like me—watching with the sound off.) Given the affluence of CNBC's audience, these seemingly small numbers did not interfere with the profits of its corporate parent, GE. With negligible production costs, a tacky studio, reporters earning a fraction of what their colleagues earned at NBC, and guests eager to appear gratis, CNBC was a cash cow.

And the questions are never too taxing. When AOL and Time Warner announced their disastrous merger in January 2000, the twin CEOs, Steve Case and Gerald Levin, appeared on the network's *Power Lunch* program. Faber asked Levin the question then on everyone's mind. "Eighty percent of the cash flow of this combined company will come from your company and yet your shareholders will own only 45 percent. Why were you willing to sign off on a deal like that?" Levin answered by noting, "The market cap of AOL was twice that of Time Warner." As I write these words, the stock of the combined company is down over 80 percent. The merged company is worth less than the assets of Time Warner alone. Levin essentially gave away the company to AOL, though he paid himself a whopping 2001 salary of $148 million. As the *New York Times* reported in July 2002, "The bitterness and resentment that employees on the Time Warner side have toward their sister division at AOL are straining the company's ability to cooperate—which, after all, was the promise of the merger."[37] It is regarded by some as among the worst mergers in business history.

Of course Faber could not see into the future during his *Power Lunch* interview. But he could have asked a follow-up question, such as, "But what if, as so many people currently believe, AOL is wildly overvalued owing to this Internet stock bubble we all worry might be about to pop? Time Warner is a real company with genuine assets and a distinguished history. Isn't this all a bit risky?" (The editors of the *Onion* knew well enough to headline their account "AOL Acquires Time-Warner in Largest Ever Expenditure of Pretend Internet Money.") To be fair, the softballs actually lobbed were par for the course everywhere. The headlines on CNN's *Moneyline* read "Mighty AOL" and "AOLectric." On *CNN Newsstand* the announcement was "a global powerhouse is born."[38]

It was bad manners on any network to ask a tough question—much less a tough follow-up—to a CEO on any of the many market-oriented programs at the time, but particularly so on CNBC. Most of CNBC believed that to worry aloud about bubbles and even valuations was a bit outré. This was a good news network. Its ubiquity turned its on-air personalities into celebrities. Faber, Joe Kernan, Ron Insana, and particularly the famed "money-honey" Maria Bartiromo, who is the only financial journalist to become the heroine of a song by the founder of the punk band, the Ramones. Even so the network's signal personality was probably not Bartiromo, but the hedge-fund manager, journalist, and all-purpose celebrity, James Cramer. The manic, volcanic Cramer was willing to say almost anything on the air in a constant quest for attention for himself and his financial Web site, TheStreet.com.

Cramer's journalistic ethics remain a matter of considerable dispute. He happily came on the air to promote stocks he was actively trading. In his column in *Money* magazine, he hawked stocks in which his fund's position was as high as 10 percent. He was the constant topic of much argument about the limits of ethical journalism when it came to money and stock markets, but nobody seemed to know what these limits were—or even if they existed anymore. *GQ, Worth, Time, Smart Money*, and *New York* all hired Cramer to be their financial columnist during this period.[39] *Good Morning America* could not live without his commentary, which he often gave on the same days he appeared on CNBC's *Squawk Box.* In a book published in early 2002, Nicholas Meier, an employee of Cramer's between the years 1994 and 1998, charged his boss with frequently using CNBC's Bartiromo and David to talk up the price of stocks his fund purchased. According to Maier:

> Jim's strategy was to put in his order to buy a stock . . . and then dial Maria. As soon as she announced the news on television, the stock would often jump. Jim then . . . peel[ed] off whatever we had bought. Jim was, essentially, both helping and using Maria. He'd give her the scoop, and before things settled down, she spread the news that was likely to get the stock running. We weren't just using the news but making it. No sooner would Maria be thanking us for the help than we'd be getting a payback—a quick hit thanks to our friends at CNBC.[40]

Impressively, in terms of both chutzpah and perspicacity, Cramer would complain on his Web site, TheStreet.com, that Bartiromo never mentioned that when a brokerage house was upgrading a stock—and thereby popping its price upward—it was also handling its banking business.[41]

Cramer admits to such shenanigans as described by Meier but only up to a (fully legal) point. "We became merchants of the buzz," he explained in his own compulsively readable memoir of the period, "getting long stocks and then schmoozing with analysts. . . . We would work to get upgrades or downgrades because we knew cynically, that Wall Street was simply a promotion machine."[42] He also admits to speaking with Bartiromo daily, as she would call to find out what he knew about as yet unpublicized analyst reports on various companies. When Cramer deduced that CNBC was about to move a stock in an up or down direction, he would trade ahead of the rest of us who did not know about it until it was announced on the air. "Yeah, I did that game," he told a reporter. "It's found money." But Cramer insisted that he never traded on explicit advance notice of an analyst's report before its release, and he never planted a story to be able to take advantage of the pop in its stock price he knew would ensue.[43]

Even supposing Cramer to be entirely innocent of any illegal action, and I do, those shenanigans to which he freely admits say quite a bit about just how far journalistic ethics strayed during the boom. Cramer is very much a political liberal. But this term bears precious little relevance when it comes to market machinations and business journalism. (Cramer did not believe, for instance, in investing in socially responsible companies per se, or shunning polluters or tobacco stocks.) During the stock market boom, the entire business journalism profession appeared to become unmoored from the fundamentals of its profession in perfect proportion to the sky-high stock market. Again to be fair, journalists were no more or less caught up in the bubble hysteria than were traders, investors, and analysts; everyone really, except the workers and investors whose pension funds were being gambled away on reporting that turned out to be lighter than air.

Moreover, some of the same executives who were celebrated CNBC anchors on the air were privately cooking their books in order to defraud their investors and abscond with millions of untoward gains. In just one week of 2002, we saw the results of years of willful media blindness: Arthur Andersen, Enron's auditor, found itself convicted of obstructing justice. Tyco International's chief executive, L. Dennis Kozlowski, was charged with massive tax evasion and accused of secret pay deals with underlings, in addition to charging the company for his almost unimaginably luxurious lifestyle. The cable giant Adelphia Communications admitted phony numbers and making surreptitious loans to shareholders. Its heads, the notorious Rigas family, were charged with using the company as their own private piggy bank to buy themselves a lifestyle that even managed to dwarf that of Kozlowski.

Xerox Corp. was forced to pony up a $10 million fine for purposely overstating revenues. Dynegy and CMS Energy Corp. simultaneously bought and sold electricity solely for the purpose of stoking trading volumes. Merrill Lynch and Company paid $100 million to settle New York State charges that analysts misled investors. Wal-Mart workers in twenty-eight states joined together to sue the company for demanding that they file phony time-clock records to avoid overtime payments. Three Rite-Aid corporation executives were charged with a securities and accounting fraud that led to the largest restatement of earnings ever—or at least for two days, when WorldCom Inc. announced that it was restating earnings by nearly four billion dollars over a period of five quarters, following the discovery of "massive fraud" in its earlier statements. This figure soon grew to more than nine billion. Even before the revelations of the WorldCom and Wal-Mart cases, wags were wondering if the business pages would henceforth be merged with papers' police blotters. The scope of exposed malfeasance, *Wall Street Journal* columnist David Wessel observed, exceeded anything the United States had witnessed since the Great Depression.[44]

These were, lest we forget, many of the same companies whose CEOs were portrayed as fearless revolutionaries just one zeitgeist earlier. As the acquisition-mad chief of WorldCom, Bernard Ebbers was termed "a long-distance visionary" by a 1997 *New York Times* profile. The Paper of Record portrayed Ebbers as a "blunt, folksy . . . entrepreneurial stepchild of the telecommunications revolution," a former "high-school basketball coach" who "even mows his own lawn." WorldCom was, the *Times* assured us, "poised for the future as the Internet and telephone communications converge." *Business Week* concurred. Its moniker for the hard-chargin' CEO, later ousted for allowing the largest fraud in reported history, was "Telecom Cowboy." This was rather modest praise, however, compared to the magazine's treatment of Tyco International's Dennis Kozlowski, whom it termed "The Most Aggressive CEO." The cover boy was shown to relax "by piloting his 130-foot J-class sloop, *Endeavour*, in international regattas." The better to "sail smoothly through the economic slowdown." To *Forbes*, George Shaheen, the CEO of Andersen Consulting, was a "Digital Messiah." Barely two years before Global Crossing went belly up, *Forbes* hailed its CEO because "an entire managerial dream team has signed on because of Gary Winnick's ability to dish out immense wealth."[45]

It is hardly coincidental that these scandals took place at the same time CEO compensation spun out of control. In 2000, for instance, Jack Welch of GE took home $144 million; Stanford Weill of Citigroup, $90 million; Rueben Mack of Colgate, $85 million; and Louis Gerstner Jr. of IBM, $102 million. The top ten CEOs in earnings for 2000 averaged $154 million; a 2000 percent increase—adjusted for inflation—compared with twenty years earlier.[46]

Even given the outlandishness of these examples, they pale in comparison to what might be termed the Woodstock Festival of corporate fraud: Enron. Writing in the *Columbia Journalism Review* in early 2002, Scott Sherman undertook the unenviable job of excavating the journalistic rubble left in the wake of Enron's collapse. He came up with an impressive number of what might be termed anthropological artifacts from a time when giants were said to walk the streets of Houston. His highlights include:

- The *New York Times* termed Enron "a model for the new American workplace."

- *Business Week* examined one of its pioneering ventures and pronounced its risks "remarkably small."

- A *Los Angeles Times* business columnist celebrated the fact that energy was no longer characterized by "a staid business of regulated monopolies" but had become a "beehive of financially savvy companies" led by Enron.

- A *Wall Street Journal* reporter quoted analysts proclaiming: "The real story isn't the earnings. . . it's what lies ahead" (Goldman Sachs); "This isn't your father's natural-gas company. . . ." "We see continued momentum. . . ." "They have a massive infrastructure built." (PaineWebber). CEO Jeffrey Skilling was also quoted, adding, "It's absolutely astounding. . . . It feels like we're being swamped with new opportunities."

- *Fortune* announced, "Imagine a country-club dinner dance, with a bunch of old fogies and their wives shuffling around halfheartedly to the not-so-stirring sounds of Guy Lombardo and his All-Tuxedo Orchestra. Suddenly young Elvis comes crashing through the skylight, complete with gold-lamé suit, shiny guitar, and gyrating hips. Half the waltzers faint; most of the others get angry or pouty. And a very few decide they like what they hear, tap their feet . . . start grabbing new partners, and suddenly are rocking to a very different tune. In the staid world of regulated utilities and energy companies, Enron Corp. is that gate-crashing Elvis. Once a medium-sized player in the stupefyingly soporific gas-pipeline business, Enron in the past decade has become far and away the most vigorous agent of change in its industry."

- *Business 2.0* hit the newsstands in August 2001 with the announcement "The Revolution LIVES," as Enron CEO Jeffrey Skilling shared its cover. He resigned the next day.

- *Red Herring* followed a month later advising "Forget about Microsoft. America's most successful, revered, feared—and even hated—company is no longer a band of millionaire geeks from Redmond, Washington, but a cabal of cowboy/ traders from Houston: Enron."

Business magazines love to issue rankings and give out rewards, believing their readers desire information that resembles—in presentation anyway—the allegedly hard data of a corporate report. For six years in a row, industry insiders voted Enron "Most Innovative" among *Fortune*'s "Most Admired Companies," which claims to be "the definitive report card on corporate reputations." (*CJR*'s Sherman noted, "In February 2001, Enron ranked second in 'quality of management' as well.") In January 2000, *Business Week* named Ken Lay one of "25 Top Managers" of 2000. Lay and Skilling both made it into *Worth*'s "50 Best CEOs" (I was a columnist there at the time). In 2001, the "hypersmart, hyperconfident" Skilling came in at number two and was lovingly described by Lay, who said, "I'm not sure he has a nonstrategic bone in his body." But Skilling was a virtual slacker in the media compared with the impression created by the fawning coverage of "Kenny Boy" Lay. *Fortune* termed him a "revolutionary." *Worth* turned to an analyst who proclaimed that Lay enjoyed "the best combination of vision and execution of anyone." Jeffrey Skilling, meanwhile, could hang on his wall *Fortune*'s proclamation terming him "the most intellectually brilliant executive in the natural gas business," unless he preferred the homier version in which same magazine described him as "a lively, impish character who disdains the huge, serene, high-walled office he occupies atop the Enron building, forty stories above downtown Houston. 'Too quiet. Too removed,' he complains. (His kids often play Koosh ball in it and store their racquets in a corner.)"

But the business media's romantic attachment to Enron was so large that the love needed to be spread around beyond just Lay and Skilling. Rebecca Mark, who had headed up Enron's international initiatives and who is reported to have cashed in $79.5 million worth of the company's stock, was described by *Forbes* in 1998 as having "honey-blonde hair, big brown eyes and dazzling white teeth that offset a toast tan," and likened her to "a movie star." Lou Pai, a top Enron executive who managed to make $354 million after dumping five million shares of Enron of the company stock in 1999 and 2000, was described in *Forbes* in July 2000 as "bursting with competitive energy." The magazine added, "Skilling calls him 'my ICBM.'"[47]

Although Enron celebrations dominated the media, one or two journalists did manage to chisel tiny cracks in its empire. Significantly, the *Economist*, a non-American publication that warned continuously during the creation of the stock-market bubble that much was amiss, published a short but critical examination in 1998 and again in 2000. By far the most prescient article ever to appear on the company was published in the unlikely location of the *Texas Journal*, a four-page, stand-alone insert on September 20, 1998, in the *Wall Street Journal*. After spending four full months researching Enron's immensely complicated balance sheets—which, after all, were designed for the express purposes of confusing not merely journalists but analysts and accountants and stock brokers and SEC officials—Jonathan Weil, a thirty-one-year-old staff reporter, came to the following lonely conclusion:

> What many investors may not realize is that much of these companies' recent profits constitute unrealized, noncash gains. Frequently, these profits depend on assumptions and estimates about future market factors, the details of which the companies do not provide, and which time may prove wrong. . . . The heart of the situation is an accounting technique that allows companies to include as current earnings those profits they expect to realize from energy-related contracts and other derivative instruments in future periods, sometimes stretching over more than 20 years.[48]

Weil and the *Journal* had the Enron story in a nutshell but nobody noticed—not even at the *Journal*. The young reporter had delved into the story only after receiving a tip from someone inside or close to the company. He was not assigned to the story and received no particular encouragement from his editors, who did not even think to run the story in the national edition of the paper once he wrote it. They had the biggest business story of the decade, but they lost it inside their own paper because somehow, they could not see it. Apparently nobody could. Bethany McLean of *Fortune* produced another skeptical piece in March 2001, based, as she told Sherman, on a tip she received from the inside, never even having heard of the Weil/*Texas Journal* piece. The behavior of the executives to whom she spoke might have alerted her editors, however, to the possibility that something fishy was going on. The company treated tough-minded questions in a manner that reminds one of a crooked union or a local crime family. When McLean tried to speak to Skilling, he insisted that her queries were "unethical" and hung up the phone. Enron executives flew to New York to answer her questions. Soon, Lay was on the phone to *Fortune*'s managing editor, Rik Kirkland, trying, unsuccessfully, to get the piece spiked.[49]

Writing in the *LA Times*, David Shaw listed a number of points that might have inspired a bit of digging had anyone been paying attention to business fundamentals. These included: the "major, longtime discrepancy between Enron's profits and its cash flow"; the "remarkably low" return on investment "for such a high-risk venture, and the increasing incomprehensibility of its financial statements. Its financial statements were incomprehensible." Incredibly, when Skilling resigned in August 2001 without even going to the trouble of inventing a cover story, no one thought to wonder why. How did it happen? As Jonathan Weil explained, it was the unspoken habit of journalists who covered business during this period to "outsource their critical thinking skills to Wall Street analysts, who are not independent and, by definition, were employed to do nothing but spin positive company news in order to sell stock." In this regard they could hardly have proven themselves to be more gullible. After all, as Weil told Sherman, "There was hardly a Wall Street analyst covering the stock whose firm was not getting sprinkled with cash in some form or another by Enron."

Is it fair to mock those journalists who sang the praises of this dishonest company— given that no one on Wall Street nor elsewhere in corporate America seemed to have any idea of just how shady its operations were? Yes and no. Journalists do not enjoy subpoena power. Were it not for the collapse of technology stock prices, through which Enron funded its own complex partnership arrangements, it's not likely that the fraud would have been discovered at all. The company was dancing on the borders of all previously known accounting practices and then jumping far across them. It covered its tracks with incomprehensible terms like "share-settle puts," "reverse contingent forwards," "synthetic equity," and "trapped appreciation."[50] What's more, Enron's statements were incomprehensible to everyone, including many of the high-powered accountants who signed off on them and institutional investors who put hundreds of millions of dollars at the company's disposal. Journalists helped in the creation of an alternate reality for Enron as they played patsy to its plots of deception.

Part of the problem is that most journalists work for large conglomerates that tend, on a much smaller scale, to employ some of the same practices used by companies like Enron—albeit probably not the criminal ones.[51] But more important is the fact that, as Jeffrey Madrick pointed out, Enron's rise "touched all the big media buttons: globalization, the new economy, derivatives, trading deregulation, and the Internet.

Enron's story was consistent with the biggest economic story, which was the much reported belief that America was in the throes of a 'new economy' and that high technology would remake the economy, with information as its main asset."[52] True or not, journalists loved this story. The term "new economy" popped up in a Nexis search just 325 times in print business press in 1995. Five years later, that number was 22,850.[53] Mortimer Zuckerman, real estate mogul and owner of *U.S. News & World Report*, would not allow the word "bubble" into his magazine. Its business writers, columnist Philip Longman noted, "concentrated on articles like the April 3, 2000, cover story—one that, even after the NASDAQ had begun to crash, explained how 'new tools' for evaluating a company's worth (such as ignoring its lack of profits) could justify a continuing bull market."[54] With each celebration, it became harder and harder to retain one's skepticism and go against the grain.

More than simple journalistic gullibility was at work here. A number of high-profile journalists found themselves showered with Enron cash in exchange for extremely little work. To some this might look like a bribe—either to hawk Enron's goods or to look the other way should anything appear amiss. Without exception every reporter or editor who got paid by Enron insists that he or she did nothing improper and need not apologize. This includes even those who never disclosed their financial relationship with Enron and allowed themselves to comment on issues of immediate concern to the company, such as the California energy crisis of summer 2001, which the company appears to have manipulated in order to line its own pockets. Among the members on Journalism's Team Enron were:

- Lawrence Kudlow, a *National Review* contributing editor and CNBC co-host with Jim Cramer, received $50,000 via two $15,000 speaking fees and a $20,000 subscription to his New York economic research firm. He did not disclose these payments when he wrote about Enron for *National Review*.

- *Weekly Standard* editor William Kristol received $100,000 for serving on an Enron advisory board. The fact of his service (but not the size of the payment) was disclosed by the *Standard* in an extremely positive article on Enron written by *Standard* contributing editor Irwin Stelzer, also paid by Enron, who recruited Kristol to the board on behalf of Kenneth Lay. Among Stelzer's conclusions: "What Enron and Lay deserve to be remembered for is leading the fight for competition. . . . Enron fought to allow customers and suppliers to strike whatever bargains they found mutually advantageous. . . . Enron did challenge and defeat the establishment."

- *Wall Street Journal* columnist Peggy Noonan cannot remember how much she was paid and was apparently too busy to look it up on her tax forms, when questioned by an inquiring reporter. She said she believed it to be somewhere between $25,000 to $50,000 for assisting in a speech for Lay and in writing captions for the company's annual report.[55]

• Paul Krugman, columnist for the *New York Times*, received a $37,500 payment from Enron before becoming a *Times* columnist. At the time, he was a full-time economics professor and consultant to numerous companies. When writing about Enron for *Fortune*, he mentioned the financial relationship but not the exact size of the payment. Upon being hired by the *Times*, he ended the financial relationship with the company and began—as did most writers—to write about the company far more critically. He mentioned the payment the first time he mentioned Enron in his column, but not in subsequent, strongly worded criticisms of the company.[56]

Engaging in a kind of obsessive journalistic witch-hunt, Andrew Sullivan used his Web site to fancifully accuse Krugman of "absconding with $50,000 worth of dirty money from a criminal enterprise" and he returned to the fact of this alleged crime perhaps at least fifty times—I lost count—on his Web site. But as Eric Boehlert pointed out in Salon, Krugman received his payments as a working economics consultant long before Enron's problems were apparent and long before he became a *Times* columnist. He disclosed them, and he could hardly have written more harshly about the company if they had stolen his money and tortured his dog. In contrast to the liberal Krugman, the CNBC conservative, Kudlow, continued to cash Enron checks as the company was beginning to crash and burn. The *Weekly Standard*'s Stelzer and Kristol received far higher payments from the company than Krugman did and found precious little to criticize. Nothing at all about the size of Kristol's payment has ever appeared in the magazine he edits, whereas Krugman himself revealed the size of his payment in the *New York Times*.[57] Once again, it seems, it is the conservatives who "abscond" with both the story and the money while the rest of the media is left to worry about the corruption of the so-called "liberal media."

To the Republicans' delight, journalists treated Enron's collapse primarily as financial, rather than as a political matter. Reporters accepted the administration's argument that Enron was a "business scandal" rather than a political one, despite the myriad ties between the corporations' executives and top Bush officials, including a close friendship and political/financial relationship between Kenneth "Kenny Boy" Lay and the president. While the administration and Enron-funded members of Congress knew better than to try to save the company once its various misdeeds were revealed, they acted energetically to help it when they believed it was still an ongoing concern. For instance, Vice President Dick Cheney consulted Lay about how to handle

California's energy crisis, while the company was secretly gouging the state.[58] Cheney also defended the company against charges that it was doing what it, in fact, did, saying the charges were so much paranoid conspiracy theory. "We get politicians who want to go out and blame somebody and allege there is some kind of conspiracy, whether it's the oil companies or whoever it might be, instead of dealing with the real issues," he complained. Here he was echoing exactly the deceitful claims of Lay himself, who explained on *Nightline*, "Every time there's a shortage or a little bit of a price spike, it's always collusion or conspiracy or something. I mean, it always makes people feel better that way."

Many media conservatives took the same line. Charles Krauthammer wrote that only "silly" Californians "think that the rolling blackouts are a conspiracy by the power companies to raise rates." William Safire chimed in that the enormous rise of energy prices—due in this case to deliberate market manipulation—was "as natural as breathing." He averred that "populist interference with the [electricity] market's self-correction would lead to worse shortages and rationing, to inflation and wage control." Meanwhile, as the columnist Joe Conason noted, internal documents revealed these strategies, and company nicknames like "Fat Boy," "Death Star," and "Get Shorty" revealed that Enron was gaming the system to "launder electricity and falsify congestion on the power grid, in order to rob tens of billions of dollars from California consumers and businesses."[59]

While reporters treated Enron as a "bipartisan" scandal, and George Bush ridiculously claimed that the company supported his 1994 opponent, Ann Richards, for governor of Texas, clearly it was far more significantly a product of Republican largesse and conservative ideology. Enron executives were financially friendly with the Democrats, but they were all but wedded in unholy matrimony to the Republicans, and particularly Texas Republicans like George W. Bush and Dick Cheney. "Not in memory has a single major company grown so big in tandem with a presidential dynasty and a corrupted political system," wrote the Republican political analyst Kevin Phillips in the *Los Angeles Times*.[60] Certainly many Democrats were guilty as well. Vice-presidential candidate Senator Joe Lieberman was particularly important in writing the kinds of corporate tax loopholes that Enron and others used to avoid paying any taxes for four of the previous five years. But a sense of proportion remains in order: 72 percent of Enron's political donations went to Republican candidates. As an investigation by the Center for Public Integrity has demonstrated, "No politician in America was closer to Enron than George W. Bush."[61] This was true both before and after Bush became president—at least until Enron became politically radioactive. Ken Lay personally interviewed some of the candidates for the Federal Energy Regulatory Commission, for which he also submitted names.[62] Congressman Henry Waxman, a Democrat, found a full seventeen policies proposed by the vice president's Energy Task Force that were "either advocated by Enron or benefited Enron."

Almost none of these policies were disclosed as originating with Enron at the time they were being offered by the company and accepted by Cheney and the members of his staff. Even long after the scandal unfolded, Thomas White, who was vice chairman of Enron Energy Services when it allegedly hid $500 million in losses and manipulated the California energy crisis, was still secretary of the Army, despite having been cited by the Senate Armed Services Committee for violating his signed ethics agreement. As Frank Rich pointed out, "The record of Enron contacts by him and countless other administration officials remains incomplete and in constant revision. What information does dribble out often emanates from the White House counsel, Alberto Gonzales, who himself had an attorney-client relationship with Enron while a partner at Vinson & Elkins in Houston."[63]

Even after Enron's fall, some journalists seemed to think the multi-millionaires who bilked the company were more worthy of their sympathetic attention than the thousands of employees and investors whose lives were ruined by their subterfuge. When Lisa Myers, the NBC Capitol Hill correspondent, interviewed Linda Lay, wife of Kenneth, she allowed the woman whose husband had been graced with cash payments totaling $103,559,793 in 2001, while the company was going under, to cry that she and her husband were "fighting for liquidity." "We don't want to go bankrupt," Lay pleaded. "Other than the home we live in, everything else is for sale." When Myers politely inquired about what happened to all those millions, Mrs. Lay answered, "There's nothing left. Everything we had mostly was in Enron stock." Meanwhile not only Mrs. Lay, but the couple's children, Mr. Lay's former wife, and his pastor were also put on the air to sing praises to the man who, as Myers put it, "led Enron to great heights and to ruin." Myers later defended her journalistic integrity to Felicity Barringer of the *New York Times* by claiming, "I dealt with her on the broad strokes of every significant issue of potential misconduct that had been raised about her husband. But you cannot go into all the minutiae."[64] Among the "minutiae," however, as columnist Rich would point out in the same newspaper, was the fact that Mrs. Lay was apparently lying. The Lays continued to enjoy ownership of no fewer than eighteen properties in Texas and Colorado, only two of which were up for sale at the time of the interview, and were happily sitting on at least $10 million in non-Enron stocks.[65]

Myers was hardly alone in extending sympathy to the perpetrators of these crimes. For yet another example of how conservative bias is considered so natural and unworthy of mention in business reporting, consider the example of Lou Dobbs, whose *Moneyline* on CNN is its biggest money maker, commanding 250 percent of the network's usual advertising fee. As Anne Glover, senior vice president of corporate marketing and communications at the Hartford Financial Services Group, told the *Wall Street Journal*, she buys ads mainly to run on *Moneyline* and avoids putting them on breaking news because she "would rather place my advertising somewhere where [she] can be a little more sure of the editorial content of the show." The audience-premium CNN charges allows the network to earn vastly larger sums than its competition on Fox, even when CNN's ratings lag behind those of the "fair-and-balanced" network in terms of ratings. [66]

With Lou Dobbs and his many imitators, ad-buyers like Glover can rest easily. The CNN anchor is not only a pro-Enron, pro-Arthur Andersen conservative, he is willing to humiliate and vilify his own reporters on the air should anyone contradict his biases. On one program, for example, correspondent Ted O'Brien interviewed Charles Lewis, of the Center for Public Integrity, who noted that "the business community in general and the energy industry in particular have traditionally supported Republicans two-to-one or three-to-one, in terms of campaign contributions, for ideological reasons, because of deregulation and the role of government in general."

This apparently infuriated Dobbs, who, following a commercial break, proceeded to grill his correspondent about his guest's views. He demanded of O'Brien, "We do have a sense that Enron not only contributed to Republicans but mightily, as well, to Democrats, wherever it served the political purpose of the company, isn't that correct?" O'Brien said that it was, however, "More to Republicans than to Democrats, but certainly to both parties, and especially in Texas, its home base. But it's not surprising, especially the contributions to the Republicans, which support causes that have always helped large industries and particularly the energy industry, and such issues as deregulation." Dobbs, however, could barely control his anger on the air and proceeded to reprimand the reporter: "The one thing we don't want to ever be accused of here is, of course, participating in creating, if you will, in the court of public opinion, making it a hanging court. So many questions here that I think it's really incumbent on us to be careful. There is enough here to create huge questions, serious questions, perhaps criminal indictment, and I just want to make sure we are balanced in keeping it all in perspective, Tim. Thank you."[67]

It was an extraordinary display of un-anchor-like bad manners, but it proved to be only the beginning of Dobbs's concerted campaign to use his program as a kind of PR infomercial for the accused corporations. In a commentary on the March 18, 2002, show, Dobbs, who had been generously remunerated by Andersen for speaking gigs, whose previous show on CNN had been sponsored by the accounting firm, and whose company, Space Holdings (in which he held a minority interest), used Andersen as its corporate auditor, whipped himself into a near frenzy over the Justice Department's decision to indict the firm. He warned that "the effect of the indictment will be to destroy the firm and the livelihoods of most of those 85,000 innocent people" and noted that neither Enron Corporation nor its executives, whose dealings with Andersen got the accounting firm in trouble, had yet been charged with a crime. Andersen circulated Dobbs's comments to the White House, the Justice Department, its remaining clients, and to journalists, quite naturally, as they made the company's case more effectively than it could do so itself. Ten days later, Dobbs complained, "Just as I don't blame the firm of Andersen for the misdeeds of a few, I don't blame the many fine men and women who serve our country at the Justice Department. But I do blame those few people at Justice who made this horrible decision to punish the many at Andersen for the acts of a few." When James O'Toole of the University of Southern California School of Business came on the program to make a rather mild argument for reforms at Andersen, Dobbs was, again, rude and furious. He lectured his guest, "Professor, I'm sorry, I think you've been given extraordinarily bad information. And I am sorry that whatever sources you've used for that, but that's just simply inaccurate." The other panelists Dobbs chose that day were Thomas Donohue, head of the U.S. Chamber of Commerce; Rep. John LaFalce; and Philip Livingston, CEO of Financial Executives International—defenders of Andersen, all. Every one of them derided the Justice Department's decision to indict the accounting firm.[68]

Dobbs is a lifelong Republican who contributed money to George Bush's presidential campaign and makes no apologies for this. In 1992, he admitted to receiving $15,000 for his role in infomercials for Shearson Lehman, Paine Webber, and the Philadelphia Stock Exchange. In exchange for PaineWebber's money, he praised the firm's "twin tradition of integrity and client service." When called on this by other journalists, Dobbs adamantly denied any conflict as "nonsensical." In his own defense, he implicitly noted that he enjoyed an even larger conflict of interest over the fact that he had been making corporate speeches for even more money.[69] CNN criticized him and Dobbs apologized, but this did not seem to dent the network's faith in his abilities nor his own in the value of his own opinions. In 2002, during the July 4 weekend, Dobbs was invited to be a guest panelist on ABC's *This Week*. In September, Dobbs, an AOL Time Warner employee, was graced with his own column in *Time*'s competitor, *U.S. News and World Report*. This was done during a deep advertising recession, while the entire *U.S. News* staff was asked to endure a 10 percent cut in pay. Conservative bias, it seems, is as natural as the air that business journalists breathe, and the news, just as polluted. And the result? Just like the folks on cable, let's give the last word to James Cramer, speaking on CNN's *Reliable Sources*: "The forty-five million people who had their 401(k)s and believed that these people were objective analysts that were actually trying to make you money. I feel sorry for them. The game was . . . rigged."[70]

# 9

## The Clinton Administration

WHEN CONSERVATIVES COMPLAIN about liberal bias in the media, they often have a lot on their minds, but ultimately, their concerns usually focus on one thing: politics, specifically electoral politics. Liberals and Democratic politicians, goes the argument, are treated with kid gloves, but conservatives and Republicans enjoy the barely concealed hostility of the chattering classes. If these sentiments had any normative validity, then you would expect to see a press corps with special sympathy for Bill Clinton's presidency, since his was the first Democratic administration in twelve years, and only the second in twenty-four. Alas, you didn't.

A full review of the Clinton administration's relationship with the elite media could take up the entire length of this book and would find room for blame on both sides. Almost never in any of Clinton's self-pitying complaints about the treatment he received from the press did he acknowledge his own responsibility: dishonesty, indiscipline, arrogance, and occasional incompetence—all of which colluded to create at least some of the problems that dogged him. But even if he had, it's hard to know how much it would have mattered. While Clinton himself bore responsibility for many of the travails he experienced as president, his problems were intensely exacerbated by a constant drum of hostility directed at him by the journalistic profession's most powerful and influential members. This, combined with the apparently irresistible tabloid aspects of the scandals of his administration, combined to create a media tsunami that engulfed the U.S. political system and unmoored it from the country at large.

During the 1992 campaign, Bill Clinton proved a remarkably popular candidate with the media. The affection demonstrated by such influential reporters as Joe Klein, Sidney Blumenthal, and Martin Walker helped to spread the good word. *New York Times* editorial page editor Howell Raines found himself complaining of what he termed "the extraordinary burst of journalistic fawning" the media sent Clinton's way during the campaign.[1]

Journalists fell in love with the president of their imagination. As a candidate, Clinton would call in the middle of the night for their advice. He liked staying up all night and shooting the breeze. He read their work and often complimented them on their insight, and picked up some of their favorite themes. The bigfoot columnists and reporters, like Klein, celebrated the candidate who "loved to talk about serious things" and "seems to be up on every social program in America."[2] They eagerly awaited the arrival in Washington of a regime that appreciated their vast knowledge of "the process" and enjoyed their company at state dinners followed by late-night bull-sessions in the private residence. To be fair, candidate Clinton gave them every reason to fantasize.

The romance quickly went sour. The charming seducer who loved journalists and respected their calling disappeared into the Arkansas governor's mansion on Election Day and never came out again. He was replaced by a guy who hated reporters when he bothered to think about them at all. Clinton viewed the media's inability to grasp the significance to "real" people of his programs such as universal health care and expanded day care with fury and contempt. And he deeply resented the media's desire to focus so much attention on the so-called scandals of which he believed himself to be unfairly accused.

Even without the hurt feelings, there are good psychological and sociological reasons for the elite media to turn on a Democratic candidate almost immediately, just as the media are generally happy—at least initially—to romance a Republican one. Reporters and editors see Democratic candidates—Ivy-educated, socially liberal, and economically centrist—as people very much like themselves. But reporters are almost never asked to face the kinds of difficult choices that a president must make every day. Many continue to believe themselves to be morally purer than politicians as a result. What's more, they resent all of the fealty presidents (or presidential candidates) command, particularly when so many feel that they could do the job better themselves. Oftentimes, they will turn on such a politician with the vengeance of a lover scorned. This cycle repeats itself every election year and then some. Mickey Kaus termed this phenomenon to be "an artifact of pro-Democrat bias, if not the actual dreaded 'liberal' bias."[3] But it does not require actual bias of any kind as an explanation. All it requires is an ex-classmate—or someone very much like him—anywhere near the White House.

Despite the incessant howls about the SCLM, most independent observers would grant that the Clinton team just could not catch a break from the media. Whether the president was falsely accused of holding up planes at LAX for getting a haircut or allegedly raping and battering a woman decades ago, no accusation was too trivial or too outrageous to be swallowed by the media and trumpeted to the country at large. Clinton had a lot to answer for as president, including most particularly, in my view, his economic program, which sold out the people who elected him, his willingness to go ahead with a punitive version of welfare reform, and his unconscionable inaction when a small effort on the part of his administration might have prevented much of the genocide in Rwanda.[4] But these were not the issues for which he was called to task. The very idea of the media worrying about poor tortured Rwanda—genocide or no—takes us into an alternate universe.

The level of hostility directed against Clinton by punditocracy bigfeet was truly a wonder. George Will—an apologist for a president who sold missiles to terrorists and then lied about it, for instance—termed Clinton to be if not "the worst president America has had" surely "the worst person to be president."[5] Demonstrating that fanatical Clinton-hatred proved a smart career move during this period, Michael Kelly of the *New Yorker, New Republic,* the *Washington Post, National Journal,* and *Atlantic Monthly* wrote that the singular "source of Clinton's uniqueness as president is the nearly unbelievable degree of his essential unfitness to be president—his profound immaturity, his pathological selfishness, his cynicism, above all his relentless corruption."[6]

In fact, when judged on the basis of its predecessors, the ethical standards practiced by the Clinton administration look pretty good, even if you leave out Nixon. The total number of convictions experienced by the Reagan administration, which, like the Clinton administration, enjoyed two terms in office, was thirty-two, of which two were overturned on appeal. Fourteen of these were related to the Iran/Contra scandal; sixteen to the HUD housing scandals; and two to illegal lobbying of the Administration by ex-officials. During the single-term George H. W. Bush Administration, seven officials were indicted, five were convicted, and five officials were pardoned before they could be sentenced or convicted. For the Clinton administration, the sum of officials indicted is zero.[7]

---

When the Monica Lewinsky story finally broke in January 1998 on Matt Drudge's Web site, the mavens of the elite media could not have been happier if they had collectively discovered a cure for cancer. Inspired by personal anger at the president, as well as the thrill of appearing "relevant" again after years of being told that politics had lost the imagination of the vast majority of Americans, a kind of unconstrained glee came over the media not unlike what one might experience when the boy or girl who dumps you in high school is then expelled for smoking pot. The fact that lots of people smoke pot, including perhaps you yourself, is of no importance. The point is that "justice," however loosely construed, must be served—or in this case meted out. Clinton did what a lot of people in America do, which is to commit adultery and then lie about it when caught. True, he lied to a grand jury—which most of us do not—but precious few of us ever face grand juries when we commit adultery, much less Torquemada-like investigators with $73 million in funding to try to nail us. Ironically, at the time of the Clinton scandals, many of the top editors and executives of extremely powerful news organizations and media organizations were either in the midst of—or had just completed—well-publicized affairs outside of marriage. I raised this point on MSNBC one day, naming a few of the institutions—but none of the names—in question. I learned pretty quickly from my immediate superiors never to make that mistake again. The media decide what is "fair game," and hence, we are not.

I will spare you, dear reader, one more recounting of those nauseating events that enraptured the nation during these unhappy times, except insofar as these relate to the SCLM and its attendant arguments. For the sake of a story about a man lying about a blow job, the *Washington Post* frequently broke its own famed two-source "Watergate" rule and relied in most cases on anonymous "background" sources. Many stories were written in the passive voice, or were a few steps removed from the actual source, as in "were said to be" or "there were reports" or "were reported to be. . . ." Robert Kaiser, the *Post's* assistant managing editor, admitted that the paper ran stories with "only the vaguest sourcing" during the early days of the scandal.

What was true of the *Post* was true everywhere. With a degree of overkill that is all but unfathomable today, on a single day following the outbreak of the news, the *Washington Post, New York Times,* and *Los Angeles Times* combined managed to publish a total of 47,500 words on this single topic in fifty-seven separate stories.[8] The media's bloodstream was infected from the start. Lucianne Goldberg's malicious fantasies were published unchecked in the *New York Post*, alongside Matt Drudge's lies. Seventy-two percent of the statements about the scandal made on *Good Morning America* and *World News Tonight* during the early days were based on anonymous sources or fell into the category of punditry. For NBC News, it was 81 percent; for CBS, 70.[9] *Nightline* did fifteen shows in a row on the scandal, but with a more respectable 48 percent reliance on anonymous sources or punditry.[10] Some of the lowlights included:

- The *Washington Post*, ABC News, *Newsweek,* and *Time* reported that Monica Lewinsky had implicated Vernon Jordan in an attempted conspiracy to get her to lie to the Paula Jones grand jury in return for Jordan's help in finding a job. On ABC, Jackie Judd reported it as follows: "ABC News has obtained what is potentially one of the most damaging pieces of evidence indicating a cover-up" and then made reference to the "talking points" that, she informed viewers, "seem[s] to have been drafted by a lawyer" and "allegedly handed to [Linda] Tripp." This accusation was later proven to be baseless.

- NBC News, Fox News, and the *Washington Times* all reported that the White House—or someone close to the White House—had provided Monica

Lewinsky with a set of "talking points" to help her mislead the Paula Jones grand jury. This charge was later proven false.

- ABC News and NBC News both broke into their daily broadcasts on Super Bowl Sunday with reports that a third party had interrupted President Clinton and Monica Lewinsky in the act. NBC based its report on the ABC report. On the basis of these reports, the same banner headline appeared in the *New York Post* and the *New York Daily News*. It read, "Caught in the Act." The *Post* insisted that "the witnesses [plural] are Secret Service agents." Again, no witness ever materialized.

Tim Russert allowed *Meet the Press* to succumb to these same dangers, inviting Matt Drudge to join an august panel of William Safire, Michael Isikoff, and Stuart Taylor at the outset of the scandal. Respectfully asked for "his take" on events, Drudge employed his NBC-supplied microphone to berate *real* journalists for failing to match his own sleazy insinuating tactics. He then offered up even more unverified information about other women who had claimed to have sex with Clinton and who were about to come forward, and then he held up a copy of Rupert Murdoch's *New York Post* claiming "hundreds" of women who might eventually be witnesses. Neither Russert, nor Isikoff, nor Safire, nor Taylor saw fit to challenge Drudge. (Fox's Roger Ailes observed this bizarre performance and immediately asked Drudge to do his own show on that network.)

What drove the story until Kenneth Starr's final report was finally delivered in September was invariably triple hearsay: what leakers say Monica Lewinsky told Linda Tripp about what Clinton or Vernon Jordan said or did to Lewinsky. Starr's office did its share of leaking, if not always to *Newsweek*'s Isikoff, then usually to Susan Schmidt of the *Post* or Michael Weisskopf of *Time*. (The two later co-authored a book in which the prosecutor was treated as a patriotic, self-sacrificing hero.) Other favored reporters of the prosecutor's office were: Christopher Ruddy, the Richard Mellon Scaife-funded fantasist who imagined Clinton guilty of murder plots, and Ambrose Evans-Pritchard, whose unsubstantiated accusations from London often made their way back into print in the United States via reports on the *Wall Street Journal* editorial page.[11] The prosecutor's office would often use these leaks—sometimes even before they appeared—to put pressure on the White House to cave in to its demands.[12]

The media proved remarkably pliant in the prosecutor's hands, in part out of admiration for Starr himself and in part out of a near unanimous distaste for the president. They almost never informed readers who was leaking to them and what the leaker might be after. The *New York Times* even appeared willing to mislead its readers for the purposes of passing on the Starr team's damaging accusations against Clinton. In this case, reporter Don Van Natta Jr. wrote in the paper that Starr spokesman Charles Bakaly had "declined to discuss" the investigation with the *Times*. When Bakaly later found himself indicted for violating grand jury secrecy rules, explicitly because federal Judge Norma Holloway Johnson deduced that he had been "the direct source," or at least a "confirming source," for much of the information found in the *Times* article,[13] it was clear who Van Natta's source had been. Over the course of the trial, during which Bakaly was eventually acquitted, he admitted to having met with Van Natta a minimum of three times and confirmed information Van Natta had reported elsewhere. In her decision, Judge Johnson condemned the *Times*'s tactics, noting, "The impression that this journalistic sleight of hand produced is quite troubling for what it shows about the reliability of anonymously attributed information."[14] When, at a social gathering, I asked Joe Lelyveld, then the *Times* executive editor, just how it had happened, he declined to defend the paper's actions and later wrote a scathing critique of press coverage of the scandal in the *New York Review of Books*—albeit excepting his own institution from criticism.[15]

"We're in a new world in terms of the way information flows to the nation," James O'Shea, deputy managing editor for news of the *Chicago Tribune*, explained. "The days when you can decide not to print a story because it's not well-enough sourced are long gone."[16] I was witness to this phenomenon while at MSNBC. A producer would come tell the anchor of a new detail that had been published on some Web site somewhere. No one in the newsroom possessed any independent knowledge of its veracity. And yet it would be broadcast, albeit with a few caveats, on the basis of the fact that it was already "out there." I remember hearing these exact words being spoken, for instance, with regard to the "eyewitness" story of Lewinsky and Clinton that was later proven false.

The conservative punditocracy's performance would prove even more embarrassing than that of the larger SCLM. "We are now in the final days," William Kristol, for instance, intoned on ABC's *This Week* during the first week of the crisis. "If the President lied to the American people about having a sexual relationship with an intern, and if it's very clear he's lied, I think he's finished." When this did not pan out, Kristol stalled for time. On CNN's *Larry King*, a week later, he admitted, "I'm a little surprised. I'm not sure that people have really thought that through. . . . I think it will be different in a month." A month later came this announcement: "The whole dynamic will change once the truth is known."[17]

But the days stretched into weeks, and later into months without a popular groundswell for impeachment. Kristol blamed Americans for letting him down. "They're wrong," he explained. "The majority of the American people, at this stage, is wrong." William Bennett also failed to hide his disappointment. He complained on *Meet the Press* that Americans had grown too "complacent," or too "prosperous," or too "fixed on the Dow Jones."[18]

The pundits were clearly at a loss for an explanation, so blinded were they by a hatred for the president. Sounding less like sophisticated political analysts than Sunday school pedants, pundits like Stuart Taylor of the *National Journal* complained on *Meet the Press*, "I'd like to be able to tell my children, 'You should tell the truth.' I'd like to be able to tell them, 'You should respect the President.' And I'd like to be able to tell them both things at the same time." His colleague on the program, William J. Bennett, spoke of the "moral and intellectual disarmament" that befalls a nation when its president is not "being a decent example" and "teaching kids the difference between right and wrong." "We have a right to say to this president, 'What you have done is an example to our children that's a disgrace,'" he added. This view was seconded by Cokie Roberts, who "approach[ed] this as a mother." "This ought to be something that outrages us, makes us ashamed of him." (Her children were fully grown, but perhaps unusually sensitive.)[19] On the *McLaughlin Group*, the panel spent some time actually discussing whether Bill Clinton was, in fact, Satan. I am not making this up.

The elite media's attitude toward the Clintons appeared akin to be that of Old Money (or power) toward some Ozark hick who failed to pay proper heed to their superior social grace and aristocratic breeding. As David Broder would later explain to the famed Georgetown hostess and sometime reporter Sally Quinn, "He came in here and he trashed the place, and it's not his place." Other pundits made similar points. "We have our own set of village rules," said David Gergen, editor at large at *U.S. News & World Report*, who worked for both the Reagan and Clinton White House. "We all live together, we have a sense of community, there's a small-town quality here. We all understand we do certain things, we make certain compromises. But when you have gone over the line, you won't bring others into it. That is a cardinal rule of the village. You don't foul the nest."

In a "community" where everyone thinks pretty much the same thoughts, actual reporting is beside the point. Thus Americans were treated to CNN analyst Jeff Greenfield reporting on CNN on what White House staffers were "thinking" but not saying. The network's Wolf Blitzer told viewers that "several" of Clinton's "closest friends and advisers" have concluded "he almost certainly did have a sexual relationship" with Lewinsky "and are talking among themselves about the possibility of a resignation." Toe-sucking political consultant Dick Morris intimated to a reporter that none of this would have happened if Hillary weren't a lesbian.[20]

The liberal *New York Times* editorial page, under Howell Raines, reached new heights of rhetorical dudgeon toward the president during this period. "Until it was measured by Kenneth Starr," thundered the voice of the paper of record, "no citizen—indeed, perhaps no member of his own family—could have grasped the completeness of President Clinton's mendacity or the magnitude of his recklessness." Meanwhile, the only problem with Starr's investigation, opined the *Times*, was "legal klutziness . . . . In the main, Mr. Starr did his legal duty . . . whatever Mr. Starr's failings, they will never achieve the grand malignancy of Mr. Clinton's folly and miscalculations." As Michael Tomasky pointed out, as of December 1999, the day after the House Judiciary Committee voted the fourth and final article of impeachment—this alleged bastion of Upper West Side knee-jerk liberalism had published some fifty-five editorials on matters re Monica Lewinsky. Exactly two were primarily concerned with Kenneth Starr's investigative techniques. The other fifty-three expressed varying degrees of outrage at Bill Clinton.[21] (Recall also, that it was the *Times*'s own investigative sleuth, Jeff Gerth, who got the entire Whitewater ball rolling, with a March 1992 story that ended up insinuating a great deal more than could ever be proven.)[22]

Like the *Times*, most of the punditocracy found itself bored by allegations of abuse in Kenneth Starr's office. The prosecutor, Sally Quinn noted, "is a Washington insider, too. He has lived and worked here for years. He had a reputation as a fair and honest judge. He has many friends in both parties. Their wives are friendly with one another and their children go to the same schools." He was a great source for journalists and, as a judge, handed down a decision in a libel case that saved the *Washington Post* many millions of dollars. The denizens of Sally Quinn's "community" could not help but like him and trust his judgment.

The American public remained remarkably serene in the face of the mounting hysteria of their televised interlocutors. When the Starr Report was released, quickly followed by the president's videotaped testimony, the public grew even more adamant in its rejection of the egregious invasion of privacy that both represented, despite the media's investment in the prosecutor's heroic feat. A CNN/Gallup poll measured the president's approval rating at 62 percent in the wake of the report's release, while support for Congressional Republicans fell precipitously. Soon, the president's popularity began to rise. Two in three Americans—67 percent—told pollsters they approved of the job that Clinton was doing as president, up from 63 percent in a *Post*-ABC News survey conducted in the last week of September. These numbers were far higher than those enjoyed by Ronald Reagan at a similar moment in his presidency and higher than those for George W. Bush as I write these words, in October 2002, despite the enormous "bounce" he receives for being a war president and the near-universal media consensus regarding his political invincibility.

Alas, pundits are slow learners and virtually all predicted a smashing Republican victory in the November 1998 midterm elections, rather than the six-seat loss the party endured in the House of Representatives.[23] "We were all wrong, all the time," admitted George Stephanopoulos on ABC's *This Week*, and indeed they all were.[24] In L'Affaire Lewinsky, the U.S. media had displayed not only a profound disconnect from the values of the nation, but also moral values that were well to the right of the "live and let live" ethos that seemed to animate most of the country with regard to the president. Far from being the liberal caricature offered by conservatives, the media showed themselves to be in the grip of a smug, hypocritical Puritanism. Here was the essential divide between the nation and the elite media during the presidency of William Jefferson Clinton and it is difficult—if not impossible—to see how anyone could blame it on a "liberal media."

# 10

## The 2000 Election

ONE CAN ANALYZE THE MEDIA coverage of the 2000 presidential election from any number of perspectives, and none of them will be fully satisfactory. This chapter will examine just one, rather prolonged, question: How did it happen? How did one of the most experienced candidates in our history somehow "lose" to one of the least qualified? At the moment of the election, the qualified candidate enjoyed twice as much experience in government as the unqualified one, even were the latter to serve two terms as president. The qualified one served in the military; the unqualified one (and his running mate) took a privileged pass, with the presidential candidate failing even to show up for his National Guard duty and the vice-presidential candidate saying he had other "priorities." The qualified candidate also held positions on virtually all the major issues—including, for instance, abortion, affirmative action, Social Security, Medicare, tax policy, education, the environment, health care, prescription drugs, and gun control to name just a few—that were, according to every published poll, much closer to those of a majority of voters than those held by the unqualified one. And finally, the experienced candidate with the popular positions who served in Vietnam was also the representative of an administration that—while a bit colorful—was among the most successful of any in recent American history. During the final months of its eight years in office, median household income had reached an all-time high; the unemployment rate was at its lowest point in three decades; the rate of violent crime was down; and the once-mountainous deficit had become a massive surplus.[1]

It is not entirely fair to say that the qualified candidate and Vietnam veteran with the popular positions representing the successful administration actually lost to the relatively unqualified one with the unpopular positions, who ducked Vietnam and did not have much of a record. Al Gore did win the popular vote and certainly was the clear favorite of those voters who went to the polls to cast their fully-legal-but-nevertheless-disqualified ballots in Florida on that fateful Election Day. Nevertheless, the question remains: How is it possible, given all of the above, that the 2000 election was somehow close enough to allow the U.S. Supreme Court to hand it to George W. Bush?

Like most worthwhile questions, the above has no simple, or even single, answer. Certainly one piece of the puzzle can be found in the near-universal judgment that the Bush folks ran an impressively disciplined campaign, with a candidate who stuck to his script and did what he was told. The Gore campaign, on the other hand, never really settled on a single strategy. In literally thousands of tiny ways that take on accumulated significance over the life of a campaign, the Gore camp saw itself outclassed by the Bush team. In-again, out-again top Gore adviser Tony Coelho conceded, "Karl Rove and Karen Hughes outmaneuvered and out-strategized us. We weren't in the same league."[2] A second partial answer can be found in the person of Ralph Nader and his followers in the Green Party. The former consumer crusader's kamikaze campaign not only cost Al Gore votes in crucial battleground states, including Florida, he also robbed the Democratic Party of much of its activist base, making the vote a near tie, despite 52 percent of the electorate having voted against George Bush.

But even with these disadvantages, Gore could and should easily have won the election by a much more considerable margin than the easily reversible one he eventually managed. And he might have, but for one key and frequently overlooked reason: the almost universal hostility he inspired in the reporters and editors who covered the race.

---

The romantic ideal of covering a U.S. presidential election is not an emotion likely to survive the actual experience. I have briefly reported on four of them, and every time, I find myself amazed at the inanity of the "process." All events are carefully staged to reveal as little about the candidate, his abilities, or his politics as is possible. Reporters are kept at a distance and expected to take down, virtually verbatim, the "message of the day." It is irrelevant whether this message has anything to do with what might even generously be termed an "issue." But to question the false pretenses under which candidates labor for your vote is to risk whatever access you enjoy to the candidate and his advisers. And so this rarely happens.

Recall, for instance, during the 2000 campaign, how George W. Bush repeatedly found himself surrounded by small black and brown children during the day's photo op. Recall also that the pictures emanating from the stage at the Republican convention were frequently dominated by such images. And yet Bush enjoyed almost no support at all from the minority voters these children were obviously chosen to represent. In fact in July 2002, the GOP's only elected black U.S. representative resigned, reducing the party's number to zero. And yet, network producers and print photographers have not only been known to go along with the party's deliberate deception on this point, they have, on occasion, even conspired to extend it. During

Robert Dole's 1996 convention speech, network camera operators could not find any actual black people to portray as delegates who were really delegates. So as a favor to Dole and the Republicans, they focused on their own employees. The aspiring emperor may be naked, but he looks awfully well-dressed on TV.

Such blatant manipulation is viewed with a kind of cynical appreciation by the cogs in the media who conspire to pass it along. Everyone understands "how the game is played" and so nobody gets too upset when the rules are bent to deceive voters. And they have a point here. After all, what difference would it make whether the black and brown children who surround Bush during photo ops were genuine Bush supporters rather than staged props? Who cares what a bunch of kids think of the president and who cares what the president thinks about a bunch of kids? Doesn't every politician on earth love children, or at least pretend to on TV? Should Americans be choosing their president on the basis of whether he is genuinely liked by a few dozen or even a hundred children? What do they know? The very idea is absurd. And yet it is upon this level of absurdity that our campaigns are conducted.

Because campaigns are not expected to pay too much attention to the actual details of policy proposals, particularly on television, and yet are conducted almost entirely in the guise of "news," this same media can, under the right conditions, make or break a candidate with voters through the manner they choose to portray him or her. But whether the candidate is portrayed favorably or negatively is, in large measure, a function of how well the campaign employs the various carrots and sticks at its disposal. The former include: access to the candidate, juicy "tick-tock"—that is the inside kitty of how a given decision was reached—and not least of all, food. (Skimp on the catering budget and you can just about kiss your candidacy goodbye.) The sticks are pretty much the same in reverse. If reporters displease a campaign, they will be frozen out from the stuff that gives campaign reporting its flavor: access, background, and the sense of being treated with even a modicum of dignity and respect.

Though the Bush campaign never achieved the gold standard of coverage enjoyed by John McCain, whose mutual love affair with the media fueled his success in the early Republican primaries, it excelled at almost all of the above. The embarrassing degree of devotion shown to the conservative Republican McCain is yet another piece of evidence that is unassimilable into the "Liberal Media" storyline, except as Mickey Kaus would have it, "the exception that proves the rule."[3] Bush proved likable and available to reporters on the campaign plane, though never to discuss substance. He clowned around for their benefit. Alexandra Pelosi, who served as a self-described "onboard librarian" as an NBC producer, made a home movie/documentary about the campaign plane entitled *Journeys with George*. The film succeeds marvelously in communicating the president's likability, but it also demonstrates why Pelosi says her "idealism about journalism died" out on the campaign trail.[4] She shows us reporters complaining about staged snowmobile rides and the other inane pseudoevents they are forced to cover, and yet to which they submit without apparent protest. In between feedings, we see the assembled pack laugh at Bush's funny faces, hound Bush for his autograph, and pose for photographs to send home to mom. The reporters kid around with the candidate and he kids back, going so far as to christen them with their own presidential nicknames. (Frank Bruni of the *New York Times* was "Pancho" and sometimes "Panchito." CNN's Candy Crowley was "Dulce," Patricia Wilson of Reuters was "Outback Woman." And Carl Cameron of the *Christian Science Monitor* was "Camarones"). Bush is an all-purpose candidate when it comes to enchanting his would-be Boswells. As you see in Pelosi's documentary, which aired on HBO in November 2002, he sets them up on dates, worries about their favorite baseball teams, and, in the case of the filmmaker herself, even offers up a kiss in pursuit of her write-in vote in the California primary.[5]

Most important for our purposes, however, is the fact that in just a few behind-the-scenes minutes, Pelosi manages to encapsulate the underlying theme of the media coverage of the entire election: As her documentary begins, we witness Richard Wolffe of the *Financial Times*—not exactly a bastion of the so-called "liberal media"—babbling excitedly about his eagerness to cover "the greatest story in the world," featuring "big issues, big stakes." A bit later in the film, we find Wolffe admitting, "Most of our time is spent doing really stupid things, in stupid places with stupid people." If one were to try to sum up the coverage of the campaign in a single sentence, it would be hard to outdo Wolffe: "The Gore press corps is about how they didn't like Gore, didn't trust him. . . . Over here, we were writing only about the trivial stuff because he charmed the pants off us."[6]

Bush charmed his press plane and Gore repelled his; in an important sense, this is all we need to know to answer the question posed at the top of this chapter. For, to make sense of the daily events of a campaign—and to put them into a context in which they presumably have some relevance to an election that might be far off in the future—reporters require a storyline. Because all the reporters are traveling on the same plane, eating the same food, covering the same events, following up on the same press releases, and most of all, reading one another's copy, reporters find themselves, as if by osmosis, sticking to the same script. What's more, there is more than osmosis at work. Back home, their editors and producers are all reading the coverage in the *Times*, the *Post*, and the newsweeklies. So too are network producers, who that night repeat the gist of these bigfoot narratives, but with visuals. These images further reinforce the narrative power inside the rest of the pack. The strict story line receives further fortification from the cable chatfests, as these focus relentlessly on the agreed-upon narrative of the day. And the entire process repeats itself beginning with the morning news shows the following day. It is an endless loop that requires the political equivalent of a large-scale earthquake to upset. As Joan Didion explained, the journalists' consensus narrative is comprised of numerous "understandings, tacit agreements, small and large, to overlook the observable in the interests of obtaining a dramatic story line." To retain the story's simple narrative structure, she noted, reporters, producers, and editors are forced to ignore "the contradictions in reporting that which occurs only to be reported." "Tree it, bag it, defoliate the forest for it, destroy the village for it," Didion wrote, but only if it fits into "the narrative."[7]

The narrative for election 2000 went roughly as follows: "Al Gore is a smug, self-regarding goody-goody, who is always trying to impress everybody in the room with how smart he is, which is why he ends up lying about himself and his record all the time. George W. Bush, by contrast, is a rather likable, if oddly Waspy, fellow, who does not really take this politics stuff too seriously. He may not be qualified to be president, and we really have no idea what he did for most of his life, but that's not so important. What matters is that he does not go around putting on airs like that supercilious prince. What's more, Bush is new. Gore is old. It's time—ha, ha—for him to go." The enforcement of the above narrative as if by dictatorial decree resulted in the postulating of a single question to guide the electorate choice for the presidency: "For Al Gore, it was 'Is he too annoying/dishonest to be president?' For Bush, it was 'Is he too stupid?'" Cokie Roberts put it nicely when, in defense of her colleagues, she helpfully explained, "The story line is Bush isn't smart enough and Gore isn't straight enough."[8] Virtually nothing else, including the fact that the two men represent wholly different constituencies, differing philosophies of governance, and differing futures for the country was considered to be relevant to the main story line.

In one of the most revealing moments of Ms. Pelosi's film, as she is filling out her absentee ballot to vote in California, Bush tries to sweet-talk her into voting for him. She peppers him with questions about his policies regarding "the little guy." Bush doesn't get it. "I am the little guy," he proclaims. "Have you ever seen me next to my brother?" Pelosi told a reporter, "I wanted to laugh in his face. You are the governor of Texas and your father was president. You are trying to sell yourself to me as the little guy? I kept giving him a chance to make his pitch, and he could never do it."[9] Bush tries to close the deal by giving her a kiss on the cheek. It didn't work on Pelosi, but its equivalent seems to have done the job on the rest of the plane. No less tellingly, the folks at ABC's *The Note* read this comment and complained, "Hey, NBC in 2004, how about not assigning any avowed liberals to cover the presidential campaign?"[10] This reflexive reaction was so ingrained in the SCLM that these usually careful and thoughtful critics did not even attempt to demonstrate how Ms. Pelosi's politics might have affected NBC's coverage. Their rules for the media clubhouse could not have been more simply stated: "No liberals allowed."

*The Note*'s concerns may have been misplaced regarding Pelosi, in part because genuine issues proved to be of such low priority to reporters covering the campaign that the *New York Times* correspondent Frank Bruni managed to write an entire book about his experiences as a Bush campaign reporter without mentioning any. *Ambling into History* contains nary a word about health care, Social Security, tax cuts, the Middle East conflict, missile defense or, God forbid, global warming. Bruni appeared to excuse himself and his colleagues by noting that political reporters don't write about issues during a campaign because they undertook to do so a year earlier, back when few people were paying attention. During the actual campaign, all that matters is who is ahead, who is screwing up, and what tactical ploy each side is likely to launch in response to the other side's tactical ploy. Bruni does nothing to address the contradiction in this situation, nor his own enormously influential role in covering it; however, nor does he see any problem with its results.

Bruni's book does offer the occasional glimpse of the press plane's inner workings, though he does not appear to understand how they might have affected his own judgment. "We were prisoners in a gilded cell, which we called 'the bubble,' because it was so separate from everyday life and had an atmosphere all its own," he explained. "We were following, not leading—herded like sheep, lured like lemmings. Small wonder that we got so cranky. Small wonder still that we got so silly."[11] But instead of examining his own work and that of his colleagues for its undeniable "silliness," he went on to blame not himself and his colleagues—or even the candidates and consultants who put so much energy into their collective manipulation—but the voters themselves. "Modern politics wasn't just superficial because the politicians made it so. It was superficial because the voters let it be."[12] The idea that journalists have a responsibility, in a democracy, to help educate voters beyond what they might demand to know—and after all, how can they know what they don't know—apparently does not occur to Bruni at all.

Blaming the voters is about as critical of the process as Bruni allows himself to be. Otherwise, his memoir on the campaign trail functions not as analysis, but as artifact of the art of political seduction. Candidate Bush puts his arms around "Panchito" Bruni and coos, "You know we love you." He looks across a crowded room at the author and mouths, "I love you, man." Rarely in political history have the sounds of sweet seduction been so richly rewarded. A visit to the Gore camp, in contrast, is a horror show. There is no access offered whatsoever, not even, get this, for the *New York Times*. Gore failed Bruni and his own campaign because, as Bruni told it, "He made no effort. His energies were channeled into his campaign trail remarks, so dense with knowledge, so showy with digressions. He sweated the big stuff and muffed the small stuff."[13] Imagine that.

Aside from dressing down voters for not stopping him before he gets silly again, Bruni finds room to criticize only one of his colleagues in the entire book. Apparently, Mike Allen of the *Washington Post* offended Bruni when he joined the press crew from the Bill Bradley campaign and filed a dispatch contending that "after five months in firm command of the presidential race, George W. Bush suddenly finds himself on the defensive, behind in the polls and struggling to fend off attacks." Bruni was merciless toward Allen because he found Bush's demeanor and confidence "off-kilter" at a time when Bruni thought Bush had his mojo working. Even worse was the fact that other reporters briefly ignored Bruni's sympathetic coverage and began "following suit" with Allen's, because, Bruni contemptuously noted, this is how "tough-minded, keen-eyed reputations are made."

The new flavor of Kool-Aid briefly proved so addictive that soon even Bruni found himself lacking the courage of his own complaisance. He was soon "rejoining the pack, because the assertion that Bush was flailing was so rampant in the newspapers and newscasts that it had transmogrified into the fact that Bush was flailing."[14] And since virtually all television producers and many national editors of local and regional newspapers take their cues about what's important in a campaign from the *Times* (and the *Post*), the willingness of the *Times* bigfoot to treat the election as the equivalent of a junior high popularity contest signaled to the rest of the media that contentless coverage would be the order of the day. After all, if the *New York Times*—the American media's undisputed Leader of the Pack—is not going to bother with the demanding task of issue-based coverage, why should anyone else?

The anecdotal evidence presented intentionally by Pelosi and inadvertently by Bruni was reinforced by a series of studies by Princeton Associates for the Committee of Concerned Journalists and the Project for Excellence in Journalism of the Pew Charitable Trust, which examined the content and quality of 430 stories from major news publications, programs, and Web sites during the 2000 election campaign. The first of these—based on the five major newspapers and nine programs on five television networks over the two-week period leading up to the Iowa caucuses and the New Hampshire primary—found that few of the 430 stories they examined "explored the candidates' past records in office with more than a passing reference."[15] Ditto the coverage of the October debates, scrutinized in a later study; 70 percent of stories studied by the committee during this crucial period focused on either the candidates' television performances or their strategies. Fewer than 10 percent attended to such matters as the candidates' policy differences, while a miniscule 1 percent focused on either candidate's vision for his presidency.[16] To take just one extremely important example, in the lead story in the *New York Times* following the third and most crucial presidential debate, readers were forced to wade through twenty-two full paragraphs before reading a word of substance with regard to either candidate's policy positions. Even there, as veteran journalists Bill Kovach and Tom Rosenstiel noted, coverage was cast not in the context of the issues themselves, but strictly in terms of how they "played" as political theater. ("One of the more heated exchanges was over reducing the cost of prescription drugs. . . .")[17]

This issueless coverage coincided perfectly with the strategy of the Bush campaign. After all, for Gore to be elected, all voters had to do was vote either for the man who was more qualified for the job or the one whose politics they happened to share. For Bush to win, these two criteria—considered to be central in most political science classes with regard to elections—had to be lain aside. The underlying message of Bush's campaign went something like this: "Forget all that stuff about qualifications, experience, intelligence, politics, records, issues, and so on. Ignore the fact that these two candidates represent significantly different political philosophies and have, on many key issues, conflicting views on how to approach our problems as a society, or on just what constitutes a problem. And especially forget the fact that on most of these you agree with Al Gore. Remember only this: Our guy may not be quite up to snuff when it comes to the serious policy stuff, but he's a good guy, and if he came over to your house for dinner, he wouldn't bore everybody at the table trying to prove that he was smarter'n you were. . . ." And the Gore team's response? Well, it changed from day to day. This is another way of saying it had no response at all.

Part of the credit for Bush's low expectations belonged to Ronald Reagan, the topic of many a dewey-eyed tribute during the Republican primary season. Both Bush and McCain battled to claim the mantle of the Gipper. John McCain termed himself "a true Reagan Republican." George W. Bush retorted, "It is not Reaganesque to say one thing and do another."[18] The rose-colored nostalgia for a president who could not recognize his own son at his high school graduation set a bar for Bush that would have been difficult for him to miss if he had been genuinely retarded. Bush could not help but perform up to this minimum level of competence. After all, all that was required of him was to give a decent speech at the Republican convention—something any minimally trained actor could do—and to "hold his own" in three debates against Gore. Well aware of the advantages of being consistently underestimated, Bush explained to David Letterman, "A lot of folks don't think I can string a sentence together so when I was able to do so, the expectations were so low that all I had to do was say, 'Hi, I'm George W. Bush.'"[19]

Gore, meanwhile, was in a bind. Deemed by the media to be irredeemably unlikeable, he needed to win the election on the issues. Suffice it to say, however, that given the interests and priorities of those same media through which these issues must be discussed, this proved to be no simple task. During the presidential debates, for instance, moderator Jim Lehrer twice explained to viewers that the two candidates held essentially indistinguishable views on domestic issues. "As a practical matter, both of you want to bring prescription drugs to seniors, correct?"[20] he introduced one question. "[W]ould you agree that the two of you agree on a national patients' bill of rights?" he offered up in another. Had Lehrer been paying attention, he would have been aware that Gore favored the key bill before Congress which both the pharmaceutical industry and the Republican presidential candidate opposed. But Bush did not want the public to understand these differences, because given the popularity of the issue, it was far easier to position himself as the beneficiary of presumed (but phony) consensus. When Gore tried to distinguish between "his" bill—Dingell-Norwood—and the one Bush was advocating, the pundits and traveling press acted as if the distinctions raised were the silliest in the world—as if Gore was trying to show off by being able to pronounce the name of the bill's sponsors. That same week *This Week* with Sam and Cokie kept flashing photos of the bill's two sponsors, as if they were anchoring "Weekend Update" on *Saturday Night Live*.[21] (As president, Bush, backed by the insurance industry, was able to convince Norwood to drop his sponsorship of the bill and reverse sides. This eventually led to the bill's defeat, thereby demonstrating the effectiveness of this media-enabled three-card-monte style of campaigning when it came to actual policy issues.)

Media coverage of the debates was so egregious it shocked even journalists who were clearly on the Bush team. On CNN's *Inside Politics*, the conservative Tucker Carlson mused on the phenomenon:

> I mean, you know, and it's interesting—I mean, there is this sense in which Bush is benefiting from something, and I'm not sure what it is. Maybe it's the low expectations of the people covering him. You know, he didn't drool or pass out on stage or anything, so he's getting credit for that. But there is this kind of interesting reluctance on the part of the press to pass judgment on it. I think a lot of people—they don't, necessarily, break down along ideological lines—believe that, you know, maybe Bush didn't do as good a job as he might have. And yet, the coverage does not reflect that at all. It's interesting.[22]

Carlson's views were seconded by virulent Gore hater Christopher Hitchens, who chalked up the press coverage to a fearful media "determined to avoid" charges of "liberal bias."[23] Chris Matthews, another Bush partisan, who would later observe of Al Gore that he "would lick the bathroom floor" to be president, and "He doesn't seem very American, even," was nevertheless shocked at the indulgence offered the incompetent George W. Bush:

> I couldn't believe the number of people who chickened out last night. It was clear to me—and I'm no fan of either of these guys entirely, and I can certainly say that about the one who I thought won last night, that's Al Gore—I thought he cleaned the other guy's clock, and I said so last night. All four national polls agreed with that. . . . I don't understand why people are afraid to say so.[24]

Frank Bruni even managed to criticize himself, apparently without being aware of it, for his indefensibly pro-Bush spin. As Bob Somerby pointed out, Bruni wrote in his 2001 book that the debate had been a dispiriting debacle for Bush:

By any objective analysis, Bush was at best mediocre in the first debate, in Boston. . . . In all of [the debates], he was vague. A stutter sometimes crept into his voice. An eerie blankness occasionally spread across his features. He made a few ridiculous statements. . . . I remember watching the first debate from one of the seats inside the auditorium and thinking that Bush was in the process of losing the presidency.[25]

But back where it still mattered—on page one of the *New York Times*—on what did Bruni focus? Certainly not on Bush's "ridiculous statements," but his personal distaste for Al Gore. As if channeling the governor's own resentful thoughts, Bruni wrote:

It was not enough for Vice President Al Gore to venture a crisp pronunciation of Milosevic, as in Slobodan, the Yugoslav president who refuses to be pried from power. . . . Mr. Gore had to go a step further, volunteering the name of Mr. Milosevic's challenger, Vojislav Kostunica. Then he had to go a step beyond that, noting that Serbia plus Montenegro equals Yugoslavia. . . . And as Mr. Gore loped effortlessly through the Balkans, barely able to suppress his self-satisfied grin, it became ever clearer that the point of all the thickets of consonants and proper nouns was not a geopolitical lesson. . . . It was more like oratorical intimidation, an unwavering effort to upstage and unnerve an opponent whose mind and mouth have never behaved in a similarly encyclopedic fashion.[26]

One question one might ask is, if Gore was, in fact, "barely able to suppress his self-satisfied grin," how did Bruni know this? The "grin," such as it was, even according to Bruni, was imaginary on his part, and hence so was the self-satisfaction.

In addition to refusing to pay attention to the many substantive issues that separated the two candidates, the media also aided the Bush campaign by conducting what looks very much in retrospect to be a campaign of character assassination against Gore, which they conducted almost as if to draw the public's attention away from the far more serious character defects in his Republican opponent. I write "in retrospect" because even though this topic was one of my "beats" during the election, and I wrote about it at some length, I really had no idea how extensive and irresponsible it had been until I looked back at it in a semi-systematic fashion. (And I write as someone who has little affection for Al Gore, and who supported his opponent Bill Bradley.) Fortunately, the numbers provided by the Pew/Committee study, undergirded by the reporting of independent-minded journalists Eric Boehlert of Salon and Robert Parry of www.consortium.com and the constant chronicling of the top reporter's work by an old Gore friend from college, Bob Somerby of the DailyHowler.com Web site, have allowed me to do just that.

First, the numbers. With regard to the overall coverage, a study by the Project for Excellence in Journalism and Princeton Survey Research Associates examined 1,149 election stories over the course of the campaign. The researchers discovered:

> The most common theme of the campaign was that Gore was scandal-tainted. This accounted for 42 percent of all the assertions about Gore's character. The second most common assertion about Gore was that he was a liar. These accounted for 34 percent of stories about him. The least common of the major themes, accounting for 14 percent of assertions, was that he was competent, experienced, and knowledgeable.[27]

The study also noted "the press has been far more likely to convey that Bush is a different kind of Republican—'a compassionate conservative,' a reformer, bipartisan—than to discuss Al Gore's themes of experience, knowledge, or readiness for the office." It additionally found that "Journalists' assertions about Bush's character were more than twice as likely than Gore's to be unsupported by any evidence. In other words, they were pure opinion, rather than journalistic analysis."[28] As Kovach and Rosenstiel pointed out, to the degree that election coverage ignored the issues, which was almost always, the election became Bush's to lose: "This focus on campaign-as-theater redounded to Bush's benefit. Bush, by most judgments, ran the better campaign."[29]

How to explain the disparity? Part of it can be blamed on the many mistakes of the Gore campaign. But it's not clear that a competent management team would have changed matters much. The more obvious, and explosive, conclusion, that the disparity in coverage was due to a political bias in favor of Bush and against Gore, is one I'm not comfortable arguing. I have no evidence, and I do not believe, that reporters prefer a conservative Republican to a centrist Democrat in the White House. Rather, ideology does not really enter into it. However, reporters do expect more from Democratic candidates, because they relate to them better. Reporters and Democrats are from Venus. Republicans, particularly Bush Republicans, are from Mars, if not an entirely alien universe. They pledged fraternities and secret societies in college and drank martinis dressed in Brooks Brothers button-downs, instead of smoking pot and traveling to Dead concerts in jeans and t-shirts like any normal college kid. They did not worry about grades, because they didn't have to. They were set up. Later on, they usually went into business and only entered politics as a kind of family trust, rather than out of a passion for the issues.

Mike Kinsley described the journalists' mounting affection for Bush as it crystallized around the time of the Republican convention in August:

> George W. wears well. He's not a total bozo. His scalawag side and his sincere side are both appealing, both apparently genuine, and the flavors mix superbly, each

making the other digestible. His comically aristocratic answer to doubts about his grasp of the issues—in effect, "I have people for that sort of thing"—comes off as amiable anti-intellectual populism. His preppy disdain for vulgar ideological passions and grubby policy details is well-suited to a contented people in a prosperous time. . . . He shares his father's attitude that politics is a game, along with the preppy ethic that one should be serious about games and casual about life. The best thing about George W. is his non-neurotic attitude that he's playing this game to win, but he won't fall apart if he doesn't. The worst thing about him is almost the same: Nothing is at stake except winning the game.[30]

George W. Bush, like his father, is clearly a recognizable Republican archetype, if not the only kind. But there is probably not a single national Democratic politician or a well-known political reporter about whom anyone could say the same.

Reporters were also almost universally disgusted with Gore's efforts to squirm away from the many White House scandals that they believed had tainted him beyond redemption—from fundraising phone calls, excused by the lack of a "controlling legal authority," as Gore cluelessly claimed, to his boss's Oval Office blow jobs and insufficient contrition. And during the course of the campaign, Gore did little to challenge these assumptions, retreating into a Secret-Service-protected cocoon, seeming to embrace Clinton on certain days while going to great pains to "distance" himself on others, without ever explaining just what he thought of Clinton's misdeeds and thereby disposing of the subject. He ended up getting the blame for Clinton's blow jobs without receiving any of the credit for Clinton's economy—quite an achievement, when you think about it.

But even the contempt that familiarity can breed does not explain the hostile and journalistically irresponsible treatment endured by the Gore campaign. The easiest explanation at hand is the fact that the vast majority of the reporters who covered Gore simply hated his guts. They thought him supercilious, superior, snotty, smug, and generally a pain in the ass—the kind of kid who would tell the teacher that the clock had been set forward and it was really not yet time for recess. *Washington Post* White House reporter Dana Milbank later offered this reasoned, mature explanation:

Gore is sanctimonious and that's sort of the worst thing you can be in the eyes of the press. And he has been disliked all along and it was because he gives a sense that he's better than us—he's better than everybody, for that matter, but the sense that he's better than us as reporters. Whereas President Bush probably is sure that he's better than us—he's probably right, but he does not convey that sense. He does not seem to be dripping with contempt when he looks at us, and I think that has something to do with the coverage. [31]

The man who narrowly lost the competition to be executive editor of the *New York Times*, Bill Keller, was no less scholarly, but like any good pundit, multiplied his own resentments by fifty million. "One big reason 50 million voters went instead for an apparent lightweight they didn't entirely trust was that they didn't want to have Al Gore in their living rooms for four years," Keller wrote on the paper's op-ed page. His evidence: During the 2000 campaign, his three-year-old daughter "went around chanting the refrain: 'Al Gore is a snore.'"[32] (Imagine where she might have learned that?)

It's weird how much the press corps hated Gore. Weirder still, however, given the strictures of journalistic objectivity, is how little compunction they felt about showing it. At an early New Hampshire debate between Gore and Bill Bradley, they openly booed him, the strictures of journalistic objectivity be damned. "The 300 media types watching in the press room at Dartmouth were, to use the appropriate technical term, totally grossed out," *Time* magazine reported. "Whenever Gore came on too strong, the room erupted in a collective jeer, like a gang of fifteen-year-old Heathers cutting down some hapless nerd."[33]

Only a universally shared consensus could possibly explain moderator Judy Woodruff's amazingly hostile opening question to Al Gore in the January 26 New Hampshire debate:

The first question goes to Mr. Gore. Most people believe that you are an honorable man, but when it comes to electoral politics your critics, including some Democrats, say that you will do almost anything to win, including reinventing yourself, using consultants no matter what their reputation, and running not just a tough, but a mean-spirited campaign. Newspaper editorials here in New Hampshire and around the country accuse you of distorting Mr. Bradley's record. Is this really necessary to win your party's nomination?[34]

When Gore, given exactly sixty seconds to respond, attempted to explain that he had not distorted Bradley's plan, Woodruff resumed her aggressive attack:

Well, Mr. Vice President, there have been, evidently, several distortions of Mr. Bradley's record. And I'm going to cite just two of them. You charged, for example, that his health care plan would eliminate federal standards for nursing homes. It would not. . . . Now was this a matter of misinformation, or were you just being political?

In fact, as James Brosnan, Washington bureau chief of the *Memphis Commercial-Appeal*, later explained, "Bradley's health care plan does leave nursing home standards vulnerable, because, as Gore explained to a surprisingly ignorant Judy Woodruff . . .

the federal government cannot force states to maintain those standards unless it pro-vides federal aid to nursing home patients, which Bradley's plan would not do."[35]

In the race to deconstruct Gore's personality, literally nothing was considered by reporters to be too trivial (or under-reported) to be thrown at the Tin Man. In an extended biographical essay published by David Maraniss and Ellen Nakashima on the front page of the *Washington Post*, later published as *The Prince of Tennessee*, the authors write that young Tinny was "prone to tattling." "Prone to tattling?" asked Bob Somerby.[36] A seven-year-old boy is "prone to tattling," and this is somehow rel-evant to his qualifications to be president? And what is the evidence? It turns out to be a single anecdote by someone said to be a friend of Gore's now deceased older sis-ter, some time in the mid-1950s.

The authors continue: "His compulsion to adhere to the expected order extend-ed beyond the common practice of snitching on an older sibling." Somerby invited his readers to "marvel" at the psychiatric language—[the reporters'] belief that they are equipped to make such a statement, forty years later. . . . The notion that young Gore has a "compulsion to adhere to the established order" is a judgment no psy-chiatrist—let alone novelist—would make on the basis of such evidence. But the judgment did express the press corps's conventional wisdom that there is something unnatural about our stiff, cautious veep. Here are some more examples of the young tyke's compulsive anal-retentiveness. According to Maraniss/Nakashima, young Al left for school "at precisely the same time each morning." (Did the school's starting time change?) He engaged in after-school athletics that "could end as late as 6." As late as 6! My goodness! Somerby writes, "Is there any high school in this country where after-school sports may not last that late? But to the writers, the desire to paint Gore as an under-age robot turns this into a major surprise." It gets worse: "If there was uneasiness among the St. Albans faculty about the senator's son," noted Maraniss/Nakashima, "it was that perhaps he was too constrained by circum-stances." This is, Somerby notes, "quite a construction." Was there, in fact, "uneasi-ness among the St. Albans faculty about the senator's son at the time?" The authors do not say.[37]

Reporters did not like Gore sartorially, either. They mocked him, fairly, I suppose, for taking advice from the high-priced feminist writer/consultant Naomi Wolf about his earth-tone wardrobe. But even his choice of suits managed to piss reporters off. Chris Matthews guffawed to his guest during a November 1999 *Hardball* about Gore's buttons. (No, really.) "What could that possibly be saying to women voters, three buttons?" he asked. "Is there some hidden Freudian deal here or what? I don't know, I mean, Navy guys used to have buttons on their pants. I don't know what it means."[38] Indeed, Matthews thought this observation so witty he repeated it on five subsequent nights. Meanwhile, *Washington Post* scribe Marc Fisher objected to the fact that Gore donned a brown suit that, according to Fisher, was "of a sort that is alien to virtually every American."[39] It is a weird enough observation for a political reporter to make about any candidate's suit, much less a quiet brown one.

But even this dimestore psychoanalysis by non-psychologists of an imaginary seven-year-old, and unsupported semiotic musings about the alien fashion forms, somehow manage to shine in comparison to the actual reporting of the campaign. Writing in *Rolling Stone*, Eric Boehlert described an (admittedly silly) event that took place one month after the campaign formally began, in July 1999. The vice president paddled down the Connecticut River in New Hampshire to spread "his green theme of protecting the environment" while posing for the obvious photo-op. Any hope he had of communicating his message to actual voters, however, went overboard when Bill Sammon of the Moonie-owned *Washington Times* reported that local authorities had granted Gore a special favor when they released nearly four billion gallons of water from a nearby dam into the drought-stricken river in order to keep the vice president's boat afloat; alleged cost: $7 million. As Boehlert noted, the reporter's larger point could hardly have been clearer: "In a clumsy abuse of power, Al Gore, a supposed friend of the environment, gladly wasted precious natural resources to stage-manage a political event."[40]

The rest of the press corps found this story irresistible. In the wake of the *Washington Times* report, the *New York Times* detailed the "mishap" that underscored, Boehlert noted, Gore's "physical tightness and the gracelessness" of the entire Gore "operation."[41] The *Washington Post* ridiculed "Gore's Four Billion Gallons for a Photo Op,"[42] *Newsweek* dubbed it the "photo op from hell,"[43] and CNN covered the "wave of criticism after floodgates are opened on a New Hampshire river to keep Al Gore afloat."

Too bad almost nothing about the story was true. Boehlert noted that no one from the Gore campaign ever asked for the water to be released. (Concerned about security, the Secret Service did.) The correct figure for the amount of water released, moreover, turned out to be just 500 million gallons, rather than four billion. The local utility company that operates the dam was already dumping millions of gallons of water into the parched Connecticut River every day, but for Gore's trip, this routine exercise was moved up a few hours. The alleged $7 million price tag also turned out to be imaginary, as the water was not wasted, but rather was sent through hydroelectric turbines that generated power, which the utility companies were able to sell.

But the "liberal media" were just getting started. In its coverage of a January 2000 New Hampshire debate with Bill Bradley, the famously liberal *Boston Globe* twisted Gore's words beyond recognition and would not let go. During the questioning, Gore explained that he had "always supported Roe v. Wade" (and "a woman's right to choose"), but at one time had opposed federal funding. Got it? Yes, always, on abortions; evolution from "no" to "yes" on the separate issue of federal (that is, taxpayer) funding for them. In the *Globe*, however, as Bob Somerby noted, Walter Robinson and Ann Scales referred to Gore's "puzzling ... metamorphosis on abortion."[44] Writing on page one a day later, Jill Zuckman and Bob Hohler explained, "Gore, at the Wednesday debate, said he has 'always' supported Roe v. Wade, the decision that created the federal right to abortion." They continued, "but Gore, early in his career, voted several times on bills designed to bar federal funding of abortions," and "Gore, however, years ago amended his stance, and now supports abortion rights across the board, including federal funding for abortion."[45] In both cases, however, none of Gore's statements required any amendment. Being for a woman's right to choose is not the same thing as being for federally funded abortions, a distinction that should not tax the brain cells of someone smart enough to be an election reporter for the *Boston Globe*.

Alas, it was. The following day, on January 30, Zuckman, together with Michael Kranish, followed up that "Gore, who said in Wednesday's debate that he has always supported abortion rights, conceded in an interview yesterday that his position on federal funding of abortion, which he initially opposed in Congress, has 'evolved.'" But where, once again, is the "concession?" Where is the contradiction? In the same story the authors write, "The abortion issue continued yesterday to be the top issue between the Democrats. Bradley again attacked Gore for having said as a congressman in 1987 that abortion was 'the taking of a human life,' while Gore insisted that he is strongly in favor of abortion rights. Bradley's attack was intended to raise questions about Gore's overall credibility."[46] Once again, the *Globe* reporters saw no need to allow a little reporting to get in the way of what seemed like a good story. Somerby did, and what he found was that in the 1987 letter in question, Gore wrote that abortion was "arguably the taking of a human life"—which of course it is, since so many millions of people argue just that. But the *Globe* reporters apparently felt it improved the story to drop the crucial qualifier that Gore had so studiously added. Amazingly, as Somerby pointed out, when Gore was quoted, later in the article, correcting the writers on what he had said, Kranish and Zuckman complained that Gore "seemed to choose his words carefully." This was apparently their idea of a yet another Gore character flaw.

The *Globe*'s careless coverage of the Gore campaign would prove to be exemplary rather than exceptional. Witness the frenzied media mania over Al the Exaggerator's alleged claim to have "invented the Internet." The truth is this: In 1999, Gore told CNN's Wolf Blitzer, "During my service in the United States Congress, I took the initiative in creating the Internet." Note the qualifier. He was a congressman, talking about what he did in Congress. And Gore, as much as anyone else (and perhaps more) really did take the legislative initiative in helping to bring to birth the Internet. He educated himself about the complicated questions involved and gave a series of extremely influential speeches on the potential of the coming "information super-highway," as both a congressman and a senator. Gore was a major supporter of the technological research that helped convert the military communications system, Arpanet, into what is now the Internet. Vinton Cerf, often called "the father of the Internet," and even Newt Gingrich, have vouched for Gore's key legislative role in helping to shepherd the Internet to life.[47]

The phrase that Gore claimed to have used—"invented the Internet"—actually first appeared in a Republican Party press release. Reporters simply swallowed it whole and regurgitated it at every opportunity. According to one Nexis search, the term "invented the Internet" appeared alongside the words "Al Gore" in 1,684 separate articles between March 1999 and Election Day.[48] (And that was just the articles, not the talk shows and so forth.) The *New York Times* even termed the Republicans' Internet campaign as "clever" and "ingenious." "In all likelihood, his exaggerations reflect a yearning for a kind of approval and admiration that he never got from his dad," explained right-wing Gore biographer and amateur psychologist Bob Zelnick.[49] Per usual, however, the Gore campaign proved wholly unequal to the challenge of combating these misportrayals. Amazingly, it actually participated in perpetuating them. Gore let the Internet story build for a week before finally addressing it by making a joke about having "inventing the camcorder."[50] This gave the story further "legs."

At a campaign union event, Gore told the assembled workers that his mom used to sing him to sleep as a child with the anthem, *Look for the Union Label*. *USA Today*'s political columnist Walter Shapiro reported that the anecdote "must be labeled untrue,"[51] as the song had been written in 1975, twenty-seven years after Gore's birth. This too was picked up everywhere. On October 6, 2000, *New York Times* reporter Richard Berke made reference to the union ditty in a lengthy examination of Gore's "tendency to embellish." He noted that "Mr. Gore recalled a childhood lullaby that did not exist."[52] Again, Gore was kidding, but no matter. Shapiro's own paper got a hold of the tape and reported, on its editorial page. "A review of the videotape gives plausibility to that explanation," but of course, this was a week after the original claim and the media had "moved on."[53] The story also proved another rule. Not only can the press not take a joke—when it comes to Al Gore, they cannot even understand one.

Throughout the campaign, media pundits sought to invent an anti–Gore issue by accusing the vice president of having "used Willie Horton" against Michael Dukakis during his abortive presidential campaign in 1988. Bob Somerby discovered examples of the accusation in the election reporting and commentary of Robert Novak, Paul Gigot, William Kristol, Roger Simon of *U.S. News and World Report,* Tony Snow, Rush Limbaugh, Sam Donaldson, and the *Washington Post*'s Dan Balz.[54] Unfortunately for this group, among many others, Gore never mentioned William Horton. He did once criticize Massachusetts' prison furlough policy during a debate, but this is hardly a controversial notion, since it was a strange and, to most, ultimately indefensible policy. The problem with Willie Horton—as exploited by the presidential campaign of George H. W. Bush—was its clearly racist implications, something that cannot possibly be tied to Gore's criticism of a foolish furlough program. But what the heck, as late as October 2002 Fox's Sean Hannity was still complaining on the air, "Al Gore brought Willie Horton to the American people."[55]

The press also had something of a collective fit over a comment Gore made about having traveled with James Lee Witt, head of the Federal Emergency Management Agency, to Texas during some wildfires there. Gore tied the trip to one particular fire, but misremembered the date. In fact, the vice president had made seventeen trips accompanying Witt. He did not happen to make one on the date he thought he remembered, and this turned out to be the key story of the entire debate.[56]

The above examples pale in comparison to the ones that ought to be taught in journalism school as cautionary tales: Love Story and Love Canal. The alleged *Love Story* "lie" with which reporters had so much fun appeared virtually everywhere. The *Globe's* Robinson and Scales naturally seized on the story, claiming Gore "has also said that he and his wife, Tipper, were the models for the movie 'Love Story,' only to be contradicted by author Erich Segal." And here is Bruce Morton on CNN's *Inside Politics*: "Then there was 'Love Story.' Gore once claimed the two characters in the movie 'Love Story' were based on his wife Tipper and himself. The author said, 'News to me,' and Gore backed off."[57] Numerous *New York Times* op-ed columnists were especially enamored with the story as well.

But the story was not merely indescribably silly, but also patently false. It began when, during a 1997 plane ride, Gore came back to the press section and spent two hours "swapping opinions about movies and telling stories about old chums" to a bunch of reporters, including Karen Tumulty of *Time*. The two "old chums" mentioned in her profile turned out to be Segal, the *Love Story* author, and Gore's college buddy, Tommy Lee Jones. This tale eventually made its way into a single sentence of a seven-page election profile that claimed Segal "used Al and Tipper as models for the uptight preppy and his free-spirited girlfriend in Love Story."[58]

The story, once again, was false. Gore had never told the reporters that he and Tipper had been the models for the main characters in the book. Tumulty later explained that Gore had said only that Segal had told some reporters in Tennessee that the characters had been based on the Gores. Two other reporters who were present for the conversation concurred with her recollection. And Gore was right. Seventeen years earlier, the *Nashville Tennessean* had reported just these alleged facts based on an interview with Segal. Unfortunately, the paper had misquoted Segal. It turns out that both Al Gore and Tommy Lee Jones had been models for the Oliver Barrett character. But Tipper was not a model for poor Jenny Cavilleri. Gore's only mistake had been to believe what he read in his local newspaper and remember it correctly. To give an idea of this silly story's staying power, it turned up four times in Ann Coulter's 2002 number one best-seller, *Slander: Liberal Lies About the American Right*, years after it had been thoroughly debunked by Eric Boehlert in Salon, Bob Somerby in the Daily Howler, Robert Parry in the *Washington Monthly*, and Sean Wilentz in the *American Prospect*.[59] Note that there is nothing wrong with any of these claims that a little reporting—much less a moment's thought—would not have solved, assuming it mattered at all in the first place.

But even this sad comedy of incompetence looks good when compared to the journalistic fiasco that was Al Gore and Love Canal. This incredible story, helpfully reconstructed by Robert Parry, began on November 30, 1999, when Gore addressed a group of Concord, New Hampshire, high school students about the ability of individuals to make important differences in their communities. To offer an example, Gore spoke about a teenage girl from Toone, Tennessee, which had been experiencing problems with toxic waste. The young girl had brought the issue to the attention of Gore's congressional office in the late 1970s. Here is what Gore actually said to the New Hampshire students: "I called for a congressional investigation and a hearing. . . . I looked around the country for other sites like that. I found a little place in upstate New York called Love Canal. Had the first hearing on that issue, and Toone, Tennessee—that was the one that you didn't hear of. But that was the one that started it all." As a result, Gore proudly noted, "We passed a major national law to clean up hazardous dump sites. And we had new efforts to stop the practices that ended up poisoning water around the country. We've still got work to do. But we made a huge difference. And it all happened because one high school student got involved."[60]

As Parry noted, the context of Gore's comment was clear. What sparked his interest in the toxic-waste issue was the situation in Toone—"that was the one that you didn't hear of. But that was the one that started it all." After learning about the Toone situation, Gore looked for other examples and "found" a similar case at Love Canal. Gore was not claiming to have "discovered" Love Canal, except in the sense that he was looking for examples that were similar to the problems of Toone—"the one that started it all—in order to hold a hearing and eventually address the problem of hazardous dump sites.

A day later, the *Washington Post* reported the story as follows: "Gore boasted about his efforts in Congress 20 years ago to publicize the dangers of toxic waste." It quoted Gore: "'I found a little place in upstate New York called Love Canal,' he said, referring to the Niagara homes evacuated in August 1978 because of chemical contamination. 'I had the first hearing on this issue.' . . . Gore said his efforts made a lasting impact." Then came Gore's quote, transposed from "That was the one that started it all" into "'I was the one that started it all,' he said."[61] The *New York Times* picked up the same phony quote and ran with it.

When folks in charge of opposition research at the Republican National Committee saw these quotes, no instructions were necessary. The Republican blast fax, sent under the name of the party chair, Jim Nicholson, read: "Al Gore is simply unbelievable—in the most literal sense of that term. . . . It's a pattern of phoniness—and it would be funny if it weren't also a little scary." No one noticed at the time that the RNC had also doctored Gore's quote, fixing his grammar to increase the likelihood of it sounding like an empty boast. The new Gore quote: "I was the one who started it all."[62]

Then the story really took off. "Let's talk about the 'love' factor here," smirked Chris Matthews on *Hardball* that night. "Here's the guy who said he was the character Ryan O'Neal was based on in 'Love Story.' . . . It seems to me . . . he's now the guy who created the Love Canal [case]. I mean, isn't this getting ridiculous? . . . Isn't it getting to be delusionary?" Matthews happened to have a qualified guest on that night, Lois Gibbs, the Love Canal resident who campaigned tirelessly to call attention to the Love Canal scandal. She responded to Matthews's jokey questions, "I actually think he's done a great job . . . he really did work, when nobody else was working, on trying to define what the hazards were in this country and how to clean it up and helping with the Superfund and other legislation."[63]

Tough luck, lady. *Hardball* followed up that evening with a clip that showed what Gore actually said, but even so, deliberately altered its context by beginning with "I found a little town . . . ." Matthews felt this too was beyond hysterical. "It reminds me of Snoopy thinking he's the Red Baron," he guffawed. "I mean how did he get this idea? Now you've seen Al Gore in action. I know you didn't know that he was the prototype for Ryan O'Neal's character in 'Love Story' or that he invented the Internet. He now is the guy who discovered Love Canal." "What is it?" Matthews asked, barely able to contain himself. "The Zelig guy who keeps saying, 'I was the main character in "Love Story." I invented the Internet. I invented Love Canal'?" The next day's *Washington Post* carried a story by Ceci Connolly that placed this new episode in the popular "Gore the Liar" context. "Add Love Canal to the list of verbal missteps by Vice President Gore," she wrote. "The man who mistakenly claimed to have inspired the movie 'Love Story' and to have invented the Internet says he didn't quite mean to say he discovered a toxic waste site."[64]

Rupert Murdoch's *New York Post* could barely contain its outrage. "Again, Al Gore has told a whopper," its editors opined. "Again, he's been caught red-handed and again, he has been left sputtering and apologizing. This time, he falsely took credit for breaking the Love Canal story. . . . Yep, another Al Gore bold-faced lie." The magnitude of this story did not elude the *Post*'s editors. They knew that Gore's "lies" hid something larger and even more sinister. "Gore's lies are not just false, they're outrageously, stupidly false. It's so easy to determine that he's lying, you have to wonder if he wants to be found out." Meanwhile, on ABC's *This Week*, George Stephanopoulos noted, "Gore, again, revealed his Pinocchio problem." Cokie Roberts did not disappoint her many fans, adding, "Isn't he saying that he really discovered Love Canal when he had hearings on it after people had been evacuated?" she asked. This prompted William Kristol to chime in with the phony RNC version of Gore's quote: "I found a little place in upstate New York called Love Canal. I was the one that started it all."[65]

Eventually, on December 7, the *Washington Post* finally published a partial correction of its initial false story, buried like a sunken treasure chest as the very the last item in a corrections box. Nevertheless, the *Post* continued to mislead its readers about what Gore actually said. The *Post* correction, as Parry noted, read: "In fact, Gore said, 'That was the one that started it all,' referring to the congressional hearings on the subject that he called." But the antecedent for the word "that" was once again misreported. Gore was not referring to the discovery of the problem, but to the Toone toxic waste case. The *Times* also ran a correction, and again, it never bothered to explain the proper context nor meaning for Gore's wholly fully accurate statement that had somehow turned him into a national laughing stock.

Meanwhile the story continued to spread independent of any relationship to truth, much less genuine reporting. *National Journal*'s Stuart Taylor Jr. cited the Love Canal case as proof of "the Clintonization of Al Gore, who increasingly apes his boss in fictionalizing his life story and mangling the truth for political gain. Gore—self-described inspiration for the novel *Love Story*, discoverer of Love Canal, co-creator of the Internet." Naturally, the Gore team screwed up here too. The veep was humble, instead of angry, in response to the media's malicious incompetence. He called a reporter to say he was sorry if his Love Canal comments had not been clear enough. Sadly but symbolically, the truth of Gore's words could not be heard anywhere in the media until a group of the students who had actually been present at the meeting came up with the idea of issuing their own press release. They headlined it, in response to a David Letterman routine entitled "Top Ten achievements claimed by Al Gore": "Top Ten Reasons Why Many Concord High Students Feel Betrayed by Some of the Media Coverage of Al Gore's Visit to Their School."

Even so, the virus would not die. One month before election day, AP reported, "Gore's exaggerations have placed him more centrally than warranted at the creation of . . . the Love Canal toxic-waste investigation."[66] So too did the *Washington Post*, whose indefensibly sloppy reporting started the entire mess. Yet eleven months after the incident took place and just three weeks before Election Day, the paper explained that Gore's "clumsy" statements "suggesting he discovered the Love Canal disaster" set up his campaign's credibility problem.[67]

All of these incidents combined to drive an election narrative that could not have proven more helpful to Bush and the Republicans, despite its distant relationship to any known facts. On NBC News's profoundly misnamed "Truth Squad Report," Lisa Myers observed of a presidential debate, "Though both candidates took liberties with the truth, Al Gore seems most on the defensive today, accused by Republicans of embellishing." Moderator Jim Lehrer asked Bush about his campaign's accusation that his opponent was "a serial" exaggerator and Gore about his campaign's charge that the Texas governor was a "bumbler." Bush stood by his campaign staff. Gore proved defensive about his, claiming he hadn't seen the commercial in question. This only made him seem more slippery to the audience, no doubt, which was too bad, since Lehrer's information was wrong. While the Bush campaign regularly accused Gore of prevaricating, the Gore commercial to which Lehrer referred did not exist.[68] The moderator eventually apologized, but the damage was done. Gore's credibility ratings began to decline on September 19 and dropped below 50 percent on October 12, never to recover. Before the avalanche of "credibility" stories started burying Gore's message, he held a ten-point lead over Bush in the polls.[69] This was, in the view of many in the media, as it should be. Reporting on ABC's *World News This Morning* on October 17, Gary Langer noted that following the debate, "The number of registered voters who think of Gore as honest and trustworthy is down from 63 percent to 49 percent." But, my oh my, Langer found "a more surprising result" as well. "Bush's credibility rating is down as well."[70] Well, never mind that. It didn't fit the story line and was never mentioned again.

By the time Election Day finally arrived on November 6, many pundits and reporters appeared shocked to discover that Al Gore was still alive. As Eric Boehlert reported, "Just days before a badly outspent Gore strung together hard-fought, and often come-from-behind, wins in tossup states like Minnesota, Iowa, New Mexico, Delaware, Pennsylvania, Washington, Michigan, Wisconsin, Maine and perhaps even Florida, Joe Klein of the *New Yorker* suggested, 'The wasting of Gore has been a stunning, and quite unexpected, phenomenon.'" (Appearing on MSNBC, Klein told host Brian Williams with a straight face that Gore's tendency to get "goofy" in public was a "serious" problem for the candidate.) *Newsweek*'s Howard Fineman professed to detect "Gore's growing frustration" in the candidate's "hoarse" voice. In *USA Today*, Walter Shapiro described the "limitations of Gore's natural charm and charisma" that led him to be "running scared" and "thinking small." James Warren of the *Chicago Tribune* wondered "if Vice President Al Gore secretly fears some Election Day avalanche."

The press planes continued the kind of coverage that had so distinguished them during the campaign's previous year. At the *New York Times*, for instance, Boehlert noted, "Katharine Seelye spent last week squeezing in her last mocking jibes. Describing Gore as 'grasping,' Seelye spun freely when she reported that the candidate 'made an appeal based on what he described as his hard work for the state—as if a debt were owed in return for his years of service.'" Meanwhile, over at Bush central, Alison Mitchell's *Times* coverage professed to find the governor surrounded by an "aura of confidence." Frank Bruni spoke of a candidate who saw himself grandly "as the country's best hope for bridging ideological divides, healing partisan wounds and making sure Americans could gaze upon the White House with unfettered respect."[71]

It is an unfortunate characteristic of journalists, who are called upon to gather so much information and make sense of it under sometimes crushing pressure of deadlines, that most are also loath to admit mistakes—even if it means compounding them forever. When Eric Boehlert sought to contact some of the journalists responsible for the flagrant perversions of Gore's words and misreporting of his actions, none mentioned any regrets. The *Washington Post*'s Ceci Connolly, he noted, screwed up Gore's Love Canal quote in her first article on the topic; she then used the twisted quote to mock Gore for lying about his record in a follow-up, adding two more malevolent misinterpretations in the same sentence: "The man who mistakenly claimed to have inspired the movie *Love Story* and to have invented the Internet says he didn't quite mean to say he discovered a toxic-waste site."[72] Among many other errors, she mis-stated Gore's draft status at the time of his enlistment in order to make it appear as if he had done so because he was going to be drafted. (Gore had not even received his lottery number at the time of his enlistment.)[73] Her coverage was so egregious that, together with Seelye, she was singled out by the conservative *Financial Times* in London as "hostile to the [Gore] campaign" and refusing to hide her "contempt for the candidate."[74]

How does Connolly explain her many mistakes, all of which redounded to the benefit of the Bush campaign? "We have an obligation to our readers to alert them [that] this [Gore's false boasting] continues to be something of a habit," she told the AP at the time of her original reporting.[75] Later on, she took refuge in the general defense, "I was very tough on Al Gore the same way I was tough on George W. Bush when I covered him briefly" during the campaign. Here is an example of her "toughness" on Bush during the few days with which she traveled with him. In a "letter from California," titled "Evoking Memories of Reagan, Bush Melds a Jaunty Manner with Talk of Compassion," Connolly wrote that Bush "evoked memories of another governor-turned-president: Ronald Reagan." With "just a bit of swagger for the party faithful," Bush proved a "cheerful patriot" with a "sunny disposition" who "jauntily plays to the cameras and crowds."[76] This is decided contrast to his opponent, the "boring" liar, "programmed to the point of seeming robotic," possibly possessing a "rarely seen human side."[77]

Bill Sammon, the *Washington Times* reporter who wrote the phony story about the Connecticut River trip and later authored an anti-Gore book for the conservative publisher, Regnery, defended his articles by arguing that they made "a point about Gore's political reflexes, [which are] to spin furiously and resort to deception."[78] Per usual, *Time*'s Margaret Carlson proved more honest than the rest. Speaking on the radio to Don Imus, she explained, "You can actually disprove some of what Bush is saying if you really get in the weeds and get out your calculator, or you look at his record in Texas. But it's really easy, and it's fun, to disprove Gore. As sport, and as our enterprise, Gore coming up with another whopper is greatly entertaining to us."[79]

So entertaining, actually, that they never let go of their mythic Al Gore. Years later, in late September 2002, members of the press corps found themselves offended that Al Gore would dare to speak out against President Bush's war plans with Iraq. Fox's Brit Hume began an account of Gore's speech with an apparent misportrayal of Gore's position on the 1991 war, excising from a Gore speech a key paragraph that allowed Hume to portray Gore as having flip-flopped. On the basis of this dishonest presentation, all of Hume's assembled guests enjoyed a laugh at "Gore the liar" who could not tell the truth no matter how hard he tried, by recycling these same discredited stories:

> BILL SAMMON: It's inexplicable. It's puzzling why he would flip-flop on something so easily checkable.
> MORTON KONDRACKE: He invented the Internet. He's got a bad memory.
> CHARLES KRAUTHAMMER: He's the guy who told us about prescription drugs, the mother-in-law and the dog.[80]

As Joe Klein would conclude of the media, around the time these comments were made, "The default position on Al Gore appears to be ridicule. He opens his mouth and is immediately assumed cynical, tactical, self-serving, self-pitying, awkward, embarrassing, unintentionally hilarious, or all of the above."[81] (That Klein himself had been guilty of coverage that reflected these same feelings during the 2000 election only strengthens the power of his observation.) Meanwhile this same media had apparently concluded during the 2000 election season, that George W. Bush, like "another George W.," could not tell a lie. Contrary evidence was deemed to be irrelevant. As Cokie Roberts helpfully explained, Bush deceptions were not part of "the story line. . . . In Bush's case, you know he's just misstating as opposed to it playing into a story line about him being a serial exaggerator."[82]

I happened to write a column about this very characteristic of the media coverage in October 2000, and hence, I don't think there can be any argument that knowledge was lacking in the media at the time about Bush's lack of honesty about his past and policies. After all, as I wrote back then, "I am no Bob Woodward." It did not take any superior investigative efforts on my part to learn what followed:

1) Bush is not honest about the policies he supports.

• Bush declared "I don't want to use food as a diplomatic weapon from this point forward. We shouldn't be using food. It hurts the farmers. It's not the right thing to do." This despite the fact that he does support using this exact diplomatic weapon against Cuba.

- Bush promised "to have prescription drugs as an integral part of Medicare," when, in fact, this is true of the Gore Medicare plan, but not of the Bush plan.

- Bush explained, "I hope our European friends become the peacekeepers in Bosnia and in the Balkans. I hope that they put the troops on the ground, so that we can withdraw our troops and focus our military on fighting and winning war," ignoring the fact that 85 percent of peacekeeping troops in Kosovo are already European.

2) George Bush is not honest about his record as governor of Texas.

- Bush took credit during the debates for a Texas HMO patients' bill of rights that he vetoed in 1995 and that became law in 1997 without his signature after he opposed it again.

- Bush took credit in the same debate for a hate crimes bill that, as governor, he opposed.

- Bush overstated health care spending for the poor in Texas, by insisting it was $4.7 billion, failing to note that a full $3.5 billion of this amount derived not from his government but from charity care and local institutions.

3) George Bush is not honest about his past.

- As a director of Harken Energy Corporation, Bush failed to comply with SEC regulations regarding the legal deadlines for revealing his purchasing and selling of the company's stock. As a result, Bush was profitably able to conceal the fact that he was buying and selling hundreds of thousands of shares of stock.

- Bush as president also appears to have misled the SEC when he insisted that he had dumped his failing company's stock in 1990 without any knowledge that the stock was about to tank. In fact, he had been warned of the trouble at least twice and was on Harken's internal audit committee.

- While Bush claims publicly to "do everything I can to defend the power of private property and private property rights," he and his partners in the Texas Rangers arranged for Texas authorities to expropriate private land to allow the investors to build their new baseball stadium. When some owners resisted, or balked at the low prices being offered, their land was condemned and expropriated by force of law. This occurred on 270 acres of land, even though only about seventeen acres were needed for the ballpark. The rest was used by Bush and Co. for commercial development and has provided the basis of Bush's personal fortune.

4) Bush cannot be trusted to tell the truth about service in the Texas Air National Guard, either.

• As the *Boston Globe* has reported, in his autobiography, *A Charge to Keep*, Bush said he flew with his unit for "several years" after finishing flight training in June 1970. His campaign biography states that he flew with the unit until he won release from the service in September 1973, nine months early, for graduate school. But both claims are false. Bush flew with the 111th for 22 months, until April 1972, and never flew again. Bush and his campaign have said that he performed "alternative" duty at the 187th Tactical Reconnaissance Squadron in Montgomery from May to November 1972, while he was working on a Senate race in Alabama. But, the *Globe* notes, Bush's own records contradict that assertion. In May 1972, Bush sought a permanent transfer to a postal unit in Alabama that didn't require weekend drills or active duty. Guard headquarters overruled that decision. Bush did not do any drills from May through September 1972. In September 1972, Bush won approval to do temporary "alternative" training at the 187th Squadron in Montgomery. He was cleared to attend weekend drills in October and November. But two of the 187th's officers said Bush never appeared. One of them, retired Brigadeer General William Turnipseed, says he is "dead-certain he didn't show up." Bush, who refuses all interviews on the subject, says he was there, but can't remember anything he did. His campaign can find no records to corroborate this.[83]

At the time I wrote this, I was, like everyone else, unaware of Bush's secret DUI arrest, and of the contention by *Dallas Morning News* reporter Wayne Slater that he had asked Bush point-blank whether or not he'd ever been arrested since 1968, and Bush had told him no. This twenty-four-year-old story was the one that the media did decide to focus on, and typically, it is the one with the least degree of substance or relevance to his qualifications to be president.

When the Harken story finally became news, in the summer of 2001, it must have come as quite a shock to most Americans, who had heard next to nothing about these same actions back when they had the opportunity to pick their next president. As the scrupulously nonpartisan but enormously press-savvy authors of ABC News's *The*

*Note* wrote, during the middle of the crisis of confidence in Bush's leadership during the 2002 market crisis,

> Of course, one of the many, many inequities in the press treatment that Bush got compared to Gore in 2000 involved the searing level of scrutiny that Gore got for personal and professional items and actions on which Bush went untouched. We aren't proposing that anyone go back now and figure out why there doesn't seem to be much of a record that the president actually served his time in Alabama during his National Guard days, but isn't it amazing that the story could change from 'the SEC ate my homework' to 'my lawyers ate my homework' so blithely, during a holiday week, after being elected?[84]

As of late 2002, Bush had still managed to skirt these questions before a remarkably uncurious press corps. Of course, as Erich Segal might put it in a sequel to *Love Story* about reporters smitten by George W: "Campaign love means never having to say you're sorry."

# 11

## Florida

THE MEDIA IMPOSE A NARRATIVE STRUCTURE on Election Day even nar-
rower than that for the campaign. It can be summed up in a single sentence: "The
system works." The winner wins, the loser loses, the new guy gets a sudden shot of
"gravitas" while the also-ran is invited to pose for American Express commercials if
he's lucky, erectile dysfunction pills if he's not. The newscaster has not yet been born
who hasn't felt compelled to marvel aloud at the fact that America has a presidential
election every four years without the presence of tanks in the streets. The media have
no back-up plan in the case of elective dysfunction. The systems "works" whether it
works or not.

The conclusion to the election of 2000 presented the media with a set of inassim-
ilable challenges to its narrative, however; and these turned out to be challenges they
were unprepared to meet. The Bush team understood its task in a way the Gore team
never did. It was able to construct a coherent story and—just as important—stick to
it, in a fashion that appealed to reporters' need for narrative simplicity and coherence.
This resulted in coverage of the election calamity that was heavily biased on behalf of
the presumed winner, now-President George W. Bush, and a significant slighting—if
not outright denial—of the many pieces of the puzzle that could not somehow be
forced into the story of the triumph, once again, of American democracy.

In the days before the election, the Bush team and a few sympathetic pundits
began to worry that Gore might actually outpoll Bush in the Electoral College, while
losing the popular vote. In a *New York Daily News* article entitled, "Bush Set to Fight
An Electoral College Loss," Bush operatives explained, "The one thing we don't do is
roll over. We fight." In league with the campaign—which was already preparing talking points about the Electoral College's essential unfairness—a massive talk-radio
operation would be encouraged. "We'd have ads, too," said a Bush aide, "and I think
you can count on the media to fuel the thing big-time. Even papers that supported
Gore might turn against him because the will of the people will have been thwarted."
Local business leaders would be urged to lobby their customers, the Bush aide

explained; members of the clergy would be asked to speak up for the "popular will," and pro-Bush Democrats would be urged "to scream as loud as they can. You think 'Democrats for Democracy' would be a catchy term for them?" asked a Bush adviser. CNN commentator Jeff Greenfield reported that conservative pundits were already being briefed "shortly before taking to the airwaves about the line of attack to be taken in the event that Bush wound up losing the electoral count despite a popular vote lead. The denials of Bush adviser Karl Rove notwithstanding, friend of the campaign Ken Duberstein admitted, "It was part of the talking points."[1] (Gore officials, the same article noted, were making no such plans.)[2] Chris Matthews, too, worried of Gore that, "knowing him as we do, [Gore] may have no problem taking the presidential oath after losing the popular vote to George W. Bush."[3]

Of course Gore won the popular vote by about 537,000 votes, a slim margin to be sure, but far larger than that enjoyed by either John Kennedy in 1960 or Richard Nixon in 1968. That was the end of any talk of the relevance of the popular vote to the presidency. Gore also won, without a doubt, a plurality of the intended votes of Floridians on Election Day. Yet he did not manage to win the election. Per usual, a significant proportion of the fault for this lies with the Gore campaign itself, which, like the Palestinians, "never missed an opportunity to miss an opportunity." But also as we've seen, the Bush campaign pretty much had the press in its pocket. From Fox's inviting Bush's cousin to falsely call the election to NBC bigfoot Tim Russert terming him to be "president elect" long before any such judgment was defensible on the basis of the evidence, Bush enjoyed a degree of deference from the national media that was matched only by the contempt accorded his hapless opponent.

---

Any sensible analysis of the battle over Florida must take into consideration two essential points: First, the actual vote was a statistical tie, well within the built-in margin of error of any system of immediate measurement. Second, the Republicans were always going to find a way to win, by whatever means turned out to be necessary.

The people who sell the voting systems that tallied 3.45 million votes in the contested state tout their counting machines as 99.99 percent accurate under ideal conditions. But in Florida, that tiny error rate alone could have misread 345 votes, which, for long periods, was more than George Bush's allegedly winning margin.[4] A 330-vote margin out of six million Florida votes cast is approximately equivalent to a one-vote margin in a city with 40,000 people and 18,000 voters. And in Florida, 2000, we were a long way from any sane person's idea of "ideal conditions."

All of this is true even though more Floridians, unquestionably, went to the polls intending to vote for Al Gore on Election Day than for George Bush. Almost certainly, more legal votes were actually cast for Al Gore than for Bush, although many of these were successfully disqualified by Republican officials. Before Election Day, Secretary of State Katherine Harris had hired a GOP-connected database company to purge the state's voter rolls of thousands of mostly minority citizens, many of whom the company falsely categorized as felons. In Seminole and Martin Counties, Republican election officials allowed Republican operatives to doctor absentee-ballot applications, while Democrats were not granted the same right. According to journalist John Lantiqua, "In all, some 200,000 Floridians were either not permitted to vote in the November 7 election on questionable or possibly illegal grounds, or saw their ballots discarded and not counted. A large and disproportionate number were black."[5] At the end of August 2002, the state of Florida agreed to settle a voter discrimination lawsuit with the NAACP, instead of facing the prospect of attempting to prove that Bush had been allowed to get his vote totals fair and square. Miami-Dade, Broward, Leon, Volusia, and Duval counties settled earlier rather than face trial.[6]

The Gore team was outmatched by virtually every measure. According to records the Bush campaign reluctantly and belatedly submitted to the Internal Revenue Service, the Republicans poured $13.8 million into winning the battle, which was about four times what the Gore campaign spent. (And this was only its "official" count.) Meanwhile, in Washington, Republicans on the House Armed Services Committee helped the Bush campaign obtain private contact information for military voters, violating the tradition of impartiality of the military and directly involving Congress in a partisan hunt for pro-Bush votes.[7] Neither side could honestly be said to demand an honest count; rather both merely tried to find a method that would put their man on top. In this regard, the Gore campaign demonstrated both its amorality and incompetence, while the Bush campaign demonstrated only the former.

The ultimate outcome in Florida was never in doubt. The Republicans were always going to win it, somehow. They wanted it worse and they had the means to make their desires into reality. Republicans controlled the Florida governorship; the office of secretary of state, which ruled in its favor on every single occasion offered; the legislature, which was preparing to hand the election to Bush no matter how the vote count eventually turned out. The party also controlled the U.S. Congress, should it come to that, and, as we all now know, the U.S. Supreme Court. The only important significant institution the Republicans could not control, the Florida Supreme Court, was proven irrelevant by the ones they did. Al Gore would have had to be an extraordinarily audacious popular leader and a tactically brilliant politician to challenge this near iron-lock on the process. Suffice to say, Al Gore was neither. Even so, an alert, fair-minded media could at least have helped even up the sides in Florida, forcing the winners (and losers) to do in daylight what they accomplished in the cover of darkness. They could have defended the institutions of democracy against those who sought to undermine them in pursuit of victory. They could have, in other words, demanded at least a modicum of accountability on behalf of the nation whose rulers were being chosen. Alas, if they had been capable of, or even interested in, achieving such lofty aims as these, this book would hardly be necessary.

When Fox News hired John Ellis to work on its election desk, they could not know that he intended to be in constant contact with his cousins, Jeb and George W. Bush, on Election Night. Nor could they know that he would likely brag to Jane Mayer of the *New Yorker*, "It was just the three of us guys handing the phone back and forth— me with the numbers, one of them a governor, the other the president-elect. Now that was cool."[8] But it taxes one's imagination to believe that the so-called "fairand-balanced" folks at Fox were unaware of Ellis's loyalties. His mother is George H. W. Bush's sister—Ellis had, in fact, honorably resigned as a *Boston Globe* columnist because, he wrote, "I am loyal to my cousin" and "I put that loyalty ahead of my loyalty to anyone else."[9]

Under Ellis's guidance, Fox called both Florida and the election for Bush at 2:16 A.M. Anchors of NBC, CBS, CNN, and ABC each followed within four minutes. As Tom Rosenstiel, director of the Project for Excellence in Journalism, noted at the time, Fox's call precipitated all the other networks' calls. "That call—wrong, unnecessary, misguided, foolish—has helped to create a sense that this election went to Bush, was pulled back and he is waiting to be restored."[10]

Meanwhile, on every network, multimillion-dollar anchors lurched from mistake to mistake, managing in most cases to get it wrong three times in one night. At CBS, Dan Rather set a Texan-sized standard of goofiness by offering "a big tip and a hip, hip, hurrah and a great big Texas howdy to the new president of the United States" and instructed viewers to "Sip it. Savor it. Cup it. Photostat it. Underline it in red. Press it in a book. Put it in an album. Hang it on the wall."[11] The other networks also gave the election to Bush, as did the Web sites of the *New York Times*, the *St. Louis Post-Dispatch*, and the *Washington Post*. If you went to bed at ten in the evening, you were pretty sure Gore won the election. If you stayed awake until 2:30 (as I did), then Bush was the victor. By the morning, the only winner was chaos.

When the Bush family consigliore, James Baker, arrived in Florida at the behest of Dick Cheney three days after the election, the alleged difference between the two candidates had fallen from 1,784 votes to just 327.[12] Any number of mishaps—including the elderly Jewish vote in Palm Beach going to Buchanan—were necessary for Bush even to make it close. The exit polls for Florida had essentially been correct. Gore had clearly won the intent of Florida voters, and if that state's election laws had been disinterestedly enforced, he would have won its electoral votes as well.

The Republican strategy never wavered: "No manual recounts, period. The election was over and Bush won. End of Discussion. Let the transition commence." The Gore team's message, as usual, changed every day. "Let's count this county, no that county, no this one; manual recount here, but not there." Gore never went for the obvious opportunity to demand a complete manual recount of all Florida's votes. He did say he would agree to one in the impossibly unlikely event that the Bush team requested it, but, like Bush, he preferred those recounts he expected to win. In doing so, he blew the opportunity to capture the nation's imagination with the only solution that might have won him the day.

Despite its simple message, the Bush team's task was a great deal more complicated than it appeared. The law was almost entirely on the side of Gore and the recounts. Florida not only explicitly permitted manual recounts, they had been used frequently for a variety of elections, including the one that preceded the current term of its Republican senator, Connie Mack. Indeed, a majority of states either mandated or permitted manual recounting when the difference between two candidates was small enough. By coincidence, one of these states, Texas, had a governor named Governor George W. Bush who only recently had put his signature on the bill. The Texas standard was exactly the same "intent of the voter" standard under use in Florida.[13] It was this standard that the Bush team needed to prevent were it to have any hope of winning the vote.

So Jim Baker had a problem. He needed to control the media's narrative in Florida in such a way that the laws on the books and virtually every legal precedent would be ignored and the incomplete vote certified, while, in the process, his candidate's presidency could be legitimized. There was another option open to Bush, winning the hard way—by political fiat in the Florida legislature, the U.S. Congress, or the U.S. Supreme Court—but such a naked political ploy might damage the legitimacy of a Bush Restoration beyond repair.

Baker addressed this problem by remaining on the attack and sticking like glue to his disciplined message. "The American people voted on November 7. Governor George W. Bush won thirty-one states with a total of 271 electoral votes. The vote here in Florida was very close, but when it was counted, Governor Bush was the winner. Now, three days later, the vote in Florida has been recounted. Governor Bush is still the winner." With no recounts yet under way, the Gore team was already guilty, according to Baker, of "efforts to keep recounting, over and over, until it happens to like the result." The vice president wished to "unduly prolong the country's national presidential election," with its "endless challenges," and "unending legal wrangling."[14] Perhaps most impressive, as Win McCormick argued in the *Nation*, Baker managed to maintain this narrative in the media, while the Bush campaign nakedly contradicted it with its actions. For instance, a day after Baker complained of his opponents' "endless challenges" and "unending legal wrangling," the Bush campaign filed the first lawsuit over the election—designed to block any manual recounts, the opening salvo in the very "legal wrangling" to which Baker alluded. The *Washington Post's* headline on the story read, "Both Sides Increase Legal Wrangling As Florida Begins Slow Hand Recount." But even with 1,636 words at their disposal, David S. Broder and Peter Slevin never were able to pinpoint any legal action instigated by the Gore campaign.[15]

The ability of the Republicans to ensure a media echo of its essential story line was, in retrospect, intensely impressive. When, for instance, the governor of Montana, a Bush surrogate, went on *Meet the Press* to assert, without proof, that during the hand recounts, "Ballots have been used as fans" and "have Post-it notes stuck on them," Sam Donaldson reported as fact, on ABC's *This Week,* that "ballots were used as fans" and had "Post-it notes stuck over presidential spots." Much as they had when Gore tried to make his points in the presidential debates, the folks at ABC's *This Week* thought Gore's efforts to ensure a full count of the ballots to be the stuff of slapstick comedy. Cokie Roberts guffawed at the notion of "It is so much going on with the chads and holding them up to the light and all that stuff that it's becoming a laughingstock." Donaldson returned her volley with the quip, "Ask not what your chad can do for you, ask what your chad can do for your country." When ABC's Jackie Judd was asked to explain the vote-counting process, she averred that doing so would be over her head. "Do you have an hour?" she responded. "It's pretty complicated."[16]

Baker and the Republicans had any number of weapons in their arsenal, from the governor's office on down. Just as useful, but little remarked upon, was the Republican army of activists willing, on the spur of the moment, to create what *Wall Street Journal* columnist Paul Gigot admiringly termed a "bourgeois riot" whenever necessary.[17] As IRS documents would later show, these rioters were flown in from out of state on private jets lent to the Bush campaign by supportive corporations, like Enron and Halliburton, put up gratis in local hotels, and entertained by Wayne Newton singing *Danke Schoen,* all courtesy of the Republican Party. Many were specifically recruited by House majority whip Tom DeLay and given directions from a communications-equipped Winnebago by party operatives keeping abreast of where their services might be best deployed.

The volunteers' value as rioters was best demonstrated when, on November 22, a Miami-Dade canvassing board attempted to undertake the hand-recounts the courts had ordered. With just a few phone calls, the Republican street operation produced hundreds of "volunteers" who, according to *Time,* created a mob scene . . . screaming . . . pounding on doors and . . . [threatening an] alleged physical assault on Democrats," "The Republicans marched on the counting room en masse, chanting 'Three Blind Mice,' and 'Fraud, Fraud, Fraud' . . . let it be known that 1,000 local Cuban-American Republicans—a group to whom violence as an instrument of political intimidation is not exactly unknown—were on the way." The mob chased down the chairman of the local Democratic Party because it falsely believed he had tried to steal a ballot. He required a police escort to escape. Another Democratic aide said he was punched and kicked by the Republican goons. Still others were trampled to the floor as the mob tried to break down the doors of the room outside the office of the Miami-Dade supervisor of elections where the votes were being counted.[18]

Few "riots," bourgeois or otherwise, have been as well coordinated as this one. In any case it had its intended effect. Longtime GOP operative Roger Stone oversaw phone banks urging Republicans to storm downtown Miami. The city's most influential Spanish-language radio station, Radio Mambi, called on the hard-right Cuban-American community to head downtown to demonstrate. As *Time* noted, "just two hours after a near riot outside the counting room, the Miami-Dade canvassing board voted to shut down the count."[19] No legal charges were ever filed, either against the rioters or their Republican paymasters. (The payments were documented in the hundreds of pages of Bush committee records released to the Internal Revenue Service after a lengthy period of resistance and refusal, in July 2002.)[20] As author Jeffrey Toobin demonstrated in a lengthy investigation of what took place, while some of the board members may have wished to deny it, "the only reasonable conclusion, then, appears to be that the board members stopped counting out of fear—for their personal safety and their political future."[21] The board could easily have hand-counted 10,750 ballots in five days had they been able to do so unmolested. Eight judges set aside just twelve hours to do it after the Florida Supreme Court finally instructed them to do so. But when they finally resumed, it was without enough time to complete their work and still meet the deadline. Florida Secretary of State Katherine Harris ultimately rejected these results, and thereby handed the rioters—and George W. Bush—his victory.

In public, the Bush camp maintained the fiction of the alleged independence of these operations. "If citizens of the United States are voluntarily objecting to the process where the rules change, and where Democratic officials take these ballots behind closed doors where they can't be observers," the Bush camp's lawyer, now solicitor general, Ted Olson, said of the court-ordered recounts, "I think American citizens are entitled to do that sort of thing."[22] But even as the Republicans endorsed the riots, they managed to blame them on the Democrats, convincing even some liberal journalists to join in the phony blame game. Gigot celebrated the rioters for acting like "Democrats." Noemie Emery in the *Weekly Standard* blamed Al Gore's "provocation," consisting of "an invasion of lawyers . . . the theater of mobs and protests, the frenzied attacks on public officials, the purposeful suppression of the votes of servicemen, the playing of the race card, and the whipping up of hatred against [Gore's] opponents."[23]

A more impressive artifact of Orwellian doublespeak would be difficult to imagine. Alas, more were produced, even by liberals. Al Hunt demanded of Al Gore that he "give the hook to Jesse Jackson, with his phony claims of African-American disenfranchisement."[24] The claims were far from phony, as later reporting would clearly demonstrate, but ever-sensitive to the opinions of the punditocracy, Gore soon called Jackson and asked him to leave the state.[25] Of course Gore's good manners did him no good with his intended audience. With truly impressive audacity for a newspaper whose members celebrated the Republican riot, *Wall Street Journal* editors advised, "If Mr. Gore wants to assure an honest count, he should discourage these voters from a public protest at this time." Michael Kelly, who appears to disapprove of physical labor in principle, complained in the *Washington Post*, "Thanks for whoever's bright idea it was to ship union goons into Palm Beach County; tense times are always made better by the presence of large, muscular men bellowing, "No recount, no peace!"[26]

At first, a group of pundits played "good cop" with Al Gore, hoping to convince him to drop out by appealing to his better nature. Mike Barnicle, now of the New York *Daily News,* argued that Gore should do the right thing and give up. "This could be Al Gore's moment." The *Wall Street Journal* editors tried this route: "In the debates, Vice President Gore spoke of his as a life dedicated to the highest ideals of public service. He may get his chance to prove it." Of course, he had to give up to do so. Meanwhile, NBC's Tim Russert declared that Gore "can't extend it too long, nor can he become a whiner about Florida."[27]

Long before the Supreme Court ended the election, the media were already positing a Bush presidency. On December 3 and December 10, the panelists on ABC's *This Week* made at least twenty-seven references to Bush's future presidency. Tim Russert did so nineteen times, going so far as to refer to Dick Cheney as "vice president."[28] Russert asked Cheney if he thought Gore was being a "sore loser" on December 3, nine days before the court's decision. That same week, on ABC, Sam Donaldson tried to elicit a concession from Joe Lieberman. Cokie Roberts tried to get one from campaign representative George Mitchell. As Kathleen Hall Jamieson and Paul Waldman demonstrate in their study, *The Press Effect*, "In the five Sunday shows aired by the three networks, the word 'concede' appeared in twenty-three questions." In twenty of them, the hypothetical conceder was Al Gore. In the others it was, well, no one.[29]

One of the most frequently made arguments for a Gore concession—made first by Bush and Baker but repeated by partisans in the media—drew an analogy to the election of 1960. Richard Reeves, biographer of both Richard Nixon and John F. Kennedy, wrote an op-ed in the *New York Times* that told the story of Nixon's alleged unwillingness to contest the close election for the good of the nation. William Bennett, William Safire, R. W. Apple, and many others made the same suggestion, using the same analogy.[30] In a display of shocking naivete for a battle-hardened veteran, Apple even quoted Nixon's own memoirs on the topic, as if the famed unindicted co-conspirator could be trusted to tell the truth about his own actions, much less his motives.[31] But as Salon's Gerald Posner and Slate's David Greenberg instructed the pundits, Nixon and his Republican allies actually mounted a massive vote challenge. Posner explained:

> Not only did Republican senators like Thurston Morton ask for recounts in 11 states just three days after the election, but Nixon aides Bob Finch and Len Hall personally did field checks of votes in almost a dozen states. The Republicans obtained recounts, involved U.S. Attorneys and the FBI, and even impaneled grand juries in their quest to get a different election result. A slew of lawsuits were filed by Republicans, and unsuccessful appeals to state election commissions routinely followed. However, all their efforts failed to uncover any significant wrongdoing.[32]

Another oddity of the media coverage of Florida was its constant warnings about the consequences of testing the patience of a nation alleged to be on the verge of a national nervous breakdown. The Baker/Bush team worked hard to create this crisis atmosphere in the hopes of increasing the pressure on Gore to relent for the good of the country, the markets, and the maintenance of world peace. Constitutional rule in America was frequently claimed to be in peril by one or another pundit or reporter, the longer the count continued. *Newsweek* ran a cover with a rip in the Constitution and the word "CHAOS" emblazoned on it. *U.S. News & World Report* ran the same cover without the rip.[33] Tim Russert warned, "We could have chaos and a constitutional crisis."[34] Tom Brokaw followed up on *Today* warning, "If the Florida recount drags on, the national markets are at risk here. National security is involved."

"Another week and no more," R. W. Apple warned Gore on the front page of the *New York Times* just two days after the election (and more than a month before the case was finally settled). "By next weekend," he announced, "a group of scholars and senior politicians interviewed this weekend agreed the presidential race of 2000 must be resolved, without recourse to the courts."[35] ABC's *This Week* warned of "turmoil" as CBS's *Face the Nation* feared a political process "spinning out of control." Always, the danger was blamed on Gore, who was said by the hosts of both *This Week* and NBC's *Meet the Press* to be willing to do anything to win.[36]

David Broder compared the period unfavorably with that immediately after the assassination of President Kennedy. The pundits seemed to believe, as ABC's Cokie Roberts explained, that we were living though "the most partisan time that we have seen in our lives." She professed to be privy to polls "showing that the longer it goes on, the less people have confidence in the accuracy of the count." In fact, every single poll taken at the moment of Roberts's November 19 comments demonstrated that strong majorities of voters preferred an "accurate" count to a "quick" one.[37] The pub-

lic also favored, by these same outsized majorities, manual recounts of disputed counties. As late as November 19, just 10 percent agreed with the assessment that the
United States faced a "Constitutional crisis."[38] Even on the day after the Supreme
Court decision that ended the recount, the *Washington Post* continued to report, "The
latest polls taken before the decision . . . showed continued strong public support for
counting Florida ballots as fully and accurately as possible."[39]

In one of the most significant events of the recount, the media joined in a
Republican effort to force the Gore campaign to count the ballots of military voters
who by law should have been excluded. The Republican accusations were led by
Mark Racicot and Norman Schwarzkopf, the latter complaining, "It is a very sad day
in our country when the men and women of the armed forces are serving abroad and
facing danger on a daily basis . . . yet because of some technicality out of their control, they are denied the right to vote for president of the United States who will be
their commander in chief."[40] Another word for "technicality" might be "law," but this
did not appear to interest anyone in the media. Peter Jennings reported on ABC that
the Democrats were being "banged around on the ground, at least anecdotally, for
interfering as best they can with the absentee ballots from the military and trying to
knock them out." The ever-dependable Ms. Roberts complained of Democrats
"seeming to be trying to take votes away from our men and women in uniform, who
are serving the country in danger's way overseas." In fact the Republicans had with-
drawn their suit of the issue, likely because they knew that votes postmarked after the
deadline or without postmarks at all were clearly ruled out of order by Florida election law. The *New York Times* reported that the Bush lawyers had failed to present
"any evidence" for legal arguments to allow the ballots before Judge L. Ralph Smith
of the Leon County Circuit Court.[41] What's more, a later extensive post-election
investigation by the *Times* found considerable circumstantial evidence for monkey
business on these and other overseas ballots by the Republicans.[42] But the echo chamber they created was so strong that Democratic vice-presidential candidate Joe
Lieberman felt compelled to concede the issue under pressure, like that described
above, from the media. Since the number of ballots in question was 680, and Bush's
alleged margin of victory turned out to be just 537, this concession alone could con-
ceivably have cost Gore his victory.[43] Entirely appropriately, Lieberman's forfeit of this
key argument in Gore's favor was made directly to Tim Russert on *Meet the Press*.

In addition to a loser who concedes, Christopher Hanson pointed out, "The
media's System Works narrative requires an official winner, and this is where Florida's
ballot 'certification' ceremony came in handy." When, on November 26, Katherine
Harris, Florida state co-chair of the Bush campaign, working in conjunction with
members of Governor Jeb Bush's staff and kitchen cabinet, decided to go ahead and
certify the state for Bush in her capacity as secretary of state—before the certification
was thrown out by the Florida Supreme Court—the media might have covered this

story in any number of fashions. The ceremony might have pointed to the powerful forces in the state arrayed in Bush's camp. While the media did not yet know that Harris had opened up her office to a team of Republican consultants and strategists, they still might have highlighted Harris's many bizarre decisions and announcements in conjunction with her undeniable partisanship.[44] Instead they played it straight, to the delight of the Bush campaign. The *New York Times* declared on page one, "George W. Bush stepped out tonight for the first time as president-elect."[45] Tim Russert said on MSNBC: "He has now been declared the official winner of the Florida election . . . and therefore is the forty-third president of the United States."[46] Dan Rather described Bush's "victory speech," in which he "outlin[ed] some of the things he intends to do after he is sworn in as president."[47]

The media happily swallowed almost everything the Bush forces threw at them. When it leaked potential cabinet choices, the media took the bait. A "working lunch" with advisers to discuss the future of the administration, an obvious spin-laden photo-op, was treated like the real thing. *Time* passed along the Bush flacks' depiction of their man as "the very picture of rugged ease, reading the new Joe DiMaggio biography, jogging daily, clearing cedar from a path where he and Laura like to ramble—much the way Ronald Reagan found peace chopping wood"[48] Not only did the system work, as CJR's Hanson smartly noted, it "works well enough to give us a new Morning in America."[49]

Treatment of the two campaigns' behavior also varied widely. When Gore's campaign manager, William M. Daley, said he believed that Gore "should be awarded a victory in Florida and be our next president"—something Baker was saying pretty much every day on Bush's behalf—the *Washington Post* reacted in horror. Its editorial page termed Daley's remark "a poisonous thing to say in these extraordinary and unsettling circumstances, and Mr. Gore makes a huge mistake if he fails to promptly disown it."[50] In this regard the *Post* echoed the furiously pro-Bush *Wall Street Journal*, whose editorial writers quoted Daley and thundered, "In your ordinary banana republic, this would be recognized as a Gore coup d'état."[51]

Oddly, Daley's boilerplate seemed to excite a great deal more antipathy than repeated comments by top Republicans that they would not abide by Florida's choice if it ultimately did not go their candidate's way, period. Robert Dole was one of the milder ones. He spoke only of boycotting a hypothetical Gore inauguration, but of course, he had no real power to assert in any case. Those who did were clearly ready to use it. House Majority Whip Tom DeLay circulated a memo to congressional Republicans laying the groundwork for Congress to reject Florida's electors if the state made the mistake of sending ones the Republicans didn't like. House Majority Leader Dick Armey told the Associated Press, "We in the House must be aware of one fact: In the end, when the final analysis is brought to the House, it is our duty to accept or reject that." Armey and DeLay also both endorsed proposed, and clearly unconstitutional, legislation that would require state officials to include retroactively all military absentee ballots as part of the final vote.[52]

The degree of fury directed at Al Gore by conservative and some not-so-conservative pundits for his attempts to contest Bush's coronation during this period was indeed something to behold. It had no analogy whatsoever on the liberal side, beyond the confines of a few, extremely marginal publications and Web sites. The bow-tied and bespectacled George F. Will seemed to be spoiling for the kind of fight that cannot be won by being the first person in the room to cite Edmund Burke. On November 12, he insisted, "all that remains to complete the squalor of Gore's attempted coup d'état is some improvisation by Janet Reno, whose last Florida intervention involved a lawless SWAT team seizing a 6-year-old."[53] Several days later he thundered, "Gore's attempted coup," his "slow-motion larceny," based on "manufactured votes," threatened a "stolen" election.[54]

Will was hardly alone. Gore's decision to fight for Florida "made the poisonous political atmosphere in Washington even more toxic," said Fox News's Tony Snow on November 12, 2000. At the *Weekly Standard*, the VP was a "jerk," who was "self-obsessed, conniving and dangerous"; "certainly divisive and ruthless, and wholly obsessed with achieving his ends"; and "compulsively mendacious."[55] The *Washington Post*'s Michael Kelly, who had been fired as editor of the *New Republic* over his inability to moderate his hysteria toward the Clinton/Gore team, complained of Gore's "revolting" campaign as filled with "hacks and political thugs."[56] Comparing Gore's attempt to get a fair count in Florida to an attack of napalm, he wrote, again in the *Washington Post*, "If he doesn't get his way he threatens to delegitimize democracy itself. Got to burn that village down."[57] "Even if Gore ultimately loses in Florida," Kelly wrote, grasping for inappropriate superlative after superlative, "with the help of reasonably sympathetic coverage from a largely Democratic and liberal national press corps, [Gore] has managed to spin his extraordinary, radical, unprecedented behavior as reasonable—and legitimate."[58]

William Bennett joined in the fun, complaining in the *Wall Street Journal* that, "The Gore campaign has begun to poison the wellspring of American democracy." Bennett worried about the "early consequences: street demonstrations, protests," but failed to notice that these were largely bought and paid for by the party to which he professed his fealty. Bennett, too, declared the process "illegitimate if Al Gore becomes president," and screamed on CNN's *Capital Gang*, "If you don't call the kind of thuggish tactics that the Gore campaign is doing right now for what they are, I think the notion of objectivity in the media is gone."[59] Again, such statements and sentiments became nearly boilerplate within the conservative punditocracy. When the Florida Supreme Court ruled to allow the recounts to continue, *Weekly Standard* editor William Kristol bellowed that should Gore gain "office through an act of judicial usurpation . . . we will not 'move on.' Indeed, some of us will work for the next four years to correct this affront to our constitutional order."[60]

As Thomas E. Mann, the moderate head of governmental studies at the Brookings Institution, observed at the time, the pundits' reaction to the election contest was not exactly unprecedented. Rather it recalled "the worst of the impeachment fervor, unbridled self-righteous defiance and venom, bordering on conservative McCarthyism with accusations of traitorous behavior."[61] To those pundits who did not view Gore as a figure of unbridled evil, he was at best one deserving of only mockery. The unpopular Gore did himself no favors by constantly phoning pundits and bigfoot reporters during this period to plead his case, so strong was their personal distaste for the hapless candidate. As Jeffrey Toobin noted, on CBS's *60 Minutes* on December 3, Leslie Stahl all but baited the vice president, lecturing him, "You're not really reaching the public with this argument. . . . You've been making it over and over: 'Every vote has to be counted.' There is more of a sense that you're asking, you know, to change the rules of the game." When Gore tried to reply that the public was demonstrating "a remarkable amount of patience and determination to see that all the votes are counted . . . ," Stahl cut him off. "But it's slipping," she informed him, citing no evidence. "It's slipping."[62]

Nowhere could Gore catch a break. When the VP decided to leave his house and go for a walk with his family, this was considered the height of lunacy by some in the punditocracy. Maureen Dowd wrote of "Sisyphus pushing his burden to Starbucks" and saw "the man has gone from being Powerful Second-in-Command of Prosperous, Happy Country to Obsessive Loon Whose Monomaniacal Quest Has Led Him to the Edge of Madness." Dowd could not help but admit in her missive to Gore, "We know you won. W. hasn't given it much thought. Jeb and Katherine know better than anyone that you won. Even Trent Lott, sashaying around W.'s ranch in that unforgettable plumed cowboy chapeau and jeans ensemble, knows you won." But she deemed this to be irrelevant. Why? Because Dowd, like virtually every one else on the planet it seemed, found Gore's manner annoying. "Why aren't people who think you deserve it more outraged to see you denied it?" she asked. "Because the more you insist you're a winner who somehow found a million different weird ways not to win, the more you seem like a loser."[63]

The groundwork explained above proved invaluable to the Bush camp in its attempt to establish its legitimacy when the U.S. Supreme Court finally handed it the election. A truly independent media, much less an allegedly liberal one, might have investigated some of the following questions in the context of the court's decision: Did it matter that Clarence Thomas was appointed by Bush's father and had a wife working with Bush's transition team? What of the fact that Antonin Scalia's sons worked in the same firm with Bush's lawyers? What of the comments made by Justice

Sandra O'Connor at a Washington dinner party on Election Day, complaining of the Gore team's tactics, and informing partygoers that Gore's then-perceived victory was "terrible" because, as her husband helpfully explained, she had hoped to retire from the court and did not want Al Gore appointing her successor.[64] Might any of these justices have considered recusing themselves, merely for the sake of propriety? Whatever happened to that beloved old journalistic standby, "the appearance of a conflict of interest"? In the case of these justices, appearances may or may not have been deceiving, but because the conservative team had only a one-vote majority, it was forced to ram through its selection of Bush, all appearances be damned.

When one considers the various logical limbs onto which the court's conservative majority had to crawl in order to hand the election to their man, the transparency of their desire to give the Republicans a victory—no matter what—becomes apparent. Consider the following: The conservative court ignored the lower federal courts, which had four times rejected similar stay requests from the Bush campaign on the grounds that the Bush team could not prove any irreparable harm to their man. And yet a Supreme Court that was so deeply committed to the ideology of states' rights that a former federal appeals court justice (and renowned legal scholar), John T. Noonan Jr., accused it of presenting a "danger to the exercise of democratic govern-ment," decides—just this one time—to overthrow a state court's election laws as interpreted by that state's highest judicial body.[65] The Supreme Court does so, more-over, on the basis of a novel legal theory—the notion that different counting stan-dards violate the equal protection and due process provisions of the federal Constitution, a theory that, if applied nationally, would bring into question virtually every state's counting methods. Finally, the court did not even try to hide its partisan agenda. It refused to allow the decision to serve as precedent and deliberately released it a bare two hours before Florida's "safe harbor" deadline of December 12, thereby making it impossible for the Gore team to contest. (It would take longer than two hours just to read the decision and its many dissents.)

Moreover, the court deliberately misinterpreted the meaning of the "safe harbor" clause—which is to allow, but not require—a self-protective action. (The Electoral Count Act of 1887 stipulates that states that send electors, chosen according to rules in place Election Day, cannot have those electors rejected by Congress, but it does not mandate that the states behave that way.) As a result, the majority could not cite any actual, germane Florida statutory law to support its contention that the counting must be ended immediately.[66] And it was forced to ignore the precedent of Hawaii in the election of 1960, when that state arranged for its Electoral College votes to be reversed following their mistaken certification, because an audited count discovered that Kennedy, not Nixon, had been its actual winner.[67] Writing bravely in the *Weekly Standard,* John DiIulio Jr., who would later briefly head up the Bush faith-based ini-tiative office, warned "the arguments that ended the battle and 'gave' Bush the presidency are constitutionally disingenuous at best. They will come back to haunt conservatives and confuse, if they do not cripple, the principled case for limited government, universal civic deference to legitimate, duly constituted state and local public authority."[68] He was absolutely alone among conservative pundits in admitting this.

While a smattering of mostly liberal print pundits did express outrage at the court's nakedly partisan performance, most media types pronounced themselves pleased with the script's ending. ABC's Cokie Roberts announced, positing no evidence, "People do think it's political, but they think that's OK. They expect the court to be political, and they wanted the election to be over."[69] Once again, Americans were instructed to be thankful: we once again managed to avoid the tanks. Former Supreme Court reporter Fred Barbash argued "legitimacy lives" because nobody tried violence, which was not entirely true.[70] Former *New York Times* executive editor Max Frankel described as "good" the demonstration that we can settle our political arguments in the courts, rather than the "streets."[71] The *Washington Post* editorial page added, "On a day when many Americans still were angry or depressed by the 37-day battle over the presidential election results, [Secretary of State-designate Colin] Powell usefully reminded us that the United States remains the center of, and inspiration for, a revolution for democracy in the world."[72]

Al Gore could have kept on fighting, but what was the point? "The spin of the morning news was 'It's over,' his campaign manager informed him."[73] The candidate who won a national majority and almost certainly a majority in Florida was being forced to concede the presidency on the basis of a Supreme Court decision handed down by conflicted justices that was so weak on grounds of logic and evidence that the court voided its validity as a precedent. The media's triumph was complete.

Following the court's announcement, a group of eight newspapers invested nearly a million dollars to hire the National Opinion Research Center at the University of Chicago to undertake a detailed study of the Florida vote, to discover, if possible, who really won. The Bush administration always opposed this action and treated the ultimate correctness of the court's intervention as all the legitimacy it needed. And, during the long period before the results of the count were announced, the news outlets that funded the study communicated a decided impression that they were not terribly eager to call the president's (and hence the system's) legitimacy into question either. September 11 made this impression unmistakable. A top *New York Times* correspondent, Richard Berke, admitted as much when, shortly after the attacks, he declared the outcome of the recount to be "utterly irrelevant" and worried that its release might "stoke partisan tensions."[74]

Berke was right to be concerned. Shortly before the September 11 attacks, a Gallup Organization poll found that nearly half of Americans surveyed remain convinced that President Bush either "won on a technicality" or "stole the election." They were right, though this would have been difficult to discern based on the coverage the eventual release of the recount report received. The headlines read: "Study of Disputed Florida Ballots Finds Justices Did Not Cast the Deciding Vote" (*New York Times*) and "Florida Recounts Would Have Favored Bush" (*Washington Post*). These were misleading at best. What the NORC researchers discovered was the Gore legal team's incredible incompetence. The lawyers happened, it turned out, to choose just about the only counting argument that would have lost Gore the election even had the court ruled in his favor. Lead member David Boies had explicitly ruled out a more inclusive recount of Florida's votes—one that not only would have elected his man, but would have been immeasurably more fair to the people of Florida. Instead Boies asked the court to count "undervotes" but not "overvotes." Using that method, Bush did indeed outpoll Gore and the court's intervention did not ultimately make a difference. It was, perhaps, a perfect coda to a perfectly awful campaign.

But buried beneath the misleading headlines was the inescapable fact that Al Gore was the genuine choice of a plurality of Florida's voters as well as of America's. As the AP report put it, "In the review of all the state's disputed ballots, Gore edged ahead under all six scenarios for counting all undervotes and overvotes statewide." In other words, he got more votes in Florida than George Bush by almost every conceivable counting standard. Gore won under a strict-counting scenario and he won under a loose-counting scenario. He won if you counted "hanging chads," and he won if you counted "dimpled chads." He won if you counted a dimpled chad only in the presence of another dimpled chad on the same ballot—the so-called "Palm Beach" standard. He even won if you counted only a fully punched chad. He won if you counted partially filled ovals on an optical scan and he won if you counted only fully filled ovals. He won if you fairly counted the absentee ballots. No matter how you counted it, if everyone who legally voted in Florida had had a chance to see their vote counted, Al Gore was our president.[75]

But by the time of the release of the report, the mainstream media had grown so protective of President Bush's legitimacy that many were willing to tar as crazy anyone who took the trouble to read the report carefully. To this reader anyway, they put one in mind of a husband who is doing everything he can to try to get his wife not only to forgive, but also to forget a past infidelity. The *Washington Post*'s Howard Kurtz reported, "The conspiracy theorists have been out in force, convinced that the media were covering up the Florida election results to protect President Bush. . . . That gets put to rest today." Kurtz scoffed as well at the notion that anyone still cared about whether Bush had stolen the presidential election. "Now," he wrote, "the question is: How many people still care about the election deadlock that last fall felt like the story of the century—and now faintly echoes like some distant Civil War battle?"[76] Following suit, the Associated Press even rewrote its own history. In September 2002, the news service carried a story from Florida that read: "Some unofficial ballot inspections paid for by consortiums of news agencies showed Bush winning by varying margins." But when the recounts were initially released in November 2001, the news service's editors had acknowledged, "A full, statewide recount of all undervotes and overvotes could have erased Bush's 537-vote victory and put Gore ahead by a tiny margin ranging from 42 to 171 votes, depending on how valid votes are defined."[77] Meanwhile CNN's Candy Crowley fell back on that old reliable, "Maybe the best thing of all is that messy feelings at the Florida ballot have only proved the strength of our democracy. . . ."

In fact, had the Supreme Court not intervened for Bush, it seems quite likely that Gore would have won the count despite his own side's incompetence. Leon County Circuit Judge Terry Lewis informed an *Orlando Sentinel* reporter that he had never fully made up his mind, but he was considering the "overvote" standard that would likely have given the count to Gore.[78] *Newsweek*'s Michael Isikoff also discovered a contemporaneous document by Lewis demonstrating exactly this intent.[79] Hence those newspapers that reported even the narrowest victory for Bush without a Supreme Court intervention may have been wrong. Once again, the so-called "liberal media" was spinning itself blind for the conservative Republican. But to point this out was to be termed a "conspiracy theorist" by the same "liberal media." Let's give the last word to the editors of the conservative London-based *Economist*, who, unlike their American counterparts, managed to read the results of recount with a clear eye, and hence, felt duty-bound to publish the following correction of its earlier coverage: "In the issues of December 16, 2000, to November 10, 2001, we may have given the impression that George W. Bush had been legally and duly elected president of the United States. We now understand that this may have been incorrect, and that the election result is still too close to call. The *Economist* apologizes for any inconvenience."[80]

# 12

## W's World

JOURNALISTS AND PRESIDENTS, especially Republican presidents, both prefer to portray the media under a mutually self-serving myth as an allegedly cynical, heartless, anti-authoritarian left-wing animal. The president and his people play along because the myth brings them as much sympathy from the largely inattentive public as it does from their fiercely ideological supporters. The idea of an indefatigable press, rumbling for trouble, also connects to the right's apparently universal wellsprings of self-pity and imagined persecution. The media enjoys the stereotype because it ennobles their self-image and disputes their own fears of being stenographers in the unstoppable spin machine. Of course, the stereotypes against which the myth is written are not always true of every reporter or every member of every administration. But those reporters who make careers of breaking through barriers of incessant spin and media to establish themselves as independent voices are few and far between. Journalists, like most people, go along to get along.

The result of this mutually reinforcing myth is that presidents are popular with the media and the public until proven otherwise. The campaign over, they are given a "clean slate" regardless of what happened on the campaign trail. As David Carr, former correspondent for Inside.com, now a *New York Times* media reporter, observed shortly after the Florida debacle, "In order to tee themselves up for the coming four years, reporters have to find a way to turn the nincompoop they bashed throughout the election into something resembling the leader of the free world. That's a bit of a lift with George W., who doesn't exactly send out statesman-like vibes." Carr went on to observe, however, that Bush had done himself a favor by choosing to vacation in Florida with his father and brother Gov. Jeb Bush immediately after the Supreme Court decision, thereby offering the media the opportunity to indulge in a plethora of Henry V allusions. "The rules of the press pool dictate that you are never close enough to engage in genuine dialogue with the target," Carr wryly noted, "so reporters can't ask impertinent questions like, 'Shouldn't you be back in Texas with your hospitalized daughter?' Or, 'Doesn't this seem like a good time to be catching up on Cliff Notes for World Peace?'"[1]

The Osric-like coverage goes beyond the widely acknowledged "honeymoon peri-od" and can last indefinitely—as it did under John Kennedy—or at least until it is in the interest of one side or the other to upset this cozy arrangement. (The Clinton presidency was the exception that proved the rule in this regard. His honeymoon occurred during the campaign.) Presidents and the media enjoy an informal agree-ment entitling every occupant of the Oval Office a certain amount of hero worship merely for being there.

The White House and the media need one another in order to be successful in their jobs. The White House depends on the media to make its case to the public; the media need the White House to fill their airtime and news columns. It is in neither side's interest to push the other too far. But the administration maintains a major advantage in the power calculus, particularly if it can maintain a united front, because it is sin-gular and the media are plural. This is where the Bush people truly excelled. As David Brooks complained of the Bush crew: "They don't leak. They don't gossip. They don't stab each other in the back. . . . It's a nightmare."[2] Unity allows administration spin-ners to divide and conquer. The top members of Clinton administration, for instance, treated leaks as a form of personal therapy, detailing every single screw-up and then some to almost any reporter who would listen. Josh Micah Marshall noted in the neoliberal *Washington Monthly*, "Even successful legislative battles like the 1993 budg-et reconciliation bill—the measure that set the stage for declining deficits and the groundwork for sustained growth—were drawn out with an almost masochistic relish and always left within a hair's breadth of failure. The Bush guys do none of this. As a result, they exude a kind of cocky confidence and competence regardless of whether it's authentic."[3] There's just no story there, beyond the boring policy stuff, which most reporters prefer to leave to wonks at the Brookings Institution.

Unlike Republicans, reporters just about never play as a team. The authors of ABC's *The Note* write, with considerable justice, "If we could change one thing about Washington journalism, we would ask White House reporters to not help out the press secretary, in contradiction to the public interest, by interrupting a colleague who is trying to elicit important information or establish a non-answer for the public record."[4] Moreover, the Bush team plays a kind of hardball that the Clintonians were never able to master. When *Houston Chronicle* reporter Bennett Roth asked press spokesman Ari Fleischer about underage drinking by the president's daughters, Fleischer informed him, Don Corleone-style, that his question had been "noted in the building."[5] The implication was clear to all: More such unfriendly questions and Roth would be cut off, unable to do his job, and useless to his employers. The out-cries of solidarity from Roth's colleagues in the press corps in the face of this public threat would not have disturbed the sleep of a napping newborn.

Clinton proved the exception to the rule, but in truth, much of what the media reports about the White House, any White House, is little more than spoonfed public relations pabulum. When NBC contracts to broadcast, more than a year into George W. Bush's first term, a special hour about an alleged day in the life of the "real" *West Wing*, Tom Brokaw must claim the broadcast will not be "an infomercial for the White House" to defend his own reputation and that of his network's news division. But of course it is. Otherwise, the profoundly image-conscious and message-disciplined Bush White House communications operation would not allow it to take place. Certainly no one at NBC News is sufficiently naïve to labor under the illusion that Karen Hughes and Karl Rove were about to leave their president's public image at the mercy of a bunch of journalists and network executives. Rather, the deal works as follows: NBC agrees to provide twelve camera crews along with an invaluable hour of prime-time air; the White House provides the "actors" playing idealized versions of themselves, going about their business in exactly the manner we all wish they would. Maybe the conditions of this deal are spelled out on paper somewhere; maybe not. It really doesn't matter. Like the actors playing wrestlers in a WWF grudge match, all the players understand the ground rules before anyone enters the "ring."

NBC has offered this same deal to all recent presidents, but few managed the opportunity as well as Rove and Hughes for Bush. For the January 2002 production, the White House came up with what the *New York Times* noted was "an unusually full schedule of public activities for Mr. Bush's day on camera." Instead of the usual single public event per day, NBC's "typical day" included: a meeting with labor leaders at Teamster headquarters; a bill-signing ceremony in the East Room; a photo-op with the president of Lithuania in the Oval Office; a 4-H award presentation in the Roosevelt Room, and finally, a cocktail party for Republican members of Congress in the White House residence. In addition, viewers saw the famously relaxed-about-work George W. Bush working out in the gym, stopping in on a meeting of his Council on Bioethics, and walking into the famed Situation Room for a top-secret national security briefing. White House spokesman Ari Fleischer insisted that the perspective offered to NBC viewers was "as real as it gets." This was clearly nonsense, as even Hughes admitted, since NBC's "typical" day contained "an education component" that was added at the last minute to round out the administration's domestic pitch. One cocktail party guest, New York Representative Peter King, later described the experience as similar to attending the Academy Awards.[6]

---

Like most lucky people, George W. Bush helped make his own luck, particularly with regard to charming the media. Consider the coverage of the brief China "crisis" of spring 2001: A U.S. spy plane collided with a Chinese fighter, killing its pilot. I dwell a bit on this now-forgotten incident to demonstrate that Bush, the unelected conservative Republican, received extremely indulgent coverage from the so-called "liberal media" long before September 11. In fact, Bush's behavior was often examined with little more critical distance than I employ when critiquing the art projects of my four-year-old daughter.[7]

Recall that the Chinese held twenty-four U.S. soldiers and demanded an apology. Even the hint of such an admission would have likely crippled the Clinton administration among punditocracy hawks, who dominate all discourse in times of perceived military threat. But the Bush administration managed to say "sorry" to the Commies and paid almost no political price whatever. Moreover it succeeded in manipulating the media to the point where its incompetence was portrayed as heroism, despite the amazingly thin gruel it offered up in support of this case. The *Washington Post*, for instance, presented readers with a twenty-six-paragraph, front-page analysis of Bush's talks, replete with inside anecdotes designed to make the president appear somehow simultaneously in charge and comfortable with delegation of details.[8]

Never mind that no *Post* reporters were present during the events they so breathlessly reported as fact. To question the official version of events handed out by the president's propaganda machine is apparently no longer part of the job description. As Josh Marshall pointed out of this incident, "Sadly enough, such articles are too often the result of an unspoken, almost Faustian arrangement. Official sources provide the essential inside details and reporters then regurgitate the official line, giving up their independence and skepticism for a quotation from the boss that he might or might not actually have said."[9]

Bush actually screwed up quite a few times during this crisis, but you'd be hard-pressed to learn this from the press coverage. For no apparent reason, and perhaps without even knowing what he was doing, the president appeared on ABC's *Good Morning America* to announce that the United States would do "whatever it took" to defend Taiwan if China attacked. This pledge, long desired by the Taiwanese, had been specifically avoided by every U.S. president since the beginning of the nation's "two-China" policy in 1979, owing to the concern that it might embolden Taiwan's rulers to start a war. Various administration spokespeople tried to pretend that U.S. policy remained unchanged, but nobody really knew for certain whether Bush was trying to change it or even if he understood it in the first place. But the Chinese surely noted it in *their* buildings. "This shows that the United States is drifting further down a dangerous road," averred Foreign Ministry spokeswoman Zhang Qiyue. "It will . . . harm peace and stability across the Taiwan Strait, and further damage U.S.-China relations."[10] Even so, Bush enjoyed oceans of SCLM slack. As an April 13 *Los Angeles Times* news analysis put it, "Bush Gets High Marks for Low-Key Approach."[11] Just about the only vocal criticism to be found in the media during this period came from the right. Writing in the *Weekly Standard*, for instance, Robert Kagan and William Kristol thundered about "the profound national humiliation that President Bush has brought upon the United States." With his hemming and hawing, they complained, "President Bush has revealed weakness. And he has revealed fear. . . . The American capitulation will also embolden others around the world who have watched this crisis carefully to see the new administration's mettle tested."[12] (To read these words in hindsight would be to see an implication that perhaps Mr. bin Laden was among those "emboldened" by the administration's "capitulation." And we can imagine that exactly such an accusation might have been leveled by these very authors—if it had been President Clinton "capitulating.")

In addition to papering over Bush's still-unexplained decision to shoot off his mouth, what was almost as odd in the incident with China was the White House spinmeisters' strategy for portraying George W. Bush as "deeply involved" in the solution of the crisis. The word was that while Bush let the diplomatic team do its own work, he stayed abreast of things by peppering his staff with questions. These were dutifully relayed by the media, and consisted of the following: "Do the members of the crew have Bibles? Why don't they have Bibles? Can we get them Bibles? Would they like Bibles?" He also inquired, "Are they getting any exercise?" The *Guardian*'s Jonathan Freedland wondered why in the world Bush's aides wished to "confirm the satirists' caricature of Bush as a 'know-nothing fundamentalist fitness freak.'"[13] But it worked.

That the elite media—much less the SCLM—chose to celebrate the performance of an unelected president who apparently lacked the intellectual curiosity to learn the finer points of his job may inspire a bit of cognitive dissonance on the part of those seeking to make sense of American politics, but there it is. And it would prove the rule, rather than the exception, of Bush's pre-September 11 presidency. Frank Bruni, whose issueless *New York Times* coverage of Bush's campaign had proven so indulgent that it inspired Bush to frequently tell Bruni that he "loved" him, continued the kind of reporting on Bush's presidency that would earn any politician's affection. On a trip to Mexico where Bush met with that nation's new president, Vincente Fox, Bruni professed to spy Bush's boots "peek[ing] out mischievously" from beneath his trousers. He did not elaborate as to what variety of mischief said boots might have in mind. On a later trip to Europe, Bruni seemed to find absolutely everything Bush said or did to be unspeakably fabulous. The reporter noted that upon meeting Tony Blair, Bush "broke into a smile, indulged a mischievous impulse and offered him a greeting less formal than the ones the British leader usually hears. 'Hello, Landslide!' Mr. Bush shouted out. It was a reference—an irreverent, towel-snapping one at that—to Mr. Blair's recent re-election, and it recalled the playful dynamic . . . when he cracked during a news conference that he and Mr. Blair liked the same brand of toothpaste."[14] It was odd to say the least. Past *New York Times* coverage of presidential missions abroad have not, by and large, celebrated "irreverent towel-snapping" comments to leaders of other nations. The "playful dynamic" of the toothpaste "crack" might just as easily have been termed a "doltish" or "obnoxious frat-boy" crack. And, since Tony Blair actually did win his job in a landslide, it's hard to see just what is so "irreverent" about pointing it out. (Now if the Prime Minister had greeted the unelected/court-appointed Bush as "Landslide," I might have laughed.)

Ari Fleischer could not have scripted the *Times* presidential coverage more generously. "Still pumped up," according to Bruni, Bush professed to detect "a willingness for countries to think differently and to listen to different points of view," though he offered no evidence. Finally, speaking of Bush's strange meeting with Vladimir Putin, Bruni still felt compelled to celebrate the apparently amazing fact that Bush refrained from drooling all over himself at a state dinner. "Rarely," Bruni wrote of Bush and Putin, "have the two nations' leaders so surpassed the limited expectations of their meeting." Nowhere, however, does the reporter bother to explain how rarely; whose expectations; how limited; limited by whom to what? (Beware, dear reader, of the passive voice.) Bush did indeed, after a fashion, surpass people's expectations on this trip when he claimed to be able to see into the soul of Russian President Vladimir Putin and find a friend, though one suspects that Bruni did not have the viewers of the Psychic Friends Network in mind when parceling out his praise. Perhaps it's a bit unfair to focus so closely on Bruni, as clearly this is the kind of coverage his editors deemed appropriate and the *Times* wanted. Indeed, why else assign to cover the presidency a man whose book-length pre-election examination of the man and his work informs readers of the exact number of seconds that George and Laura Bush danced at each of their nine Inaugural Balls but contains nary a word about what the president intended to do the next day when he finally sat down at his desk to get to work?[15]

The kid-gloves approach to Bush puzzled many, as the SCLM myth had grown into a monolith by the time of the Bush presidency. Early in the administration, *Washington Post* White House correspondent John Harris felt compelled to explain the apparent contradiction in the form of a kind of public mea culpa. "The truth is," he wrote, "this new president has done things with relative impunity that would have been huge uproars if they had occurred under Clinton. Take it from someone who made a living writing about those uproars." He made the following comparison:

Take the recent emergency landing of a U.S. surveillance plane in China. Imagine how conservatives would have reacted had Clinton insisted that detained military personnel were not actually hostages, and then cut a deal to get the people (but not the plane) home by offering two "very sorrys" to the Chinese, while also saying that he had not apologized. What is being hailed as Bush's shrewd diplomacy would have been savaged as "Slick Willie" contortions.

Try to recall this major news story during Clinton's first 100 days: Under pressure from Western senators, the president capitulated on a minor part of his 1993 budget deal, grazing fees on ranchers using federal lands. A barrage of coverage had an unmistakable subtext: Clinton was weak and excessively political and caved to special interests. Bush has made numerous similar concessions on items far more central to the agenda he campaigned on, such as deemphasizing vouchers in his education plan and conceding that his tax cut will be some $350 billion smaller than he proposed. For the most part these repositionings are being cast as shrewd rather than servile. Do you suppose there would have been an uproar under Clinton if Democrats had been rewarding donors with special closed-door briefings by Cabinet secretaries? The *New York Times* reported the other day that GOP donors received just such a briefing with Health and Human Services Secretary Tommy Thompson as thanks for their efforts. Far from an uproar, the story has had only a faint echo. Clinton's "donor maintenance" coffees led to a year of congressional inquiries.[16]

Harris could not note, because it had not yet happened, that while the Clinton fund-raisers were front-page/lead-the-news-every-night affairs for years, they were chicken feed compared to Bush's uncovered fund-raising efforts. Federal Election Commission records demonstrated that between January 2001 and mid-August 2002, for instance, despite a four-month moratorium he set following September 11, George W. Bush raised $100.03 million. Clinton, for all the outrage he generated, raised just $38.7 million during the same period of his first term.[17] That's more than two-and-a-half times as much money with a tiny fraction of the number of unflattering stories written. (Howard Kurtz termed Clinton officials' defenses of these efforts as attempts "to defend the indefensible.")

The media, as we have seen, turned parsing Bill Clinton's words into an obsession, hoping to catch the president in a lie about whether or not he had sex with Monica Lewinsky. "We have our own set of village rules," complained David Gergen, editor at large at *U.S. News and World Report*, who had worked for both Ronald Reagan and Richard Nixon, as well as Clinton, and therefore could not claim to be a stranger to official mendacity. "The deep and searing violation took place when he not only lied to the country, but co-opted his friends and lied to them."[18] Chris Matthews explained that, "Clinton lies knowing that you know he's lying. It's brutal and it subjugates the person who's being lied to. I resent deeply being constantly lied to."[19] Pundit George Will, a frequent apologist for Reagan, went so far as to insist that the president's "calculated, sustained lying has involved an extraordinarily corrupting assault on language, which is the uniquely human capacity that makes persuasion, and hence popular government, possible. Hence the obtuseness of those who say Clinton's behavior is compatible with constitutional principles, presidential duties and republican ethics."[20]

As president, however, George W. Bush regularly lied about far more significant matters relating to both war and peace, and the media could barely bring themselves to make note of them. In fact, in a front-page story devoted to this very topic in the *Washington Post*, the writer, Dana Milbank, could not bring himself (or was not allowed by his editors) to pen the words, "The president lied." Instead, readers were treated to complicated linguistic circumlocutions like: Bush's statements represented an "embroidering of key assertions." Presidential assertions were clearly "dubious, if not wrong." The president's "rhetoric has taken some flights of fancy . . . taken some liberties . . . omitted qualifiers," and "simply outpace[d] the facts."[21] But "Bush lied"? Never.

---

The attacks of 9/11 initially appeared to cause a tectonic shift in virtually every aspect of American politics and the media that covered it. Anchor people started sprouting American flags on their lapels, and in their station's new logos. Behind the scenes, network and newspaper executives agreed to a variety of administration requests to withhold information from the public, and Fox's Roger Ailes sent secret strategic advice to the President.

As is natural in times of war or quasi-war, political dissent and even truthful reporting on those in power became a luxury that many believed to be unaffordable, and so the right seized on its political opening. Ari Fleischer seemed eager to shut down all criticism of the U.S. government when the ABC comedian, Bill Maher, called American pilots cowards for "lobbing cruise missiles from 2,000 miles away." The comment was actually a critique of the Clinton Administration's policies, not of Bush's, and a transparently foolish one at that. (How many missions had the millionaire comedian flown?) But Fleischer used the opportunity to warn against all forms of criticism of any U.S. government action. Americans, Fleischer said, "need to watch what they say, watch what they do."[22] This ominous warning was echoed by Attorney General John Ashcroft, who insisted at a congressional hearing a few days later that any criticism of the administration—be it on grounds of the protection of civil liberties, pragmatic considerations, or anything else—would "only aid terrorists—for they erode our national unity and diminish our resolve. They give ammunition to America's enemies, and pause to America's friends."[23]

Many conservatives took up the cause, seeking to silence anyone and everyone who was ever heard to utter a critical word about the United States of America under the guise of the need for wartime unity. CNN's Robert Novak ruled out the very possibility of patriotic dissent. In a response to the e-mail of a viewer, who wrote, "It is patriotic to debate foreign policy, especially when we have troops on the ground whose lives depend on our making sound policy," Novak replied, his history askew, "It was people like you who undermined our forces in the Vietnam War and brought Communist tyranny to a country that doesn't deserve it." Similarly, in response to Senate Majority Leader Tom Daschle's criticisms, Fox's Sean Hannity attacked Daschle, not for the substance of his words, but because he was "communicating to our enemies that this nation is divided, that we lack resolve and that we have forgotten September 11." To be fair, these pundits were only echoing the comments of Senate Minority Leader Trent Lott, who issued a "Red Alert" press bulletin, stating "How dare Senator Daschle criticize President Bush while we are fighting our war on terrorism, especially when we have troops in the field."[24]

According to the American Council of Trustees and Alumni, an organization founded by Second Lady Lynne Cheney and featuring Democratic Senator Joe Lieberman on its board of directors, in a report issued after the attack, America's professors were "the weak link in America's response to the attack." The report criticized those who allegedly invoked "tolerance and diversity as antidotes to evil." The Rev. Jesse Jackson earned censure for remarking to an audience at Harvard Law School that America should "build bridges and relationships, not simply bombs and walls." Stanford historian Joel Benin was guilty of observing to students, "If Osama bin Laden is confirmed to be behind the attacks, the United States should bring him before an international tribunal on charges of crimes against humanity." And Wasima Alikhan of the Islamic Academy of Las Vegas made the organization's not-so-little list because of his publicly stated view that "Ignorance breeds hate."[25]

Along similar lines, on the first anniversary of 9/11, the conservative, Moonie-owned *Washington Times* ran an unforgivably misleading story by a reporter named Ellen Sorokin about the teaching plan offered to its members by the National Education Association. The front-page article falsely accused the NEA of advising teachers not to blame "terrorists," or anyone else for that matter, for the 9/11 attack. Not one of the quotes attributed to the NEA actually appeared on its Web site or was spoken by any of its officers. Rather they appeared in an essay in one of the NEA's many hundreds of links, and even these were taken out of context and, it turned out, had been posted accidentally on the pre-release version of the site. Sorokin wrote her story without even seeing the final version. No matter. The lie was picked up and trumpeted by Matt Drudge on his Web site, by the *London Times*, by John Gibson substituting for Bill O'Reilly, by Sean Hannity on *Hannity and Colmes*, by Tucker Carlson on *Crossfire*, by Kate Snow and *New Republic* editor Peter Beinart on CNN's *Late Edition*, and in op-eds by Abraham Cooper and Harold Brackman in the *Los Angeles Times* and Mona Charen in the *Baltimore Sun*. George Will took the occasion of its publication to term the NEA a "national menace" and "as frightening, in its way, as any foreign threat."[26] John Leo denounced the NEA in his column in *U.S. News and World Report*, and then went on Lou Dobbs's *Moneyline* to issue this slanderous statement, using extremely vague language to make this grave charge with no evidence: It's "always hanging in the background that somehow America invited this somehow," he said, "as if you got punched by a stranger on the street. It's somehow it's your fault for making more money or being more successful. And I think that's the aura of the NEA's philosophy."[27]

On the Internet, the superpatriots' attack was led by Andrew Sullivan, British expat and former *New Republic* editor. In language that seemed deliberately evocative of that employed by the late Senator Joseph McCarthy during the Red Scare of the 1950s, Sullivan implored Americans to distinguish between the kinds of citizens who could be trusted and those who sought to undermine the country from within. In the first category he identified "the middle part of the country—the great red zone that voted for Bush." Among Gore voters, however, Sullivan professed to spy a "decadent left in its enclaves on the coasts [that] is not dead—and may well mount a fifth column."[28] It apparently did not concern Sullivan that not only were Gore voters more plentiful in America than Bush voters but that one of those "decadent enclaves"—the island of Manhattan—had actually suffered the consequences of the terrorists' attack. Many of Sullivan's former colleagues objected to the broad-based McCarthyite overtones of his attack, and so Sullivan responded by naming names. "These people," he wrote, "have already openly said they do not support such a war, and will oppose it. Read Sontag and Chomsky and Moore and Alterman and on and on, and you'll see that I'm not exaggerating."[29] In fact, Sullivan was not exaggerating. Like McCarthy, he was simply lying. While Susan Sontag wrote a short essay in the *New Yorker* that many people, including myself, found to be objectionable for its insensitivity to the victims of the attack, she never said she opposed the war.[30] The "Alterman" to which Sullivan refers—the author of this book—also supported the war from the outset and has never said or written otherwise.[31]

Admittedly, the self-appointed chiefs of the conservative thought police in the war on terrorism had an unenviable task on their hands. The war on terrorism proved categorically different from other wars in recent U.S. history because it was started by a physical attack on the mainland of the United States. We did not choose the war; it chose us. Excluding matters of purely operational importance, such as those involving ends and means, the war did not inspire any politically significant dissent. Indeed, the most vocal members of "Blame America" were on the political right, bedrock supporters of the president and his party. Jerry Falwell appeared on the *700 Club*, hosted by Pat Robertson on the Christian Broadcasting Network, and announced to a still-grieving nation, "God continues to lift the curtain and allow the enemies of America to give us probably what we deserve." "Jerry, that's my feeling," Robertson responded. "I think we've just seen the antechamber to terror. We haven't even begun to see what they can do to the major population." Falwell then added that the American Civil Liberties Union has "got to take a lot of blame for this," again winning Robertson's agreement: "Well, yes." Then Falwell broadened his blast to include the federal courts and others who he said were "throwing God out of the public square." He added: "The abortionists have got to bear some burden for this because God will not be mocked. And when we destroy 40 million little innocent babies, we make God mad. I really believe that the pagans, and the abortionists, and the feminists, and the gays and the lesbians who are actively trying to make that an alternative lifestyle, the ACLU, People for the American Way—all of them who have tried to secularize America—I point the finger in their face and say, 'You helped this happen.'"[32]

The White House naturally distanced itself from these amazing words of some of its bedrock supporters, and the ensuing outcry inspired both men to apologize, if not exactly retract. Robertson, meanwhile, retained his status as an honored political commentator. When George Bush made a much-awaited speech outlining his Middle East policy in the spring of 2002, for instance, Robertson was the very first "expert" to whom CNN turned for illumination.

But on the left, as the neoliberal editor of Slate, Jacob Weisberg observed, opposition to the war and blame for the United States for causing it was at best insignificant. The *New Republic* created an "Idiocy Award" for those making allegedly anti-war or anti-American comments. Winners included: Katha Pollitt, Alice Walker, Michael Moore, Oliver Stone, Karlheinz Stockhausen, Arundhati Roy, the syndicated political cartoonist Ted Rall, and the novelist Barbara Kingsolver, who was quoted out of context. The *Weekly Standard* created the stupidly named "Susan Sontag Awards" for the same offense and chose from much the same menu: the novelist Alice Walker, filmmakers Oliver Stone and Michael Moore, the German composer Karlheinz Stockhausen, the Indian writer Arundhati Roy, and Ted Rall. Another article in the magazine went after Katha Pollitt for a nutty column in which she tried to convince her daughter not to fly an American flag. Andrew Sullivan piled on with his own version of the "Sontag Awards," published on his popular Web site, which included, almost without exception, the very same individuals as those mocked by the *Weekly Standard* and the *New Republic*. As Weisberg pointed out, this motley collection did not a movement make. Stone and Moore are movie directors. Roy and Stockhausen aren't even American. "The sins of the others," Weisberg wrote, "fall somewhere short of lending aid and comfort to the enemy. Kingsolver published something in a Milwaukee newspaper (allegedly) equating patriotism with terrorism. Walker wrote something incoherent in the *Village Voice* about how 'the only punishment that works is love.' I'm not sure many people have even heard of Ted Rall." Susan Sontag, he noted, referring to her Salon interview, had actually defended the war. "In other words, anti-war villain No. 1 isn't even against the war, much less in sympathy with the other side."[33]

Nevertheless, the combination of these cops on the beat had the effect of silencing those with even the mildest of unpopular opinions. CNN chief Walter Isaacson warned his staff, "If you get on the wrong side of public opinion, you are going to get into trouble." This view was reinforced by a report by Alexandra Stanley, in the *New York Times*, who cautioned that "Most viewers are in no mood to listen to views they dismiss as either loopy or treasonous."[34] And when Ted Koppel invited Roy to give her critical views, he felt compelled to offer this warning to his viewers: "Some of you, many of you, are not going to like what you hear tonight. You don't have to listen. But if you do, you should know that dissent sometimes comes in strange packages."[35]

Indeed, it became, in many instances, impossible for any public figure to make even a common-sense observation about the war. The case of David Westin, the president of ABC News, is instructive in this regard. On October 23, 2001, Westin spoke to a class at Columbia University's Graduate School of Journalism. Asked if the Pentagon were a legitimate target for attack by America's enemies, he said, "I actually don't have an opinion on that . . . as a journalist I feel strongly that's something I should not be taking a position on." Four days later, the Westin speech was shown on C-Span, where a member of the Media Research Center caught it and put excerpts in the center's daily "CyberAlert." (The center was apparently undertaking what Brent Bozell, its chief, explained in a fund-raising letter would be its "new and vital mission" of "training our guns on any media outlet or any reporter interfering with America's war on terrorism or trying to undermine President Bush."[36]) Meanwhile, Fox's Brit Hume spotted the item and mentioned it on *Special Report* the same evening. The *New York Post* then picked it up, together with the Drudge Report. It then caught the attention of Rush Limbaugh, who devoted over an hour to voicing his outrage about it on his radio program. With Limbaugh's show still in progress, an e-mail to the center followed. "I was wrong," the network president explained. "Under any interpretation, the attack on the Pentagon was criminal and entirely without justification."[37]

Westin's capitulation was particularly dispiriting to those who look to the network media to defend freedom of speech in this country, given the inanity of his alleged defense. The answer to the question he was asked is obviously "yes." There are millions of people all over the world whose interpretations of the attack lead them to believe it was justified, however wrong they may have been. But even leaving that aside, the question is a no-brainer. How can anyone say the Pentagon is not a legitimate target for an attack in case of war? War is the entire reason the building exists. By what conceivable definition of war could it be excluded as a potential target? The shock of the 9/11 attack derived from the fact that most of us were not even aware that we were at war with Al Qaeda. Once we did, we fought back on its turf, seeking to destroy its would-be pentagons. What was most depressing about Westin's answer was his willingness to drop any pretext of objectivity upon having his patriotism questioned by conservative ideologues. It was more evidence—if any was necessary—of just how effective the right-wing assault on the U.S. media and free speech had become.

Conservatives, meanwhile, thrilled to the transformation they perceived in the media, a media they had been attacking on September 10 as working hand-in-glove with liberalism and Satanism. Peggy Noonan wrote, "As I watched television I became aware . . . that the great leaders in our time of trauma were the reporters and anchors and producers of the networks and news stations. What cool and fabulous work from Peter Jennings, Dan Rather and Tom Brokaw, what stunning work from Brit Hume and Aaron Brown, Katie Couric and Diane Sawyer" and so on.[38] L. Brent Bozell III called the September 11 reporting "media coverage at its best" and lauded "Tim Russert adorned with the red, white and blue ribbons on *Meet the Press*, CNN continuously running graphics of a waving American flag in its broadcasts, and Fox's Shepard Smith on Saturday night, casting journalism rules to the wind as he reported on the pending reopening of the stock market only to launch into a national pep talk about the patriotic duty to buy, not sell, on Monday morning." Dan Rather, formerly conservative public enemy number one, announced to viewers of the David Letterman program that the reason the terrorists and their supporters viewed America with such unbridled hostility was simple: It was "because they're evil," and "they're jealous of us." Even Bernard Goldberg, author of *Bias*, praised the post-9/11 media to the sky, writing:

> On September 11, 2001, America's royalty, the TV news anchors got it right. They gave us the news straight, which they don't always do. They told us what was going on without the cynicism and without the attitude. For that, they deserve our thanks and admiration.[39]

Judging by conservatives' reaction to 9/11, their critique that the media was too liberal to report the news objectively has been thrown out the window. What conservatives wanted, apparently, was a mainstream media that reported and discussed the news from their own conservative perspective. In the aftermath of 9/11, that is what they got.

While most of us were still trying to sort through the horrific emotions of the moment, the media seemed to choose only the most belligerent voices to broadcast. Former Secretary of State Lawrence Eagleberger told CNN: "There is only one way to begin to deal with people like this, and that is you have to kill some of them even if they are not immediately directly involved in this thing." *Time* magazine's Lance Morrow demanded that the nation "relearn a lost discipline, self-confident relentlessness—and to relearn why human nature has equipped us all with a weapon (abhorred in decent peacetime societies) called hatred."[40] Charles Krauthammer announced in the *Washington Post*, "This is not crime. This is war."[41] Eliot A. Cohen declared (mistakenly) in the *New Republic*, "This is our generation's Pearl Harbor. In all likelihood, the price in human life will prove even greater."[42] And Seth Lipsky, writing in the *Wall Street Journal*, got so excited, he started coming up with all kinds of places we could bomb. "There will be no shortage of targets," he wrote, "from Afghanistan to Iran to Iraq to Syria to the Palestinian Authority. Or even, for that matter, Saudi

Arabia, which proved so recalcitrant in cooperating in our investigation of the bombing of an American barracks."[43]

Wholly missing from the media's endless regurgitation of the horrific events, for instance, were voices of scholars who, while not pacifists or even (God forbid) leftists, knew enough about history and diplomacy to ask at least some difficult questions about whether "war" in the traditional sense would be the most effective response to achieve our purposes and defend our country. If you watched your television or read your op-ed pages during this time, you would have found endless commentary from the likes of Eagleberger, Krauthammer, and Cohen. Try as you might, however, you would not have found say, Sir Michael Howard, perhaps the world's most renowned living military historian. Articulating a view that eventually appeared to gain a consensus in Europe but was rarely even discussed in the United States, Howard offered up a strikingly different analysis of how to address the threat. "To 'declare war' on terrorists, or even more illiterately, on 'terrorism,'" he explained:

> is at once to accord them a status and dignity that they seek and which they do not deserve. It confers on them a kind of legitimacy. Do they qualify as 'belligerents'? If so, should they not receive the protection of the laws of war? This was something that Irish terrorists always demanded, and was quite properly refused. But their demands helped to muddy the waters, and were given wide credence among their supporters in the United States.
>
> But to use, or rather to misuse the term 'war' is not simply a matter of legality, or pedantic semantics. It has deeper and more dangerous consequences. To declare that one is 'at war' is immediately to create a war psychosis that may be totally counter-productive for the objective that we seek. It will arouse an immediate expectation, and demand, for spectacular military action against some easily identifiable adversary, preferably a hostile state; action leading to decisive results.[44]

Nowhere on television, however, was the wise Harvard political scientist, Stanley Hoffmann, who observed in the *New York Review of Books* that despite all of the televised fulminating, the most elementary kinds of distinctions were being ignored, and hence all kinds of options were excluded from consideration. "Some of the terrorists and their supporters are religious fanatics who see in the U.S., the West, and Israel a formidable machine for cultural subversion, political domination, and economic subjection. The kind of Islamic revanche bin Laden projects in his statements is both so cosmic and based on so peculiar an interpretation of the Koran that there is very little one can do to rebut it," Hoffmann wrote. "But there is a great deal one can do to limit its appeal. This kind of an ethics of conviction feeds—like so many other forms of totalitarianism—on experiences of despair and humiliation, and these can be understood and to some degree addressed."[45] Part of the problem with the kinds of views expressed by Howard and Hoffmann—views that probably represented a consensus view in most of Western Europe—was their inherent complexity; they could not, as television demands, be reduced to a sound bite. But another part is that these views did not flatter the jingoistic impulses of the conservative superpatriots who succeeded in hijacking our post-September 11 public discourse. And the mainstream media, ever fearful of conservative attacks on their patriotic bona fides, paid them no mind.

―――――――――

By far the most significant beneficiary of September 11 from a media/political standpoint was President Bush. Even in "normal" times, Peter Wolson, a former president of the Los Angeles Institute and Society for Psychoanalytic Studies, has explained, "The public has a need for an idealized hero. The public wants the president to succeed, even though there may be envy and lots of other conflicted feelings. There's a wish that the president will be a strong, powerful father figure."[46] In the case of a trauma such as 9/11, this kind of nascent hero worship might be applied directly to the media, temporarily transforming George W. Bush from the military's commander-in-chief to the media's as well. Rather even appeared on David Letterman's program and announced, "George Bush is the president, he makes the decisions, and, you know, as just one American, if he wants me to line up, just tell me where."[47] As David Carr observed at the time, "There's been a collective decision to re-imagine the president, and the media is fully cooperating. Journalists are very anxious to help him construct a wartime presidency, because we may be at war and he's the only president we have."[48]

Made nervous by never-ending conservative attacks on their values and patriotism, the media reacted to the events of September 11 as if accused of a crime of which they secretly believed themselves to be guilty. The evidence of this "crime" could be seen in their overcompensation, orchestrated to demonstrate their patriotism like a community of new immigrants for an enemy nation, all to the benefit of Bush and his administration. CNN, for instance, ever defensive about its alleged anti-American agenda, could not get enough of the president, no matter what he was doing or where. According to one study, beginning January 1, 2002, CNN carried 157 live events featuring administration officials. Over the same time, the network carried only seven events featuring elected leaders of the Democratic Party. This was a clear break from previous administrations. For the first fifteen months of the Bush administration, for instance, CNN cut into regular programming approximately 150 times to feature Bush speaking live. Most of these features showed the president addressing extremely partisan audiences, pushing the Republican domestic agenda. In comparison, during the final fifteen months of Bill Clinton's presidency, the network did so just eighteen times. Of the 150 cut-ins, a mere 44 turned out to be primarily related to the war. (Note that even before September 11, CNN had already broadcast sixty-five of Bush's speeches live.)[49]

Moreover, the tone of the coverage of Bush's presidency after September 11 could hardly have been kinder if it had been vetted by his mother. On a relatively trivial level, as Maureen Dowd noted, "Garry Trudeau has pulled his featherweight-Bush cartoons. Barbra Streisand has taken anti-Bush diatribes off her Web site. David Letterman has been as diplomatic as Colin Powell. 'Saturday Night Live' will tone down its scorching Bush satires."[50] But the seminal organs of the media stood as if at attention to their newly anointed commander in chief. A typical post-9/11 *New York Times* headline read "To Reassure World, Bush Flies Confidently and Forcefully Without a Net."[51] A typical *New York Times* editorial found the president to be "a different man from the one who was just barely elected president last year, or even the man who led the country a month ago. He seemed more confident, determined, and sure of his purpose and was in full command of the complex array of political and military challenges that he faces in the wake of the terrible terrorist attacks of Sept. 11."[52] A typical punditocracy exchange found Tucker Carlson accusing Paul Begala of making "a treasonous statement" on *Crossfire* when the latter stated his opinion that Tony Blair was "the finest leader in the free world."

In the aftermath of 9/11, even Bush's weaknesses became virtues. Making a virtue of necessity, Frank Bruni found that the president's effect "wasn't that of the ignorant or aloof" but came from someone bolstered by his religious faith, a "keen sense of destiny," and a "ready acceptance of fate." "An unthreatening, easygoing man for unthreatening, easygoing times," Bush was transformed by the terrorist attacks, in Bruni's decidedly straining-for-praise formulation, "into one of the most interesting presidents in decades."[53]

Believe it or not, the Bush people even got the members of the media to go along, however briefly, with the notion that Bush had somehow morphed into a Daniel Patrick Moynihan–type politician/intellectual, though why they thought this was a good idea was never clear. Nevertheless, when Bush offered up the commencement address at Ohio State in the spring of 2002, a *Washington Post* reporter announced, "The president who spoke here today was not the same president who spoke in New Haven a year ago." The reason? "Bush aide John Bridgeland told reporters this morning that the president's speech, serious and grave, was inspired by the writings of Alexis de Tocqueville, Adam Smith, George Eliot, Emily Dickinson, William Wordsworth, Pope John Paul II, Aristotle, Benjamin Rush, Thomas Jefferson, George Washington, Abraham Lincoln and Cicero." Bridgeland also said that he had discussed Nicomachean ethics in the Oval Office with the president, as well as the Patrick Henry–James Madison debate." Beyond Bridgeland's claims, however, the newspaper failed to present any evidence of these soaring claims about the awakening of Bush's intellectual capacities, as the president did not mention any of these in his speech.[54] Nor was this new respect for scholarly learning consistent with the actions of the man who publicly, just a few weeks earlier, had responded to a U.S. reporter's questioning the president of France in French—as is proper, after all; foreign reporters do not question Bush in Czech or Romanian—"Very good, the guy memorizes four words, and he plays like he's intercontinental. I'm impressed."[55]

The media also seized on 9/11 to render irrelevant the question of Bush's tarnished legitimacy. Employing decidedly unorthodox criteria, Chris Matthews accorded Bush his personal seal of presidential legitimacy on the basis of a call-and-response speech Bush made to a group of rescue workers who cheered him at Ground Zero in Manhattan. The president yelled "I can hear you, and the rest of the world hears you, and the people (cheers and applause) and the people who knocked these buildings down will hear all of us soon." As Matthews explained it, "With that spontaneous retort, George W. Bush became this country's unchallenged leader. His communion with those firemen on that third day after the horror brought him the broadly accepted legitimacy that was denied him earlier. Those brave firemen, elevated to a kind of secular national priesthood, gave Bush what the oath administered by Chief Justice Rehnquist on Jan. 20 and the 5–4 Supreme Court decision about Florida's votes could not." (In fact, in August 2002, the International Association of Fire Fighters voted unanimously to boycott a national tribute to firefighters who died on September 11, in an angry response to Bush's rejection of a bill that included $340 million to fund fire departments. "Don't lionize our fallen brothers in one breath and then stab us in the back," the association's general president, Harold Schaitberger, told President Bush. No word from Matthews on how the vote affected Bush's legitimacy.[56])

Matthews's theological justification of the Bush presidency found an even more bizarre echo in the words of one of the punditocracy's top cardinals, if not its papal equivalent, NBC's Tim Russert. On *Meet the Press*, Russert inquired of first lady Laura Bush whether she thought her husband had become president due to divine intervention. To her everlasting credit, Laura Bush declined to credit the Almighty with inspiring Katherine Harris's and Antonin Scalia's anti-democratic escapades. But Russert persisted, and his other guests, Rudy Giuliani and Theodore Cardinal McCarrick of the Archdiocese of Washington, took the bait. The former mayor responded, "I do think, Mrs. Bush, that there was some divine guidance in the president being elected" while the latter, a presumed expert on God, chimed in, "I don't thoroughly agree with the first lady. I think that the president really—he was where he was when we needed him. And he's still there where we need him now."[57]

The media's underlying refrain in the aftermath of 9/11 seemed to be "Thank God that Al Gore somehow managed to lose that election." Both Howard Fineman of *Newsweek* and Richard Berke of the *New York Times* wrote up post-attack stories in which even Gore supporters were said to be belatedly coming to their senses. Many were now "privately expressing satisfaction that Mr. Gore, who tried to make his foreign affairs expertise an issue in the campaign, did not win." Neither Fineman nor

Berke's stories contained a single named Democrat supporting this contention. Instead we heard from Democrats eager to praise Bush's performance in public and from a few who chose to snipe at Al Gore in private. In many ways, such "stories" perfectly replicated the dynamic of the coverage of the 2000 election, particularly now that Bush's only recognizable flaw in that context—his lack of intellectual sophistication—had become transformed into a virtue, when it was not being denied entirely. Berke said in his story that "the bluntest assessments were from Democrats who spoke on the condition that they not be identified. Several said the nation was fortunate to have Mr. Bush in power, and they questioned whether Mr. Gore would have surrounded himself with as experienced a foreign policy team as Mr. Bush did." But this is demonstrable nonsense. Gore's secretary of state would almost certainly have been Richard Holbrooke; his national security adviser, Leon Fuerth. Both enjoy reputations for being extremely experienced and respected in their respective areas of expertise. As for the rest of Gore's potential team, excluding Joe Lieberman, a punditocracy favorite, it is entirely unknown. But it is doubtful, for instance, that Gore would have appointed a man to head the Justice Department like John Ashcroft, who in May 2001 testified "our No. 1 goal is the prevention of terrorist acts," and who then proceeded to refuse an FBI budget request to add 149 field agents, 200 analysts, and 54 translators to its counterterrorism team, despite the fact that the FBI then had only one analyst monitoring Al Qaeda.[58] (Mr. Ashcroft managed to stay on the ball, however, when it came to harassing growers of medical marijuana in California and prostitutes in New Orleans.)

Appearing on Fox News, the *Post's* Ceci Connolly, who tortured Gore with her biased and inaccurate *Washington Post* coverage throughout the 2000 campaign, would still not give up the bit in her mouth. She thought a speech of Gore's devoted to domestic issues "didn't seem quite appropriate," coming after September 11.[59] Her comment, however, begged the obvious question of just what Gore had ever done in Connolly's career of covering him that she had found appropriate. ABC's *The Note* picked up another of these examples in late September, more than a year after the attack. Noting, "You can never go wrong comparing the dynamics of adult life to high school," the authors described Bush as "cool and popular, which means he can get away with some pretty amazing things." Just imagine, the authors wrote, "if Bill Clinton, in a speech in which he asserted that security isn't a political issue, and that good women and men of both parties are working to make America safe, also said the following . . . regarding the stalled homeland security bill: 'The House responded, but the Senate is more interested in special interests in Washington and not interested in the security of the American people.'" This was the same day, one can't help but observe, that the "annoying and unpopular" Al Gore "gives what was on some levels a serious, substantive speech in San Francisco yesterday and gets chastised by the White House and the Republican National Committee for playing politics, a storyline followed to some extent by the TV and newspaper coverage. . . . Chalk it up, say ABC's perspicacious, nonpartisan analysts, to "another day of Goofus and Gallant in the insider media."[60]

Consider the astonishing explosion of invective unleashed in September 2002 by Gore's calm and soberly delivered warning that echoed the concern of at least three four-star generals given to Congress on the same day. (These attacks were offered, one cannot help but observe, by a group of pundits who, unlike Gore, had probably never seen the inside of a mess hall, much less an Abrams tank.) The *New York Post* headlined its editorial, "Al Gore, Wimp." Sean Hannity noted, "He's sweating profusely. . . . He seems very angry at different points in the speech. He didn't look presidential. I didn't see any gravitas, any leadership." He added, "Are we watching something similar to appeasement before our eyes?" Charles Krauthammer found the speech to be "a disgrace—a series of cheap shots strung together without logic or coherence." Never to be outdone, Michael Kelly went Krauthammer one or two better, unleashing a string of invectives that appeared designed to make Ann Coulter look like Isaiah Berlin. Kelly termed Gore's speech "dishonest, cheap, low, hollow . . . wretched . . . vile . . . contemptible . . . a lie . . . a disgrace . . . equal parts mendacity, viciousness and smarm."[61]

Al Hunt, the token moderate on the *Wall Street Journal* editorial page, made a congruent political argument, in which the court's selection of Bush, while perhaps not the result of the Hand of God, nevertheless turned out to be a lucky break for the nation. According to his logic, this was owing to the fact that U.S. conservatives had grown so uncivil in their opposition to Democratic presidents that they placed these feelings ahead of their patriotic feeling for the country. The far right—including, no doubt, the folks on the other side of the page from Hunt—would have been merciless in their attempt to exploit September 11 as a stick with which to beat President Gore, just as they had used the war in Kosovo to pummel President Clinton. Hunt noted that House Republicans refused to pass a resolution supporting American troops, even after the fighting in Kosovo was well under way. Republican leaders Tom DeLay and Don Nickles both suggested that the atrocities in Kosovo were more Clinton's fault than Milosevic's. [62] In other words, Hunt was thankful for Bush because conservative hysteria made America ungovernable for anyone but conservatives.

As a final favor to President Bush, and presumably national unity, the media acted as if guided by an unspoken agreement not to look terribly carefully into any potential administration screw-ups that might have contributed to the nation's vulnerability on September 11. The clearest example of this tendency can be found in the ten-part, 40,000-word epic poem Bob Woodward and Dan Balz produced for the *Washington Post*, based on extraordinary access from the president, the National Security Council, the State Department, and the Department of Defense. The impression this report created was not unlike that of an official Soviet-era account of the Great Patriotic War. As the *Washington Monthly*'s Nicholas Confessore wrote of the series, "In the *Post*'s breathless account of the days after 9/11, the president and his staff are always resolute, action is always decisive, and pressure is always met by grace."[63] As with Woodward's study of the Central Intelligence Agency, which managed to miss completely the selling of arms to the Ayatollah and the use of the money to fund a secret war, America's most famous investigative reporter again failed to notice the big story. Later, dozens of reports would reveal that the national security establishment had received any number of warnings that, if properly understood and acted upon, might have allowed the nation to prevent the attacks or certainly prepare for them in a more effective manner. A systemic failure occurred inside the FBI, the CIA, the National Security Agency, the National Security Council, and their coordinating bodies, which are supposed to streamline the information collected and provide it in a timely manner to those officials whose job it is to address it.[64] But even with their unique access to everyone on the Bush team in the intelligence community and in the Pentagon—or perhaps because of it—the Woodward/Balz story managed to miss this most crucial aspect.

In a macro sense, the entire relationship of the president and the media seemed the mirror image of that endured under Bill Clinton. In contrast to the mockery that Sidney Blumenthal, Joe Conason, and a tiny band of not terribly influential brothers received for their diehard support in the media for Bill Clinton, during Bush's presidency there seemed to be no appreciable limits on the hero worship that punditocracy conservatives and moderates un-self-consciously showered on the president after September 11, 2001. Even Secretary of Defense Donald Rumsfeld, whom many in the media had viewed, when appointed, as a Seventies retread deeply out of touch with the demands of the modern-day job, found himself painted in heroic hues. "Rummy," who kept the tightest reign on war news in many a generation and who professed a desire to jail unauthorized leakers—found himself fawned over— "America's stud"; a "sexy symbol"; and a "babe magnet"—by the very journalists whose reporting he sought to suppress.[65] Who knows how many of her colleagues Cokie Roberts spoke for when she admitted to being "a total sucker for the guys who stand up with all the ribbons on and stuff and they say it's true and I'm ready to believe it."[66]

The desire of many in the media to contrast the behavior of George Bush with that of the previous occupant of the Oval Office led to some extremely questionable journalistic practices, even in matters that had nothing to do with the war or the patriotism it inspired. For instance, during the frenzy of reporting on Enron—a company whose top executives were among Bush's closest and most generous supporters—the decidedly undependable Drudge Report ran an item arguing that the Enron CEO,

Ken Lay, whom Bush had termed "Kenny Boy," "also played golf with President Bill Clinton and slept in the Clinton White House."

Like so much of Drudge's "reporting," this January 11 item was entirely unsourced. Two days later, the *Chicago Tribune* reported, "Lay was no stranger to the Clinton White House, playing golf with the president and staying overnight in the Lincoln Bedroom." A day later, *Weekly Standard* editor Fred Barnes made the same claim in primetime on Fox News. "Ken Lay not only played golf with Clinton, he spent a night in the Lincoln Bedroom," Barnes announced. That same evening, CNN allowed Bush campaign consultant Alex Castellanos to inform *Crossfire* viewers that "Ken Lay slept in the Lincoln bedroom," with Clinton as his host. Castellanos repeated the claim on ABC's *This Week* (where former Clinton aide Paul Begala denied its veracity). David Bossie made the claim on the "liberal" Greta van Susteren's Fox News broadcast about the same time. The same story eventually found its way into the pages of the *Washington Times*, the *Arkansas Democrat-Gazette*, the Newhouse News Service, and other papers and newspapers in Korea, Australia, and Britain, including the *Times* of London.[67] On February 1, the *New York Times* disseminated the same story. Note that not one of the people who made the claim, be they Republican operatives or reporters behaving in the role of Republican operatives, had actually seen any evidence to support it. They hadn't seen any because there was none. Ken Lay never did sleep in the Lincoln Bedroom while Bill Clinton was president, as Joe Conason, Brendan Nyhan, and others repeatedly pointed out.[68] All any reporter had to go on was the Drudge Report, whose unreliability had at that point been well established. And yet this trashing of the previous Democratic president in order to protect the reputation of the current Republican one was somehow carried out by the "liberal media" that was allegedly trying to subvert the nation on behalf of its own left-wing agenda. I have to admit that at times, it is enough to drive a genuine liberal to distraction.

With the media cowed by a combination of conservative criticism and patriotic self-censorship, it seemed as if there was almost nothing George Bush could not get away with during early portions of his presidency, no matter how incompletely or hypocritically his administration performed. Al Hunt said as much in April 2002, when, in noticing once again the ever-so-gentle treatment that Bush's foul-ups were receiving, he wrote, "Imagine the outcry if Mr. Clinton's United Nations representatives voted against the Israelis on a Saturday morning and the president was trotted out only hours later expressing a different view. Or if President Clinton sent his vice president on a highly publicized overseas mission that turned out disastrously. Remember 'amateur hour' in foreign policy? And what a hypocrite Clinton would have been called if, as a supposed free trader, he raised taxes, in the form of higher tariffs, to placate important electoral and contributor bases."[69] Imagine too the outcry that Clinton would have experienced had he tried to blame his troubles in the Middle

East on George H. W. Bush and then lied about it when he was caught. (George W. Bush quote No. 1: "Well, we've tried summits in the past, as you may remember. It wasn't all that long ago where a summit was called and nothing happened, and as a result we had significant intifada in the area." Bush quote No. 2: "Somebody told me there's a story floating around that somehow I am blaming the Clinton administration for what's going on in the Middle East right now. . . . I appreciate what President Clinton tried to do. He tried to bring peace to the Middle East.")[70]

The media never relented in examining—quite properly, in my view—the barely legal shenanigans the Clintonites employed to soak their contributors and fund their campaigns. Yet as ABC's nonpartisan authors of *The Note*, observed in September 2002, "Under most indices, this President [Bush] is more 'political' than Bill Clinton ever was." [71] You'd never know it from the press coverage. Imagine, now, for a moment, the outcry that Bill Clinton would have caused in the media had he explicitly tried to exploit a tragedy like September 11 to bolster his political fundraising. Yet the Republican National Committee planned to make as much as $30 million at a Presidential Gala featuring Bush and Vice President Cheney, in which donors were rewarded with a September 11 photo of Bush aboard Air Force One: "The photos depict 'the defining moments of The First Year of the George W. Bush presidency," according to the party's direct mail. It continued, "The pictures show the gritty determination of our new president at his inauguration; a telephone call from Air Force One to Vice President Cheney the afternoon of Sept. 11, 2001; and President Bush's historic State of the Union speech before a joint session of Congress that united a nation and a world." [72] (Imagine, moreover, the outcry from conservatives if President Clinton had disappeared from view on a day like September 11 and left Al Gore to run the government, only to offer a desperate nation a patently phony explanation?)

Of course there were exceptions to the herd-like behavior, and these tended to prove the rule. As Frank Rich pointed out in his October 27, 2001, *New York Times* column:

> This was an administration that will let its special interests—particularly its high-rolling campaign contributors and its noisiest theocrats of the right—have veto power over public safety, public health, and economic prudence in war, it turns out, no less than in peacetime. When anthrax struck, the administration's first impulse was not to secure as much Cipro as speedily as possible to protect Americans, but to protect the right of pharmaceutical companies to profiteer. The White House's faith in tax cuts as a panacea for all national ills has led to such absurdities as this week's House "stimulus" package showering $254 million on Enron, the reeling Houston energy company (now under S.E.C. investigation) that has served as a Bush campaign cash machine. Airport security, which has been enhanced by at best cosmetic tweaks since Sept. 11, is also held hostage by campaign cash: As Salon has

reported, ServiceMaster, a supplier of the low-wage employees who ineptly man the gates, is another G.O.P. donor.[73]

Rich picked his particular set of issues quite early in the aftermath of the attack. Given his space constraints, this was a quite respectable set of choices. But of course there were many more, had the media been interested in pursuing them. Josh Marshall tallied up a just a few of them ten months later:

The White House's cocky bullheadedness turned Vermont Sen. Jim Jeffords into an Independent and gave the Democrats the Senate. Its budget predictions were in shreds well before September 11. Social Security privatization went bust long before the market did. During the California energy crisis, the administration refused for months to cap wholesale energy rates. This ill-advised move looked like payback to price-gouging energy firms like Enron and drove California even further beyond Republican reach, probably for years to come. Instead of disengaging from the Middle East peace process, as Bush had promised, he is ever more mired in its problems. When, predictably, bloodshed spilled out of control, the administration rushed forth one peace plan after another, each with a half-life measured in weeks. The president talked tough against McCain-Feingold; then he signed it. And after September 11, he insisted, against the advice of almost every expert, that the country didn't need a cabinet-level homeland security agency, instead entrusting this vital task to an adviser, Tom Ridge, who lacked experience and authority and quickly became a Washington laughingstock. Seven wasted months later, Bush burst forth with a brand-new plan: a cabinet-level homeland security agency.[74]

Much the same case, Marshall noted, can easily be made with regard to Vice President Cheney, whose reputation for tough-minded competence seemed entirely impervious to redress when considered in light of his record of failure. Again, Marshall noted:

The Cheney-led energy task force produced an all-drilling-no-conservation energy bill that went nowhere. The task force's real legacy was to mire the administration in a thicket of congressional investigations and private lawsuits, all springing from Cheney's insistence on Nixonian secrecy. His major foreign policy gambit—last spring's shuttle-diplomacy mission to the Middle East to secure support for an invasion of Iraq—was a debacle. The tough-talking VP went to the region to line up the Arab states behind the United States against Saddam; days after Cheney's return they were lining up behind Saddam against the United States. Less well known, but no less embarrassing, was Cheney's leadership of the pre-9/11 anti-terrorism task

force. In spring 2001, rather than back congressional efforts to implement the findings of the Hart-Rudman commission, Cheney opted to spearhead his own group,
to put the administration's stamp on whatever reforms occurred. But the task force
did almost nothing for four months until terrorists struck on September 11. More
recently, it was Cheney who advised Bush not to include any serious corporate
reforms in his July speech on Wall Street, the one that sent markets plunging.[75]

To be fair to the journalists, the Bush White House was a difficult one to cover. As
Nicholas Confessore noted in an examination of Bush-media relations, the administration would simply withdraw cooperation from those reporters whose questions it
did not appreciate. They tried to have reporters removed from their beats if they felt
reporting was too aggressive. Virtually without exception, they refused to offer any
substantive information and spoke in vague platitudes when asked specific questions.
They complained about photo placement. They complained about background pictures. They complained about networks paying too much attention to Bill Clinton's
opinions. They consistently interfered with reporters' ability to do their jobs by failing to respond to the most basic questions with straight answers, preferring to adhere
to a degree of secrecy that, again, had few if any precedents in recent American history—going well beyond any demonstrable or even conceivable justification on the
basis of national security.[76] One *Washington Post* journalist in Afghanistan, Doug
Struck, who was pursuing a story about civilian casualties from U.S. operations, was
told by the U.S. commanding officer there, "This is an ongoing military operation.
If you go further, you would be shot."[77] Once Struck wrote of the incident, a
Pentagon spokesman tried to discredit his story, saying that Struck had only been held
back for his own safety. But the *Post* correspondent called the Pentagon's version "an
amazing lie," adding that "it shows the extremes the military is going to to keep this
war secret, to keep reporters from finding out what's going on."[78] For understandable
reasons, perhaps, given the shocking nature of what took place on September 11,
many journalists could not separate their patriotic emotions from their professional
responsibilities. They allowed themselves to be exploited, as a result, for propaganda
rather than informational purposes.

Within a surprisingly short period of time, in any case, media life returned to relative normalcy following the shock of the attacks. Advertisers voiced discomfort
about having their products placed alongside smoking embers and crying widows,
and so the television media quickly embarked on new scandals to unearth. Among
these were the confirmed death of that old standby, poor Chandra Levy, and an imaginary epidemic of child kidnapping. International coverage, once again, fell back to
its pre-attack levels, which is to say all but non-existent.[79] But the center of political
gravity in politics, and the media, had shifted rightward. The recently passed military

budget was much higher; toleration for civil liberties, much lower. Bush was in a far stronger position to get what he wanted from Congress, while his critics were much chastened—and hesitant—in taking him on, irrespective of whether any one particular program had any relevance to the war on terrorism. Missile defense, for instance, sailed through Congress with nary a peep of dissent despite the fact that it was irrelevant to the kind of low-tech, non-national threat the terrorists posed. Bush attempted to tie his energy plan, his trade plan, and even his tax plan to the need to fight terrorism. Osama bin Laden, Mullah Omar, and virtually all of the Al Qaeda leadership may have remained at large. So too did the infamous "anthrax mailer," whoever he or she or they may be. Bush declared that the "evildoers" could "run, but could not hide," but in fact they could do both. (Bush could not even bring himself to mention Dr. Evil's name in a speech after July 8, 2002, though his replacement evil, Saddam Hussein, did get quite a few mentions.[80]) Despite Ashcroft's largely successful efforts to use the war to enforce a long-time right-wing assault on civil liberties, U.S. homeland "security" remained a sick and scary joke. Still, it was considered bad media manners—if not downright disloyal—to bring this up in public.

Dan Rather was among the few journalists to admit openly that the media had made a terrible error in deferring to the president, noting, "We haven't lived up to our responsibility. . . ."We haven't been patriotic enough to ask the tough questions." He was joined by CNN anchor Aaron Brown, who spoke of Ashcroft's detention policy and noted, "If we don't ask these questions, then history will record our country and our behavior in a very unkind way."[81] By September 2002, the costs of the media acquiescence to the atmosphere of conservative superpatriotism were everywhere evident. The nation was fighting one war in Afghanistan and appeared to be about to enter another in Iraq. Yet, because of the Bush administration's penchant for obsessive secrecy, coupled with the media's misplaced deference, the nation was not much more knowledgeable about our path than it had been thirty-eight years earlier when Lyndon Johnson sent U.S. troops into combat in Vietnam by retaliating for an imaginary attack. I wrote a column for the *Nation* on the topic in September 2002 and listed some of the issues for which Americans still did not have answers—and for which the media, with a few significant exceptions, had all but given the Bush administration a pass, and thereby failed in their fundamental constitutional charge to help create an informed citizenry in both war and peace. The questions included:

- Why did the Bush national security team ignore the Al Qaeda briefing it received from President Clinton's national security adviser, Sandy Berger, in the fall of 2000?

- Why did the president ignore the August 2001 intelligence briefing warning him of the likelihood of an Al Qaeda hijacking?

- Why, in August 2000, was the FBI unable to locate Al Qaeda operatives Khalid al-Midhar and Nawaq al-Hazmi, both of whom had been placed at a terrorist planning meeting by Malaysian intelligence in December 1999? Hazmi was listed in the San Diego telephone directory and Midhar was using a credit card with his name on it. Both were active at the San Diego Islamic Center.

- Why didn't the National Security Agency have foreign language expertise to translate the words "Tomorrow is zero hour," spoken by Al Qaeda operatives and picked up in real time on September 10, 2001?

- What was really up with George Bush flying around the country on September 11? If the administration thought it had a "credible threat" to Air Force One, why the hell did he fly on Air Force One?

- What's up with those "loose" and missing Soviet-era nukes in Russia, Ukraine, and elsewhere? Why is the White House cutting funding for the Nunn-Lugar program, designed to protect them?

- Speaking of Ground Zero, does anyone know if it's safe to breathe the air down there? Anybody know how all those contaminants—mercury, asbestos, benzene, and so on, combining in unprecedented chemical cocktails—affect the long-term health of children, pregnant women, old people? Who is monitoring the health effects on the rescue workers? Who made the decision to reopen downtown so quickly, knowing so little?

- How did Bush decide on war with Iraq without consulting the uniformed military, the intelligence agencies, the United Nations, NATO, the Republican national security establishment—including both of his dad's secretaries of state and his national security adviser—the Republican Party in Congress, the Democratic majority, or just about anyone who did not already want to go to war with Iraq?

- Does the administration have any hard evidence of Iraq's nuclear program? Its CBW and WMD delivery capabilities? And why is Hussein not considered to be deterrable, the way, say, Joseph Stalin was?

- Regarding the nation's right to go to war preemptively, do, say, China, India, and Pakistan enjoy the same right?[82]

Politically, the media's deference to George W. Bush proved particularly handy when, in the summer of 2002, the collapse of the stock market and a nationwide recession eventually displaced the war against terrorism as the primary story driving political coverage. Here was a story in which the president, for reasons both of personality and ideology, was particularly vulnerable. For one thing, the corporate crooks who had ripped off billions from their shareholders and were destroying investor confidence with their phony accounting schemes were among Bush and the Republican Party's most high-profile supporters. Second, as Paul Krugman tirelessly demonstrated, Bush had been guilty of many of the same kinds of offenses—albeit on a far smaller scale— while heading up Harken Oil in the 1990s.

The Harken story had every conceivable element of a prized media scandal, and certainly more than were present in the relatively (in comparison to Harken) penny-ante Arkansas-based financial shenanigans that inspired nearly 3,000 pages of *Wall Street Journal* editorials and, eventually, the only impeachment trial of an elected president in the nation's history. Among the journalistically mouth-watering details were:

- Harken engaged in Enron-like financial manipulation to boost its earnings. Struggling in 1989—with Bush on its audit committee—the company decided that instead of revealing its true financial straits, it would loan money to a group of insiders who had formed a partnership under the name International Marketing & Resources. IM&R then used the funds to purchase 80 percent of a Harken subsidiary called Aloha Petroleum Ltd. This move succeeded in hiding $10 million worth of debt. The Securities and Exchange Commission ruled the transaction phony and forced the company to restate its 1989 earnings. As a member of the audit committee (and a functioning adult who takes his professional responsibilities even remotely seriously), Bush must have seen the company's balance sheets and discussed its finances in detail. And he must have examined the audit reports prepared by Arthur Andersen. Other members of the audit committee have certainly admitted as much. When asked about the particulars of the Aloha deal, he responds, "I had absolutely no idea." But as Paul Krugman points out, "If Mr. Bush didn't know about the Aloha maneuver, he was a very negligent director." As the *Washington Post* later reported, "Bush was deluged with confidential information about the financial plight of a Texas oil company before he sold the majority of his holdings and triggered a federal investigation, according to Securities and Exchange Commission records."[83] As the *LA Times* reported,

Alfred King, former managing director of the Institute of Management Accountants and former adviser to the Financial Accounting Standards Board, noted, "The people at Enron could have gone to school on this thing. . . . They [Harken] sold to themselves and recorded a profit. That's exactly what Enron did on a number of those off-balance-sheet transactions. On this one transaction at least, it's almost identical."[84]

- Bush took two low-interest loans totaling $180,375 from Harken Energy Corp. in 1986 and 1988 while he was a member of the board of directors, engaging in a practice he later condemned as president to stem corporate abuse and accounting fraud. "I challenge compensation committees to put an end to all company loans to corporate officers," he said.[85]

- Moreover, Bush had signed a document in 1990 saying he wouldn't sell any stock for at least six months but then unloaded the stock in less than half that time, cashing out for $848,560, just before Harken's debt was disclosed and its value tanked.[86] Just one week before Bush's windfall sale, lawyers sent letters to all the Harken directors warning them not to cash in any stock if they were in any possession of negative information about the company.[87] The SEC investigated the trade but took no action. This decision may or may not have had something to do with the fact that the SEC chief then was Robert Breeden, appointed by Bush's father who was then president. The SEC's general counsel—the person charged with the decision about legal action—had previously been George W. Bush's personal lawyer. Dan Bartlett, the White House communications director, said Bush "was fully cooperative, waived attorney-client privilege and made himself available for a telephone or in-person interview." But in truth, Harken proved particularly uncooperative. Two SEC investigators said in a 1991 internal memo, "Harken has asserted the attorney-client privilege and refused to produce documents concerning its policies covering the purchase, sale or ownership of Harken securities by officers or directors." The investigation was so lax, in fact, that Bush was never even personally interviewed about the case. Bush would later claim that his sale was fully "vetted" by the SEC, but the *Dallas Morning News* has quoted a 1993 letter from the SEC to Bush's lawyer emphasizing that its decision "must in no way be construed as indicating that (Bush) has been exonerated." Bush invited reporters to examine the minutes of relevant meetings, saying, "You need to look back on the director's minutes," but the White House refused to ask Harken or the SEC to release them. The identity of the mysterious buyer of Bush's overvalued stock has never been revealed.[88]

- Bush offered up no convincing answers for his actions beyond what he calls "an honest difference of opinion," noting "sometimes things aren't exactly black-and-white when it comes to accounting procedures." At first the president said it was because the SEC lost the paperwork. Later he said it was a lawyer mixup. When the questions became overly uncomfortable, he took refuge in ridiculous homilies such as: "I believe people have taken a step back and asked, What's important in life? You know, the bottom line and this corporate America stuff, is that important? Or is serving your neighbor, loving your neighbor like you'd like to be loved yourself?"

- Amazingly, Vice President Cheney engaged in many of these same practices while CEO of Halliburton. Cheney made an $18.5 million profit selling his shares for more than $52 each in August 2000; sixty days later, the company surprised investors with a warning business was way down, sending shares down 11 percent in a day. About the same time, it announced it was under a grand jury investigation for overbilling the government. Cheney's actions inspired another SEC investigation, undertaken while he was serving as vice president and overseen by Bush's appointee, Harvey Pitt.[89]

The Harken sale appears to have every appearance of the kind of corrupt crony capitalism that SEC investigations are supposed to catch. Perhaps this appearance is deceiving, but given the stakes—and the fact that George W. Bush ran for president in part on his reputation for business acumen—one would think this had the makings of a major story. After all, in his first bid for governor of Texas, Bush bragged of a business career that had to be judged a success "by any objective measure." The press picked up this theme for him and ran with it during the 2000 election. To cite just one example, a week before the election, pundit Robert George testified on CNN, "We are in a very much, a strong business-oriented economy and I think the experience of a businessman, like George W. Bush, I think, is actually good in a president."[90]

Compared to the millions gained in the Harken and Halliburton cases, the Clintons' $30,000 (failed) Whitewater investment looks mighty puny indeed. But the media proved remarkably uncurious about the story about the former compared to the latter. The Bush administration, Harken Oil, and the SEC stonewalled with regard to the relevant documents, inspiring barely a peep of protest. This despite the fact that the single most important issue at the moment these questions were being asked was that of "corporate responsibility" in the wake of the billion-dollar debacles at Enron, Arthur Andersen, WorldCom, Tyco, and others. But here was Howard Kurtz on his CNN show, *Reliable Sources*, falsely claiming that Bush "was ultimately cleared by the SEC," a view that was seconded by his guest Martha Brant of *Newsweek*. Kurtz seemed to be doing his best to ridicule the very idea that anyone would care about Bush's honesty in making his fortune. "Where is the evidence," he asked "that George Bush's history as an oilman or his contributions from industry have anything whatsoever to do with the misaccounting, as he put it? Isn't the press trying to rope him into these corporate scandals? . . . Do you think it was fair for reporters Wednesday to pepper Ari Fleischer with questions about this 1989 SEC case involving George W. Bush?" Of course no evidence yet existed, which is exactly why more investigation was needed, given the strong circumstantial evidence of wrong-doing—that is, after all, the entire purpose of so-called investigative reporting—but Kurtz would have none of it.

Remember CNN is the "liberal" network, alternately called either "Communist Network News" or "Clinton Network News." Over at "fairandbalanced" Fox, its media program, *Fox Newswatch*, left this line of argument to one of its right-wing panelists, James Pinkerton, a former policy aide for George H. W. Bush. He trotted out those old war-horses of "predictable" response of a "liberal press corps" that "is out to get Bush and always has been." Pinkerton posited that "probably 90 percent of them voted for Al Gore," offering no evidence, "and they never believed much in capitalism." As he spoke, Pinkerton gestured toward a correspondent for the *Nation* and promised "as we'll hear more of in a moment."[91] His obvious implication here is that the tiny leftist opinion magazine—for which I write a column—is representative of the entire mainstream media, an intellectually indefensible belief that I can only wish had any credence.

Naturally, the *Wall Street Journal* editors saw nothing wrong with anything Bush undertook while in private industry. "We took our own very close look at the Harken story back in 1999," they explained, "scrutiny that made us none too popular with the Bush campaign. What we found is some interesting Saudi connections on the finance side, but on the corporate ethics side absolutely zero. . . . While a putative scandal is always open to fresh disclosures, what excited the press pack this week was already known when voters cast their ballots. An informed election, it seems to us, wipes the slate clean."[92]

Also stepping up to the plate in defense of ignoring the story were the allegedly liberal editors of the *Washington Post*. The editors warned that Congress shouldn't let Harken "distract" members from corporate reform, as if there were any relationship between these two tasks. What the editors really meant is that the media should not distract itself. Congress, they well know, is set up to deal with many items simultaneously. That's why, as any decently educated high school freshman can tell you, it has committees with names like "Appropriations," "Government Operations," "Armed Services," and "Foreign Relations." Moreover, the *Post* editorial demonstrated remarkable naivete in describing the head of the SEC who closed the Bush investigation as "a Republican who knew Mr. Bush's father."[93] Hello? Breeden not only "knew" Bush's father, he got his job from him. As Salon reported, Breeden was "a devoted admirer of President Bush," according to a *New York Law Journal* profile at the time of his nomination. (The *Journal* noted that one of Breeden's three sons shared a Bush family name, Prescott.) One friend told the magazine that Breeden's admiration for Bush was "something of a passion for him," adding, "He would have done just about anything for the vice president's chances of becoming president." Seeing the photos on the SEC director's wall, one person termed George H. W. Bush "Breeden's Mao." Before becoming SEC chairman, Breeden spent time working in the Washington office of the influential Texas law firm Baker Botts, partially founded by the great-grandfather of James A. Baker III, who served as secretary of state for George H. W. Bush and Florida operator-in-chief for W. Another one of the firm's founding partners was Robert Jordan, who represented Bush during the SEC investigation.[94]

Back in January 1994, the very same editorial page insisted upon the creation of a special prosecutor for Whitewater despite its admission that "there has been no credible charge in this case that either the president or Mrs. Clinton did anything wrong." That was not the point, the editors advised. The Justice Department could not be depended upon to do a fair and thorough investigation because, as the paper put it, "To whom do they report?" That question apparently lost its relevance by the time Bush became president, with regard to SEC chairs appointed by both father and son.[95]

It would not be fair to say the media ignored the Harken story. They were prodded by Paul Krugman's columns in the *New York Times* to ask a few uncomfortable questions of Ari Fleischer and the president himself, as Kurtz's comments indicate. This went on for a couple of weeks. But Bush stonewalled here just as successfully as he had during the campaign stonewalled the charge that he had used cocaine in the 1980s; a brief frenzy took place and then the media lost interest.

The comparison with the Clintons' Whitewater escapades is truly damning. As Krugman noted, "Harken's fake profits were several dozen times as large as the Whitewater land deal—though only about one-seventh the cost of the Whitewater investigation."[96] For following the Bush decision to stonewall the investigation and release no new documents, nor request that Harken nor the SEC do so, the media simply let the story lie, as if Bush had indeed been exonerated by a tough-minded SEC investigation, rather than by a lax one conducted entirely by family friends and filial appointees. In contrast, as Eric Boehlert has noted, during the Whitewater frenzy in 1995, the government's Resolution Trust Corp. commissioned the highly respected law firm of Pillsbury, Madison & Sutro to conduct its investigation. At a cost of $3.8 million, it discovered, "The evidence is unequivocal that, concerning almost all of the fraudulent transactions, the Clintons were unaware of McDougal's criminal conduct." It found, "The Clintons' investment in Whitewater was financially unsuccessful. They invested a substantial amount of personal funds and realized no profit from the venture." Yet the media continued to swirl around the story, demanding to know how much the president and first lady knew about McDougal's criminal activities, and whether they made any money from them. The investigation, for journalistic purposes, was simply ignored.[97]

---

As a citizen, I must admit, I don't particularly care what Bush did before he was president. I only care about the job he does while in office. But the contrast between the treatment he and Vice President Cheney have received and that meted out by the media to the Clintons is enough to make one wonder if the media have not made some sort of silent pact among themselves to torment only Democratic presidents.

In the midst of the media's brief flurry of interest in Harken, ABC's nonpartisan and extremely politically savvy Web publication *The Note* warned its fellow journalists: "Since the Republican party is the only one of our two major political parties in America who believes the press is routinely biased against them, when such a frenzy is going on for a GOP administration, the press needs to be extra careful in making sure that perspective and fairness are maintained."[98] Talk about "working the refs." Between the fear of appearing to tear down a national icon during wartime and the effect of decades of fielding attacks by politically minded conservatives drumming to a beat of their own invention, the elite media has so internalized the false message of their own "liberalism" that they were openly holding back on the Republicans, as if in fear of where the truth might lead. The media's gentle treatment of George W. Bush and his administration was, in many ways, a tribute to decades of hard spadework by conservative activists undertaken specifically for this purpose. And given its effect across the broad swath of American politics in the late 1990s and early 2000s, they had every right to take pride in their work.

By the time of the first anniversary of the 9/11 attacks, as *Wall Street Journal* reporter John Harwood quietly noted, most Americans were worse off than they had been on the day George Bush took office. "The Dow Jones Industrial Average has declined by nearly 2000 points since he took office; unemployment has risen to 5.7% from 4.2%. In the six quarters of the Bush presidency, growth of gross domestic product has averaged 1.1%, down from 3.6% in the last six quarters of the Clinton presidency. In the *Journal*/NBC poll, only 38% of Americans believe the country is safer than a year ago."[99] Partially as a result of these developments and partially because of the enormous tax cut Bush pushed through Congress based on transparently phony economic assumptions, the federal budget had gone from surplus to massive deficit. Meanwhile, the number of Americans living in poverty saw its largest increase in more than forty years, median household income declined, and the number of Americans living without health insurance spiked upward. Every single one of these trends proved a reversal of the progress of the Clinton years.[100] Abroad, the Middle East peace process—a deal nearly closed by Clinton—was in flames. America's allies were increasingly alienated by the nation's refusal to abide by international agreements and its insistence upon a ham-handed unilateralism in world affairs. And much of the sympathy engendered by the attacks of 9/11—attacks that might have been at least partially anticipated had the administration been paying closer attention to their warning signs—had been dissipated by Bush's demand for backing for a preemptive war against Iraq. Of course many of these events were well beyond the ability of any administration to control, particularly in light of the events of 9/11. But certainly not all of them. And the ironclad rule—at least until the advent of the second Bush administration—of American politics is that administrations get credit in good times and blame in bad times, regardless of causal connection or the lack thereof.

Yet Bush and the Republicans scored a smashing victory in the mid-term elections of 2002, making him the first president since 1882 to see his party actually gain seats in the House and Senate in an off-year election. Part of the reason, of course, was money. The Republicans, according to FEC records, spent $184 million more than the Democrats did in these elections, and that did not include the vast resources afforded by Bush's control of the executive branch. Another obvious reason was the dispirited, all-but-voiceless performance of the Democrats. But a no-less-significant factor in the Republican victory was a media that, as if by unspoken consensus, declined to hold the administration responsible for almost any aspect of these unhappy developments. Naturally, many in the media sought to portray the election of 2002—in which fewer than 40 percent of Americans participated and money made an obvious difference, to say nothing of September 11—as a vindication of the Supreme Court's decision to hand the 2000 election to Bush.[101] The logic is a bit hard to follow, except when we remember that establishing Bush's legitimacy has been a desperately pursued priority of the punditocracy since the moment the court handed him his tarnished prize.

Given the media's role in helping George Bush to claim the presidency, both during the regular election as well as in Florida—in addition to the enormously gentle treatment accorded his presidency—one recalls the saliency of a slogan that could be found on Republican bumpers during the 1992 election. It read "Annoy the Media: Re-elect George Bush." Given the power of the "liberal media" myth, despite an avalanche of evidence to the contrary, one suspects that we will see its reappearance in 2004. A more intellectually defensible bumper-sticker would read as follows: "Annoy the Media: Re-elect Al Gore."

# 13

## The (Really) Conservative Media

ONE REASON THAT MANY PEOPLE, including some liberals, believe the myth of the liberal media is that they do not know how extensive and influential the conservative media is. It is not simply that when you add up the circulation/penetration of the Fox News Channel, the *Wall Street Journal* editorial page, the *New York Post*, *Washington Times*, *Weekly Standard*, *National Review*, *American Spectator*, *Human Events*, www.andrewsullivan.com, the Drudge Report, Rush Limbaugh, the entire universe of talk radio, and most of the punditocracy, you've got a fair share of the media. The ability of these deeply biased and frequently untrustworthy outlets to shape the universe of the so-called "liberal media" gives them a degree of power and influence that exceeds their already considerable circulations.

As we have seen in earlier chapters, nefarious political operatives, masquerading as journalists, helped turn the Clintons' unprofitable $30,000 investment in a failed savings and loan into a politically paralyzing, $70 million constitutional crisis. But they could not have done it without the full cooperation of such mainstream media outlets as the *Washington Post* and ABC News, which have grown increasingly cowed by false complaints of liberal bias and, hence, progressively more sympathetic to the most outlandish conservative complaints.

When *Washington Post* White House reporter John Harris noted that he and his fellow White House correspondents were proving far more sympathetic to the conservative George W. Bush than they had ever been to the "liberal" Bill Clinton, he chose as his main culprit "conservative interest groups, commentators and congressional investigators" who, beginning in 1993, "waged a remorseless campaign that they hoped would make life miserable for Clinton and vault themselves to power." This movement had been in the works for decades and had helped turn the tide in Washington toward conservatism as early as 1978, when Jimmy Carter was forced to switch directions in mid-presidency and embrace a host of measures that he had previously found to be anathema. But during the previous decade and a half, conservative interest groups had grown both more powerful and more conservative, outpacing liberals at first and soon matching and eventually exceeding in many cases the resources of the old establishment. Liberals have no such movement, not a fraction of the money, and what troops they possess can boast much less organizational discipline than that enjoyed by the right. As Harris noted, the left lacks the ability (if not the inclination) to weave all "manner of presidential miscues, misjudgments or controversial decisions" into a fabric of alleged scandal. As a result of the context created by the conservative warriors, Harris argued, "stories like the travel office firings flamed for weeks instead of receding into yesterday's news. And they colored the prism through which many Americans, not just conservative ideologues, viewed Clinton." I quote Harris at length because, working within the belly of the so-called beast, he knows that of which he speaks:

> For the most part, Clinton's foes and their contemptuous views of him were within the bounds of fair debate. But Democrats are not likely to give as good as they got. They simply aren't as well organized. And they are not shouting as loudly.
>
> Few liberal commentators see themselves self-consciously representing an ideological movement the way many conservatives do. The Brookings Institution tilts liberal but is not an ideological arsenal in the way the Heritage Foundation is. Who is the liberal version of Rush Limbaugh, who so colorfully rallied opposition to Clinton? Nor is there an obvious Democratic version of Rep. Dan Burton (R-Ind.), eager to aim the investigative apparatus of Congress at the White House. Bush is also catching a break from his own side: Clinton's nomination of a gay man as ambassador to Luxembourg caused outrage on the right; Bush's naming a gay AIDS czar was met largely with silence on Capitol Hill.
>
> In Clinton's first term, Rep. Richard K. Armey (R-Tex.) turned to Democrats and said, "Your president is just not that important to us." This underscores the irony that Bush, whose ascension was clouded by questions over whether he really won, has been accorded more legitimacy by the opposition than Clinton was—or than Gore would have been had he become president while winning the popular vote.
>
> The discrepancy also illustrates how Bush and his aides miss the point with their constant boasting about how Bush has "changed the tone" in Washington after the coarsening Clinton years. Clinton disgraced himself through his personal behavior and by then taking flight from honor and accountability. But Washington's snarling public tone was caused more by his opponents; he was as ready to meet with Republicans as Bush is with Democrats. Little of his rhetoric ever matched the vitriol that congressional Republicans aimed at him.[1]

Franklin Foer of the not-so-liberal *New Republic* shares Harris's basic analysis of an objectively pro-conservative Republican Washington media, but believes that reporters let themselves and their colleagues off the hook too easily by blaming outside pressure groups. The problem, as Foer diagnoses it, is that "after years of listening to conservatives complain about their bias, and years of living in fear of overzealous media critics, liberal reporters have been completely cowed."[2] Of course the two hypotheses are not exactly contradictory. Conservatives have spent billions during the past three decades, both to pressure the mainstream media to move rightward and to create their own parallel media structure, which serves the same purpose as it provides an alternative viewpoint both to the faithful and the gullible. Unbeknownst to millions of Americans who continue to believe that the media are genuinely liberal—or that conservatives and liberals are engaged in a fair fight of relative equality—liberals are fighting a near-hopeless battle in which they are enormously outmatched by most measures. Just take a look, for example, at the power and influence exercised within the media by the self-described "wild men" of the *Wall Street Journal* editorial page.[3]

For twenty-nine years before he stepped down in 2001 to become a columnist for the paper, Robert Bartley led his *Journal* editorial page staff in the practice of a kind of journalism alien to most newspapers and newsmagazines. It was not typical editorial page opinion-mongering. It was not the objective style of reporting to which all national newspapers, including the *Wall Street Journal*, aspire. It was something else entirely; a reported polemic, written in a style akin to a Sunday sermon on hellfire and damnation, or perhaps a politically inverted Alexander Cockburn column. Michael Kinsley, a former columnist for the page, calls the page's methods "Stalinist" and couched in "intellectual dishonesty."[4] Alex Jones, head of the Shorenstein Center at Harvard, termed Bartley's pages "perhaps the most influential, most articulate, most ferocious opinion page in the country."[5] Its power, *New Yorker* editor David Remnick noted, is "amplified by the audience it reaches every day—five and a half million of the nation's best educated and most influential citizens."[6] In January 2002, the *Journal* added the viewers of CNBC to its Dow Jones–powered global reach, as that station inexplicably chose the editors to present a weekly version of the extremist opinion-mongering it offers in print on a daily basis, with no balance from a single moderate, much less an actual liberal. Given this influence, it seems likely that if you added up every genuinely liberal voice in the American political discourse—every single newspaper pundit, talk-show co-host, opinion magazine columnist or writer, and Internet scribbler—you would not have accumulated even one half of the power enjoyed on a daily basis by the *Journal*'s firebreathing staff.

Under the curiously soft-spoken Bartley's direction, the *Journal*'s editorial pages did more than make American journalistic history; they made political and economic history too. During the late 1970s and early 1980s, as the economic historian Wayne Parsons observed, "without [the *Journal*'s] support it is difficult to see how the supply-side argument could possibly have achieved such a leading position in the economic policy debates." The amazing story of the *Journal*'s near single-handed promotion of a theory from economic outer space—one that lacked a single well-known and respected proponent in the economic profession at the time of its adoption by candidate and then President Ronald Reagan, has been told many times.[7] When, after twelve years in which supply-side-inspired deficits threatened to strangle future growth, Bill Clinton was forced to clean up the economic mess, Bartley had no doubt about what would happen. Clinton's proposals, he predicted, would "cripple" the economy. When the plan passed, the paper promised, "[W]e are seeing the early signs of the stagflation that we knew so well during the Carter presidency." "Hysteria" would not be too strong a term to describe the *Journal*'s reaction to the Clinton plan. The headline, "The Class Warfare Economy" was attended by a cartoon of a guillotine. The tiny rise in the nation's top marginal tax rates to a level where they remained the second lowest in the industrialized world did not turn out well for the editors. The Clinton years resulted in an unbroken expansion of the economy in which the vast majority of its benefits were tilted toward the very wealthy, the people on whom "class war" had allegedly been declared.[8]

The *Journal* editors are so deeply committed to the far-right propaganda they espouse, they frequently contradict the reporting in their own newspaper. For instance, in 1980 a *Journal* reporter broke a story proving that an alleged $100 million administration cost offered up by a group of California oil firms protesting a new state tax, was, in fact, a wildly exaggerated estimate of the expense of administering the tax. Two days later, the editorial page noted, "according to one estimate, enforcement of the tax would cost taxpayers $100 million. . . ." Four years later, Washington bureau reporter David Rogers discovered that the CIA had been illegally mining Nicaragua's harbors. The story ran on page six and was picked up by the *Washington Post*. Six days afterwards, the editorial page, standing foursquare behind the contra war, criticized members of Congress for leaking the information to the *Post*.[9] More recently, the paper's reporters won a Pulitzer Prize for exposing the misleading statements of tobacco company officials, leading to massive jury awards in tobacco liability cases. Meanwhile, Bartley and company ridiculed tobacco regulations as "further government-imposed nuisances, whose chief direct effect will be to make millionaires of a few more lawyers."[10]

In August 2002, Bartley wrote a column in favor of war with Iraq in which he insisted that because the Bush administration had succeeded "for the first time exerting American leadership to unify the factions opposing Saddam." In uniting the Iraqi opposition, "The pieces are now in place to liberate Iraq."[11] A day later, the *Journal* ran a heavily reported page one story that popped Bartley's hot air balloon. "The tension among Iraq's opposition groups amounts to a significant impediment as the Bush administration speaks more publicly about ousting Mr. Hussein," the *Journal* reporters explained, offering the kind of evidence entirely absent from his op-ed.[12] Readers of only the editorial page might have been surprised, a day later, to discover that the most powerful Kurdish chieftain in northern Iraq, Massoud Barzani, had refused the Bush administration's invitation to attend its meeting.[13] But one suspects the paper's readership among America's titans of industry are well aware as to which portions of the paper to trust when real money is on the line.

When it comes to the editors' ideological opponents, all gloves come off and most journalistic rulebooks go out the window. During the 1984 election, for instance, the *WSJ* editorial pages ran a story rejected by the newspaper about alleged connections between Geraldine Ferraro and the Mafia, based on her husband's business dealings. In the following election, it published rumors about Democrat Michael Dukakis's psychological state that originated with known nut-case Lyndon LaRouche and dealt mainly with Dukakis's brother.[14]

*Journal* editors like to paint the media as soft on Communism, though the only credible example to which they can easily point is Rupert Murdoch's defense of China. (See below.) And while, to its credit, the *Journal* has been tough on Murdoch, its contributors have also been genuinely soft on fascism. The brutal Chilean dictator, Augusto Pinochet, they argued, "saved his country," transforming it from "a Communist beachhead to an example of free-market reform."[15] That the so-called "Communist beachhead" was actually a democratically elected government, the editors do not mention. Former editor Jude Wanniski termed the death-squad leader and priest killer, Roberto D'Aubuisson of El Salvador to be the victim of a "McCarthyist" media cabal and "one of the most successful propaganda hoaxes of the decade." (Wanniski has also developed a decidedly soft spot for another would-be fascist, Louis Farrakhan, and serves as perhaps his most high-profile champion in America.) It's not easy, in the eyes of the editors, for any right-winger to go too far. But when it happens, it usually turns out to be the fault of leftists. For instance, when, in 1993, a right-wing terrorist murdered an abortion doctor named David Gunn in Pensacola, Fla., the editors blamed . . . the Sixties' New Left: "We think it is possible to identify the date when the United States . . . began to tip off the emotional tracks," they explained. "The date is August 1968, when the Democratic National Convention found itself sharing Chicago with the street fighters of the anti–Vietnam War movement." The protesters, they went on, were responsible for "lowering the barriers of acceptable political and personal conduct."[16] In other words, Jerry Rubin made me do it. Again, if, for the sake of balance, the Dow Jones corporation and CNBC wished to balance their politics with the equivalently extreme views from the left, they would have a hard time finding anyone at all in the United States, save perhaps Alexander Cockburn, who by sheer coincidence, no doubt, is also a former *Wall Street Journal* editorial page columnist.[17]

The *Journal* editors, moreover, play by journalistic rules of their own making. In a lengthy examination in the *Columbia Journalism Review*, Trudy Lieberman examined six dozen examples of disputed editorials and op-eds in the paper. She discovered that "on subjects ranging from lawyers, judges, and product liability suits to campus and social issues, a strong America, and of course, economics, we found a consistent pattern of incorrect facts, ignored or incomplete facts, missing facts, uncorroborated facts."[18] In many of these cases, the editors refused to print a correction, preferring to allow the aggrieved party to write a letter to the editor, which would be printed much later, and then let the reader decide whose version appeared more credible. Almost never is the record corrected or do the editors admit their errors.[19]

The page's cavalier attitude toward facts and corrections is matched by an impressive ferocity of language. Frequently, its content is closer to a Rush Limbaugh radio rant or an Ann Coulter outburst than the Olympian tone employed by editorial writers on Fifteenth Street or in Times Square. Citizens who support consumer and safety regulation are termed "no-growth specialists, the safety and health fascists who try to turn real and imagined hazards to some political end." One editorial even referred to "so-called acid rain." To *Journal* editorial writers, the rest of the media—including presumably the paper's own reporting staff—is not merely liberal, but, as Mark Helprin wrote in its pages, "slavish[ly] obedien[t]" to Democratic liberals. This has, he insisted, "quintupled the arrogance of the most arrogant people in America, a triumphalist coterie of graduate students who accord to the hard left the same uneasy respect that most people reserve for the clergy, and grow teary-eyed over bats, squirrels and caribou as with barely concealable pleasure they sacrifice whole regions of rednecks."[20]

Aside from the Chicken Little-like role vis-à-vis the Clinton economic plan, the primary task the paper set for itself during the 1990s was the responsibility for publishing virtually every anti-Clinton rumor ever started, no matter how farfetched or lightly sourced. When White House aide Vincent Foster committed suicide in a park outside Washington in 1993, he left a note saying "the *WSJ* editors lie without consequence."[21] (The *Journal* had been insinuating nefarious activity on Foster's part.)

Politically, having the imprimatur of the *Journal* and its first-rate reporting staff gives its editorial pages far greater credibility and significance than they could possibly have achieved by mere force of argument. Many of the arguments made on its pages would be permanently relegated to the extreme fringes of political debate were it not for their appearance in one of the world's greatest newspapers. Nevertheless it was the *Journal*'s embrace of these strange tales that helped keep conservative hopes alive long enough for Kenneth Starr's investigation to find something—or anything—with which to impeach Bill Clinton.

The strange pursuit of poor Vince Foster, in death as in life, is a case in point. While it is obviously a bit unfair to blame the *Journal* writers for Foster's suicide—though he may have—their journalistic values with regard to his case left a great deal to be desired. "Until the Foster death is seriously studied, a Banquo's ghost will stalk . . . the Clinton administration," one long editorial warned, paying particular attention to Mrs. Clinton's movement on the day of Foster's death, as if to cast her as a contemporary Lady MacBeth.[22] The *Journal* also praised other media outlets' outlandish pursuits with regard to this paranoid endeavor. Its assistant features editor, Erich Eichman, later books editor, expressed "a debt of gratitude" for the *New York Post*'s irresponsible speculation that Foster's gun had been put in his hand after his death and the body had been moved to the spot where it was found.[23] Two days afterward, the editors imagined a vicious physical attack on a reporter whose notes were allegedly stolen, no doubt to prevent the disclosure of some other dastardly deed. This piece was entitled "Censored in Arkansas" and argued that *Harper's* reporter L. J. Davis had met with foul play while reporting a story on Whitewater in Little Rock. But the *Journal* editors turned out to have played fast and loose with the facts, once again, though the facts themselves are quite confusing. Davis lost some pages of his notes after waking up unconscious in his hotel room. He told a reporter he did not remember much beyond that and admitted to having downed at least four martinis on the night in question.[24] But the hotel manager later explained, "We have records that he was down here [at the hotel bar] at 10:30 that night," which was supposed to be the end of when he said he had been unconscious. The hotel bartender confirmed the manager's version and put the number of martinis Davis consumed at six. Davis, meanwhile, quite understandably, never mentioned the incident in print, thinking it insignificant and not trusting his own memory. He says he asked the *Journal* to print a retraction of its wild allegations, but of course it refused.[25]

The Foster "murder" may have disappointed, but two months later, the paper went back to the paranoid well, this time on behalf of the infamous Jerry Falwell videotape, "The Clinton Chronicles," in which Clinton was blamed for Foster's murder, Davis's alleged assault, and even a mob-related killing during his Arkansas governorship. While the paper pretended to disassociate itself from the film's nuttiest charges— "finding no real evidence of a Clinton connection, and feeling the President of the United States is entitled to a presumption of innocence, we decline in the name of responsibility to print what we've heard"—it still felt compelled to print the 800 phone number so that its readers might obtain their own copy.[26]

One of the prime movers of the *Journal*'s anti-Clinton obsession was John Fund, who spent a great deal of time meeting with members of the Arkansas Project and some of the more notorious figures in the Paula Jones lawsuit and "Get-Clinton" conspiracy. Fund acted as kind of a father figure to many of them, helping to guide their strategy in secret while simultaneously writing editorials in the *Journal* accusing Clinton of all manner of unproven malfeasance. It was a complicated balancing act; it could not last. In a tale that appears almost too weird to write down, it seems that a woman named Melinda Pillsbury-Foster, with whom Fund had had an affair more than twenty years ago, sent her young daughter, Morgan, to look up Fund when she went to New York. One thing led to another, and the results appear to have been a live-in relationship and an abortion.

Anyway, Fund's relationship with the daughter of his ex-girlfriend did not exactly work out, inspiring mother and daughter to take their revenge by uploading onto the Web a taped telephone call in which John attempts to reconcile his support for Morgan's abortion with his "family values" politics. Mrs. Foster then informed the media that John and Morgan had decided to wed after all. This turned out to be false, but the next thing you know, Fund was gone from the *Journal*'s editorial page and was apparently the victim of a series of bizarre but quite public campaigns designed to destroy his reputation—up to and including an arrest (with charges later dropped) for battery that included a restraining order. (Irony of ironies, the Rush Limbaugh ghost-writer is also cited in David Brock's book, among other places, as a likely source for Matt Drudge's false and malicious claim that Sidney Blumenthal was a wife-beater, though Fund denies this.) Fund denies the charges and, in the view of this writer, is almost certainly innocent. (I have always found him to be very much a gentleman in his personal dealings.) Still, the charges demonstrate the difficulties that so many conservatives face—the pot-smoking, draft-dodging, multiply adulterous, deadbeat dad named Newt Gingrich; Henry Hyde, who broke up another man's family at age 40 in his "youthful" adulterous fling; adulterers Robert Dole and Robert Livingston; to say nothing of men of the cloth such as Jim Bakker and Jimmy Swaggart—who seek to enforce their hypocritical moralistic standards on the rest of us as they ignore them. The fact that the media take these people seriously, while knowing of the hypocrisies that lie beneath their charges—is further evidence of the foolish fiction that promotes the SCLM myth.

---

When Robert Bartley turned over the keys to the editor's office, he did so to Paul Gigot, a former speechwriter for James Baker during the Reagan administration and the page's Washington columnist. Gigot achieved a kind of infamy when, in November 2000, he celebrated the violent Republican riot that shut down the vote counting in Miami-Dade County and helped pave the way for the Supreme Court's handing of the presidency to George. W. Bush. (See Chapter 11.) Still, he is not quite as nutty as Bartley and has even been known to do some reporting as a columnist in Washington, which tended to keep his analyses tethered, however tenuously, to earth. With Bartley gone and Fund removed from the page, the editorialists had to work hard to retain their reputation for loopiness. They did, however, have the advantage of enjoying the services of another former Reagan speechwriter, Peggy Noonan, who has set a standard that is hard to beat.

Noonan does not appear to research her columns. She just gets feelings about people and goes with them. ("Is it irresponsible to speculate? It is irresponsible not to,"[27] she wrote.) These feelings tend to match her political prejudices, particularly in the case of people of whom she happens to disapprove. "When I first met Hillary Clinton she was a plain, dumpy woman with glasses and a shawl. I thought she was sweet," she wrote. But "people have worked on her clothes and her image; she's gone through a lot and come out cold and ambitious. Neither she nor Bill loves America. They don't want the presidency to help the country but to use it as a platform to power."[28] (*Journal* editorial writers have a thing about Hillary Clinton. Mark Helprin once used the pages to compare her to a "900-pound boyfriend of a voluptuous girl hitchhiker.")[29]

Al Gore was no better, Noonan decided. He was, she wrote, "not fully stable" and "altogether as strange and disturbing as Bill Clinton."[30] What's more, he was a liar. Once again, how did Noonan know? She just knew. Before the 2000 election, she wrote, with regard to partial birth abortion, the vice president "supports something he knows to be sick and wrong." The same was true regarding education. Gore, Noonan declared, somehow "knows [that] the most hopeful proposal of our time to make government schools better is the school liberation movement—including scholarship vouchers," but "Al Gore lies and says vouchers are bad." On Social Security, you guessed it: "Al Gore knows that it is responsible and constructive to allow greater freedom and choice in Social Security. . . . But he lies and says it's bad."[31] Lucky for Gore and the Clintons that they are not Arabs. Noonan supports a war against, well, she is not quite clear against whom, because "bad guys" tend to breed too quickly. "I tell you this," she explained to a reporter for the *Spectator* (UK). "It looks like the bad guys are breeding and proliferating pretty well already. You might say, quite literally, that at least an attack will keep a few of them from breeding at all."[32]

Noonan likes to play the pundit game of attributing the things she "knows" to "everyone." For instance, when the Bush White House was actively seeking to deceive reporters and the nation with its phony "vandalism" scandal, she told readers, "Everyone I know is talking about the 'pranks' of the departing Clinton-Gore crew on the incoming White House staff—the W's pried off the keyboards, the garbage left in the vice president's offices. You just know when you read about it that it's worse than anyone is saying—the Bush people being discreet because they don't want to start out with complaints and finger pointing." The story, which turned out to have virtually no basis in fact, proved to Noonan that "The Clintons were at heart vandals."[33]

Many observers thought Noonan outdid herself in late 2002 when she penned a mock–Paul Wellstone column from beyond the grave. Wellstone stood foursquare behind just about everything the *Journal* and Noonan opposed. But with the wisdom that comes with death—"You learn things here quickly . . . . You can literally see the big picture. You can see people's souls."—she informs Wellstone's supporters that the late senator disapproved of his memorial service. "You hurt a lot of people," Noonan has Wellstone's ghost telling those who loved him. "You offended and hurt and antagonized more than half the country. . . . Some of you need to get a good psychologist . . . ." It gets better. Noonan recruits a few other dead guys to make her case: "Jack Kennedy was here, and you're not going to like this, but he said what he said the day Nixon had his meltdown in '62. He looked at you and said, 'No class.' John Adams is here too. He turned away from you in disgust. 'Faction!' is what he said. It was no compliment." Her Wellstone admits to being sorry for what Peggy has him say, but like any good dead left-ist populist Democrat being channeled by a right-wing corporatist Republican, he was only saying these harsh things "because I care about you."[34]

The Wellstone-from-beyond-the-grave column might be considered Noonan's high point were it not for the masterpiece she crafted during the "Elian" episode of 2000, when she managed to set a standard for a combination of childlike hero wor-ship and downright silliness that belongs in textbooks devoted to either quality. In that famous episode, in which a group of Miami Cubans did not wish to return a child whose mother had been killed at sea to his father in Cuba—with the support of the very same "family values" crowd among U.S. conservatives—Noonan complained that her hero, Reagan, would never have allowed his justice department to enforce the law and the court's decisions to return the child. Moreover, he "would not have dis-missed the story of the dolphins [sent by God to rescue Elián, according to some of the young boy's protectors/kidnappers] as Christian kitsch, but seen it as possible evi-dence of the reasonable assumption that God's creatures had been commanded to protect one of God's children." She concludes, "But then he was a man."[35] Indeed.

---

The *Wall Street Journal* editors enjoy the backing of the Dow Jones Corporation and CNBC, and even with their more than five million readers, a few hundred thousand viewers, and the uncounted numbers who read their opinions on the Internet, via www.opinionjournal.com, they have to be considered relative pikers compared to the empire amassed by the veritable Wizard of Oz, Rupert Murdoch. With a net worth hovering in the area of $5 billion, the Australian national's News Corporation has holdings that include:

- Fox Broadcasting Network;

- Fox Television Stations, including over twenty U.S. television stations, the largest U.S. station group, covering more than 40 percent of U.S. TV house-holds;

- Fox News Channel;

- A major stake in several U.S. and global cable networks, including fx, fxM and Fox Sports Net, National Geographic Channel, Fox Kids Worldwide, and Fox Family Channel;

- Ownership or major interests in satellite services reaching Europe, the United States, Asia, and Latin America, often under the Sky Broadcasting brand;

- 20th Century Fox, with its library of over 2,000 films; 20th Century Fox International, 20th Century Fox Television, 20th Century Fox Home Entertainment, Fox Searchlight Pictures, Fox Television Studios;

- Over 130 English-language newspapers (including the *London Times* and the *New York Post*), making Murdoch's one of the three largest newspaper groups in the world;

- At least twenty-five magazines, including *TV Guide* and the *Weekly Standard;*

- HarperCollins, Regan Books, Zondervan Publishers;

- Fox Interactive, News Interactive, www.foxnews.com;

- Festival Records;

- The Los Angeles Dodgers.

While most of Murdoch's corporations are registered abroad to avoid taxes—News Corp. pays a paltry 7.8 percent effective tax rate in the United States—Murdoch gets more for his money as he is able to use the proceeds of one to support the other.[36] Politically and commercially, he is determined to put "synergy" to work. Murdoch's magazines and newspapers support his television programs and movies and vice versa. His reporters make up news that other companies would have to pay public relations firms millions to try to place. No newspaper in America is less shy about slanting its coverage to serve its master's agenda—be it commercial or political—than the *New York Post.* Judging by the *Post,* almost every Fox program is either "jaw-dropping," "megasuccessful," "highly anticipated," or all three.[37] Columnist Gersh Kuntzman once revealed that editors consider page two to be the "Pravda Page." "When there's a major [Murdoch] business deal going down, with no interest to readers," he explained, "it's on page two. Or when [then-conservative New York Senator Alfonse] D'Amato makes a pronouncement of no particular interest to readers, it's on page two." Oftentimes, this tendency turns the paper into kind of an extended inside joke in the media, where it is carefully read because of its obsessive media-oriented gossip. For instance, the *Post* declared the film *Titanic,* a Murdoch property, to have received "the first endorsement of any Hollywood movie by a Chinese official."[38] The paper did not mention just who believed it or why this mattered. The entire article was based on a premise so farfetched—that the entire Chinese nation was agitating to see the sappy film a full month before it was scheduled to open—that the article read as a kind of satiric self-criticism session of the kind that Maoists used to undergo in the days when they plotted to overthrow the evil government of "Amerika."

Once famous for its loveably nutty "Headless Body in Topless Bar"–type headlines in the early 1980s, Murdoch's tabloid has lost him perhaps hundreds of millions of dollars over the years at a rate of $10 million to $30 million per annum. (Actual figures are a closely guarded secret.) But despite its down-market definition of news, the paper still provides Murdoch with an entree to the media elite because of its great gossip pages, and, hardly incidentally, its terrific sports section. Curiously, in a city that is so fierce about its cultural pride, in late 2002 the *New York Post* was run largely by Australian imports. The *Post*'s current editor, hired in 2001, is Col Allan, a man who brags about peeing in the sink during editorial meetings and enjoys the nickname "Col Pot" back in Sydney. Allan took just six weeks to decide to fire the *Post*'s only black editor, Lisa Baird, who was fighting a losing battle with breast cancer at the time. He also fired the paper's only liberal columnist, that feisty New York institution, Jack Newfield, preferring the columns of Victoria Gotti, the sexy daughter of a murderous mob boss.[39] Allan also demonstrated his tin ear for New York politics quite early in his tenure when, upon Jim Jeffords's decision to switch sides in the Senate and vote with the Democrats—thereby giving that party a one-vote majority—he headlined the front page "Benedict Jeffords." New York, someone might have pointed out to him, has two Democratic senators and voted for both Al Gore and Bill Clinton by so large a margin that they barely needed to campaign there. Its denizens were not exactly angry about a switch in the Senate that gave their side more power.

Murdoch made no attempt to hide his paper's political agenda. Rudy Giuliani, who all but forced TimeWarner to add Fox News Channel to its local roster of stations, was second only to Leonardo in the *Post*'s pantheon of heroic Italians. Hillary Clinton, the "rejected wife," who proved the cause of "a veritable crime wave in the White House" and who, while running for senator, "couldn't find the Bronx unless she had a chauffeur, and couldn't find Yankee Stadium with a Seeing Eye dog," was, to say the least, treated rather less generously.[40] To the degree that any racial problems existed anywhere in New York, they were always the fault of black people, who demand special treatment or merely raise a ruckus for its own sake—all of these views shared by many on the right. All Israelis were noble warriors; all Palestinians, vicious terrorists. These, however, were predictable prejudices for a right-wing ideologue. The most interesting bias exhibited by Murdoch media properties was that on behalf of Communist totalitarianism—at least of the variety practiced in Beijing.

Initially Murdoch held conventional views about murderous Communist dictatorships and praised the manner in which modern telecommunications "have proved an unambiguous threat to totalitarian regimes everywhere." But when Beijing shut down his satellite broadcasts, Red Rupert switched sides, telling critics: "The truth is—and we Americans don't like to admit it—that authoritarian societies can work." When the Chinese complained about how the BBC portrayed them, Murdoch booted it off his Asian satellite network, Star TV. "The BBC was driving them nuts," he was quoted as saying. "It's not worth it."[41] Sucking up to the killers soon became a family affair. Murdoch's son James even found some kind words to say about the Reds' enforcement of anti-religious repression.[42]

Murdoch's publishing companies were put to work for the commies as well. Murdoch gave over a million bucks to Deng Xiaoping's daughter for an unreadable propagandistic tome that no sane person could ever have imagined would become a best-seller in the West.[43] When Chris Patten's tough-minded memoir of his years as the governor of Hong Kong threatened to upset the Chinese, however, Murdoch canceled the contract and attacked its author. His explanation? "We're trying to get set up in China. Why should we upset them?"[44]

Amazingly, Murdoch would not even take his own (adopted) nation's side in a conflict with the Chinese. During the hostage crisis of April 2001, while the Chinese were refusing to release U.S. soldiers, the paper seemed to undergo a personality transplant, all but ignoring the biggest story in the world.[45] *Post* editorials, which usually declare war every time someone sneezes near the Stars and Stripes, were almost completely mum. John Podhoretz, who later advised George Bush to invade Iraq merely to get the corporate accounting scandals off the front page, was the perfect diplomat.[46] Steve Dunleavy, who, as the *Post*'s almost insanely belligerent columnist, usually thinks of foreign policy as a subset of bar-fighting, proved to be remarkably patient and thoughtful in his discussion of the crisis. "Until happiness is restored to 24 American kids and their families, let's keep our sabers safely and silently sheathed," wrote the newly sissified tough guy. "Careless rhetoric can prove disastrous to freedom, as President Jimmy Carter harshly learned during the Iran hostage crisis."[47]

In 1985 Murdoch acquired 20th Century Fox Studios, in much the same way he acquired the *New York Post:* with lots of cash and some crucial political interventions from the politicians he funded. He combined the company with the fledgling Metromedia television stations to launch America's first new broadcast network since the early days of television. Fox was given every break imaginable throughout the 1980s on the grounds that a new television network should be encouraged. Finally, in 1994, following nearly ten years of indifference, the Federal Communications Commission checked into the network's ownership to see if it was foreign-owned. It was; Murdoch's News Corporation was actually an Australian company, not an American one, as he had portrayed it. But rather than allow the commission to enforce the law, according to Reed Hundt, then the FCC chair, conservative Republicans "lambasted me for the audacity of having looked into the question."[48]

While some of what the Fox network produced has been genuinely great—most notably *The Simpsons*—much of its programming appears devoted to answering the question "just how low can you go?" Conservatives like William Bennett and Pat Robertson enjoy condemning liberals for the promotion of casual sex and alternative lifestyles at the expense of society's bedrock social institutions like marriage and courtship, but Robertson has no more powerful and influential enemy in this regard than his business partner in the Fox Family Channel. In the spring of 2000, the network that had invented *Studs*, a dating show with stripping men, managed to amaze even its critics with *Who Wants to Marry a Millionaire?* Here, women were invited to prostitute themselves and debase the institution of marriage for the greater glory of Fox's ratings. (It almost didn't matter that the program's producers went about this task entirely incompetently, as the alleged "millionaire" was no such thing, but did have a few restraining orders in his past. The marriage was never consummated but the "bride" did get to pose naked in *Playboy*.) A year afterward, Fox managed to outdo itself in the cultural debasement sweepstakes with the debut of *Temptation Island*, in which four "committed" couples were dumped on an island and filmed "canoodling" in various combinations.[49]

From the outset, the network's "news" programs demonstrated a similarly catholic interpretation of the term "family values" when it came to reeling in viewers (and hence profits). Its original flagship, *A Current Affair*, erased much of the journalistic rulebook. As Burt Kearns, one of its top producers, later recounted, in order to get a copy of a tape alleging to show the actor Rob Lowe having sex with some young women of "jailbait" age, at the 1988 Democratic convention in Atlanta, the producers lifted footage from an Atlanta station and claimed it as its own, paid a club owner for the sex tape even though he had no legal ownership, and physically destroyed the evidence in the face of a lawsuit. As Kearns put it, "The Rob Lowe tape was a milestone for the show and tabloid television. Sex, celebrity, politics, crime, morality and America's obsession with home video cameras were all rolled into one. . . .We were the fucking champions of the world." (In fact, the events caught on tape did not really take place in Atlanta but were filmed in France. There were no underage girls involved and hence, no story. But nobody ever reported that.)[50] Details aside, Kearns was right. The conservative Roger Ailes, the former Reagan/Bush aide who then went on to head Fox News Channel, said he did not believe that such shows even require a defense. "News is what people are interested in," Ailes insisted. "We're just getting the same girls to dance around shinier poles."[51]

Despite this rather tricky track record, family-values wise, when Murdoch began Fox News Channel in 1996 with Ailes at the helm, conservatives fell all over themselves to praise it. "If it hadn't been for Fox, I don't know what I'd have done for the news," Trent Lott gushed during the Florida election recount.[52] George W. Bush extolled Bush I-aide-turned-anchor Tony Snow for his "impressive transition to journalism" in a specially taped April 2000 tribute to Snow's Sunday-morning show.[53] The right-wing Heritage Foundation had to warn its staffers to stop watching so much Fox News on their computers, lest the entire system crash.[54]

The conservative orientation of Fox is invaluable to the right, not merely because Fox offers the spin on reality conservatives prefer to have people see and hear, but also because it helps pull the rest of the not-terribly liberal media in its direction. In Chapter 10, I discussed the key role played by Fox and its election analyst, George W. Bush's loyal cousin, John Ellis, in helping create the media stampede to call the election for Bush. But the hiring of Ellis was no isolated incident; rather it was symbolic of business as usual. For instance, when, just before Election Day, the media discovered that George W. Bush had been hiding a DUI conviction, Fox seemed to spin the incident even more furiously than Karl Rove and Karen Hughes. Morton Kondracke of *Roll Call*: "A footnote." John Fund of the *Wall Street Journal*: "A blip." Mara Liasson of NPR: "Yes, I agree with that. I think it's a blip." The program in question—*Fox Special Report with Brit Hume*—did not even bother to devote much attention to the potentially election-altering news. Instead it focused, once again, on troubles Al Gore had in fighting off Ralph Nader.

When it did return to the story, the FNC spin focused on the Bush campaign's charge that the Gore team had somehow engineered the leak. FNC's Tony Snow went so far as to give credence to "rumors" that the Clinton administration had been involved and predicted that this might help the Bush campaign by creating sympathy for it—and therefore "backfire" on Gore. Snow never cited a shred of evidence for any of these claims, which was wise, as none existed. Meanwhile, FNC's Paula Zahn mused aloud on the question of just how long Maine Democrats had "sat on the story." In fact, it was the local Maine newspaper, where the Bush family compound is located, that sat on the story, for whatever reason we cannot know. As Eric Boehlert noted, all this spin-oriented damage control is, indeed, a far cry from the days during the height of the Clinton scandals, when former FNC correspondent Jeb Duvall, according to his account in *New York Magazine*, was once met by a news producer who "came up to me, and, rubbing her hands like Uriah Heep, said, 'Let's have something on Whitewater today.'"[55]

Such fare is, however, the norm for a station where a special about foreign policy is hosted by Fox commentator and former Republican House Speaker Newt Gingrich; *Heroes*, an irregular series, is hosted by Gingrich's ex-colleague in the Republican congressional leadership, John Kasich; and on *The Real Reagan*, a panel discussion on Ronald Reagan, hosted by Tony Snow, all six guests were Reagan friends and political aides, plus the ever-present Ollie North.[56] Fox's coverage of the conflict in Afghanistan is similarly slanted but also kind of crazily flawed. Most famous, of course, was the incident in which Geraldo Rivera missed the spot of the "hallowed ground" from which he pretended to be reporting by a mere 200 miles.

But most news organizations have displayed a bias toward the American side in covering the events in Afghanistan. Indeed, how could they not? While none beside Rivera brag about "packing heat" and laughably threaten to take out bin Laden themselves, these reporters too are Americans, who saw the tapes of the horror of September 11. Most are not only deeply patriotic people themselves, personally sympathetic to the soldiers and their cause, but also quite understandably hostile and fearful of an enemy that has been targeting journalists with a gruesome (and occasionally bloodthirsty) effectiveness. These reporters are also, in many cases, extremely sensitive to the charge that the media is anti-American, and in the cases of both Fox and CNN have been warned against appearing so. It is a baseless charge, as any quick comparison between U.S. and British or European coverage of the fighting immediately demonstrates. To take just one "for instance," on December 30, 2001, U.S. airstrikes hit the village of Niazi Kala (also called Qalaye Niaze) in eastern Afghanistan, killing dozens of civilians. The attack was major news in several U.K. newspapers, with the *Guardian* and the *Independent* running front-page stories. The headlines were straightforward: "U.S. Accused of Killing Over 100 Villagers in Airstrike" (*Guardian*, January 1, 2002); "U.S. Accused of Killing 100 Civilians in Afghan Bombing Raid" (*Independent*, January 1, 2002); "'100 Villagers Killed' in U.S. Airstrike" (*London Times*, January 1, 2002). In contrast, the *New York Times* first reported the civilian deaths at Niazi Kala under the headline "Afghan Leader Warily Backs U.S. Bombing" (January 2, 2002). Keep in mind that the *New York Times* is usually considered Public Enemy Number One by conservatives. Note also that this antiwar/anti-American accusation, while useful to conservatives seeking to force news organizations to hew to their views, has always been false. In the most famous case, that of the Vietnam War, the media has been exonerated by none other than the official history of the U.S. Army. [57] But as with the overall charge of bias, endless repetition, coupled with a multibillion-dollar propaganda offensive carried out over a period of decades, has had its intended effect. Much of the U.S. media is particularly wary of reporting any news that might be construed as "anti-American," regardless of the merit of the charge. For many, it is simply not worth the hassle.

Yet even in the deeply pro-American, patriotic context in which the U.S. media has been operating since September 11, 2001, Fox still manages to distinguish itself.

Osama bin Laden, its anchors, reporters, and guests explain, is "a dirtbag," "a monster" overseeing a "web of hate." His followers in Al Qaeda are "terror goons." Taliban fighters are "diabolical" and "henchmen." Fox is not interested in covering the civilian casualties of U.S. bombing missions. As Brit Hume explained, "We know we're at war. The fact that some people are dying, is that really news? And is it news to be treated in a semi-straight-faced way? I think not." To a considerable degree Fox's open bias in this case—and in many others—is refreshing. It is perhaps the only news station where news comes with a context, and is therefore made more understandable for consumers than the helter-skelter version to which most Americans have become accustomed. It's unfortunate, both for genuine liberals as well as for the cause of democratic discourse in the United States, that it is the only one available. And fortunately for the pro-war crowd in the United States, Rupert Murdoch has no significant investments in Iraq—nor any desire to convince Saddam Hussein to let his satellite network into that nation.

Because investments almost always appear to trump ideology in Murdoch's world—he supported Tony Blair in England against his conservative opponents and received some extremely curious favors from the government thereafter—the millions of dollars Murdoch pours into the low-circulation conservative opinion magazine, the *Weekly Standard*, is perhaps his most curious investment. Most of Murdoch's properties earn money. The *New York Post* may look like a money-loser, but it buys him a political voice in New York and with the media elite, which is extremely valuable when he needs a favor from one of the city or state's elected politicians. It also allows him to intervene directly in the copy of the newspaper, offering him the opportunity to punish enemies and reward allies. Fox News Channel, has, like its broadcast parent, turned out to be a surprisingly shrewd commercial proposition. Though its older, largely rural audience does not produce the revenues of CNN despite significantly higher ratings, it does give every indication of having become a profitable enterprise with remarkable rapidity.

But the *Weekly Standard*, unlike Fox, will never make a profit, as political opinion magazines never do. And unlike the *New York Post*, the *Standard*'s editors will not allow Murdoch to dictate its politics. When Murdoch's other publications were toadying up to the Chinese during the spy plane crisis of 2001, the *Standard* was denouncing the administration—and by extension, Rupert and James Murdoch, with fire and brimstone. When the kind of deal Murdoch was actively seeking was finally achieved by the Bush administration, William Kristol, together with Robert Kagan, thundered about "The profound national humiliation that President Bush has brought upon the United States."[58] While writing a column on the topic, I made a few calls to the magazine to determine what their policies were with regard to criticizing their owner. Kristol, executive editor Fred Barnes, and senior writer Christopher Caldwell were all apparently too busy to get back to me. Opinion editor David Tell was helpful with critical pieces about China but also demurred on the question of Murdoch per se. Senior editor and best-selling swami David Brooks was all charm and no information: "I'm sorry. I'm having some computer problems. At first I thought you were asking me to comment on the son of my employer. Must be some garble."[59] Murdoch could not have liked that.

Perhaps the owner was suckered in. In its original inception, the magazine, edited by Kristol, appeared to be exactly the same wavelength as its sugar daddy. Murdoch, recall, was trying to pay then-House Speaker Newt Gingrich more than $6 million for an unreadable book of speeches much in the fashion that he paid Deng's daughter. (The Murdoch "advance" was ruled out of order by the House ethics committee and was never paid. The book was an easily predicted flop.) The *Standard*, as it was originally conceived, appeared to be a kind of Newt Gingrich fanzine. The cover of its first issue, published in April 1995, portrayed Gingrich as Rambo, bravely swinging on a vine above a burning Capitol, and featured four pieces on Newt of the Jungle. Within two years, however, it was Gingrich and company who seemed bound for the nuthouse—or at least for disgrace and retirement. The *Standard* transferred its affection to Republican dissident and media darling John McCain, with Kristol and Kagan acting as a kind of unofficial brain trust during McCain's heady 2000 run. When Bush won, however, that was fine, too.

There is no question that the *Weekly Standard* has been home to many of the most talented political writers anywhere, conservative or no. Bill Kristol, David Brooks, Christopher Caldwell, and Tucker Carlson would have enjoyed considerable success no matter what politics they practiced. Even though the *Standard* had been a bastion of the McCain mutiny, the Bush administration swallowed its collective pride and raided it upon coming into office. Among the staffers who moved over to the administration were John DiIulio (to head up the president's faith-based initiative), Matt Reese (to work for U.S. Trade Representative Robert Zoellick), and David Frum and Ed Walsh (to join the White House speechwriting shop).

Of course things did not always work out perfectly. DiIulio quickly ran afoul of the Republican thought police when he seemed to take seriously his mandate to involve inner-city clergy to address real problems. Warned publicly for his apostasy by Grover Norquist, he was the first significant member of the administration to quit his job. David Frum lasted a bit longer, but also left under clouded circumstances. He was working as a supposedly anonymous White House speechwriter. But his wife, novelist Danielle Crittenden—who has a sideline in instructing women to use their husband's name professionally but used her own—could not bear to see hubby's genius go unrecognized. Following Bush's famous "Axis of Evil" State of the Union in 2002, Crittenden sent out a mass e-mail proudly proclaiming her husband's authorship of the phrase. Timothy Noah, Slate's gossip columnist, published the offending e-mail. ("It's not often a phrase one writes gains national notice . . . so I hope you'll indulge my wifely pride in seeing this one repeated in headlines everywhere!!") Noah also quoted Crittenden's stepfather's Canadian newspaper telling the same tale. And he cited other possible authors. Later Frum, thinking twice, decided it was Bush's idea after all. As speechwriters are not supposed to take credit for anything, even incoherent geopolitical formulations, Frum decided it would be a good time to, as the saying goes, "return to private life." Republican pooper-scooper Robert Novak blamed Crittenden's e-mail for the decision, but Frum said it wasn't so. Still, Frum did not improve his credibility with his announcement, in early 2002, that W. had already "proven himself to be one of the great presidents of American history."[60]

Under the rhetorically challenged Bush, the *Standard*'s most important function was to become the primary public voice of America's war party, no matter who was the enemy. China, the Palestinians, the Iranians, the Syrians, the Cubans, and, of course, Al Qaeda and the Iraqis would all have qualified. When, for instance, some Republicans, including some of ex-President Bush's closest advisers, dissented from the policy of a U.S. war against Iraq in the summer of 2002, Kristol and company shot back—in the language of Joe McCarthy—that "an axis of appeasement–stretching from Riyadh to Brussels to Foggy Bottom, from Howell Raines to Chuck Hagel to Brent Scowcroft—has now mobilized in a desperate effort to deflect the president from implementing his policy." Those on the left who opposed an invasion of Iraq did so not out of pragmatic considerations about its effectiveness, lack of allied support, effect on the region and its inhabitants, or moral considerations about the launching of a pre-emptive war. Rather, they were "queasy about American principles." Others, "mostly foreign policy 'realists,'" opposed it because "they're appalled by the thought that the character of regimes is key to foreign policy." A few "cosmopolitan sophisticates of all stripes," Kristol noted, using the word that Stalin chose for Jews, were on the wrong side because they "hate talk of good and evil."[61]

Kristol was hardly alone in this tactic. As John Judis noted in the *American Prospect*:

> The *Wall Street Journal* identified Scowcroft's views with those of the "anti-war left." The *New York Sun* enumerated Scowcroft's current business ties and his founding of a "front group" that includes a "PLO apologist" on its board. As for Hagel, the *Wall Street Journal*'s editorial page accused him of trying to "grab a fast headline." And in an article titled "Sen. Skeptic (R., France)," the *National Review* insinuated that the Nebraskan was more European than American in his views. But the hawks didn't expend most of their ammunition on Scowcroft and Hagel. Instead, they took aim at the *New York Times* and its new executive editor, Howell Raines. The *Wall Street Journal*, The *Weekly Standard*, the *Washington Times* and columnists Charles Krauthammer and George Will charged that the *New York Times* was promoting opposition to the administration's Iraq plans by publishing false information about the dissenters in its news pages.[62]

The idea of honest, principled, and intelligent opposition to a war against Iraq was ruled out of order by most conservative pundits, no matter what the credentials of those giving voice to it. Note also that the very idea of reporting dissent—be it within the military, the Congressional Republican Party, or the Republican foreign policy establishment that had crafted George H. W. Bush's war with Iraq—was equated, once again, with the dreaded liberal bias, as if Brent Scowcroft, James Baker, Lawrence Eagleberger, Republican Chuck Hagel, and even House Republican Whip Dick Armey had somehow switched to the "liberal" side so that they might be charged with making common cause with the *New York Times*. Krauthammer even concluded, "Not since William Randolph Hearst famously cabled his correspondent in Cuba, 'You furnish the pictures and I'll furnish the war,' has a newspaper so blatantly devoted its front pages to editorializing about a coming American war as has Howell Raines' *New York Times*." Too bad for the pundit, Hearst never said this. It is a tale that ten minutes worth of research might have prevented his repeating, but never mind.[63] (Curiously, Krauthammer, who is partially paralyzed, and Kristol—like most of the outspoken journalistic war hawks with regard to Iraq, including Bob Kagan, George Will, Rush Limbaugh, Marty Peretz, Andrew Sullivan, Jacob Heilbrunn, Christopher Hitchens, and Michael Kelly—share with George Bush, Dick Cheney, Republican Majority Whip Tom DeLay, the hawkish defense official Paul Wolfowitz, Senate Majority Leader Trent Lott, and the DOD adviser Richard Perle the quality of having managed to avoid military service of any kind during their entire lives. Hence, they are entirely innocent of any understanding of its character from the ground up. In the case of the vice president, who required four separate deferments to stay out of harm's way while the unlucky amongst his generation went off to fight and die to defend "freedom in South Vietnam," he has explained that he "had other priorities in the 60s than military service.")[64]

It should surprise no one that when both the *Times* and the *Washington Post* egregiously underreported a massive antiwar demonstration in Washington in late October 2002 with a crowd estimated by local police to be well over 100,000 people, not one of the above pundits bothered to complain. The *Times* was forced to run an embarrassing "make-up story" in which it admitted its earlier (buried) story on the demonstration, which claimed merely "hundreds" of demonstrators, had been profoundly misleading. The *Post* received a hard slap from its ombudsman, Michael Getler, who complained that the paper had "fumbled" the story of the biggest antiwar demonstration since the 1960s. Hypocrisy aside, the apparent lack of sympathy evinced by the editors of both papers would appear to put a crimp into the arguments of anyone accusing these media titans of an antiwar bias, which is perhaps why the hawkish pundits who focus obsessively on the coverage of Iraq in both papers, decided to ignore it entirely.[65]

No one—not even *Times* superhawk William Safire—was more important in the media debate over Iraq than the *Weekly Standard's* William Kristol, McCarthyite language or no. When, in late August 2002, Vice President Cheney finally laid out a case for war, the *Washington Post's* Dana Milbank quoted Kristol and Kristol alone for analysis. "The debate in the administration is over,"[66] he declared in apparent triumph. "The time for action grows near." Of course it did not hurt that the pro-war side also had Howard Kurtz, asking this dumb question on its behalf: "By the way, do you think there were any Hill hearings on removing Adolf Hitler?"[67] (Mr. Kurtz does not seem to be aware that it was Hitler who declared war on the United States, not the other way around.) As James Capozzola nicely put it on the Web log Rittenhouse Review, "That's the liberal media at work."[68]

---

The notion of a conservative network capable of enforcing such a line on its members, drawing the mainstream media into its ideological corner, and mau-mauing even many liberals into parroting its line might be just a pipe dream today were it not for the generosity of one man. As of September 2002, sixty-nine-year-old Richard Mellon Scaife was, according to *Forbes*, the 209th richest person in America, with a personal fortune of just over a billion dollars.[69] On a list of the strangest people in America, he might rank a bit higher. Had Scaife decided to commit his fortune to chasing orchids or beautifying his native corner of western Pennsylvania while writing the occasional six-figure check to the Republican Party, he would merely qualify as one more eccentric conservative billionaire. Instead Scaife put his fortune at the service of a group of visionary right-wing intellectuals and activists. His efforts proved so successful that it is not too much to say that the United States is a different country because of them.

A somewhat bulky, handsome man with hypnotic blue eyes, Scaife lives what a *Washington Post* writer once called "a life thickly insulated from the workaday tribulations of ordinary citizens."[70] At that time, he had houses in Pittsburgh; Ligonier, Pennsylvania; Nantucket, Massachusetts; and Pebble Beach, California; and a private DC-9 jet with which to shuttle between them. He is apparently so shy and insecure that he never talks business unless surrounded by a bevy of assistants. Even then, underlings do most of the talking.

Scaife rarely if ever grants interviews, so most of his motivations must be intuited. When journalist Karen Rothmyer tried to interview him for a *Columbia Journalism Review* profile in the early 1980s, Scaife avoided her every inquiry. When she finally caught up with him on a Manhattan street as the billionaire departed a meeting of the First Boston Corporation, Rothmyer inquired as to why he chose to dedicate his fortune to the cause of conservative politics. Scaife replied in a booming voice, "You fucking Communist cunt, get out of here." He then volunteered his opinion that she was ugly and that her teeth were "terrible," before warning, "don't look behind you."[71]

It's too bad that Scaife is so reluctant to speak to journalists because, politics aside, he is a fascinating guy. After William F. Buckley Jr., he is perhaps the single most important private citizen in the contemporary conservative movement. And yet to those who know him, he appears to be wholly uninterested in political ideas. When one journalist asked over a dozen conservative intellectuals receiving Scaife monies if they could recall a single book he ever mentioned, they all came up empty-handed. They did know he liked flowers and took an interest in geography. His penchant for conspiracy theories was also mentioned. As for newspapers, most of Scaife's reading, according to those closest to him, focused on the gossip columns.[72]

Scaife has certainly had ample opportunity to read about himself while scanning the gossip pages. Using his wealth and fame, he has scandalized polite society over and over during his career, carrying on an open affair while married and having at least two of his adversaries—including his brother-in-law—die under mysterious circumstances. This billionaire is also comically impecunious. He goes over the expenses submitted by his employees and has been known to strike out the cost of airport taxis and hotel shirt-laundering. He even wrote Richard Nixon 334 $3,000 checks to avoid the obligatory gift tax.

Scaife's great-grandfather Thomas Mellon founded the financial empire that bears his name. Mellon mused in 1885, "The normal condition of man is hard work, self-denial, acquisition and accumulation; as soon as his descendants are freed from the necessity of such exertion they begin to degenerate sooner or later in both body and mind." He would appear to be a prophet of sorts about his own family. Richard Mellon Scaife was raised by his mother, a "gutter drunk," according to her daughter Cordelia, and an ineffectual father in a family that excelled, in Scaife's sister's words, only in "making each other totally miserable."[73]

Richard grew up around Pittsburgh surrounded by buildings and institutions named either "Mellon" or "Scaife" or both. An important building at the University of Pittsburgh, where Scaife studied, is called Scaife Hall. Another university in town also has a Scaife Hall. Its name is Carnegie Mellon. Scaife's uncle, R. K. Mellon, proved adept at expanding the family fortune in the years after World War Two, but he thought little of his brother-in-law, Alan Scaife, and would not allow him near any important aspects of the business. As Richard Scaife would later put it, "My father was sucking hind tit." A failure in his own business ventures, Alan Scaife died a year after his son's graduation from college, and his son sold his corporation "for a dollar." In 1974, Scaife expressed some of his feelings about his family when he donated a new wing to the Carnegie Museum in Pittsburgh in honor of his mother. While she had always considered herself to be "Sarah Mellon Scaife," he insisted that the new structure be named the "Sarah Scaife" wing. Shortly thereafter, he also had the name "Mellon" removed from the foundation that bore his mother's name.

Like his father, Richard Scaife was refused any substantive responsibilities in the family business by his uncle. He had been thrown out of Yale University in an alcohol-fueled incident in which he rolled a beer keg down a stairwell that broke both of a fellow student's legs and nearly left him crippled for life. Scaife managed to make it through the University of Pittsburgh, but one suspects this achievement was not unrelated to the presence of his father in the chairman's seat of the university's board of directors. Richard Scaife spent much of the years that followed as a mean drunk without any visible career or profession. According to Mellon family biographer, Burton Hersh, Scaife nearly drank himself to death, time and again.[74]

Due to the U.S. tax law, Scaife was forced to become a philanthropist to protect his share of the family's wealth, lest large parts of it went to the IRS. In 1957, when *Fortune* magazine tried to rank the largest fortunes in America, four Mellons— including Richard's mother—were among the top eight. Sarah Scaife and, after her death in 1965, Richard Scaife, earned huge tax deductions from their trusts and foundations. Sarah Scaife's causes focused on family planning, the poor and disabled, hospitals, the environment, and various good works in and around Pittsburgh. Her most famous gift went to the University of Pittsburgh research laboratory during the late 1940s, when Jonas Salk happened to be there working on the formula for his successful polio vaccine. Richard Scaife would not help cure polio, but he would, eventually, help impeach a president.[75]

Scaife's first donations to conservative groups began in 1962 with relatively meager grants to the American Bar Association's Fund for Public Education for "education against communism," and shortly thereafter, to the Hoover Institution, the Center for Strategic and International Studies, and the American Enterprise Institute.[76] But 1964 proved to be a kind of rude political awakening for Scaife. An enthusiastic Goldwater supporter, that summer he ferried the candidate on his private plane to the annual Bohemian Grove retreat, where wealthy businessmen and male political leaders frolic together in the Northern Californian woods, happily peeing on plants.[77] Scaife was extremely excited about the possibilities of a Goldwater presidency, and he may have let his hopes triumph over his ability to judge the likely course of events. Few people were surprised in November of that year when Johnson trounced the conservative Republican. Most pundits blamed the candidate's conservative views and connections to the conservative movement as the cause. The *New York Times*'s James Reston wrote that Goldwater's conservatism "has wrecked his party for a long time to come." Also at the *Times*, Tom Wicker wrote that conservatives "cannot win in this era of American history." The *Los Angeles Times* interpreted the election outcome to mean that if Republicans continued to hew to the conservative line, "they will remain a minority party indefinitely." Political scientists Nelson Polsby and Aaron Wildavsky speculated that if the Republicans nominated a conservative again he would lose so badly "we can expect an end to a competitive two-party system."[78]

According to one of Scaife's associates, the billionaire became convinced that politically, no genuinely conservative candidate could succeed in a nationwide election without first overcoming the advantage that liberalism appeared to have both in the media and in the war of political ideas that provided politicians their ideological foundation. By most measures, Scaife had precious little to show for his thirty-seven years by way of personal achievement. He lived, as he might put it, on his own family's "hind tit" as a drunk and a patsy for conservative fund-raisers. In 1969, however, he began to create his own independent power base by paying approximately $5 million to buy the *Tribune-Review* of Greensburg, Pennsylvania, a daily paper with just over 40,000 circulation in the county seat of Westmoreland County.

Scaife became the paper's publisher and soon established what would become his trademark management style. When the Associated Press ran a story in 1972 revealing Scaife's checks to Nixon, Scaife had every AP machine thrown out of the newsroom. He fired a young reporter who, in the aftermath of Vice President Agnew's resignation, had quipped, "one down and one to go." The firing inspired ten out of the paper's twenty-four editorial employees to resign in protest, charging that Scaife had interfered "continually in the opinion of the professional staff, interjected his political and personal bias into the handling of news stories."[79] This was the first of a number of such incidents that became a regular feature of the newspaper, to the constant consternation of the professional reporters and editors who came to be employed there.[80]

But of course if all Scaife was responsible for was publishing a silly Pennsylvania newspaper, he would hardly be of sufficient concern to merit discussion here. While many rumors have been attached to Scaife's alleged efforts to purchase either CBS or the *Washington Post* for the conservative movement, as of 2002, he had attempted only one other foray as a publisher. It proved both short and ignominious. In 1973, he bought Kern House Enterprises. While registered in the United States, the company ran a London-based news agency called Forum World Features, which offered stories to newspapers and magazines worldwide, including approximately thirty in the United States. But Scaife was forced to close the business down two years later, just before press reports revealed it to be a CIA front. According to ex-CIA director, the late Richard Helms, Forum World provided "a significant means to counter Communist propaganda."[81]

Scaife's unhappy experiences with Nixon—with whom he broke just before the president's resignation in 1974—and the Kern House CIA debacle no doubt contributed to his subsequent decision to remain behind the scenes in national politics. It also taught him the folly of depending on any one politician to fulfill his vision. Though he continued to contribute to the Republican Party and to individual candidates, the bulk of his giving focused on conservative institution-building, and Scaife spread his money like manure. Of the more than 300 groups listed in the 2000 edition of the foundation guide to conservative research and pressure groups in Washington, 111 received grants from Scaife. These represent less than a third of the number of organizations to which his foundations have given grants during this period.[82]

Scaife's contributions have been so varied and numerous that one searches in vain for a consistent theme beyond a shared commitment to conservative ideology. Some are media pressure groups, some legal pressure groups. Some are intellectual, some action-oriented. Some are devoted to scandal-stoking and are driven by fantastic notions of presidential-directed killings and drug-smuggling schemes. Others support educational PBS programming featuring Nobel laureates. Some have proven tremendously successful. Many have not.

Most histories associate the founding of the Heritage Foundation with the fortune of the conservative beer magnate, Joseph Coors. This is because Coors put up the original $250,000 in seed money in 1973. Inside of two years, however, Scaife's gifts had dwarfed those of Coors, totaling more than $35 million in inflation-adjusted dollars.[83] At Heritage the joke went, "Coors gives six-packs; Scaife gives cases." In 1976, Heritage's third year of operation, Scaife ponied up over 40 percent of the foundation's total income of $1,008,557. This proved "absolutely critical" to the organization's survival, according to its president, Edwin J. Feulner.[84]

But Heritage represents just a small fraction of Scaife's giving during the past three decades. At least five additional organizations—the Hoover Institution on War, Revolution and Peace at Stanford University, the Center for Strategic and International Studies, Free Congress Research and Education Foundation, American Enterprise Institute for Public Policy Research—received in excess of ten million dollars from Scaife's foundations between 1974 and 1998. And even these together represent barely a quarter of the funds he disbursed to right-wing causes during this period.[85]

Many of Scaife's most successful gifts have been directed towards shaping the long-term contours of intellectual and political thought, both within academia and outside of it. Since 1970, Scaife put up more than $8 million to fund scholars working on "law and economics" at places like the University of Chicago, the University of Miami, and George Mason University Law School. Legal scholars who identify intellectually with this movement have labored hard to redirect the emphasis in legal education and jurisprudence toward the efficiency of the market rather than the rights of the worker or consumer. Using Scaife money, these well-funded programs have invited hundreds of federal judges to attend seminars in luxurious vacation resorts in exchange for their participation in seminars on issues such as the efficacy of market solutions to problems such as the destruction of the environment or unsafe working conditions for workers. Law and economics scholarship has grown so mainstream that one of its founders, Richard Posner, was named as the mediator on the single largest anti-trust case of the past two decades—the United States versus Microsoft—without a word of criticism in the media.

Scaife money was also instrumental in sustaining the Federalist Society, an organization that has developed into perhaps the most influential legal organization in America after the American Bar Association, and among the most conservative. Founded in 1982, the Federalists have received more than $1.3 million from Scaife's foundations since 1984. Today its membership exceeds 25,000. The society's proponents can frequently be found attacking liberal "judicial activism" while praising the allegedly "strict constructionist" judges who interpret the Constitution according to the founders' "original intent." But as Chris Mooney pointed out, the society's understanding of "original intent" is original indeed. While its name invokes the authors of the Federalist Papers, James Madison, Alexander Hamilton, and John Jay, its philosophy is more consistent with the view of these writers' opponents, the Anti-Federalists, who sought to defeat the Constitution. In other words, scholars have begun to interpret the Constitution based on the views of its opponents.[86]

Within its ranks, the society includes some of the most influential judges in America, including an extremely high percentage of those selected by George W. Bush for promotion to the federal bench. This is no surprise, since the advisers selecting the judges and making the recommendation to President Bush are either members of, or closely tied to, the society as well. So, in late 2002, were four of nine members of the Supreme Court, though it is hard to be certain, as the society refuses to confirm or deny anyone's membership. During the Clinton impeachment hearings, virtually every member of Kenneth Starr's prosecutorial staff had some connection to the society. So did a number of the lawyers who worked on the Paula Jones lawsuit.[87] At the 2002 twentieth-anniversary meeting of the society, the "Barbara K. Olson Memorial Lecture"—in honor of the anti-Clinton radical activist and author who was married to Theodore Olson and died when her plane crashed on September 11—was delivered by none other than Kenneth Starr.

Since 1996, the society has published *ABA Watch*, documenting the American Bar Association's allegedly liberal stands on abortion, the death penalty, and gun control.[88] President Bush was acting upon this legacy of criticism when he chose to eliminate the ABA's influence in the judicial selection process. As an only slightly tongue-in-cheek Grover Norquist told Thomas Edsall of the *Washington Post*, "If Hillary Clinton had wanted to put some meat on her charge of a 'vast right-wing conspiracy,' she should have had a list of Federalist Society members and she could have spun a more convincing story."[89]

Scaife has also taken a considerable interest in the media on America's college campuses. According to the *Washington Post*'s audit, Scaife's trusts and foundations have given at least $146 million to university programs, equal to more than $373 million in inflation-adjusted dollars. One of the chief beneficiaries has been the Intercollegiate Studies Institute, founded in 1953 with William F. Buckley Jr. as its first president. Through an organization called the Collegiate Network, ISI pays nearly all the costs of conservative publications on sixty campuses and offers graduate fellowships for the academically inclined. Former fellows include Antonin Scalia, Edwin J. Feulner Jr., Dinesh D'Souza, and William Kristol.[90]

The conservative faculty organization the National Association of Scholars benefited from Scaife's generosity to the tune of over $2.6 million between 1988 and

1998.[91] With an advisory board featuring Jeanne Kirkpatrick, Irving Kristol, and Chester Finn, the organization presents itself as a champion of "intellectual renewal" and "academic standards" in the face of their perceived decline at the hands of leftist academics and fashionable post-modern theories that blur the verities of our time behind a façade of impenetrable professional vernacular. The organization is more than willing, however, to play hardball politics at the campuses where it operates, particularly in the area of affirmative action, which it opposes most vehemently.[92]

Of all of Scaife's political passions, however, the one that appears most inspirational to him is his view that the liberals who allegedly control the media are in league with the liberals who control the Democratic Party to commit all manner of malfeasance against law-abiding Americans, including murder, extortion, kidnapping, drug-smuggling, and money-laundering. To this end Scaife has committed a sizable portion of his vast fortune to various organizations that profess to be able either to shed light on these forces, or even better, do battle with them. For years these gifts appeared to take a rather haphazard pattern. Scaife funded Gen. William C. Westmoreland's failed 1982 libel suit against CBS News. Beginning in 1977 he provided roughly $2 million to Reed Irvine's Accuracy in Media, a right-wing press critic, whose critiques of the alleged liberal bias in the media have led some to observe that "Accuracy in Media" bears the same relationship to accuracy in media that the Holy Roman Empire bore to holiness, Rome, and empires. (Back in 1978, Ben Bradlee famously termed Irvine "a miserable, carping, retromingent vigilante.")[93] Like Brent Bozell's Media Research Center, David Horowitz's Center for the Study of Popular Culture, and other miserable, carping, retromingent vigilantes to whom Scaife has handed millions, Accuracy in Media's constant stream of propaganda, faithfully broadcast by the media it attacks, is a major reason that so many people inside and outside of the media share the misimpression of its "liberalism."

Scaife also supported the *Public Interest* and the *National Interest*, both of which are published under the aegis of neoconservative impresario Irving Kristol. The cranky neocon art critic, Hilton Kramer, got to edit the *New Criterion*, a cultural review. Scaife also provided necessary funds for *Reason*, the official publication of the libertarian Reason Foundation, and *Commentary*, the monthly magazine of the American Jewish Committee, edited for decades by the excitable neocon, Norman Podhoretz. Scaife also gave generously to *Encounter* magazine, before it folded, which had been the house organ of the CIA during the days of the intellectual battles over the Cold War in Europe in the 1950s and 1960s. Overall, these publications have enjoyed spending more than $10 million of Scaife's inheritance. Scaife money also helped fund television documentaries on the economics of Milton Friedman, the guru of the monetarist school of free-market economics, and on Cold War themes.

Suffice to say, none of these causes ever excited Scaife like the opportunity to "get" Bill Clinton, and nothing so loosened his purse strings. Scaife attributed his support for the project to his doubts that "the *Washington Post* and other major newspapers would fully investigate the disturbing scandals of the Clinton White House." He explained those doubts: "I am not alone in feeling that the press has a bias in favor of Democratic administrations." That is why, he continued, "I provided some money to independent journalists investigating these scandals."[94]

Following Clinton's election in 1992, Scaife started handing out money to virtually every journalist who claimed to be able to prove Clinton a crook, however farfetched the story. He termed Vincent Foster's suicide to be "the Rosetta stone to the Clinton administration," telling John F. Kennedy Jr., "Once you solve that one mystery, you'll know everything that's going on or went on—I think there's been a massive cover-up about what Bill Clinton's administration has been doing, and what he was doing when he was governor of Arkansas." Scaife had ominous specifics in mind: "Listen, [Clinton] can order people done away with at his will. He's got the entire federal government behind him." And: "God, there must be 60 people [associated with Bill Clinton]—who have died mysteriously." For a while, all any conservative had to do was to come to Scaife claiming to have solved the mystery—but for a few hundred thousand dollars in necessary investigative funds—and suddenly the money spigot was turned on. For instance, in 1995, Scaife donated $175,000 to Grover Norquist's Americans for Tax Reform, which hired "experts" to dispute the authenticity of Vince Foster's suicide note and produced a widely circulated video entitled *Unanswered: The Death of Vince Foster.* Accuracy in Media received $355,000 from Scaife in 1995 as well. It broadcast the theory that Vince Foster was lured into a "sex trap" from which he fled to where his body was found."[95]

Among the most energetic pursuers of Scaife's "Rosetta Stone" was a hitherto unknown "journalist," Christopher Ruddy. Scaife hired Ruddy, after he had been fired by the *New York Post,* to continue his obsessive investigation of Foster's death in the hopes of trying to pin a murder rap on the president or those closest to him. Ruddy produced his theories on the basis of some imaginative writing, faulty logic, and vast leaps into the unknown and unknowable, both of which he claimed to know. Given that he was never able to prove any of his farfetched theories about the nature of Foster's death and was found to have made major errors when other journalists looked into them, his primary talent seems to have been to wring funds out of Scaife. He used the publicity he generated from these page-one stories to convince other, relatively more reputable journalistic establishments, most notably Sun Myung Moon's *Washington Times*, Rupert Murdoch's *New York Post*, and Robert Bartley's *Wall Street Journal* editorial page, to give his tales undeserved publicity and marginally improved credibility.

Ruddy lived in a fully Scaife-contained world. He published on page one of Scaife's *Tribune Review*. His articles were picked up by the Western Journalism Center, based in suburban Sacramento, California, which billed itself in a biweekly newsletter as a "nonprofit tax-exempt corporation promoting independent investigative reporting" and "the only national news agency supporting a full-time probe of the mysterious death of White House deputy counsel Vincent W. Foster, Jr." What this means, it seems, is that the center mostly recycled stories written by Christopher Ruddy. When CBS's *60 Minutes* devoted a segment to exposing the hoariness of Ruddy's conspiracy theories—and the gullibility of those news organizations that treated them as legitimate news stories—Scaife helped fund the creation of a video called *The '60 Minutes' Deception.* He advertised this in the *Washington Times* (with discounted rates) but also through the Scaife-funded entities Free Congress Foundation and National Empowerment Television, along with the Western Journalism Center. In 1996, Ruddy was named the recipient of the Western Journalism Center's first "Courage in Journalism Award," replete with trophy and $2,000 cash prize."[96]

Inspired by his obsession with Clinton, Scaife took seriously the advice Charles Foster Kane offered his underlings when they complained of a dearth of sensational news. He went out and made his own. Scaife's foundations provided funds to two public interest law firms staffed by rival litigators whose obsession with the misdeeds of the president and his administration were no less dogged than Ruddy's. Together, Judicial Watch and the Landmark Legal Foundation received more than $4 million of Scaife's foundations' funds. Founded in 1994 and run by the frequent cable television commentator, Larry Klayman, Judicial Watch pursued a strategy of repeatedly subpoenaing as many Clinton officials, friends of Clinton officials, and working journalists as the presiding judges in his various lawsuits against the Justice and Commerce Departments, among others, would allow. Klayman tried to unearth information about Vince Foster's death, Clinton's foreign policy, and a few other extremely unlikely conspiracies, but never managed to find any actual dirt. Meanwhile, the Landmark Legal Foundation took up the cause of Paula Jones's sexual harassment suit against the president, with its lawyers leaking information via pundit Ann Coulter's many media appearances. (She would do this frequently on MSNBC where I worked with her at the time.) In addition, an organization called the Fund for Living American Government (FLAG), a one-man philanthropy run by William Lehrfeld, a Washington tax lawyer who had represented Scaife, gave $59,000 to Paula Jones's sexual harassment suit against Clinton. FLAG received at least $160,000 in Scaife donations. Together with Landmark staffers and members of the Federalist Society, these firms helped provide low-cost legal advice to Paula Jones to keep her suit going long enough to hit proverbial paydirt with the discovery of Linda Tripp.[97]

Undoubtedly, Scaife's most costly endeavor—judged purely in terms of the unwanted publicity and negative attention he received—was the so-called "Arkansas Project" based at the *American Spectator* magazine and its concurrent "Education

Fund." Begun on a fishing trip on the Chesapeake Bay in the fall of 1993, the project managed to bilk the billionaire for millions, nearly destroy the magazine, and almost cost George W. Bush one of his most trusted advisers, his appointed solicitor general.[98] The plot was originally hatched by Scaife's top aide, Richard M. Larry, right-wing entrepreneur and public relations man; David Henderson, a friend of Larry's; Washington lawyer Steven Boynton; *Spectator* editor R. Emmett Tyrell; and Theodore Olson, who later argued George W. Bush's election case before the Supreme Court and was rewarded with the job of solicitor general. Larry had already approached at least two other organizations seeking funding for a massive investigation into alleged Clinton wrongdoings back in Arkansas, but he was turned down cold. Eventually the *Spectator* would receive nearly $2.3 million for the project alone. According to the foundation's internal accounts, three-quarters of the Arkansas Project funding, or $1.8 million, was paid out in "legal expenses" with no further explanation provided.

The project was best known for the (now) admittedly dishonest reporting of the then-right-wing ideologue/hatchetman, David Brock. As he related in his book-length mea culpa, "I had stumbled onto something big, a symbiotic relationship that would help create a highly-profitable, right-wing Big Lie machine that flourished in book publishing, on talk-radio, and on the Internet in the 90s."[99] Acting on the advice of one of his many mentors in the movement, Free Press publisher Erwin Glikes (now deceased), that "right-wing journalism had to be injected into the bloodstream of the liberal media for maximum effect," Brock leaked a copy of his fatally flawed Troopergate story to CNN—"astonished," he claimed, "to see how easy it was to suck [them] in"—where it led the evening newscast, and was further picked up from there. Scaife liked what he saw and continued to give more millions to further pollute the national discourse with baseless allegations and paranoid conspiracy theories.

Not even Brock believed his own reporting at the time. And neither did many of the people who helped publish him. Brock alleged that Olson pushed for the publication of the phony Vince Foster story because, Olson told him, the purpose was not to get at the truth but to throw mud at the Clintons and hope that something stuck. Brock wrote of Olson that "while he believed, as [independent counsel Kenneth] Starr apparently did, that Foster had committed suicide, raising questions was a way of turning up the heat on the administration until another scandal was shaken loose, which was the *Spectator*'s mission."[100] The Paula Jones story, which Brock also published without believing it, was also a strategic advance by the right. George Conway, a $1-million-a-year partner at Wachtell, Lipton, Rosen, and Katz, who was secretly helping to promote Jones's suit, explained, according to Brock, "This is about proving Troopergate." The Conway team was, it turned out, planning to grill Clinton under oath about his consensual sex life and hopefully catch him lying about it. The aim, Jane Mayer noted, was to force Bill Clinton "to face open-ended questioning under oath about his sex life, a humiliation that, long before Monica Lewinsky ever bobbed up in the Rose Garden, promised to distract and embarrass the President, drain his political and financial resources, and lead to the tantalizing payoff of a charge of presidential perjury."[101] To almost everyone's shock and amazement, it worked.

It rarely mattered to anyone that so much of Brock's story was made up or that his sources had been paid for their information and lacked even elemental credibility in the first place. Even in the rare moments when such concerns did matter to Brock, they did not matter to his editors. Brock recalled hearing an extremely complicated "Vince Foster murder scenario," at an airport hotel in Miami, along with tales of alleged drug-running out of a small airport in a town called Mena, Arkansas, that allegedly involved payoffs to Governor Clinton. The allegations had no basis in evidence, however, and he decided to ignore them. The magazine's editor in chief published them himself, managing the considerable feat of publishing lies that were beneath even David Brock.

A dearth of truth in reporting was not the only problem for Scaife's project. Its sloppy accounting methods and money-shuffling between the magazine and the foundation worried Ronald Burr, the magazine's longtime publisher and co-founder. When Burr decided to instigate an independent tax fraud audit by Arthur Andersen, Tyrell wrote back: "I do not want a 'fraud' audit of any project. I do not want any further audits until I have examined our accounting of the Arkansas Project. . . . This issue is now closed." He then informed the staff that Burr was suspected of having misallocated a million dollars of project money. Following an emergency session of the foundation's board held at Tyrrell's home, Burr was thrown overboard and replaced by Theodore Olson. Burr was allegedly paid $350,000 to sign a "mutual confidentiality" clause. The audit never took place.[102]

No one, it appears, ever discovered what became of all of Scaife's contributions. But in the wake of Burr's firing, three of the magazine's board members quit: former United States Information Agency director Frank Shakespeare, the billionaire entrepreneur Theodore Forstmann, and Heritage Foundation vice president John von Kannon.[103] Many of the magazine's highest profile writers also resigned in protest. The magazine soldiered on for a while, changing owners and editors, as its circulation fell from 300,000 during the height of the Clinton wars to fewer than 65,000 in 2002.[104]

The Arkansas Project also came close to derailing Olson's nomination as solicitor general when Brock, following a crisis of conscience, testified under oath that Olson had been far more deeply involved in the Arkansas Project than his previous testimony had indicated. Olson had claimed, "It has been alleged that I was somehow involved in that so-called project; I was not involved in the project, in its origin or its management." He was also far from forthright about his role in ghost-writing anti-Clinton screeds in the magazine and his paid role representing David Hale, an anti-Clinton Whitewater witness. But Brock had the effect of jogging Olson's memory, and he later admitted to some involvement, though not nearly as much as Brock alleged. Despite the widening hole in his credibility, Olson was narrowly confirmed in the Senate. The Democrats, having just won control of the body vis-à-vis Jim Jeffords's decision to join them as an independent, did not think it tactically smart to pick a fight so quickly. The relative silence greeting Olson's confirmation to an office so influential that its holder is frequently termed the "tenth Supreme Court Justice" demonstrated the degree of double standard at work in the SCLM. Clinton did not dare even nominate anyone with analogous involvements, much less such radical views.[105] Yet, in the Bush era, significant sections of the U.S. Justice Department were turned over to people who might fairly be termed radicals—working in league with a radical media whose practitioners knew few boundaries with regard to journalistic ethics or political morality. Again, the silence of the lamb-like "liberal media" turned out to be deafening.

Meanwhile Scaife himself also fell out of love with the project, though of course he never offered any explanation why. It might have had something to do with a November 1997 negative review of Christopher Ruddy's book, *The Strange Death of Vincent Foster: An Investigation*. Shortly after it was published, the Accuracy in Media newsletter reported that Scaife cut the *Spectator* off. It might be said that its work was done, however. While many people debased and degraded themselves on behalf of what appears to be a neurotic obsession with bringing down Bill Clinton, the mainstream media's bloodstream was successfully injected with the poison of Brock's and others' lies. The *American Spectator* provided the rumor. The mainstream did the rest.

The Arkansas Project may have ended unhappily for Scaife, but he had considerable reason to be proud of his contribution to American conservatism nevertheless. Not only did he help to create the necessary conditions to impeach Bill Clinton—and to convince the mainstream media to follow in the footsteps of the ideologues and adventurers whom he paid to blaze the trail—but he helped create an entire conservative infrastructure to carry on the fight against any president who sought to deviate from what his movement knew to be right and true. Just look at how they punish their apostates.

As he noted in his memoir, if young David Brock had come to Washington as an ambitious young liberal journalist to make his fortune in the early 1980s, he might well have been out of luck. There would have been no newspapers, magazines, think tanks, ready-made social life, mentors, and the like ready to embrace him, because of, rather than in spite of, his ideology. I am roughly Brock's age and came to Washington at about the same moment. Between 1982 and 1984, I think I earned a grand total of about $500 working as a liberal journalist, for articles in the *Nation, In These Times*, the *Washington Monthly*, the *Washington City Paper*, and *Arms Control Today*. Meanwhile the bars and softball fields of the capital were filled with young right-wingers living on generous salaries and fellowships provided by multi-million dollar institutions like the *Washington Times*, Heritage Foundation, and their various off-shoots. At the advice of one the last great independent journalists, my friend I. F. Stone, who struggled for much of his life to feed his family before becoming a great success in the late 1960s, I returned to graduate school to earn my master's and eventually my doctorate. Brock, in contrast, was embraced by a wealthy and welcoming culture that not only showered money and riches on him but also provided a ready-made social life; its only price was that he willingly lie about liberals in public and about his own homosexuality in private. Brock began by writing essays for the Scaife-funded Heritage Foundation's *Policy Review*, which then became op-eds on the Dow Jones-funded *Wall Street Journal* editorial page, which turned into a job offer from the loudly homophobic John Podhoretz, son of neocons Norman Podhoretz and Midge Decter, at the Moonie-funded *Washington Times* magazine, *Insight*, and from there, to the Scaife-funded *American Spectator*, which led to a million dollar contract from Simon and Schuster to take down Hillary Clinton. The only question he was asked, according to Brock, by Jack Romanos, then the head of S&S—an alleged bastion of the liberal publishing world—was whether Hillary was really a lesbian. He didn't even have to bother with a book proposal.

The significance of the story of Brock's cozy rise to foundation-funded riches and infamy lies in the hundreds or perhaps thousands of other young conservative journalists whose stories are similar, if not quite so dramatic. (Many of the writers who worship at the shrine of the free market would be lost if any of them were ever forced to earn their living working in it.) For instance, look at the man who hired Brock at *Insight*. John Podhoretz, together with virtually his entire family, including father, Norman, mother, Midge Decter, and brother-in-law, Elliott Abrams, has lived most of his entire professional life sucking at the teat of conservative cash, be it Moon's, Murdoch's, or Scaife's. Currently a columnist for Murdoch's *New York Post*, after having been relieved of his duties as its editorial page editor, Podhoretz uses his perch to enforce what *Slate* editor Jacob Weisberg, invoking the old Communists, has termed "the Coninturn line." When Brock experienced his crisis of conscience, John called him a "disgrace" who was engaged in "almost boundless hypocrisy."[106] The Scaife-funded polemicist and one-time Communist, David Horowitz, wrote, in *Salon*, "Brock, of course, cannot even present himself with any integrity that lasts for more than a sentence," adding that the author was "relentlessly squalid."[107] Writing in *National Review*, Ramesh Ponnuru accused Brock of "narcissism and attitudinizing, constant revisionism, and false pieties masking low cunning."[108] Earlier, his former friend and editor at the *Spectator*, Wlady Pleszczynski, had noted that in defending Hillary Clinton from the accusation of using an anti-Jewish slur, "Brock resorts to doing the only thing he's really interested in: talking about himself, reinventing himself, repositioning himself."[109] Robert Bartley termed Brock "the John Walker Lindh of contemporary conservatism." Brock had long ago been excommunicated by the Coninturn. When he failed to get the goods on Hillary Clinton, Barbara Olson told him he better not come to any of its parties. Others spread rumors that he was having an affair with a male member of Mrs. Clinton's staff. Now he was being damned, like Lindh, to Hell as well.

Harkening to Richard Hofstadter's famous examination of the "paranoid style" of American conservative politics, Weisberg detected in the behavior of these conservatives the same kind of "imitation of the enemy" that Hofstadter saw in the extreme right-wing organizations of his day. Just as the KKK modeled itself after the Catholic Church, and the John Birch Society looked a lot like the CP front organizations it believed were hiding beneath virtually every bed, "Contemporary conservatives believe that the most powerful institutions in American society are part of a liberal conspiracy. They feel this gives them license to create conservative counterinstitutions, from magazines to think tanks. But these conservative institutions—the *Washington Times*, the Heritage Foundation—are part of an ideological mission in a way that 'liberal' ones—the *Washington Post*, the Brookings Institution—are not."[110]

The *New Yorker*'s Hendrik Hertzberg noticed a similar, Communist-like dynamic at work in the world in which Brock swam when his gills tilted rightward:

Like the American and other Western Communist parties in their heyday, the American conservative movement has created a kind of alternative intellectual and political universe—a set of institutions parallel to and modeled on the institutions of mainstream society (many of which the movement sees, or imagines, as the organs of a disciplined Liberal Establishment) and dedicated to the single purpose of advancing a predetermined political agenda. There is a kind of Inner Movement, consisting of a few hundred funders, senior organization leaders, lawyers, and prominent media personalities (but only a handful of practicing politicians), and an Outer Movement, consisting of a few thousand staff people, grunt workers, and lower-level operatives of one kind or another. The movement has its own newspapers (the *Washington Times*, the *New York Post*, the *Journal*'s editorial page), its own magazines (*Weekly Standard*, *National Review*, *Policy Review*, *Commentary*, and many more), its own broadcasting operations (Fox News and an array of national and local talk-radio programs and right-wing Christian broadcast outlets), its own publishing houses (Regnery and the Free Press, among others), its own quasi-academic research institutions (the Heritage Foundation, the American Enterprise Institute), and even its own Popular Front—the Republican Party, important elements of which (the party's congressional and judicial leadership, for example) the movement has successfully commandeered. These closely linked organizations (the vanguard of the conservative revolution, you might say) compose an entire social world with its own rituals, celebrations, and anniversaries, within which it is possible to live one's entire life. It is a world with its own elaborate system of incentives and sanctions, through which—as Brock discovered—energetic conformity is rewarded with honors and promotions while deviations from the movement line, depending on their seriousness, are punished with anything from mild social disapproval to outright excommunication. [111]

The power of this conservative media world, of course, is not merely that it keeps conservatives in line who might be thinking deviationist thoughts. Rather, it skews the entire discourse toward the right because the Coninturn, unlike the Communists of yesteryear, is considered to be one of two—or perhaps two and a half—legitimate poles in the spectrum of American media discourse. Its power of gravity pulls the center rightward and leaves liberals off in outer space. Hence, its members dominate the punditocracy and receive highly favored treatment from media policemen like Howard Kurtz. And certainly no liberal can boast of such generous terms from any major television network as those enjoyed by the ideologically driven John Stossel, whose work is consistently questioned by his colleagues and yet whose diatribes are just as consistently broadcast by the network because of his strong following among right-wing viewers. Despite the sorry standards of his work, and the considerable grief and embarrassment they have caused the network, Stossel is able to spout his extremist views on ABC in the guise of genuine reporting in large measure because the conservatives have so powerfully succeeded in pushing discourse rightward, all the while whining "liberal bias."[112]

Perhaps the best illustration of the power of the far right to draw the mainstream into its web of lies and unfounded insinuations is the treatment of Brock himself. When Brock was still a lying conservative hatchetman, for instance, his work was trumpeted and celebrated in such allegedly liberal bastions as the *New York Times*, the *LA Times*, and elsewhere. When he became a liberal, however, the attack on Brock was picked up by gossip columnist Timothy Noah in the allegedly liberal *Slate*, who first called the apostate conservative a liar on the basis of having read a CNN transcript. When it was later revealed that the person who typed the transcript had made a mistake, and Brock was not lying, Noah scored Brock instead for telling the truth not "very loudly." Here, Noah was joining in a misguided attack based on the mistaken transcript that had already been joined by the Media Research Center, Andrewsullivan.com, and William F. Buckley's *National Review*. Even though Brock had told the truth on the CNN program, as Noah admitted—the issue was whether he had ever been invited on Fox during "prime time"—Noah attacked him because had he been "less concerned about staying on message and more bent on conveying the truth," he would not have spoken in such a low voice. While the conservatives were unarguably incorrect when they attacked Brock for lying, Noah argued, "the conservatives were right to view Brock's remarks as misleading."[113]

It is remarks like this one that demonstrate just how successful the Coninturn has been at intimidating allegedly liberal journalists apparently out of their wits. But Noah was hardly alone. The allegedly liberal *Washington Post* (accidentally, I assume) assigned Brock's book to be reviewed by a former writer for the *American Spectator* and published a malicious gossip item—originally reported by Matt Drudge—about his check-in to a mental health facility. (See chapter 5.) And it should surprise no one that Brock received none of that "brave contrarian who rooted for the wrong baseball team" treatment from *Post* media critic Howard Kurtz. In a 2,160 word profile, every single quote chosen by Kurtz came from right-wingers such as Wlady Pleszczynski or John Podhoretz, terming Brock to be either a liar or a psycho. Here, for instance, is the opening of Kurtz's profile. "David Brock is a liar. And a character assassin. And a turncoat. And a partisan hatchet man. And a lonely, tortured soul. And a practitioner of malicious journalism. And a bizarre guy. That, at least, is how he describes himself. . . ."[114]

The reception of David Brock's memoir, while predictable, is a relatively minor matter. It is also complicated by the fact of Brock's past dishonesty which, to say the least, opens the door to the possibility that he might be lying again, though none of his conservative critics have been able to substantiate this accusation in any significant way. But the reaction is illustrative of far more significant ones. Don't forget that following the 2000 election, at least two liberal columnists, Richard Cohen and Al Hunt, suggested that it would be best if the guy who actually lost the election be allowed to be president because the threat to social peace presented by the right was too great to justify a genuinely democratic outcome. (Cohen suggested that Al Gore give up because "Bush would be better . . . at restraining GOP Dobermans."[115] Al Hunt later wrote a column endorsing the Supreme Court's decision to hand Bush the election on exactly these grounds.)[116] These liberals had their reasons, no doubt. They had seen and heard comments like those by Paul Gigot of the *Wall Street Journal* celebrating a Republican riot to stop the vote count. There was William Kristol promising that if a fair count were allowed, "We will not 'move on.' Indeed, some of us will work for the next four years to correct this affront to our constitutional order." There was John Podhoretz fulminating, a bit ominously, in the *New York Post*, "Let him have it. Let him attempt to govern the United States when untold tens of millions of Americans consider him an illegitimate president. Let him be the president who must preside over the economic slowdown with a program that will only accelerate that slowdown and a world in which terrorists and other provocateurs will delight in testing his dimpled presidency."[117] Of course the media cannot by itself make the nation ungovernable for Democrats and liberals. But it can certainly legitimate behavior that does, no matter how unlawful or unconstitutional. This time it was America's first impeachment trial of an elected president and a close presidential election that eventually went to the wrong man. Next time, who knows? One thing is for certain, the longer we pretend that the media is actually controlled by "liberals," the easier it will be.

# Conclusion:
# An Honorable Profession

THE CURRENT HISTORICAL MOMENT in journalism is hardly a happy one. Journalists trying to do honest work find themselves under siege from several sides simultaneously. Corporate conglomerates increasingly view journalism as "software," valuable only insofar as it contributes to the bottom line. In the mad pursuit for audience and advertisers, the quality of the news itself becomes degraded, leading journalists to alternating fits of self-loathing and self-pity. Meanwhile, they face an administration with a commitment to secrecy unmatched in modern American history. To top it all off, conservative organizations and media outlets lie in wait, eager to pounce on any journalist who tries to give voice to almost any uncomfortable truth about powerful American institution—in other words, to behave as an honest reporter.

Now there is no denying that the media themselves are often their own worst enemy. Many of even the top reporters and pundits demonstrate considerable sloppiness, laziness, and irresponsibility, often coupled with an unfortunate proclivity toward a pack mentality. God forbid one of them should pay attention to a given story's historical, sociological, or macroeconomic context. When, in the autumn of 2002, the *LA Times* published an enormous story about the separation of an Honduran immigrant mother from her child, together with source notes for the entire piece, it threatened to overthrow the entire epistemological foundation of the journalistic profession.[1] But even those who labor, rather heroically, under these burdens find precious little to celebrate about their profession of late. Not even the attacks of 9/11 managed to put a crimp in the style of a media culture that is increasingly giving itself over to tabloid fluff that distracts as it simultaneously disinforms. As Frank Rich put the case with admirable succinctness: "We remain a resilient nation, and much is just as it was a year ago. Old Normal: Gary Condit, Lizzie Grubman. New Normal: Michael Skakel, Lizzie Grubman."[2]

In the fall of 2002, America found itself in the midst of an inconclusive war against terrorism, a failing economy, an exploding deficit, a crisis of confidence in the nation's corporate accountability, and a debate over whether to launch a preemptive war against Iraq. Yet according to the priorities of much of the media, the country's most pressing problem was a nationwide epidemic of kidnapping of small children. It was nearly impossible to turn on a cable news station without hearing the heartbreaking story of some beautiful young girl—be it Holly Wells, Jessica Chapman, Miranda Gaddis, Ashley Pond, Danielle van Dam, Elizabeth Smart, Samantha Runnion, Cassandra Williamson, or Nancy Chavez—who would never see her mommy and daddy again. Viewers would have been forgiven for naturally fearing the effects of this outbreak on their own families. Indeed, they were instructed as such by such popular and admired figures as Bill O'Reilly, who warned of "100,000 abductions of children by strangers every year in the United States." In fact, O'Reilly was off by a bit more than a thousand percent. The true number was fewer than a hundred and was on its way down. As Michelle Goldberg reported in Salon, in fiscal year 1999 there were 134 such kidnappings; in FY 2000, only 93, and in the first three quarters of FY2002, just 62, or one fewer a month than in the previous year.[3] In other words, this frightening fairy tale, cynically hawked as genuine news, was crowding out the stuff of war and peace, prosperity and decline, life and death.

Genuine journalists speak of such developments with regret. But they receive little support—either from within the profession or from the public at large—for the kind of journalism that brought them into the business in the first place. If September 11 taught the nation anything at all, it should have taught us to value the work that honest journalists do for the sake of a better-informed society. Thousands of journalists made the profession proud on that day, none more so than the reporters and editors of the *Wall Street Journal*, who somehow managed to put out a paper despite the fact that their newsroom had been blown up that morning. And have any of us ever known a sadder, but more honorable, death than that of the paper's beloved and heroic reporter Daniel Pearl?

But for all the alleged public spiritedness inspired by September 11, the mass public has proven no more interested in serious news—much less international news— on September 10, 2002, than it had been a year earlier. This news comes as a grievous shock and disappointment to many journalists, who interpreted the events of September 11 as an endorsement of the importance of their work to their compatriots. But as Sarah Wildman noted in the *New Republic*, Americans' curiosity about the world around them barely survived the holiday shopping season. Initially, journalists cheered to reports of "Once Insular Americans Studying Up on the World," as the *LA Times* announced in October 2001. The story would prove a triumph of hope over experience. Americans were certainly claiming to be more interested in world affairs. From September 11 through October, according to the Pew Research Center for the People and the Press, 78 percent of Americans followed news of the attacks closely.[4]

But it was not to be. According to a wide-ranging study by Peyton Craighill and Michael Dimock, interest in terrorism and fear of future terrorists attacks have "not necessarily translated into broader public interest in news about local, national, or international events. . . . Reported levels of reading, watching, and listening to the news are not markedly different than in the spring of 2000." The report found, "At best, a slightly larger percentage of the public is expressing general interest in international and national news, but there is no evidence its appetite for international news extends much beyond terrorism and the Middle East." In fact, 61 percent of Americans admitted to tuning out foreign news unless a "major development" occurs.[5]

Of equal concern to journalists and those who value their contribution to public life was the collapse of post–9/11 public support for the profession itself. In November 2001, 73 percent of those questioned spoke with admiration of the media's professionalism and 53 percent admired their morality. By June, those numbers had sunk to 53 and 39 percent respectively, lower than they been a year earlier.[6] Network news ratings were marginally higher than in the past, but its content was no less fluffy. As Peter Jennings told Howard Kurtz, in the autumn of 2002, "Are we more sensitive about not putting pieces on the air that don't have huge impact? Somewhat, but a broadcast filled up with hard, hard, hard news is very hard for an audience to subscribe to."[7] Meanwhile, newsstand sales of *Time* and *Newsweek*, which had risen 80 percent in the second half of 2001 over a year earlier, fell back to their original levels. Their content, too, returned to their pre–9/11 mix of celebrity worship, religion, dieting tips, and world affairs.

To blame journalists themselves for the media's inability to remain focused on the "spinach" of serious news over the ratings-grabbing candy of tabloid and celebrity schlock is pointless and counterproductive. Rare indeed is the journalist or editor who relishes the race to the lowest common denominator. The media were inspired by 9/11, not only by the same patriotic stirrings that most Americans experienced but also by the hope of regaining some of the industry's professional pride. "When you find yourself covering sex and sleaze stories, you're not terribly proud of it," said Clarence Page, a *Chicago Tribune* columnist. "It wasn't the kind of thing I could go home and talk to my kid about. Now my son comes to me with questions about Afghanistan. I feel proud of what I do. . . . "[8]

The most basic problem faced by American journalists, both in war and peace, is that much of our society remains unaware, and therefore unappreciative, of the value of the profession's contribution to the quality and practice of our democracy. That contribution can be summed up in an example offered by Captain Marc Hedahl, ethics teacher in the philosophy department at the United States Air Force Academy. He noted: "Most military members have used the *Washington Post* test at some point in their careers. If you are facing an ethical dilemma, then you simply ask yourself what you would do if you knew that your actions would make the front page of tomorrow's *Washington Post*. The test is easier to remember and employ than Kant's Categorical Imperative."[9]

Captain Hedahl's test reveals an important truth about society. People are not angels. Power requires watchdogs. Powerful people will often abuse their authority if they believe that no one is watching. That, in a nutshell, is why we need journalists. As Bill Kovach, chairman of the Committee of Concerned Journalists and a former curator of the Nieman Foundation at Harvard University, has explained, "a journalist is never more true to democracy—is never more engaged as a citizen, is never more patriotic—than when aggressively doing the job of independently verifying the news of the day; questioning the actions of those in authority; disclosing information the public needs but others wish secret for self-interested purposes."[10]

And yet the public demands nothing of the media companies that serve it, save entertainment. The dilemma for even the most conscientious journalistic enterprise is inescapable, and 9/11 did nothing to undermine it. As the political scientist Robert Entman lamented:

> To become sophisticated citizens, Americans would need high-quality, independent journalism; but news organizations, to stay in business while producing such journalism, would need an audience of sophisticated citizens. . . . Because most members of the public know and care relatively little about government, they neither seek nor understand high-quality political reporting and analysis. With limited demand for first-rate journalism, most news organizations cannot afford to supply it, and because they do not supply it, most Americans have no practical source of the information necessary to become politically sophisticated. Yet it would take an informed and interested citizenry to create enough demand to support top-flight journalism. The nature of both demand and supply cements interdependence and diminishes the press's autonomy. On the demand side, news organizations have to respond to public tastes. They cannot stay in business if they produce a diverse assortment of richly textured ideas and information that nobody sees. To become informed and hold government accountable, the general public needs to obtain news that is comprehensive yet interesting and understandable, that conveys facts and outcomes, not cosmetic images and airy promises. But that is not what the public demands.[11]

This apparently insoluble Catch-22 endangers not only the journalistic profession, but also the democratic world power that depends on it. Done well, journalism can be a noble, even heroic calling. Compared to professions such as law, medicine, or investment banking, it offers relatively meager pay and social status. In the greatest but most pitiless book ever written about the profession, Honore de Balzac's *Illusions Perdues,* the author terms journalism "a hell, a sink of iniquity, lies and betrayals that no one can pass through, or emerge from uncorrupted. . . ." Honest journalists are rarely appreciated by the citizens they serve, even less so by those on whom they report. In recent years, good journalism has become increasingly devalued by the very people who are supposed to support it: the media companies who own the various newspapers, magazines, television, radio stations, and Internet sites where it is produced. In journalism, as in life, virtue is increasingly deemed to be its own reward.

Captain Hedahl's *Washington Post* rule reminds us, moreover, of why we have a First Amendment. We need one. Thousands of pedophile priests would still be preying on young boys today were it not for the bravery of a few journalists in pursuing the story. For their trouble in saving these boys from sexual attacks under the cloak of the church's protection, these journalists are denounced by the same authority figures who have abused the sacred trust of their constituencies. "You can't go wrong blaming the media," explained Father Andrew Greeley, and the behavior of his own church bears him out. "By all means," thundered Boston's Cardinal Law, who himself knowingly shielded criminal priest/pedophiles, "we call down God's power on the media, particularly the *Globe*."[12] He was joined in this attack by Cardinal Oscar Rodriguez Maradiaga, a man who may be in line to be the next pope, who compared the heroic work of the journalists on this story to "the dark days of Stalinist trials of churchmen of Eastern Europe."[13] Even loyal Catholics in the media who voice their unhappiness with the betrayal of trust are not safe from anti-media opprobrium. When Maureen Dowd, a church-going Catholic columnist, did so in the *New York Times*, Catholic League president William Donohue accused her of being part of a cabal of "radical feminists" who have "long hated the Catholic Church."[14] Such attacks are of a piece with those of Linda Lay, wife of Enron's Kenneth Lay, who went on NBC's *Today* show to lie about her finances to a sympathetic interviewer following the fleecing of the company's stockholders and pensioners for hundreds of millions of dollars. Who was really at fault? Naturally, it was the media, who, according to Lay, simply sought to wreak "havoc and destruction in people's lives."[15] It seems safe to say that both the pedophile priests and the Kenneth Lays of the world would never have done what they did had they known their actions would one day be revealed on the front page of the *Washington Post* (or *New York Times*, or *Boston Globe*). What's more, we only know of these attacks because they have been recorded and transmitted honestly by the people who were their respective targets.

Many conservatives who attack the media for its alleged liberalism do so because the constant drumbeat of groundless accusation has proven an effective weapon in weakening journalism's watchdog function. Conservatives like William Kristol of the *Weekly Standard* are well aware, as he put it, that "The press isn't quite as biased and liberal. They're actually conservative sometimes."[16] But conservatives also know that if the press is effectively intimidated, either by the accusation of liberal bias or by a reporter's own mistaken belief in the charge's validity, the institutions that conservatives revere—the military, corporate America, organized religion, and the powerful conservative groups themselves—will be able to escape scrutiny and increase their influence. Working the refs works, as I hope I have demonstrated in the previous pages.

Powerful people and institutions have strong, self-interested reasons to resist the media's inspection, and the public accountability it can inspire. But the net effect of their efforts is to weaken the democratic bond between the powerful and powerless that can, alone, prevent the emergence of unchecked corruption where it matters most. These irresponsible attacks come at the cost of the kind of information citizens require to understand the political, social, and economic context of their lives. The decades-long conservative ideological offensive constitutes yet another significant threat to journalism's ability to help us protect our families and ensure our freedoms. Tough-minded reporting, as the legendary *Washington Post* editor Ben Bradlee explained, "is not for everybody." It is not "for those who feel that all's right with the world, not for those whose cows are sacred, and surely not for those who fear the violent contradictions of our time."[17] But it is surely necessary for those of us who wish to answer to the historically honorable title of "democrat," "republican," or even that wonderfully old-fashioned title, "citizen." Knowledge is power, goes the saying. Here's hoping this helps.

# Afterword:
# "Operation Iraqi Freedom"

WAR PUTS A STRESS ON ALL SYSTEMS, and few more so than journalism. Accuracy and accountability are never more necessary to a democracy than in war, but that is also when they are hardest to achieve. The natural patriotism that arises in almost all of us when our country—or the men and women pledged to protect it with their lives—is under attack not only empowers right-wing jingoes and chauvinists to silence honest debate, it also silences some of the internal debate that takes place in our own hearts and minds. Is wartime really the best time to be questioning the judgment and veracity of the president, the vice president, and the cabinet? Is it a good time to reprise the logic of those who argued beforehand that the enterprise was destined to failure? Must not those who commandeered the war know something we don't? And what of the risk of endangering lives with carelessly reported information? If "loose lips sink ships," imagine what loose broadcasts can do.

Different news organizations naturally grappled with these questions with varying degrees of honesty and integrity. To generalize about "the media" as if they were a single organism is always a mistake. (This is not even true of the individual institutions that comprise them.) In the main, however, it is fair to say that the jingoes won. The thirty-year assault on journalistic independence under the guise of assertion of liberal bias combined with journalists' natural patriotic urges to undermine the U.S. media's commitment to objectivity and "balance" in their reporting of the U.S. war against Iraq. Indeed, such accusations opened up a hole that proved large enough for the administration to drive a fully-equipped convoy of Humvees right through. Compared to the manner in which the rest of the world reported the war—and the various political battles between the United States and its allies that led to it—many of the U.S. media reports occurred inside an alternate universe in which Iraqis uniformly cheered their "liberation," the world stood by in a purported state of "shock and awe" at the prowess and perspicacity of U.S. global leadership, and nary a protester was heard to utter a single sensible sentence in opposition to the war.

While much of the difficulty of presenting a more complete and complex picture of the war is endemic to war itself—it is simply too big to fit on any television screen—

at times it appeared as though members of the media had decided to handicap themselves from the beginning for political as well as commercial reasons. Just as they did in Afghanistan, many journalists still felt the need to prove their patriotism—in part a legacy of the thirty-year attack by the far right on the very idea of honest reporting, represented as a liberal "conspiracy" that began with the reporting of the Vietnam War and continuing to the present. "Working the refs" continues to be effective, despite its having been demonstrated to be based on a patently false charge. (The U.S. Army College's official history of the conflict specifically rejects the charge.) It may not be true, but its resonance continues to make journalists—and their bosses—anxious indeed. This nervousness about their perceived patriotism combined with the journalistic deference to President Bush that emerged in the aftermath of 9/11. As CNN's Wolf Blitzer admitted on the air nearly two years after the attacks,

> Well, there's one difference between President Bush and the previous presidents, and we're about to commemorate the second anniversary of 9/11. After 9/11, attitudes have changed towards the President, the President's responsibility, and what this country needs. And I think people are willing to give the President the benefit of the doubt, knowing what happened on 9/11.[1]

Moreover, even if journalists did not have political or emotional reasons to go easy on the president, his advisers, and their war, they had commercial reasons to do so. One cannot overlook the success of Fox, whose ratings dwarfed its competitors, with the kind of jingoistic cheerleading that frequently equates reporting antiwar attitudes, either at home or abroad, with offering aid and comfort to the enemy.

Author Michael Wolff attributes the willingness of networks to favor the administration's point of view to a corporate decision to "take a dive" in exchange for favorable treatment from the Federal Communications Commission for proposed mergers and expansions that, indeed, followed immediately upon the war. (Wolff posits no direct evidence, but then again, his argument is not the kind for which evidence would likely be readily available.)[2] Others, mostly on the left, blamed the long-term corporate interests of the companies that own the networks and their fear of a retributive White House; many of these same people point to the alleged willingness of GE's Jack Welch to instruct his elections desk to call "Florida" for George W. Bush during the 2000 election despite the fact of his apparently having failed to achieve victory there—or in the national vote. (Welch denies this.) Whatever the motivation, the effect on coverage was easily observable. CNN's star correspondent Christiane Amanpour inspired the animus of her superiors when she admitted to CNBC's Tina Brown,

I think the press was muzzled and I think the press self-muzzled. . . . My station was intimidated by the administration and its foot soldiers at Fox News. And it did, in fact, put a climate of fear and self-censorship, in my view, in terms of—of the kind of broadcast work we did.[3]

The bias toward the Bush administration's arguments—rejected by the population of every nation on earth save that of Israel—was evident by the sympathy with which they were treated in all major media outlets in the United States. This was true even before compelling evidence emerged that the administration had deliberately misled the country and the world and used trumped-up intelligence well beyond the point of honest misreading.

During autumn 2002, for instance, *Washington Post* ombudsman Michael Getler thwacked his own paper for its hawkish bias during this period of coverage. He noted that the paper all but ignored the doubts of the then House majority leader Dick Armey (R-Tex.) and Brent Scowcroft, the first President Bush's national security adviser, first given voice in August 2002. So too the first public hearings on the ramifications of war, held by the Senate Foreign Relations Committee. A month later, when three retired four-star generals went before the Senate Armed Services Committee to warn against preemptive attack without first exhausting diplomatic options and gaining United Nations backing, the *Post* found this unworthy of attention. Shortly thereafter, a "widely reported" antiwar speech by Senator Edward Kennedy (D-Mass.) rated exactly one line. Millions who protested the coming war in London and Rome one weekend also failed to make the paper. The more than 100,000 protesters who converged on Washington found themselves covered only in the Metro section. Next came a decision to ignore the fact that a bin Laden audiotape described Iraqi leaders as "infidels"—something that threw a monkey wrench into administration attempts to portray Iraq and Al Qaeda as joined at the hip. A "rare story estimating the cost of the war, which was front-page news elsewhere," Getler noted, ran in the *Post* on page A19.[4]

Perhaps most significant, the *Post* buried the dogged investigative work of its tenacious reporter Walter Pincus, who consistently debunked the administration's claims against Iraq, only to see his exposés relegated to the back of the news section. As *The Nation's* Ari Berman demonstrated, on February 7, 2003, two days after Secretary of State Powell's Security Council presentation, Pincus described how foreign government officials, terrorism experts, and members of Congress undermined evidence that discredited the alleged connections between Iraq and Al Qaeda. A week later, a similar piece by Pincus and the military correspondent Dana Priest, entitled "Bin Laden-Hussein Link Hazy," also landed on page A20. A March 16, 2003, Pincus missive, "U.S. Lacks Specifics on Banned Arms," reported that American intelligence agencies were concerned about the administration's proclivity to exaggerate the alleged level of threat posed by Saddam's supposed weapons of mass destruction stockpiled; *Post* editors put it on page A17. On the following March 18, Pincus and Dana Milbank observed, "As the Bush Administration prepares to attack Iraq this week, it is doing so on the basis of a number of allegations against Iraqi President Saddam Hussein that have been challenged—and in some cases disproved—by the United Nations, European governments and even U.S. intelligence reports." *Post* editors decided that this story merited placement on page A13. Finally, nearly a month after Bush declared "mission accomplished," on May 29, Pincus and Karen DeYoung appeared on page one with a deeply investigated piece that read, "U.S. Hedges on Finding Iraqi Weapons; Officials Cite the Possibilities of Long or Fruitless Search for Banned Arms." By July 15, such stories started making the front page seven days a week—a far more aggressive effort than could be found then in the *New York Times*—but of course it was too late to influence anyone's mind when the ultimate decisions were being made.[5]

No less worrisome to those who persist in claiming a liberal bias for the *Post* were the contents of its editorial and op-ed pages: a near uniform viewpoint in favor of war. As Todd Gitlin noted, during the twelve-week period in December 2002 through late February 2003, hawkish op-ed pieces outnumbered doves by more than three to one. But this number actually understates the hawks' dominance. Gitlin observed,

> In December the total number of dovish columns, including columnists, was, to stretch the sum, two: a moral appeal by former U.S. Rep. Bob Edgar (D-Pa.), head of the National Council of Churches, and a skein of questions by William Raspberry—good, legitimate policy questions, eminently worth asking, but still questions. The number of unequivocally hawkish columns: eleven.

January's ratio was seventeen to four. Meanwhile, on the editorial side, where the paper speaks in its own voice, every single piece fell on the hawkish side, including a McCarthyite missive that accused the French and Germans of "standing with Saddam" as they tried to prevent war and maintain the inspections regime. (Note that the only German to appear on the *Post* page during this entire twelve-week debate was a Bush supporter—one of the precious few in the entire nation, where no major national candidate dared to take such a position.)[6] Virtually all coverage referred to U.S. and British troops under the deliberately deceptive nomenclature of the "coalition" when in fact it was no such thing. Only England and Australia proved willing to commit troops, materiel, or medical teams—compared with thirty-four legitimate partner nations in the previous Gulf war.[7]

Once the war began, *Washington Post* reporters distinguished themselves with some of the best reporting done anywhere. But the paper's willingness to allow the administration's agenda to shape its coverage during the fighting seeped into any number of stories, most evidently in its shameless hyping of the now infamous Jessica Lynch saga. The original front-page story, which appeared on April 3, ran beneath the subheading, "She Was Fighting to the Death." A number of "U.S. officials" had apparently informed *Post* reporters that Private Lynch had "fought fiercely and shot several enemy soldiers after Iraqi forces ambushed the Army's 507th Ordnance Maintenance company, firing her weapon until she ran out of ammunition." In the words of one of these officials, she "continued firing at the Iraqis even after she sustained multiple gunshot wounds and watched several other soldiers in her unit die . . ."She was fighting to the death," the official said. "She did not want to be taken alive."[8] Much of the rest of this media took up the theme of Lynch's spunky combativeness, transforming her into a heroic figure of nearly mythical dimensions, and her rescuers, veritable knights in shining armor. The *New York Daily News* ran a story of the "daring nighttime rescue," informing its readers, "commandos stormed the hospital, facing gunfire from guards outside. The resistance was quickly snuffed." In addition, its reporters explained, Pylelike, "Once more, as the commandos slipped out of the building, came the enemy gun blasts."[9] The airwaves were filled with tales of courage and character.

Unfortunately, it was all fiction. Following her recovery in November 2003, Lynch confirmed what had already been reported, though never in such detail. She fought no Iraqis and was not shot or stabbed; rather, her truck crashed near the Iraqi town of Nasiriya and she suffered numerous bone fractures. And while she was apparently raped before arriving at the hospital, she was well treated by Iraqi doctors in every sense of the term. Rather than holding her prisoner, one of the hospital's doctors claimed that they attempted to turn her over to U.S. forces but could not owing to U.S. gunfire directed at the ambulance carrying the wounded private.[10] Showing more courage and independence of mind than the reporters who swallowed what the Pentagon handed them, Lynch decried the "hurt" she suffered, "in a way that people would make up stories that they had no truth about." She had no interest, she said, in taking credit for things she never did and felt violated by the mutual military-media exploitation of her rescue and the symbolism they insisted it carried.[11]

Interestingly, the *Post*'s original April 3 story was coauthored by Susan Schmidt, the reporter who had proven so sympathetic to pro-impeachment Republicans and right-wing special prosecutor Kenneth Starr, often at the expense of accuracy in her reports. Months later, on June 17, 2003, the *Post* redeemed itself with an enormous investigative piece that highlighted all of the errors it had made in its initial reporting.[12] Of course, the damage had long been done—or shall we say that the propaganda victory had long been won.

Like the *Post*, the *New York Times* produced some terrific journalism in Iraq. Its editorial pages published a much wider range of opinion about the war than did the

*Post*'s, and its news pages seemed open to a wider range of possibility as well. Considered by conservatives to be ground zero of the liberal media conspiracy, in part for these reasons the *Times* nevertheless did the administration's bidding on a crucial issue by consistently hyping Iraq's alleged possession of weapons of mass destruction and even nuclear weapons. In the run-up to the war, star national security correspondent Judith Miller, together with her colleague Michael Gordon, reported in breathless tones—and sans attribution—that Iraq had "embarked on a worldwide hunt for materials to make an atomic bomb" by trying to purchase "specially designed aluminum tubes" that unidentified administration sources believed were for centrifuges to enrich uranium. Their report added, as a statement of fact, "Mr. Hussein's dogged insistence on pursuing his nuclear ambitions along with what defectors described in interviews as Iraq's push to improve and expand Baghdad's chemical and biological arsenals, have brought Iraq and the United States to the brink of war."[13]

The administration swung into action to make the most of its propaganda coup. The same day, Condoleezza Rice, the national security adviser, confirmed the *Times* story on CNN's *Late Edition*, claiming that the tubes "are only really suited for nuclear weapons programs, centrifuge programs." She also added, "The problem here is that there will always be some uncertainty about how quickly he can acquire nuclear weapons, but we don't want the smoking gun to be a mushroom cloud." Dick Cheney did much the same thing on NBC's *Meet the Press*, telling Tim Russert, "We don't have all the evidence [but it] tells us that he [Saddam Hussein] is in fact actively and aggressively seeking to acquire nuclear weapons. There's a story in the *New York Times* this morning," he continued, "this is—I don't—and I want to attribute the *Times*. I don't want to talk about, obviously, specific intelligence sources, but it's now public that, in fact, he has been seeking to acquire . . . the kind of tubes that are necessary to build a centrifuge." NBC White House reporter Norah O'Donnell followed this up by terming it an "alarming disclosure." And a day later, NBC's Andrea Mitchell stated baldly that U.S. intelligence had "blocked several shipments of aluminum tubes heading toward Iraq, the kind of tubes only used in a centrifuge to make nuclear fuel." Not one of these claims stood the test of time. On January 27, 2003, as the *Post*'s Walter Pincus later noted, the head of the International Atomic Energy Agency (IAEA) informed the UN Security Council that inspections had found that no prohibited nuclear activities had taken place at onetime Iraqi nuclear sites. Mohamed ElBaradei also told the Security Council that preliminary analysis suggested that the aluminum tubes, "unless modified, would not be suitable for manufacturing centrifuges." His March 18 final report was even more strongly worded; its conclusion was, "The IAEA had found no evidence or plausible indication of the revival of a nuclear weapons program in Iraq."[14] Once again, the damage had long been done.

Later, during the war, Judith Miller at the *Times* went even further in helping the administration make its phony case, and inspired a minijournalistic ethics scandal in the wake of the Jayson Blair fiasco by authoring a front-page story shortly after the main fighting ended in which she described an Iraqi scientist who "led Americans to a supply of material that proved to be the building blocks of illegal weapons, which he claimed to have buried as evidence of Iraq's illicit weapons programs." The scientist also allegedly explained Iraq's connections to Al Qaeda and its attempts to ship its weapons of mass destruction to Syria. Yet Miller never interviewed her source. And by the rules to which she agreed to write the story, she allowed the Pentagon to censor her work before it was published in the newspaper. This odd bit of official editing turned out to be of a piece with Miller's extremely peculiar relationship with certain members of the U.S. military; she allegedly participated in a ceremony in which she pinned a medal on one of the officers of the unit in which she was embedded, and threatened another officer with going over his head to Donald Rumsfeld when she did not approve of the unit's deployment—as well as the Iraqi exile community. In a May 1 e-mail to her colleague John Burns in Baghdad, parts of which were quoted in the *Post*, Miller explained, "I've been covering [Iraqi exile leader Ahmed] Chalabi for about 10 years, and have done most of the stories about him for our paper. . . . He has provided most of the front page exclusives on WMD to our paper."[15] That Chalabi had been indicted in Jordan for the embezzlement of millions of dollars—and clearly had a demonstrable interest in provoking an attack on Iraq since he expected to be installed by Rumsfeld as that nation's new leader—hardly made him a source on whom the *Times* should have been relying. And yet they did, to the Bush administration's delight and the detriment of the paper's credibility. Meanwhile, *Times* reporter Douglas Jehl noted in late September 2003 that internal assessment by the Defense Intelligence Agency (DIA) had concluded that almost all information provided by defectors made available by Chalabi's Iraqi National Congress had been worthless, and that Chalabi himself "invented or exaggerated their credentials as people with direct knowledge of the Iraqi government and its suspected unconventional weapons program."[16] If the DIA is to be believed, then worthless too were the headlines featured with Miller's byline during this period, including "Iraqi Tells of Renovations at Sites for Chemical and Nuclear Arms," "White House Lists Iraq Steps to Build Banned Weapons," and "Defectors Bolster U.S. Case Against Iraq, Officials Say."[17] Overall, it was a performance that put precious little wind in the sails of "liberal media bias" accusers.

Of course, the *Times* and the *Post*—together with the *Los Angeles Times*, the *Wall Street Journal*, *Time*, *Newsweek*, and a handful of other publications—set the standard for coverage across the media spectrum; it was neither the best nor the worst. Cable news coverage (which tends to take its cues from major print publications), with its ceaseless drive for higher ratings, further lowered the standard of coverage and added a few weaknesses of its own.

Fox News could hardly have covered the Iraq war—and the administration's campaign for it—much differently were its chief executive, Roger Ailes, still in the employ of the Bush family. The network appropriated the Pentagon's own slogan for the war, "Operation Iraqi Freedom," as its own. Virtually everything it presented was put in the context of a propaganda movie, driven by whatever line the Bush administration and its supporters happened to be pushing at the moment. Fox anchors described U.S. bombers as making a "grand entrance . . . into battle." Host John Gibson introduced a story about UN Secretary General Kofi Annan's argument on behalf of further weapons inspections by replying, "I can only ask: Huh?" Bob Sellers used the term "axis of weasels" to describe France.[18] The ubiquitous Geraldo Rivera—kicked out of Iraq for, in the words of Pentagon spokesperson Bryan Whitman, giving "real-time information about a unit's location, their mission and their pending activity, which would clearly aid the enemy"—found himself in Kuwait pumping his fists in the air and shouting that America's "iron fist continues its path inexorably toward Baghdad."[19] ("If he had been working for MSNBC, Fox would have wanted him tried for treason," quipped Quinnipiac University journalism professor Paul Janensch.[20])

Those who did not share Foxian enthusiasm were lucky to be treated with mere contempt. Gibson also described war protesters as "hundreds of knuckleheads." Neil Cavuto asked one military analyst, "Would you tell them to shut up or what?"[21] Those being told to shut up faired better than the journalism professor who took the trouble to write in to Cavuto to correct him on one of his many factual misstatements regarding the war. That fellow was instructed by the Fox host that he was an "obnoxious, pontificating jerk." Cavuto went on to call the professor a "[s]elf-absorbed, condescending imbecile" and an "Ivy League intellectual Lilliputian."[22]

The star of Fox's military cheering section was undoubtedly its best-known and most controversial host, Bill O'Reilly, who seemed to feel that all criticism of the Bush administration was intolerable, whether in the lead-up to the war or during the conflict itself. Familiar targets included the leftist filmmaker Michael Moore ("This guy truly despises America"), Al-Jazeera ("We're going to have to blow up these mosques, and you know what those Al-Jazeera idiots are going to do with that"), anti-war protesters who practice civil disobedience ("Well, they hate America"), Senate Minority Leader Tom Daschle ("I believe that Tom Daschle's career is pretty much over"), and French President Jacques Chirac (U.S. troops need to find Iraq's weapons of mass destruction, he said, so they can "ram 'em up Chirac's nose and go home"), to name a few.[23]

Fox outdid its rivals, CNN and MSNBC, in almost every way, measured by enthusiasm for the war or by nightly ratings. As a result of the eyeballs it commanded, its jingoistic, no-nothing approach to the war helped set the terms through which the rest of the cable universe defined the conflict as well. This was less true at CNN, which charges advertisers a premium for its desired audience, than for MSNBC, which continued to struggle during this period to define its identity. But plenty of evidence for the "Fox effect" could be found on both networks. For example, CNN's Lou Dobbs invited country singer Darryl Worley to sing "Have You Forgotten"—a song that argues for an invasion of Iraq in response to the Al Qaeda attacks of September 11, 2001—on what was apparently a special country music version of *Moneyline*. Dobbs congratulated his guest for his "wonderful" song with its "compelling" and "powerful" message, and accompanied the performance with a video collage that combined the horror of 9/11 with images of U.S. soldiers preparing to fight in Iraq. Together with Dobbs's angry comments attacking the United Nations, Dobbs seemed to endorse the false notion—frequently implied but never proven by President Bush—that Iraq was somehow related to the September attacks. When a reporter contacted Dobbs about this shameless manipulation of fact, he replied defensively. "Do I think Saddam had something to do with Sept. 11? Not at all. Do I think he supports terror? Yes, I do." Dobbs made this assertion despite the fact that any connection is also wholly unproven and denied specifically by the U.S. intelligence community. The song in question, he added, "is a pro-military song. It's about support of the U.S. military and the war against terror. Is it a problem?"[24] Recall that conservative critics continue to refer to Dobbs's CNN as the "Communist News Network."

Like Fox, MSNBC carried the flickering image of an American flag in the lower quarter of its screen. Its anchors announced, "We talk about America's Bravest here on MSNBC." The station even boasted an "America's Bravest" wall in the studio, filled with photos of military men and women sent in by their families.[25] Just before the war began, executives at GE/NBC moved to fire the antiwar talk show host Phil Donahue, the station's highest-rated anchor. An internal NBC memo reportedly complained that Donahue presented a "difficult public face for NBC in a time of war" while "our competitors are waving the flag at every opportunity," because "he seems to delight in presenting guests who are anti-war, anti-Bush and skeptical of the administration's motives."[26] To replace Donahue, the station hired in his stead former Republican congressman Joe Scarborough and the radio talk show host Michael Savage. The former, a genial extreme conservative, characterizes antiwar protesters as "leftist stooges for anti-American causes." He wondered aloud rather ominously, might it not be "time to make them stand up and be counted for their views?"[27] By the Fox-driven standards of cable TV, however, Scarborough's angry assertions barely raise an eyebrow.

But Michael Savage was another matter. When Savage, like Scarborough, accused protesters of committing sedition, or treason, he was speaking in unusually moderate terms. Before being hired by MSNBC, Savage was best known for referring to Third World nations as "Turd World nations" and complaining that the United States was "being taken over by the freaks, the cripples, the perverts and the mental defectives." Of poor immigrants, he complained, "You open the door to them, and the next thing you know, they are defecating on your country and breeding out of control." MSNBC was eventually forced to fire Savage (as was entirely predictable) when he screamed at a gay caller, "Oh, you're one of the sodomites. You should only get AIDS and die, you pig. How's that? Why don't you see if you can sue me, you pig. You got nothing better than to put me down, you piece of garbage. You have got nothing to do today, go eat a sausage and choke on it."[28] Before doing so, however, the network admonished one of its correspondents, Ashleigh Banfield, who had the temerity to point out in an off-camera lecture that perhaps Savage was not the best imaginable commentator to be given a national platform.[29] (Savage previously had termed his colleague, Banfield, "the mind slut with a big pair of glasses that they sent to Afghanistan," adding, "She looks like she went from porno into reporting."[30]) Banfield distinguished herself reporting from Ground Zero on 9/11 and later in both Pakistan and Afghanistan. By admonishing and demoting her in favor of a fellow employee who publicly termed her a "mind slut"—whatever that is—the station made clear its priorities in seeking to outdo even Fox by jumping headfirst into the depths of the gutter of extremism and verbal abuse.

Even on the high end, MSNBC's coverage did not contain much to gladden any liberal's heart. With the demise of Phil Donahue's program, Hardball's Chris Matthews is probably the most liberal commentator to have his own cable show. This itself is alarming. The fact that Matthews received (and still receives) lower ratings than those of the canceled Donahue throws yet another monkey wrench into the workings of "liberal media" theorists.

While Matthews can hardly be seen as a liberal—indeed, George W. Bush had few more sympathetic interlocutors than the starstruck Matthews when he appeared on the program during campaign 2000—he did, however, oppose the war before it took place, one of the few commentators to do so on cable television. Yet despite his dovish views, Matthews sounded like a sexually confused male cheerleader when discussing the episode in which George Bush dressed up like a fighter pilot and declared "mission accomplished" aboard an aircraft carrier that had to be rerouted for the purposes of the president's photo op. Together with former Watergate felon G. Gordon Liddy, Matthews actually discussed the size of the president's penis admiringly—Bush's, not Clinton's—or as Liddy put it, "his manly characteristic." Liddy, who once instructed his radio program listeners on how to murder U.S. federal agents, told his little buddy, "You know, all those women who say size doesn't count—they're all liars. Check that out." Matthews added, "And I've got to say, why do the Democrats, as you say, want to keep advertising this guy's greatest moment?"[31] The inanity of the discussion is only part of the problem; another is its mendacity. After all, not only was the mission far from accomplished—as we have all come to see—but the George W. Bush who disappeared from his National Guard service without explanation hardly had any business dressing up like a soldier. No president had done it before him. And he and his advisers would never have risked it were they not certain that a cowed, supine media would never call them on the many contradictions inherent in the phony picture. Still, seeing allegedly liberal pundits engaged in awestruck discussion of the president's "manly characteristic" must have exceeded their already debased expectations.

While nothing as offensive as this low discussion appeared on the broadcast networks, they nevertheless ceded the initiative in covering the war to cable stations, as advertisers do not like to see the shows they paid for replaced by gore and guts. And while many programs on the three major networks offered useful, fair-minded, and intelligent coverage—Ted Koppel's *Nightline* was the obvious standout—in the main they did not differ much from cable. The contrast with BBC broadcasts, available in many American cities, was enormous. The BBC regularly covered global reaction to the invasion, interviewed Iraqis far off the beaten path with unique stories to tell, and presented an extremely complex picture of what was taking place—particularly in view of the promises made by both the Anglo and American governments about the level of threat Iraq allegedly presented to its neighbors and to world peace in general. Americans without access to the BBC saw virtually none of this. Almost all network commentators were ex-generals who addressed themselves primarily to the success of former colleagues in achieving their military objectives. (Incredibly, CNN even allowed the Pentagon to sign off on its choice of commentators.) Civilian deaths went largely unmentioned, as did the rising level of anger toward the United States since the bombing began. The massive array of problems that likely would face a U.S. occupation of Iraq—always the basis of most opponents' objections to the endeavor—were uniformly swept aside. Apart from discussions of logistics and reports from the battlefield itself, almost all commentary was very much of a gee whiz nature, with little context to determine whether the United States was in fact achieving its stated goals of reducing terrorism, finding WMDs, or bringing democracy to the Arab world. Dan Rather, the far right's bête noir, undoubtedly spoke for many of his colleagues when he explained, "Look, I'm an American. I never tried to kid anybody that I'm some internationalist or something. And when my country is at war, I want my country to win, whatever the definition of 'win' may be. Now, I can't and don't argue that that is coverage without a prejudice. About that I am prejudiced."[32]

Rather was right. The coverage *was* prejudiced. While conservative think tanks tended to pronounce the coverage generally fair—an alarm bell in and of itself—according to a study by the progressive media watchdog Fairness and Accuracy in Reporting, nearly two-thirds of all sources used by the networks were prowar.[33] The percentage of prowar U.S. guests was 71 percent. Antiwar voices made up just 10 percent of all sources and only 3 percent of U.S. sources. In other words, the ratio of prowar American sources to antiwar was 25 to 1. Of a total of 840 U.S. sources drawn from a pool of ex- or current officials, a grand total of 4 could be deemed antiwar opinions. Of these, 2 were on PBS and 2 were on Fox. None at all appeared on any of the major broadcast networks. As for nonofficials, antiwar percentages ranged from 4 percent at NBC, 3 percent at CNN, ABC, PBS, and FOX, and less than 1 percent—1 out of 205 U.S. sources—at CBS. (For the purposes of this study, a "prowar source" was classified as such only if he or she voiced a prowar opinion. General Wesley Clark, for instance, took no public position on the war at the time, and hence was not classified in either camp.[34])

To insist that such überpatriotism is the norm for journalists during wartime—with Vietnam being the exception that proved the rule—would be misleading. Just four short years earlier, when Bill Clinton was president and the United States, together with NATO, went to war with Serbia in Kosovo, conservatives undertook exactly the same kind of public criticism of the president and the war effort that they decried as unpatriotic during the war in Iraq. Ironically, this wartime dissent was actually led by the very voices that were among the most vocal in their attacks on those who protested Iraq. For instance, Fox's Sean Hannity, who proved so contemptuous of war opponents, was heard to complain in April 1999, "Explain to the mothers and fathers of American servicemen that may come home in body bags why their son or daughter have to give up their life." Then Republican representative Joe Scarborough, now of MSNBC, complained to Fox host Catherine Crier, "This has been an unmitigated disaster . . . . Ask the Chinese embassy. Ask all the people in Belgrade that we've killed. Ask the refugees that we've killed. Ask the people in nursing homes. Ask the people in hospitals." And the famed virtuecrat William Bennett took time out from the slots at Harrah's to attack the U.S. war in Kosovo as "nuts." Like Hannity, Scarborough, and so many others, dissent was only patriotic when it matched his prejudices. Bennett said of the protesters, "Well, you shouldn't listen to these protests because they're obviously helping Saddam Hussein. . . . Saddam was much encouraged by these protests."[35]

Conservative bias and superpatriotic correctness were hardly the only phenomena tilting coverage to the right. In a move that bespoke public relations genius, the Pentagon created a program whereby journalists would cover the war while "embedded" directly into individual units of U.S. and British troops. In previous wars, journalists had grown increasingly bitter at being denied any access to the fighting; but the Pentagon consistently worried about both ensuring journalists' safety and the problem of allowing them to broadcast information that might endanger operations. The brilliance of the strategy was that it provided the access journalists craved, at the same time creating a profound emotional bond between reporters and soldiers, giving journalists a personal stake in the success of the outcome. Journalists therefore were unlikely to take a harsh view of the troops' actions, no matter what happened in the field of battle, because, as ABC's John Donovan put it, "they're my protectors."[36] "I can tell you that these soldiers have been amazing to us," explained David Bloom, a reporter for NBC who was later killed in action. "They have done anything and everything that we could ask of them and we in turn are trying to return the favor."[37] As the *Guardian*'s Gary Younge put it, "The media wasn't just physically embedded; it was politically embedded, too."[38] No wonder, early in the war, Captain Stewart Upton, a public affairs officer with the U.S. Central Command in Qatar, pronounced the Pentagon to be "extremely happy with the coverage."[39]

And even when the "embeds" had bad news to report, their superiors in New York wanted none of it on the airwaves or in their news columns. This was standard operating procedure in Murdochland, where as *New York Post* embedded reporter Jonathan Foreman noted, "On more than one occasion, I'd be writing stories about how exhausted and pissed off the troops were—I'd find they were topped by a headline like 'Troops Can't Wait To Get Their Hands On The Republican Guard'." Yet this was hardly limited to the likes of Fox and the *New York Post*. Speaking to a conference on the reporting of the war, Donovan, working for *Nightline*, recalled the night that his car was looted in Safran, and he reported that "it was unstable in the place where just yesterday people were cheering." His New York editors replied, "Well, John, could you get us some of those pictures of people cheering?"[40]

Moreover, the networks' unwillingness to put anything on the air that might shock viewers ensured that they would be offered an extremely antiseptic, Disneyfied version of the combat on the ground and in the air. "I haven't seen any destroyed tanks. I haven't seen any dead bodies. I haven't seen any disturbing images," noted Alex Jones, director of Harvard's Shorenstein press center. From the Pentagon's point of view, "it's been one magnificent recruitment video."[41] Images such as those of U.S. soldiers killed and captured were widely shown on the BBC and by commercial stations in France and Italy, where viewers are presumed to be more mature than those in the United States. Moreover, as Eric Boehlert wondered at the time, "Where was that hand-holding approach when the Black Hawks went down in Mogadishu? Virtually all those same news outlets ran pictures of a bloated U.S. G.I. corpse being dragged through the streets."[42]

There was nothing wrong with relying on footage produced by embedded journalists. Much of it was indeed riveting, and it was fairly gathered according to the rules of journalistic objectivity, at least as this was possible during wartime. But rarely did news organizations bother to put information in context for audiences. Iraqi soldiers had no reporters embedded with their units, after all, and so it was as if journalists were covering only one fighter in a boxing match. Paul Slavin, executive producer of ABC's *World News Tonight*, called embedding a "terrific experiment" but noted, "We were looking at the battlefield through 600 straws. . . . It was difficult to contextualize it."

"I certainly did not get a clear picture of the war because we were so isolated," added ABC's Don Dahler, who had been embedded with the 101st Airborne division. "My job was to look at things through a microscope, not the binoculars."[43] Temporarily, this lack of a larger context appeared to annoy the administration, when the U.S. offensive appeared to stall for lack of sufficient troops. Network commentators overreacted to the initial resistance facing U.S. and British troops, just as they would vastly exaggerate the extent of their apparent "victory." Overall, the embedding process ensured that the difficult and easily predictable problems that arose after George Bush declared victory would never be raised while the war was being covered. With little real resistance, did that mean that Hussein's forces were folding themselves back in the field for a period of prolonged guerrilla warfare? What was the Iraqi people's reaction to the destruction of their country? Did they view Americans as occupiers or liberators? What of the rest of the Arab world? Did the evidence of superior technology spur them to want to throw off the yoke of oppressive antimodernist Islam and embrace democracy and free markets—or was it having the opposite effect? Where were the "terrorists"? Where were the weapons of mass destruction? Where were the nuclear weapons? All of these questions figured directly in the administration's rationales for going to war and almost all were forgotten once the bang-bang began.

As implied by all of the foregoing, the most significant problem facing the media in reporting the war was the administration's consistent dishonesty in promoting it. After the main fighting ended, it became obvious to all but the most willfully blind that none of the administration's alleged justifications for war were supported by evidence. Virtually nothing turned up after the invasion to support even one of the administration's contentions for going to war in the eyes of its domestic and international opponents. Iraq was not "reconstituting" nuclear weapons; they had no significant quantities of weapons of mass destruction, if indeed they had any at all. Its leaders were not in league with the Al Qaeda terrorists who attacked the United States on 9/11. Moreover, the cause of democracy and human rights in the Arab world could hardly be said to have been improved by the administration's chaotic and ultimately counterproductive attitude toward reconstruction.

To tell Americans the truth about the Bush administration's willingness to deceive, deliberately, the nation into a very different war than the one it promised and repeatedly justified would have required a revolution in American journalism. At the very least, it would have demanded bad manners; not those usually associated with reporters—that is, shouting over one another, elbowing a colleague to get closer to one's interview subject, or even quoting an anonymous source reporting that so-and-so really isn't up to the job. Rather, to be an honest, objective, and fair-minded reporter of the Bush administration's policies required pointing out repeatedly and without sentimentality that just about all the men and women responsible for the conduct of this nation's foreign (and much of its domestic) affairs were without personal honor when it came to America's affairs of state. This simply isn't done in respectable journalism, and the Bush people understand this. Arthur Miller, speaking at a Nation Institute dinner, termed the willingness to use this kind of knowledge "the power of audacity," and Bush administration spokespeople used it with impressive effectiveness.

Take the case of Secretary of State Powell. Widely considered to be a man of uncommon personal integrity and a voice of reason in presidential war councils— perhaps the only such voice—Powell remained throughout the war debate the thin reed upon which men and women of good will, in America and abroad, pinned their ever-declining hopes. A war hero, a member of a minority who is known to be more moderate, thoughtful, and generally more sensible on pretty much everything than the president and the rest of those who serve him, it was Powell, after all, who fought the good fight for a multilateralist approach to foreign policy in Iraq and elsewhere.

At a meeting at the Waldorf Astoria hotel just before he was to go before the United Nations to lay out the case for war, Powell reportedly complained to U.K. Foreign Secretary Jack Straw—according to a diplomatic source quoted by the London *Guardian* who saw the transcript of the conversation—that the Pentagon's many claims could not be substantiated. (Straw has denied this.) Powell told the British foreign secretary that he had just about "moved in" with his intelligence staff to prepare for his speech before the UN Security Council, but left his briefings "apprehensive," fearing that the evidence might "explode in their faces" once the facts were known. *U.S. News & World Report* published a rather more lurid story, in which the U.S. Secretary of State was seen throwing the documents he was being given into the air in fury, declaring, "I'm not reading this. This is bullshit."[44] But read it he did. Powell's fears would be realized, just a few days after his speech when the British foreign office was forced to admit that a considerable portion of its Iraq dossier—upon which Powell had decided to rely quite heavily—had been lifted verbatim from dated academic sources and even included a portion that was lifted from a twelve-year-old American doctoral dissertation.[45]

Charles J. Hanley, an Associated Press reporter, subjected Powell's claims to detailed scrutiny in light of what was known at the time as well as later revelations and discovered that just about none of them turned out to be supportable. The satellite photos Powell showed of various buildings and vehicles in order to suggest that Iraqis were shielding chemical and biological weapons, as well as the missiles with which to launch them, were no such thing. Neither did he correctly identify the "decontamination vehicles" associated with chemical weapons. In fact, these very sites had undergone 500 recent inspections. Norwegian inspector Jorn Siljeholm told the

Associated Press on March 19, 2003, that these were actually fire trucks. No contrary evidence was ever found. In addition, the audiotapes Powell played of Arabic-speaking individuals speaking about a "modified vehicle," "forbidden ammo," and the expression "nerve agents"—the ones he insisted were intercepts of Iraqi army officers—never panned out either. Powell also mistranslated his final tape, according to the official U.S. translation. What Powell translated as "cleared out" was later explained to be "inspected," which is hardly nefarious. Much the same was true ad infinitum of the rest of the so-called proof Powell offered. There was no "dramatic confirmation" of intelligence indicating that prohibited items were concealed that way from the documents he claimed; no anthrax was ever found in Iraq after the invasion; no "biological weapons factories"; no four tons of the nerve agent VX; no "illicit chemical weapons infrastructure within its legitimate civilian industry"; no "stockpile of between 100 and 500 tons of chemical weapons agent"; no "nuclear weapons program"; and no "prohibited Scud-type missiles with a range of 600 miles." And so it goes.[46]

Most members of the media passed along these unsupportable claims unquestioningly. Gilbert Cranberg, former editorial page editor of the *Des Moines Register*, examined the media reaction to Colin Powell's UN presentation, pointing out that the secretary "cited almost no verifiable sources." Many of his assertions were unattributed. The speech had more than forty vague references such as "human sources," "an eyewitness," "detainees," "an al-Qaeda source," "a senior defector," "intelligence sources," and the like. Nevertheless, surveying the coverage of an allegedly skeptical media from some forty papers from all parts of the country, we find the following: "a massive array of evidence," "a detailed and persuasive case," "a powerful case," "a sober, factual case," "an overwhelming case," "a compelling case," "the strong, credible and persuasive case," "a persuasive, detailed accumulation of information," "the core of his argument was unassailable," "a smoking fusillade . . . a persuasive case for anyone who is still persuadable," "an accumulation of painstakingly gathered and analyzed evidence," "only the most gullible and wishful thinking souls can now deny that Iraq is harboring and hiding weapons of mass destruction," "the skeptics asked for proof; they now have it," "a much more detailed and convincing argument than any that has previously been told," "Powell's evidence . . . was overwhelming," "an ironclad case . . . incontrovertible evidence," "succinct and damning evidence . . . the case is closed," "Colin Powell delivered the goods on Saddam Hussein," "masterful," "If there was any doubt that Hussein . . . needs to be . . . stripped of his chemical and biological capabilities, Powell put it to rest."[47]

Recall that General Powell maintains the reputation for being the trustworthy senior member of the administration, and the one who least obsessed with the need to find an excuse for war with Iraq at any cost; certainly more so than President Bush, Vice President Cheney, National Security Adviser Rice, Defense Secretary Rumsfeld,

Undersecretary of Defense Wolfowitz, and the rest of the team in and around the president who were willing to stretch the truth well beyond its breaking point in attempting to portray Iraq as a credible threat to the United States.[48]

Yet despite all this, the mainstream media continued to stick to their guns, together with the increasingly discredited administration. Anyone in public life who veered from the belief that the invasion of Iraq was a noble cause, truthfully pursued by an administration committed to the public good and no other cause was treated as beyond the pale, unworthy of serious consideration or response. This was true regardless of whether the person or institution doing the accusing was aware of the many lies, exaggerations, prevarications, and so on that allowed the Bush administration to take the nation into war. An instructive case in this regard involves the treatment of Al Gore. Speaking to MoveOn.org at New York University in July 2003, Gore accused Bush of undertaking "a systematic effort to manipulate facts in service to a totalistic ideology that is felt to be more important than the mandates of basic honesty." The president, he said, was "pursuing policies chosen in advance of the facts—policies designed to benefit friends and supporters—and [using] tactics that deprived the American people of any opportunity to effectively subject his arguments to the kind of informed scrutiny that is essential in our system of checks and balances." The reaction was as swift as it was predictable. Recalling the hysterics of late *Washington Post* columnist Michael Kelly, who termed Gore's earlier September 2002 antiwar speech to be "dishonest, cheap, low . . . hollow . . . wretched . . . vile . . . contemptible . . . a lie . . . a disgrace . . . equal parts mendacity, viciousness and smarm," *Post* editors accused Gore of leading his party "off a cliff" and "validat[ing] just about every conspiratorial theory of the antiwar left."[49]

Yet on the very same day that the editors were fulminating about Gore, *Post* reporters Barton Gellman and Walter Pincus published a 5,331-word report detailing how Bush and his aides "made allegations depicting Iraq's nuclear weapons program as more active, more certain and more imminent in its threat than the data they had would support . . . withheld evidence that did not conform to their views," and "seldom corrected misstatements."[50] It's not as if the information was kept from Americans; the reporters themselves, for the most part, were doing their jobs. But as the *Guardian*'s Gary Younge pointed out, "In the political context in America, there weren't that many takers for certain kinds of information." Indeed, you can learn how little regard for the truth the Bush administration demonstrated from the front page of the *Washington Post*. Say so aloud, however, and be prepared to be smeared as "paranoid" by the paper's editors.[51]

It's worth noting, however, that in Britain, Tony Blair found himself on the ropes both within his party and in the nation generally for offenses against democracy that paled in comparison to those of George W. Bush. Blair faced an aggressive, independent-minded media whose members consider it their job, in the words of the

BBC's head of newsgathering, Adrian Van Klaveren, "to question governments . . . to hold governments to account. . . . This is not passive journalism. This is about trying to get information which others don't want us to know." The BBC may have been overaggressive in this pursuit, and careless in one very costly instance; but together with the *Guardian* it provided a level of information and critical analysis of the war— its run-up and aftermath—that had no parallel in the United States. (When Alan Rusbridger, editor of the *Guardian*, witnessed the now infamous Bush press conference in which reporters were preselected and asked only friendly questions about the war effort—"looking like zombies," in the words of ABC's Terrance Moran—he said he found himself "cringing" as he watched, both "appalled" at the pliancy of the White House press corps and amazed, given such indulgences, "that any information ever gets out at all."[52])

Among the most egregious moments in recent media history occurred when President Bush decided to celebrate the war's alleged conclusion on May 1, 2003, with a *Top Gun*–style landing on the USS *Abraham Lincoln*. Fox's John Gibson enthused that Bush had arrived in "historic, spectacular fashion." MSNBC's Bob Kur mused, "Now, a little bit more on what we're calling the president's excellent adventure today," and his colleague John Elliott observed, "It's cool. I mean, it's history in the making. . . . And that's new to me from Bob Kur, that we're calling it the president's excellent adventure. I like that. Kudos to the gang at MSNBC." On CNN, Chris Burns gave his audience the half truth that Bush once flew with the National Guard in his younger days, "so this is not a big, big new thing for him," implying not only that he had served out his full term but pretending that he had actually flown in harm's way.[53]

Unreported on the air were such details as the fact that in order to make this complicated photo op work, the navy was forced to slow down the aircraft carrier and extend by a day the sailors' almost ten-month deployment at sea, the longest by a carrier in thirty years.[54] Originally, White House officials insisted that Bush had to make the dramatic trip by fighter jet because the ship was too far out at sea to be reached by helicopter. But even with the intentional delay in its return pattern, the carrier was a mere thirty miles from shore by the time Bush arrived—well within reach of a helicopter, and without call for Bush to dress up like Tom Cruise for the cameras. Meanwhile, the cost of the expensive photo op in taxpayer dollars as well as the unseemliness of the costume quickly turned into a liability when it became clear just how *unaccomplished* the mission truly was. Within a few short weeks, more American troops had died in Iraq after the Bush pronouncement than during the initial invasion. United States forces were soon facing daily coordinated ambushes, surface-to-air missile attacks, protracted guerrilla operations, and a campaign of assassination against those locals who cooperated with their efforts to restore order.[55] Moreover, these extras in the Bush extravaganza were hardly offered scale pay. As his jet was landing on the *Lincoln*, the president's budget was quietly slashing the benefits of these soldiers over the next decade by nearly $29 billion. At the same time, his administration was restricting soldiers' medical care in the service of giving a tax break to the wealthiest Americans.[56] On Monday, July 14, 2003, the Pentagon announced that "due to the uncertainty of the situation in Iraq and the recent increase in attacks on the coalition forces," the 3rd Infantry Division—which had suffered thirty-six deaths, with many of its troops in the region since September—would have to remain in Iraq and keep fighting.[57] Rotations were being canceled and "in-country" tours were being extended to a full year. Did any of the cable stations ever mention these inconvenient facts? If so, I sure missed it.

But such coverage was the rule rather than the exception. Aside from a brief fascination with "sixteen words" in the president's 2003 State of the Union speech that dealt with the alleged purchase by Iraq of enriched uranium from the African nation of Niger that turned out to be completely bogus, the U.S. media rarely challenged the administration to prove any of its fantastic assertions about why the war was necessary or what would be likely to follow in its aftermath. When the Niger nuclear scandal finally began to break, the administration tried its usual program of stonewalling with a combination of tough talk and incoherent assertion. The phony story—which was not merely included in Bush's State of the Union speech but also, despite carefully worded denials, in CIA director George Tenet's classified briefing to the Senate Foreign Relations Committee—helped convince many fence-sitters to commit to war. Yet the story was easily identifiable as nonsense by any professional who cared to examine the evidence. Even without Joseph Wilson's now famous mission, Mohamed ElBaradei, director general of the IAEA, told the UN Security Council that he knew almost immediately that the documents were phony. Dick Cheney, who was reportedly briefed on Wilson's findings, tried to smear ElBaradei. Sans evidence, the vice president announced on *Meet the Press* in March, "I think Mr. ElBaradei frankly is wrong." Cheney continued, "I think, if you look at the track record of the International Atomic Energy Agency and this kind of issue, especially where Iraq's concerned, they have consistently underestimated or missed what it was Saddam Hussein was doing. I don't have any reason to believe they're any more valid this time than they've been in the past."[58]

In fact, a senior IAEA official had already told *The New Yorker*'s Seymour Hersh, "These documents are so bad that I cannot imagine that they came from a serious intelligence agency." Indeed, one of the letters was signed with the name of a Niger minister of foreign affairs who had been out of office for more than a decade. Another letter, allegedly from Niger's president, was so rife with obvious inaccuracies that the same IAEA official observed that its counterfeit character "could be spotted by someone using Google on the Internet."[59]

Until George Tenet—the only high-level holdover from the Clinton administration still working for Bush—was chosen as the fall guy, Donald Rumsfeld actually claimed to be unaware of the entire controversy. Even after the scandal broke, Rice and Rumsfeld appeared on the Sunday talk shows to defend Bush's deception as "technically accurate"—given the British misinformation. In fact, it wasn't even that; but so what? This was the standard by which America is taken to war?

Even after its mendacity was revealed, the Bush team remained able to rely on its many media apologists. Bob Woodward, who serves as the administration's unofficial autobiographer, took to *Larry King Live* to pooh-pooh the whole thing as just "one little piece of thousands of pieces that get sifted when they put something like this together." (No wonder why they turn the secret NSC notes over to him.) Meanwhile, the *Washington Post*'s Howard Kurtz tried to blame the entire outcry on "the left," as in, "The left is now up in arms about one sentence in George Bush's last State of the Union speech." (Just one sentence. Just one war. Just how silly can leftists be?)[60]

Eventually, even so dogged a Bush apologist as Kurtz—recommended as reliable by the web site of the American Conservative Union—could not help noticing that when in July 2003 Bush said, "Did Saddam Hussein have a weapons program? And the answer is: absolutely. And we gave him a chance to allow the inspectors in, and he wouldn't let them in," his answer bore "no relation to reality." He asked his guest on CNN's *Reliable Sources*, "Why has that not been more made of by the press?" The *Post*'s Dana Milbank, who had established a deserved reputation as the toughest of all the regular White House correspondents, answers, "I think what people basically decided was this is just the President being the President. Occasionally he plays the wrong track and something comes out quite wrong. He is under a great deal of pressure."[61] There you have it. An American president is said to be "under a great deal of pressure"—unlike, say, every other American president who has ever sat in the Oval Office—and the Washington press corps decide that "people" prefer that he not be held accountable even for his own deceitful words. And this from one of the toughest White House correspondents on the block. It is enough to make one shake one's head in amazement and despair.

It was just this unwillingness on the part of most of the mainstream media to hold the president and his administration responsible for their own words that allowed Bush, Cheney, Rumsfeld, Powell, Wolfowitz and company to prepare the country for war that existed only in their rhetoric—and perhaps imagination. In that war, Saddam Hussein had helped plan and execute 9/11 together with his close friend and coconspirator Osama bin Laden; he possessed mountains of weapons of mass destruction and was on the verge of acquiring deliverable nuclear weapons. His removal, meanwhile, would be painless and inexpensive. United States soldiers would be greeted as liberators; democracy would flourish in Iraq and all over the Middle East, and the peaceful occupation and reconstruction of Iraq would pay for itself by virtue of that nation's oil reserves. Of course, once they viewed the combination of our military prowess and the vision of our leadership, European naysayers and America's doubters throughout the world would join the chorus of congratulation. Finally, by virtue of all of this, the terrorist threat in the United States would be vastly reduced and at precious little cost.

Perhaps it's an unfair standard, but the ultimate measure of how well the press is doing is to ask, simply, How well informed are the people to whom it speaks? Without a doubt, the media face a difficulty in the consistent commitment to mendacity of the men and women in the Bush administration. Virtually everything the administration promised regarding Iraq failed to hold up to scrutiny. And yet they continued to stick to their disingenuous script. The inability of media to keep pace with the president's deliberate deceptions was evident during the debate over whether to go to war, a period in which Bush, Cheney, Rumsfeld and company actually managed to increase Americans' ignorance of the facts. For instance, a January 2003 poll found that 44 percent of respondents said they thought "most" or "some" of the 9/11 hijackers were Iraqi citizens. Only 17 percent of those polled were aware that none of them were. The answer shocked pollsters, as almost nobody had given the answer "Iraqi" in the aftermath of the attack. Moreover, a full 41 percent of those questioned believed that Iraq had already obtained the nuclear weapons the administration claimed it was pursuing. As Carroll Doherty, editor at the Pew Research Center, explained at the time, "There's almost nothing the public doesn't believe about Saddam Hussein."[62]

As the second anniversary of September 11, 2001, approached, Americans' ignorance continued to grow. Seven in ten Americans questioned insisted at the time that Hussein played a direct role in the attacks. On the one hand, this was surprising. After all, no credible evidence linking Saddam to 9/11 had appeared anywhere. On the other hand, the creation of this misperception had been at the center of the administration's strategy to win the argument for war. An in-depth study undertaken for the University of Maryland's Program on International Policy Attitudes (PIPA) and published around the time of the second anniversary of the attacks found that more than 60 percent of Americans believed one of the following misperceptions:

> There's clear evidence that Iraqi President Saddam Hussein worked closely with the Sept. 11 terrorists.
> U.S. forces found weapons of mass destruction in Iraq.
> People in foreign countries generally either backed the U.S.-led war or were evenly split between supporting and opposing it.

These findings imply a direct correlation between viewers' misperceptions and the consumption of television news as opposed to newspapers or National Public Radio. According to the PIPA figures, 80 percent of Fox News's audience and 71 percent of CBS's bought into at least one of these falsehoods. Meanwhile, only 47 percent of newspaper and magazine readers and just 23 percent of those who said they relied on PBS or NPR found themselves similarly misled. And lest we forget, phony ideas have genuine consequences. Support for Bush's war reached 53 percent among those who believed one of the lies, 78 percent among those who accepted two of them and a full 86 percent among those who embraced all three. At the same time, fewer than a quarter of people who understood the truth of the situation—rejecting all three canards—were willing to take a trip on Bush and Cheney's not-so-excellent adventure.[63]

These figures were no accident. Over and over, the Bush team made statements on this—and many other Iraq-related matters—for which they had no evidence and in many cases knew to be untrue. These related to an alleged meeting between 9/11's Mohamed Atta and a senior Iraqi intelligence officer in Prague in April 2000 that Vice President Cheney said was "pretty well confirmed," but never actually took place. Speaking on NBC's *Meet the Press*, Cheney was referring to a meeting that Czech officials said took place in Prague in April 2000. That allegation was the most direct connection between Iraq and the September 11 attacks. Amazingly, Cheney continued to harp on this connection on the very same program two years after the fact. Speaking to Russert on September 10, 2003, Cheney explained,

> With respect to 9/11, of course, we've had the story that's been public out there. The Czechs alleged that Mohamed Atta, the lead attacker, met in Prague with a senior Iraqi intelligence official five months before the attack, but we've never been able to develop any more of that yet either in terms of confirming it or discrediting it. We just don't know.

No less amazingly, Russert, who is considered the toughest interrogator on TV, simply let the accusation pass. Had he been a bit more on the ball, or at least willing to challenge the administration when it purposely put forth misinformation, he might have replied,

> Well, sir, with all due respect, that claim is based on the claim of a single uncorroborated informant to Czech intelligence. President Havel informed President Bush that the meeting had almost certainly not taken place. Moreover, when the high-level Al Qaeda leader, Abu Zubaydah, was finally captured in March 2002 in Pakistan, he informed his captors, according to a *New York Times* report, that bin Laden had personally rejected the idea of any kind of alliance with Hussein. Zubaydah's explanation was later corroborated by testimony from top-level Al Qaeda agents captured later in the spring, including one of the key planners of the September 11 attacks, Khalid Shaikh Mohammed. Farouk Hijazi, a former Iraqi intelligence operative who U.S. officials allege met with Al Qaeda operatives and perhaps bin Laden himself in the 1990s, also has denied any Iraq–Al Qaeda ties,

according to U.S. officials. Meanwhile, U.S. military forces also captured Samir al-Ani, the very man in question, in July, with no word on any meeting. Do you have any new evidence, or are you simply trying to perpetrate yet another deception on top of all those already perpetrated on the nation?[64]

Such a response, of course, by Russert is unimaginable. Nor did it occur to him to force Cheney to defend his many other false allegations in justification of the war, such as his unproven insistence that the Iraqi government "had a relationship with Al Qaeda that stretched back through most of the decade of the 90s."[65] (Or, for that matter, what about the time he told Russert that Iraq was "reconstituting nuclear weapons"?[66] Or that "simply stated, there is no doubt that Saddam Hussein now has weapons of mass destruction"? Or that U.S. troops would be "greeted as liberators"?[67]) President Bush also tried consistently to create the impression of a link between the forces of Hussein and Al Qaeda. In March 2003, he claimed,

If the world fails to confront the threat posed by the Iraqi regime, refusing to use force, even as a last resort, free nations would assume immense and unacceptable risks. The attacks of September the 11th, 2001, showed what the enemies of America did with four airplanes. We will not wait to see what terrorists or terrorist states could do with weapons of mass destruction.

Later on, he announced, "The battle of Iraq is one victory in a war on terror that began on September the 11, 2001—and still goes on. That terrible morning, nineteen evil men—the shock troops of a hateful ideology—gave America and the civilized world a glimpse of their ambitions." Bush also added,

The liberation of Iraq is a crucial advance in the campaign against terror. We've removed an ally of Al Qaeda, and cut off a source of terrorist funding. And this much is certain: No terrorist network will gain weapons of mass destruction from the Iraqi regime, because the regime is no more. In these nineteen months that changed the world, our actions have been focused and deliberate and proportionate to the offense. We have not forgotten the victims of September the 11th—the last phone calls, the cold murder of children, the searches in the rubble. With those attacks, the terrorists and their supporters declared war on the United States. And war is what they got.[68]

In fact, "they," in the persons of Osama bin Laden and his top lieutenants, got away. They continued to taunt Bush from their hideaways on September 11, 2003, two years after the attack, in a videotape broadcast by Al Jazeera. And to the degree that any cooperation existed between their forces and the secularist Hussein, it came *after* the Iraq war and as a result of it. In other words, Bush himself created the very situation against which he dishonestly claimed to be defending.

Yet on the second anniversary of September 11, many mainstream media sources continued to participate in this deliberate obfuscation of the truth, linking 9/11 and the invasion of Iraq as nakedly as any member of the Bush administration. On *CBS News*, for instance, viewers learned that the American soldiers in Iraq "are well aware that they're on the front line of the war on terror." It quoted servicemen who reenlisted because they said they wanted to "stamp out terrorism." Over and over, the networks juxtaposed scenes from the voluntary, "preventative" war in Iraq with scenes from the Al Qaeda attack on America. CNN, which had played Lou Dobbs's deliberately confusing country music video during the propaganda run-up to the war, picked as an interview subject the World Trade Center widow Ginny Bauer, who had just returned from a USO tour in Iraq. She claimed to have felt an "immediate chemistry" with the soldiers. ABC observed Iraq CEO Paul Bremer during a moment of silence for the 9/11 fallen. NBC aired a segment about a young man inspired by the Al Qaeda attacks to join the military.

Earlier, the network conducted a brief interview with Deputy Defense Secretary Paul Wolfowitz in which he warned of the continuing threat posed by Al Qaeda and explicitly linked the ongoing conflict in Iraq to that threat. Several networks reported on growing concerns that Al Qaeda may in fact have begun to operate in that country, but none saw fit to depict such developments as a consequence of a war that was sold to the public as a means of *preventing* Al Qaeda from operating in Iraq.[69] Condoleezza Rice made the original argument that we needed to go to war because Hussein posed a threat in "a region from which the 9–11 threat emerged."[70] Meanwhile, Wolfowitz was proving no less disingenuous than Cheney on this issue. "We know [Iraq] had a great deal to do with terrorism in general and with al-Qaeda in particular, and we know a great many of [Osama] bin Laden's key lieutenants are now trying to organize in cooperation with old loyalists from the Saddam regime," he told ABC on the second anniversary of the 9/11 attacks. This was false, of course, and a day later Wolfowitz qualified his remarks, telling the Associated Press that he meant to say a single contact, Abu Musab Zarqawi, who may or may not even have been a member of Al Qaeda. "[I] should have been more precise," Wolfowitz admitted.[71] True, but why bother, when journalists are generally so credulous?

In fact, the reaction by the media to Cheney's misinformation in particular forced the administration to distance itself from his remarks. A couple of days later, President Bush went so far as to admit that no evidence pointed to Iraqi involvement in 9/11, though he stuck to his "there's no question that Saddam Hussein had Al Qaeda ties," line.[72] (This too is false. There are indeed quite a few questions, and nothing significant has been proven, although this is nowhere near as egregious a claim as the 9/11 charge.)

Much of the media may not have been willing to go along so meekly with these false charges months after the war, when events started to sour on the administration's strategy and public support began to waver. But recall that the alleged Al Qaeda–Iraqi link was just one of many deceptions perpetrated on the American people to win their support for war. It wasn't just "sixteen words"; it was more like sixteen thousand. The administration manipulated the intelligence process to pretend that Iraq was building nuclear weapons and possessed large quantities of weapons of mass destruction. It trumped up the threat Iraq posed to the United States as well as to stability in the region. In a truly nutty editorial published in June 2003, *Washington Times* editors observed that "86 percent of Americans continue to be certain, or at least believe it is likely, that before the war Iraq not only had the facilities to develop weapons of mass destruction, but that it also possessed biological or chemical weapons." The editors were arguing that Americans don't care that their leaders deliberately misled them in order to convince them to enter this apparently never-ending quagmire, and so neither should the media. It's quite a trick: Lie to the American people then fall back on the fact that they bought the lies to demonstrate that truth really doesn't matter anyway.[73] Most of the media would never endorse this tactic so nakedly. But that is exactly what happened. And because the U.S. media was insufficiently aggressive vis-à-vis the lies of the Bush administration, the American people were tricked into an expensive catastrophe that will likely drain our resources of blood and treasure for decades. Perhaps it was unavoidable. After all, it is no easy task for a mere reporter or editor or even columnist to call the president a liar, even though he may be one. In any case, the result of this deference is an almost undeniable catastrophe for the country. Call it unfortunate. Call it necessary. Call it predestined. But whatever you call it, please don't call it "liberal."

# NOTES

## Chapter One

1. David Broder, *Beyond the Front Page* (New York: Simon and Schuster, 1987), p. 332.

2. Eisenhower is quoted in Stewart Alsop, *The Center: People and Power in Political Washington* (New York: Harper and Row, 1968), p. 206.

3. See Jules Whitcover, *White Knight: The Rise of Spiro Agnew* (New York: Random House, 1972), p. 47.

4. *Washington Post*, March 1, 2002, p. A02, and *Chicago Tribune*, March 1, 2002.

5. Jann Wenner and William Greider, "The Rolling Stone Interview: President Clinton," *Rolling Stone*, December 9, 1993. The irony here is that Clinton really was talking to members of the tiny "liberal" press, as represented by *Rolling Stone* magazine.

6. Bush's 1999 interview with the *National Review* is quoted in Jonathan Chait, "The Contradictions of Conservative Media Criticism," in the *New Republic*, March 18, 2002 (http://www.tnr.com/doc.mhtml?i=20020318&s=chait031802&c=1).

7. Reuters, January 25, 2002, 11:51 A.M. ET.

8. See David Domke, Mark D. Watts, Dhavan C. Shah, and David P. Fan, "The Politics of Conservative Elites and the 'Liberal Media' Argument," *Journal of Communication*, Autumn 1999, p. 46.

9. *Washington Post*, August 20, 1992, p. C1.

10. Mark Hertsgaard, *On Bended Knee: The Press and the Reagan Presidency* (New York: Farrar, Straus & Giroux, 1988), p. 4.

11. In an interview with the *Los Angeles Times*, March 14, 1996.

12. *New Yorker*, May 22, 1995.

13. The author received this subscription mailing in June 2001.

14. Author was present, and pleased.

15. See Spinsanity column, July 16, 2001, (http://www.spinsanity.org/columns/20010716.html).

16. *High Crimes and Misdemeanors* (Washington: Regnery, 1998), p. 107.

17. Alex Beam, "'High Crimes' and Misuse?" *Boston Globe*, October 18, 2001. Note that Beam reproduces passages from both documents that do, indeed, appear to be nearly identical.

18. Ann Coulter, *National Review* Online, September 30, 2001 (http://www. nationalreview. com/coulter/coulter091301.shtml).

19. Jonah Goldberg, *National Review* Online, October 3, 2001 (http://www. nationalreview.com/nr_comment/nr_comment100301.shtml).

20. Jay Bookman, *Atlanta Journal-Constitution*, February 14, 2002, p. A18.

21. Coulter said, "According to initial buoyant reports in early February, enraged travelers rose up in a savage attack on the secretary of transportation. Hope was dashed when later reports indicated that the irritated travelers were actually rival warlords, the airport was the Kabul Airport, and Norman Mineta was still with us." Quoted in Chris Mooney, "Idea Log," March 1, 2002 (http://www.prospect.org/webfeatures/2002/03/mooney-c–03–01.html).

22. I rely on Richard Cohen's reading for catching these particular insults, "Blaming of the Shrew," *Washington Post*, August 15, 2002, p. A25.

23. For instance, Michael Scherer, an assistant editor, and Sarah Secules of the *Columbia Journalism Review,* compiled just these few. There are many, many more. Coulter Claim: The *New York Times* columnist Frank Rich "demanded that Ashcroft stop monkeying around with Muslim terrorists and concentrate on anti-abortion extremists." (p. 5) Footnote: She cites an October 27, 2001, column in which Rich makes no such demands. He does chastise Ashcroft for not meeting with Planned Parenthood, which sought to offer tips on combating anthrax scares, based on its own experience with them. Coulter Claim: Liberals called the American flag "very, very dumb." (p. 4) Footnote: She cites a *New York Times* story in which a liberal history professor, Daniel Boylan, makes no claim about the intelligence of the flag. He does criticize—as "acting very, very dumb in their patriotism"—those who have criticized Hawaii for not flying an American flag over Iolani Palace, the nineteenth-century seat of the Hawaiian monarchy. Coulter Claim: She introduces a *New York Times* editorial on Supreme Court Justice Clarence Thomas headlined "The youngest, cruelest justice," then writes: "Thomas is not engaged on the substance of his judicial philosophy. He is called 'a colored lawn jockey for conservative white interests,' 'race traitor,' 'black snake,' 'chicken-and-biscuit-eating Uncle Tom. . . . ' " (p. 12) Footnote: The passage is constructed to suggest that the *Times* wrote these epithets, but the footnote refers readers to comments made in a *Playboy* article, which goes unmentioned in the book's text. See Michael Sherer and Sara Secules, "Books: How Slippery is *Slander?*" *Columbia Journalism Review,* November/December 2002 (http://www.cjr.org/year/02/6/coulter.asp).

24. See "Tapped: Fact Check Ann Coulter, a Special Edition," The *American Prospect* Online, July 26, 2002.

25. The contents of "Tapped: Fact Check Ann Coulter, a Special Edition," The *American Prospect* Online, July 26, 2002, can be found in Appendix One of this book, available at www.whatliberalmedia.com.

26. The *Wall Street Journal,* April 27, 2003 (http://online.wsj.com/article) email/,O,,SB103031135171291455,00.html) and Poynter.org (http://www.poynter.org/media news/letters.htm) August 27, 2002.

27. *New York Times*, January 10, 2002, p. E3.

28. Goldberg provided this number in his letter to the *New Republic*, April 29, 2002, p. 4. But these numbers shouldn't be taken at face value. Conservative books like Goldberg's benefit not only from a network of roughly 400 right-wing talk-radio hosts and forty cable TV programs (by Goldberg's count) eager to promote it, but also from a group of well-funded conservative organizations that buy books as a service to their members and (sometimes) to manipulate best-seller lists. Among the many conservative *New York Times* bestsellers whose numbers, according to the *Times*, were artificially inflated by bulk purchases were: *Bias*, by Bernard Goldberg (Regnery, $27.95), *Shakedown*, by Kenneth R. Timmerman (Regnery, $29.95), *The Death of the West*, by Patrick J. Buchanan (Thomas Dunne/St. Martin's, $25.95), *Absolute Power*, by David Limbaugh (Regnery, $27.95), *The Final Days,* by Barbara Olson (Regnery, $27.95), *Sellout*, by David P. Schippers with Alan P. Henry (Regnery, $27.95), *The*

*Case Against Hillary Clinton*, by Peggy Noonan (Regan, $24.00), *No One Left to Lie to*, by Christopher Hitchens (Verso, $19), and *Hell to Pay*, by Barbara Olson (Regnery, $27.95). The single liberal book to benefit from this manipulative tactic was written by an ex-conservative, David Brock: *Blinded by the Right* (Crown, $25.95).

29. *Bias*, p. 19.

30. *Bias*, p. 10.

31. *Bias*, p. 57.

32. Jonathan Chait, "The Contradictions of Conservative Media Criticism," in the *New Republic*, March 18, 2002 (http://www.tnr.com/doc.mhtml?i=20020318&s–chait 031802&c=1).

33. *Bias*, p. 12.

34. *Bias*, p. 10.

35. *Bias*, p. 12.

36. Eric Alterman, "'Whacking' the Liberal Media," *The Nation*, February 11, 2002.

37. John Leo, "With Bias Toward All," *Jewish World Review*, March 11, 2002 (http://www.NewsAndOpinion.com).

38. *Miami Herald*, March 17, 2002.

39. Goldberg admitted as much, when asked by a reporter why he chose to exempt his present employer, the liberal Bryant Gumbel, from his indictment. Goldberg explained that he was confining his examination to the three nightly news programs. In his letter in the April 29, 2002, *New Republic*, he made the claim regarding his lack of concern for politics, rather than social issues.

40. See for instance, Kurt Andersen, "The Last Gerontocracy: Why the Anchors Are So Ancient," Slate, April 9, 2002 (http://slate.msn.com//?id=2064171).

41. *Bias*, p. 189.

42. This was long after the September 11 "bounce" had disappeared.

43. *New York Times*, March 11, 2002, p. C13; March 16, 2002, p. A15; March 25, 2002, p. C8; April 3, 2002, (http://www.nytimes.com/2002/04/03/business/media/03ADCO. html), April 8, 2002, p. C10; *USA Today*, April 4, 2002 (http://www.usatoday.com/ advertising/orbitz/orbitz-window.htm). Note that O'Reilly's numbers in 2002 represented an 87 percent increase over 2001, meaning that when Goldberg originally made his assertion, O'Reilly's viewership represented barely one thirtieth of the number of people viewing the network news.

44. *Bias*, p. 56–58. See also CNN's *Reliable Sources*, February 17, 2002, and the *Washington Post*, January 19, 2002, p. A27.

45. Chait, *New Republic*, March 18, 2002 (http://www.tnr.com/doc.mhtml?i=2002 0318&s=chait031802&c=1). Chait continued to accept this false claim, moreover, in his April 29, 2002, *New Republic* exchange with Goldberg, p. 4.

46. Tom Goldstein, "The Goldberg Disputations," *Columbia Journalism Review*, March/April 2002, p. 76.

47. Bob Somerby, The Daily Howler, March 1, 2002 (http://www.dailyhowler.com/ h030102_1.shtml).

48. Bob Somerby, The Daily Howler, February 1, 2002

49. Bob Somerby, The Daily Howler, March 1, 2002. See Appendix Two.

50. Bob Somerby, The Daily Howler, January 12, 2002.

51. See Michael Tomasky, "The Savaging of the President: His Terrible, Swift Sword; Raines on Clinton," *Nation*, January 4, 1999.

52. *New York Times*, October 9, 2002 (http://www.nytimes.com/2002/10/09/opinion/09WED2.html).

53. *Washington Post*, October 10, 2002, p. A32.

54. Michael Massing, "Hawks at the Washington Post," *Nation*, November 11, 2002 (http://www.thenation.com/doc.mhtml?i=20021111&s-massing).

55. The cartoon in question can be found at (http://www.salon.com/comics/tomo/2002/05/13/tomo/index.html).

56. *New Republic*, April 29, 2002, p. 4.

57. Conducted September 5 to 8; surveyed 1,004 adults; margin of error +/- 3 percent (released September 20).

58. M. D. Watts, D. Domke, D. V. Shah, and D. P. Fan, "Elite Cues and Media Bias in Presidential Campaigns: Explaining Public Perceptions of a Liberal Press," *Communications Research*, 26 (1999), 144–175. See also David Niven, "Partisan Bias in the Media? A New Test," *Social Science Quarterly*, 80 (4), December 1999, p. 847–857.

59. *New York Times*, September 6, 2002, p. A23.

# Chapter Two

1. See David Domke, Mark D. Watts, Dhavan C. Shah, and David. P. Fan, "The Politics of Conservative Elites and the 'Liberal Media' Argument," *Journal of Communication*, Autumn 1999, pp. 35–58.

2. *Washington Post*, May 6, 2001, p. B1.

3. *Brill's Content*, September 1999.

4. The *London Independent*, April 17, 2002 (http://www.commondreams.org/views02/0417–02.htm), and the *Daily Northwestern*, April 14, 2002 (http://www.dailynorthwestern.com/daily/issues/2002/04/12/campus/c-middleeast.shtml).

5. The study in question can be found at (http://www.lyinginponds.com/boxscore.20020517.html). Krugman's response appeared on May 14, 2002, at (http://www.wws.princeton.edu/~pkrugman/).

6. Quoted in the *Nation*, March 13, 2000 (http://past.thenation.com/cgi-bin/framizer.cgi?url=http://past.thenation.com/issue/000313/0313alterman.shtml). See also Bernard Goldberg, *Bias* (Washington, D.C.: Regnery, 2001), p. 124.

7. *Bias*, p. 124.

8. See Jonathan Chait, "The Contradictions of Conservative Media," *The New Republic*, March 18, 2002 (http://www.tnr.com/doc.mhtml?i=20020318&s=chait031802&c=2).

9. Author's interview, Rome.

10. Author's interview, Paris.

11. See John Rawls, *A Theory of Justice* (Cambridge: Harvard University Press, 1999, revised ed.) and *Political Liberalism* (Cambridge: Harvard University Press, 1995).

12. Lawrence Mishel, Jared Bernstein, and Heather Boushey, *The State of Working America, 2001–2002* (Ithaca, N.Y.: ILR Press, 2003), p. 213.

13. Peter Singer, *One World: The Ethics of Globalization* (New Haven: Yale University Press, 2002), pp. 150–176.

14. The *Milwaukee Journal Sentinal*, May 8, 2002 (http://www.jsonline.com/news/metro/may02/41911.asp).

15. Robert Parry, "Media Mythology: Is the Press Liberal?" February 17, 1997 (http://www.consortiumnews.com/archive/story21.html).

16. Herbert Gans, "Are American Journalists Dangerously Liberal?" *Columbia Journalism Review*, November/December 1985, pp. 32–35. See also Gans, *Deciding What's News: A Study of CBS Evening News, NBC Nightly News, Newsweek, and Time* (New York: Pantheon, 1979).

17. See David Croteau, "Examining the 'Liberal Media' Claim: Journalists' Views on Politics, Economic Policy, and Media Coverage," *International Journal of Health Services*, 29 (3) 1999: 627–655.

18. Croteau noted that 44 percent of regular people put NAFTA at the bottom of the list of its priorities while fewer than one-fifth as many journalists—just 8 percent—did. Twenty-four percent of journalists put NAFTA expansion in the rest of Latin America among the "top few" priorities, compared with just 7 percent of the general public. More than twice as many journalists (71 percent) told pollsters they support giving the president "fast-track" authority to negotiate trade agreements without interference from Congress while, according to an October 1997 Hart-Teeter/NBC News/*Wall Street Journal* poll, the number for the public was only 35 percent and the number opposing it was five times as high. This conservative journalist/liberal public dichotomy carries over to the larger philosophical question of the proper role of corporate power in society. Just 57 percent of the journalists agreed that "too much power is concentrated in the hands of a few large companies." However, when the Times Mirror Center asked the same question of the general public in October 1995, the number who agreed was 77 percent. The number disagreeing reached 43 percent for the journalistic survey, but only 18 percent for the public. A repeat of this pattern is discernible with regard to tax fairness. Seventy-two percent of the general public, when questioned in 1992, told pollsters that Bill Clinton's tax plan did not go far enough in raising taxes on the wealthy. Fewer than half the journalists questioned agreed. See "Examining the 'Liberal Media' Claim."

19. *Washington Post*, May 12, 2002, p. W3.

20. Author's interview, April 22, 2002.

21. See www.whatliberalmedia.com, Appendix Three, Nation Media Ownership chart.

22. Transcript, *Good Morning America*, July 31, 1995.

23. Slate, December 26, 1997 (http://slate.msn.com/?id=2217).

24. Trudy Lieberman, *Slanting the Story: The Forces That Shape the News* (New York: The New Press, 2000), p. 146.

25. Rockefeller is quoted in Miles Maguire, "Business As Usual," *American Journalism Review*, October 2002 (http://www.ajr.org/Article.asp?id=2648).

26. "The Truth About Self-Censorship," *Columbia Journalism Review*, May/June 2000 (http://www.cjr.org/year/00/2/2/may-juneindex.asp).

27. "Self-Censorship: How Often and Why: Journalists Avoiding the News," April 30, 2000, Pew Research Center for the People and the Press (http://www.people-press.org/reports/display.php3?ReportID=39).

28. "The Truth About Self-Censorship," *Columbia Journalism Review*, May/June 2000 (http://www.cjr.org/year/00/2/2/may-juneindex.asp).

29. Michael Wolff, *New York*, April 29, 2002.

30. As David Shaw noted in the *Los Angeles Times*, "Gannett earns profit margins of 25 percent. Knight Ridder newspapers, like most newspapers, continue to be very profitable—a profit margin of 20.8 percent last year and, despite this year's sour economy, 18.5 percent in the first quarter of 2001, slightly better than the industry average. That is more than double the profitability of the average Fortune 500 Company." July 3, 2001, p. A1.

31. In Howard Gardner, Mihaly Csikszentmihalyi, and William Damon, *Good Work: When Excellence and Ethics Meet* (New York: Basic Books, 2001), p. 133. See also the *Los Angeles Times,* March 21, 2001, p. A15.

32. Among the exceptions were the *Wall Street Journal,* National Public Radio, and *Variety.*

33. Rather is quoted by Frank Rich in "The Weight of an Anchor," *New York Times Magazine,* May 19, 2002 (http://www.nytimes.com/2002/05/19/magazine/19ANCHOR. html?pagewanted=print&position=top).

34. *Washington Post,* February 25, 2002, p. C1.

35. *Washington Post,* February 24, 2002, p. B7.

36. Ben Bagdikian, *The Media Monopoly,* fifth edition (Boston: Beacon Press, 1997), p. xiv.

37. *Congressional Quarterly* Web site, cited April 29, 1997.

38. Carl Jenson, *Censored: The News That Didn't Make the News and Why: The 1996 Project Censored Yearbook* (New York: Seven Stories, April 1996) pp. 50–51.

39. Tom Johnson, "Excellence in the News: Who Really Decides," speech delivered at Paul White Award Dinner, October 2, 1999. Quoted in Bill Kovach and Tom Rosenstiel, *The Elements of Journalism* (New York: Three Rivers Press, 2001), p. 63.

40. Crain Communications, *Top Executive Salaries for Major Media Companies,* 2001.

41. *Good Work,* p. 131.

# Chapter Three

1. Quoted on The Drudge Report, June 18, 2002 (http://www.drudgereport.com/ flashgs.htm).

2. Paul Glastris, "Why Can't the Democrats Get Tough?" *Washington Monthly,* March 2002 (www.washingtonmonthly.com/features/2001/0203.glastris.html).

3. *Wall Street Journal,* June 7, 2002, p. W17. Varadarahan noted that no members of the Clinton administration attended Stephanopoulos's wedding. There were at least nine.

4. ABC's *This Week with George Stephanopoulos,* September 15, 2002.

5. CNN's *Reliable Sources,* September 21, 2002 (http://www.cnn.com/TRANSCRIPTS/ 0209/21/rs.00.html).

6. Glastris, *Washington Monthly,* March 2002 (www.washingtonmonthly.com/features/ 2001/0203.glastris.html).

7. Glastris, *Washington Monthly,* March 2002.

8. *Crossfire,* May 6, 2002 (www.cnn.com/TRANSCRIPTS/0205/06/cf.00.html).

9. J. Max Robins, "Fox News Returns CNN's Crossfire," *TV Guide* Online, April 30, 2002 (www.tvguide.com/magazine/robins/020429.asp).

10. Jim Rutenberg, "From 'Crossfire' to Long Afternoons on MSNBC," *New York Times,* June 12, 2002. For a discussion of Pat Buchanan's strange sympathy for Nazi war criminals, see the author's *Sound & Fury: The Making of the Punditocracy,* second edition (Ithaca, N.Y.: Cornell University Press, 2000), p. 118. (Note: all references to the book hitherto will refer to this edition.)

11. Michael Fletcher, "Study: History Still a Mystery to Many Students," *Washington Post,* May 10, 2002, p. A3, and Joan Bishupic, "Has the Court Lost Its Appeal?" *Washington Post,* October 12, 1995, p. A23 (and for the record, Moe, Curly, and Larry, though sometimes Shemp).

12. For an abbreviated history of punditry, see *Sound & Fury*, Chapters 1–3.

13. Marvin Kalb, "The Rise of the 'New News': A Case Study of Two Root Causes of the Modern Scandal Coverage," Joan Shorenstein Center for Press, Politics and Public Policy Discussion Paper, D–34 (Cambridge, Mass.), October 1998, p. 27.

14. *Sound & Fury*, p. 124.

15. Quote in James Fallows, *Breaking the News: How the Media Undermine American Democracy* (New York: Pantheon Books, 1996), p. 113.

16. *Breaking the News*, p. 103.

17. For an explanation of the history of the McLaughlin Group, see *Sound & Fury*, pp. 106–127.

18. Andrew Ferguson, "I, Pundit," the *Weekly Standard*, November 20, 1995, Vol. 1, No. 10, p. 4.

19. For a fuller explanation of the history of Will's career, see *Sound & Fury*, pp. 85–105.

20. *Sound & Fury*, p. 72.

21. *Breaking the News*, p. 38.

22. *Sound & Fury*, p. 92.

23. Tim Rutten, "Talk Is Cheap or at Least Cheaper than Newscasts," *Los Angeles Times*, June 7, 2002.

24. Paul Farhi, "The Life of O'Reilly," *Washington Post*, December 13, 2000, p. C1.

25. *Television Quarterly*, January 2001 (http://www.emmyonline.org/national/tvquarterly/default.asp).

26. "Resignation at CNN; Renewal at Fox," *New York Times*, March 15, 2001, p. C6; *Boston Globe*, March 14, 2001.

27. *Television Quarterly*, January 2001 (http://www.emmyonline.org/national/tvquarterly/default.asp).

28. Peter Hart, "The 'Oh Really?' Factor: O'Reilly Spins Facts and Statistics," *Extra!*, May/June 2001 (http://www.fair.org/extra/0205/oh_really.html).

29. Here is a copy of the e-mail sent to O'Reilly regarding his complaints: Original Message—From: Arun Rath; Sent: Thursday, May 09, 2002 3:38 PM; To: 'oreilly@foxnews.com'; Subject: your fantasy world; Bill, I'm sick of hearing you say you can't get on NPR. Our own Mike Pesca reported a long piece all about you last year, although you later denied ever hearing of him (odd that you spoke with him over an hour on tape, had him in your office and around while you were taping and later developed amnesia) AND you've turned down the requests to be on our show since then. We would still love to have you on OTM. Your claim that you can't get on NPR is self-serving bull. So put your money where your mouth is or shut up. awaiting your response, Arun Rath Senior Producer, NPR's On the Media WNYC.

30. Hart, *Extra!*, May/June 2001 (http://www.fair.org/extra/0205/oh_really.html).

31. "Nobody should begrudge any American the right to an opinion, but, hey, Rosie [O'Donnell], come on, let's think out your flaky liberal agenda a little. Are you making sense, or are you spouting propaganda? I mean, a guy named Joseph Goebbels did the same thing on the far right during World War II" (Bill O'Reilly, *The O'Reilly Factor*, (ETC) 184). Quoted by Peter Hart and Seth Ackerman, "Bill O'Reilly's Sheer O'Reillyness," *Extra!*, August 2001 (www.fair.org/extra/oreilly.html).

32. Alex Williams, "Bill O'Reilly: Bull-Fighter for New York," *New York* magazine, January 1, 2001 (http://www.newyorkmetro.com/nymetro/news/media/features/4233/).

33. The incident is described by Clarence Page in "Dummying Up: For Fear of Reading a Book about the Koran," *Chicago Tribune*, August 11, 2002 (http://www.chicagotribune.com/news/showcase/chi–0208110057aug11.column).

34. The *O'Reilly Factor*, May 24, 2001.

35. *New York Times*, April 4, 2001, p. A21.

36. Bill Kovach and Tom Rosenstiel, *Elements of Journalism* (New York: Three Rivers Press, 2001), pp. 131–134.

37. Noam Scheiber, "Chris Matthews and Bill O'Reilly v. the Working Man: Class Act," *New Republic*, June 25, 2001 (http://www.tnr.com/062501/scheiber062501_print.html).

38. Gail Shister, "More Hardball not a Senate Race for Matthews," *Philadelphia Inquirer*, June 6, 2001.

39. Christopher Matthews, "Leadership in the Moment," *San Francisco Chronicle*, November 4, 2001 (www.sfgate.com/cgi-bin/article.cgi?file=/chronicle/archive/2001/11/04/IN221955.DTL). There is something odd about the conservative punditocracy's desire to compare Bush to Hemingway, since the novelist probably wrote more books than the president has read. When George Will wrote in the *Washington Post* on March 12, 2002, that ""Bush's terseness is Ernest Hemingway seasoned with John Wesley," he inspired the following letter to the *Boston Globe* from Norman Mailer: Well, one is hardly familiar with John Wesley's sermons, but I do know that to put George W. Bush's prose next to Hemingway is equal to saying that Jackie Susann is right up there with Jane Austen. Did a sense of shame ever reside in our Republican toadies? You can't stop people who are never embarrassed by themselves. Will's readiness to turn a sow's ear into a silk purse can be cited as world class sycophancy. Here's a passage from "A Farewell to Arms." It has more going for it than "terseness." "I was embarrassed by the words sacred, glorious, and sacrifice. . . . I had seen nothing sacred, and the things that were glorious had no glory and the sacrifices were like the stockyards at Chicago if nothing was done with the meat except to bury it. There were many words you could not stand to hear. . . . Abstract words such as glory, honor, courage, or hallow were obscene beside the concrete names of villages, the names of roads, the names of rivers, the numbers of regiments and the dates." It is worth reminding ourselves that the life of a democracy may also depend on the good and honorable use of language and not on the scurvy manipulation of such words as "evil" and "love" by intellectual striplings of the caliber of our president. (See "For Whom The Will Toils," *Boston Globe* Letters Page, March 14, 2002.)

40. *Television Quarterly*, January 2001 (http://www.emmyonline.org/national/tvquarterly/default.asp).

41. Alicia Mundy, "TV Talker Matthews Confronts Post-Clinton Era," *Adweek Magazine's Special Report*.

42. Steven Battaglio, "More to Shout About," New York *Daily News*, June 6, 2002, p. 112.

43. Bill Kovach and Tom Rosenstiel, *Warp Speed: America in the Age of Mixed Media* (New York: Century Foundation, 1999), pp. 62–65.

44. Tim Rutten, "Talk Is Cheap, or at Least Cheaper Than Newscasts," *Los Angeles Times*, June 7, 2002, p. 1.

45. Ben Fritz and Bryan Keefer, "The Blowhard Next Door," Salon.com, August 26, 2002 (http://www.salon.com/politics/feature/2002/08/26/hannity/print.html).

46. Ibid.

47. Tad Friend, "It's, You Know, About Opinions and Stuff," *New York Times Magazine*, June 15, 1997, p. 34.

48. CNN's *Reliable Sources*, April 27, 2002.

49. CNN's *Reliable Sources*, June 1, 2002.

50. Marjorie Williams, "Laura, Get Your Gun," *Vanity Fair*, January 1997, p. 46.

51. See the introduction and Appendix 1 of this book on www.whatliberalmedia.com.

52. Paul Farhi, "The New Face of the Talking Head: Heather Nauert's Fast Path to Punditry," *Washington Post*, May 25, 2000, p. C1.

53. *Today Show*, July 18, 2002.

54. Quoted in Eric Boehlert, "Phil Donahue's Liberal Oasis," Salon.com, July 18, 2002 (http://archive.salon.com/news/feature/2002/07/18/donahue/).

55. Paul Farhi, "Talk Radio, Top Volume on the Right," *Washington Post*, May 8, 2002, p. C1.

56. Jeffrey Scheuer, *The Sound Bite Society: Television and the American Mind* (New York: Four Walls Eight Windows, 1999), pp. 32–40. See also Scheuer, "The Television Thing," *Dissent*, summer 1995 (www.dissent.com).

# Chapter Four

1. Michael Kramer, "The Un-Drudge. David Broder: Still Class of the Field," *Brill's Content*, November 1998, pp. 129–132.

2. Mary McGrory, "Not Worthy of Tragedy," *Washington Post*, November 23, 2000, p. A3.

3. R. W. Apple. Jr., "Gotcha! One Cheer for Politics as Usual," *New York Times*, May 19, 2002.

4. *Washington Post*, April 20, 1985.

5. *Washington Post,* December 22, 1985.

6. *Washington Post*, August 14, 1987.

7. *Washington Post*, January 14, 1990, p. B7, and January 11, 1991, p. A21.

8. David S. Broder, "Gore Means Gridlock," *Washington Post*, October 22, 2000, p. B7.

9. David S. Broder, "Autumn Showdown," *Washington Post*, August 26, 1998, p. A19.

10. Sally Quinn, "Not in Their Backyard: In Washington, That Letdown Feeling," *Washington Post*, November 2, 1998, p. E1. See also *Sound and Fury*, p. 270.

11. David S. Broder, "Truly Nixonian," *Washington Post*, August 19, 1998, p. A21.

12. David S. Broder, "A Grown-Up Choice," *Washington Post*, July 26, 2000, p. A27.

13. David S. Broder, "Gore Means Gridlock," *Washington Post*, October 22, 2000, p. B7.

14. David S. Broder, "Scoring the Debates," *Washington Post*, October 1, 2000, p. B7.

15. David S. Broder, "Gore Tells All . . . ," *Washington Post*, August 20, 2000, p. B7.

16. David S. Broder, "The Best Campaign," *Washington Post*, November 5, 2000, p. B7.

17. David S. Broder, "Burying the Hatchet," *Washington Post*, November 10, 2000, p. A45.

18. David S. Broder, "A Cloud Over Thanksgiving," *Washington Post*, November 21, 2001, p. A25

19. See for instance, Eric Alterman, "Accuracy vs. Speed," *Nation*, December 11, 2000.

20. Frank Ahrens, "On the Wealth of *Nation*: Leftist Weekly to Break Even, a Rarity for Political Magazines," *Washington Post,* June 11, 2002, p. E1.

21. Quoted in Janet Meyers, "*New Republic* Ad Pitch Leaning to the Right," *Advertising Age*, February 10, 1986, p. 32.

22. Michael Kinsley, "No Dogs or Journalists," *New Republic*, June 3, 1985.

23. The Podhoretz quote can be found in Dinesh D'Souza, "Marty Come Lately: *New Republic* Discovers Old Truths," *Policy Review*, Summer 1985. See also George F. Will, *Washington Post*, November 10, 1987, and *National Review*, December 28, 1984, p. 16.

24. For the full story of this shameful journalistic episode, see James Fallows, *Breaking the News: How the Media Undermine American Democracy* (New York: Pantheon Books, 1996), pp. 223–233.

25. Howard Kurtz, "Turning the Page: *New Republic* Editor Ends a Rocky Tenure," *Washington Post*, April 13, 1996, p. B1.

26. Howard Kurtz, "Blumenthal's Suit Has Become More Than a Drudge Match," *Washington Post*, August 03, 1998, p. D1.

27. See Peretz's interview with Benny Landau, published in *Ha'aretz*, December 9, 1982.

28. Author's interview.

29. Martin Peretz, "Israel, the United States, and Evil," *New Republic*, September 24, 2001.

30. "Louisville Slugger," *New Republic*, December 3, 2001.

31. "Armed Resistance," *New Republic*, June 10, 2002 (http://www.tnr.com/doc.mhtml?i=20020610&s=editorial061002).

32. Peter Beinart, "Faultlines," *New Republic*, October 1, 2001. The offending piece in the *Nation* was by Robert Fisk in the October 1, 2001, issue.

33. Jacob Heilbrunn, "The Powell Doctrine," *Los Angeles Times*, November 4, 2001, p. M2, and Charles Krauthammer, "Not Enough Might," *Washington Post*, October 30, 2001, p. A21.

34. Michael Tomasky, "Who is Roger Hertog?" *American Prospect*, May 6, 2002.

35. David D. Kirkpatrick, "*New Republic*'s Longtime Owner Sells Control to 2 Financiers," *New York Times*, January 28, 2002, p. C1.

36. Robert Morin and Claudia Dean, "A Liberal Bastion Gets Conservative Cash," *Washington Post*, December 18, 2001, p. A25.

37. Jeff Jacoby, *Boston Globe*, "Slander Is Just Fine When the Left Does It," December 28, 2000, p. A15.

38. Ibid.

39. Nicholas Confessore, "Hacked to Death: Jeff Jacoby, at It Again," *American Prospect* Online, January 5, 2001 (http://www.prospect.org/webfeatures/2001/01/confessore-n-01–05.html). Begala's original column appeared at (www.msnbc.com/news/495921.asp).

40. Peggy Noonan, "The Donkey in the Living Room," *Wall Street Journal*, November 17, 2000.

41. Michael Kelly, "Send in the Thugs," *Washington Post*, November 22, 2000, p. A27.

42. James Taranto; "The *Boston Globe*: Recycling Shouldn't Be a Crime," *Jewish World Review* Website, July 17, 2000; and Howard Kurtz, "At the *Boston Globe* a Question of Who's Right," *Washington Post*, July 11, 2000, p. C1; and Jonah Goldberg, "Honesty Is the Best Policy," *National Review* Online, July 10, 2000.

43. Jacoby e-mail, published on *Jewish World Review* website (http://www.jewishworldreview. com/).

44. From Sid Smith, "Conflict-of-Interest Spat Seeks a Clear-Cut Sinner," *Chicago Tribune*, July 10, 2002.

45. Geraldine Fabrikant, "Plunge in Bison and AOL Weighs on Turner Fortune," *New York Times*, August 26, 2002, p. C1.

46. See, for instance, Tim Rutten, "To Err Is Human, but to Think Out Loud . . . ," *Los Angeles Times*, June 21, 2002, p. A1, and Bill Carter, "CNN, Amid Criticism in Israel, Adopts Terror Report Policy," *New York Times*, June 21, 2002, p. C6.

47. *Reliable Sources*, July 13, 2002.

48. *Reliable Sources*, July 13, 2002.

49. *Reliable Sources*, July 20, 2002.

50. *Reliable Sources*, July 20, 2002.

51. *Reliable Sources*, July 27, 2002.

52. *Reliable Sources*, August 17, 2002.

53. *Reliable Sources*, August 17, 2002.

54. CNN's *Reliable Sources*, July 6, 2002 (http://www.cnn.com/virtual/editions/europe/2000/roof/change.pop/frameset.exclude.html).

55. Quoted in Rutenberg, "White House Keeps a Grip on News," *New York Times*, October 14, 2002, p. C1.

56. Sridhar Pappu, "The Art of the Leak," *New York Observer*, August 19, 2002 (http://www.nyobserver.com/pages/story.asp?ID=6216).

57. Quoted in Rutenberg, "White House Keeps a Grip on News," *New York Times*, October 14, 2002, p. C1.

58. Quoted in Helen Dewar and Mike Allen, "Senators Wary About Action Against Iraq," *Washington Post*, September 4, 2002, p. A1, and Alison Mitchell and David E. Sanger, "Bush to Put Case for Action in Iraq to Key Lawmakers," *New York Times*, September 4, 2002, p. A1.

59. ABC's *The Note*, September 3, 2002, (http://www.abcnews.go.com/sections/politics/DailyNews/TheNote.html).

60. Howard Kurtz, "Ari Fleischer Likes to Serve Up His Spin with a Smile," *Washington Post*, December 18, 2000, p. C1.

61. *Reliable Sources*, aired July 28, 2001.

62. Howard Kurtz, "Straight man George W. Bush's message is that everything's under control in a tightly disciplined White House that knows how to keep a secret. Ari Fleischer is the messenger," *Washington Post Magazine*, May 19, 2002, p. W14.

63. See Chapter 1 for Nunberg's work. Kurtz repeated the phony charge in an August 12, 2002, on-line news chat (http://discuss.washingtonpost.com/wp-srv/zforum/02/media backtalk081202.html).

64. Howard Kurtz, "Death by a Thousand Jabberers," *Washington Post*, June 24, 2002, p. C1.

65. Howard Kurtz, "Buzz on the Right: *National Review* Editor Rich Lowry Is Re-energizing the Magazine Many Conservatives Grew Up On," *Washington Post*, December 26, 2000, p. C1.

66. Howard Kurtz, "Right Face, Right Time: Conservative Bill Kristol Carves a Niche for Himself as the Friendly Contrarian," *Washington Post*, February 1, 2000, p. C1.

67. See Roger Angell, "The Sporting Scene," *New Yorker*, June 16, 1962.

68. See Peter Golenbock, *Amazin': The Miraculous History of New York's Most Beloved Baseball Team* (New York: St. Martin's Press, 2002).

69. Howard Kurtz, "Radio's New Right-Fielder; For Conservative Hannity, Liberal Praise," *Washington Post*, January 14, 2002, p. C1.

70. Kurtz, *Washington Post*, February 1, 2000, p. C1.

71. Howard Kurtz, "That's 'Wittmann,' with Quotes," *Washington Post*, January 22, 2001, p. C1.

72. These figures were tallied up by my *Nation* intern Timothy Waligore. Many thanks, Timothy.

73. Howard Kurtz, "The Comeback Columnist: Andrew Sullivan Continues to Defy All Expectations," *Washington Post*, April 19, 2001, p. C1.

74. Howard Kurtz, "Columnist Andrew Sullivan Bites Paper; Paper Bites Back," *Washington Post*, May 14, 2002, C1

75. Franklin Foer, "Howard Kurtz and the Decline of Media Criticism," *New Republic* Online, May 15, 2000 (www.tnr.com/051500/foer051500.html).

76. Eric Alterman, "The Conspiracy Continues . . . ," *Nation*, May 30, 2002 (http://www.thenation.com/doc.mhtml?i=20020617&s=alterman).

77. *Bias*, p. 124.

78. CNN's *Reliable Sources*, March 24, 2002 (http://www.cnn.com/TRANSCRIPTS/ 0203/23/rs.00.html). In fact, Brown was not even being attacked. He was being congratulated for something he had broadcast. But he could not get past the name of the "left-wing" pro-Clinton/Gore Web site, mediawhoresonline.com.

# Chapter Five

1. These figures are taken from a May 15, 2002, report by Scarborough Research, a joint venture between Arbitron, Inc., and VNU Media Measurement & Information.

2. Howard Kurtz, "Out There: It's 10 Past Monica, America. Do You Know Where Matt Drudge Is?" *Washington Post*, March 28, 1999, p. F1.

3. *Time*, October 19, 1992; Jim Rutenberg, "Despite Other Voices, Limbaugh's Is Still Strong," *New York Times*, April 24, 2000, p. C1; Howard Kurtz, "Limbaugh, Post-Clinton: Dining Happily on What's Left," *Washington Post*, May 7, 2001, p. C1.

4. *Washington Post*, May 8, 2002, p. C1, and the *Valley Advocate*, July 11, 2002 (http://www.newmassmedia.com/nac.phtml?code=wma&db=nac_fea&ref=21185).

5. The *Eugene Register-Guard*, June 30, 2002 (http://www.registerguard.com/ news/2002/06/30/1f.ed.col.monks.0630.html).

6. Ibid.

7. Maureen Dowd, "At Dinner with Rush Limbaugh," *New York Times*, March 24, 1993, p. C1.

8. Molly Ivins, "Lyin' Bully," *Mother Jones* (http://www.motherjones.com/mother_jones/ MJ95/ivins.html).

9. *Rush Limbaugh Show*, June 3, 2002.

10. *Rush Limbaugh Show*, June 3, 2002.

11. *Washington Post*, June 5, 2002, p. A2.

12. *Rush Limbaugh Show*, July 8, 2002, dialogue taken from the notes of *Nation* intern, Tim Waligore, July 15, 2002, based on a reading of the transcript of the show by Kit Carson of Limbaugh's staff. He refused to provide a written transcript.

13. *Rush Limbaugh Show*, July 20, 2002, as published on (http://www.spinsanity.org/posts/ 200107–3.html#21).

14. *National Review; New York*, September 6, 1993.

15. Howard Kurtz, *Washington Post*, November 21, 2002.

16. Tony Blankley, "Rush's Show Goes On," *Washington Times*, October 10, 2001.

17. Jim Rutenberg, "Despite Other Voices, Limbaugh's Is Still Strong," *New York Times*, April 24, 2000, p. C1.

18. Tony Blankley, "Rush's Show Goes On," *Washington Times*, October 10, 2001.

19. Jefferson Graham, "In 2001, the 'Big Three' Sites Got Bigger," *USA Today*, January 7, 2002, p. 3.

20. Worldnet Daily, October 8, 2002 (http://www.wnd.com/news/article.asp?ARTICLE_ID=29201).

21. www.kausfiles.com, November 1, 2002.

22. The *New York Times*, August 26, 2002, p. C7.

23. Frontpage.com.

24. Quoted in Paul Glastris, "Why Can't the Democrats Get Tough?" *Washington Monthly*, March 2002, and Michael Powell, "A Racial Transformation," *Washington Post*, March 28, 2001, p. C1.

25. www.kausfiles.com, November 1, 2002.

26. (http://www.drudgereport.com/thanks.html), June 19, 2002.

27. *Columbia Journalism Review*, January/February, 1999, www.cjr.org.

28. Quoted in Eddie Dean, "Hard Times and Jalapeno Bologna: Exclusive: Internet Rebel Matt Drudge's Early Years," Washington *City Paper*, March 13–19, 1998 (http://www.washingtoncitypaper.com/archives/cover/1998/cover0313 drudge.html).

29. Howard Kurtz, "Out There: It's 10 Past Monica, America, Do You Know Where Matt Drudge Is?" *Washington Post*, March 28, 1999, p. F1.

30. Quoted in Eddie Dean, "Hard Times and Jalapeno Bologna," p. 160.

31. (www.drudgereport.com/book/html).

32. Blumenthal would later drop the suit, citing financial constraints. Drudge received support from the Scaife-funded David Horowitz for his legal fees.

33. Kurtz, *Washington Post*, March 28, 1999, p. F1.

34. Howard Kurtz, "Fox Threatens Matt Drudge With Lawsuit Over Walkout," *Washington Post*, November 17, 1999, p. C1.

35. (http://www.drudgereport.com/affils.txt).

36. Greg Beato, Review of *The Drudge Manifesto*, *The Washington Post Book World*, October 9, 2000.

37. Quoted in *The Note* (http://www.abcnews.go.com/sections/politics/DailyNews/TheNote.html), November 4, 2002, and (http://www.pryor2002.com//11402affi.html).

38. Michelangelo Signorile, "Spreading Drudge's Sludge," *New York Press*, May 28, 2002 (http://www.nypress.com/15/22/news&columns/signorile.cfm). See also Katharine Graham, *Personal History* (New York: Alfred A. Knopf, 1997).

39. Kurtz, *Washington Post*, March 28, 1999, p. F1.

40. Bryan Keefer, "Feeding Frenzy over DSA Plan to Register Voters," (www.spinsanity.org), October 18, 2002.

## Chapter Six

1. National Committee for Responsive Philanthropy, *Moving a Public Policy Agenda*, July 1997, pp. 3–5 (www.ncrp.org/reports/moving.htm).

2. Ibid., p. 20.

3. Ibid., p. 20.

4. See David Callahan, "Clash in the States," *American Prospect*, June 18, 2001, pp. 28–30. An Adobe version of the 2000 Heritage Foundation's tax filing can be found at (http://www.guidestar.org/pdf/2000/237/327/2000–237327730–1–9.pdf).

5. Quoted by Brendan Nyhan, "Creaky Foundation," in Salon, May 10, 2002, www.salon.com.

6. Heritage Foundation Annual Report: *Leadership in the New Conservative Era*, 1995, p. 86.

7. Jacob Weisberg, "Happy Birthday Heritage Foundation," www.slate.com, January 9, 1998.

8. David Callahan, "$1 Billion for Ideas: Conservative Think Tanks in the 1990s" (Washington, D.C.: National Committee for Responsive Philanthropy, 1999), p. 22.

9. For more details, see Bill Berkowitz, "The Heritage Foundation Soars," *Z Magazine*, August 2001 (http://www.zmag.org/ZNET.htm).

10. (http://www.heritage.org/about/).

11. Cited by Brendan Nyhan in Salon, May 10, 2002, www.salon.com, and David Broder, "Thanks to Two Think Tanks," *Washington Post*, May 8, 2002, p. A21.

12. Michael Dolny, "Think Tanks Y2K," *Extra!*, July/August 2001.

13. Michael Dolny, "Think Tanks in a Time of Crisis," March/April 2002, (http://www.fair.org/extra/0203/think_tanks.html). Note: The Heritage Foundation's citations were adjusted to reflect the incidence of "false positives." Approximately 22 percent of the time the words "heritage foundation" appeared in Nexis without referring to the Washington-based think tank.

14. Michael Harrington, *The Other America: Poverty in the United States* (New York: MacMillan and Company, 1962).

15. *Washington Post*, September 22, 2002, p. F1.

16. *Los Angeles Times Book Review*, August 11, 2002 (http://www.calendarlive.com/books/bookreview/cl-bk-malcolm11aug11.story?coll=cl%2Dbookreview).

17. David Brock, *Blinded by the Right* (New York: Crown Publishers, 2002), pp. 114–115, and *New York Times*, April 26, 1993, p. C18.

18. David Brock, *Blinded*, p. 114.

19. Ibid.

20. Eric Alterman, *Sound & Fury*, second edition (Ithaca, N.Y.: Cornell University Press, 2000), p. 7.

21. *Washington Post*, September 22, 2002, p. F1.

22. Nick Confessore, *American Prospect*, January 17, 2000, www.prospect.org, and the *Washington Post*, September 21, 2002, p. F1.

23. This was 1994's *With Honors* starring Joe Pesci, about a homeless man at Harvard, released by Warner Brothers.

24. The book was co-authored with the late Richard Herrnstein, who died shortly before its publication. Its full title is *The Bell Curve: Intelligence and Class Structure in American Life* (New York: Free Press, 1994).

25. Jason DeParle, "Daring Research or Social Science Pornography?" *New York Times Magazine*, October 9, 1994, p. 51.

26. Sidney Blumenthal, *The Rise of the Counter-Establishment: From Conservative Ideology to Political Power* (New York: Times Books, 1986), p. 293.

27. Ibid., p. 293.

28. The book's full title was *Losing Ground: American Social Policy, 1950–1980* (New York: Basic Books, 1984).

29. Regarding the various flaws of *Losing Ground*, see Michael Harrington, "Crunched Numbers," *New Republic*, January 28, 1985, pp. 7–10; Robert Greenstein, "Losing Faith in 'Losing Ground,'" *New Republic*, March 25, 1985; Michael B. Katz, *The Undeserving Poor: From the War on Poverty to the War on Welfare* (New York: Pantheon Books, 1989), pp. 153–155; Michael Lind, *Up From Conservatism: Why the Right Is Wrong for America* (New York: The Free Press, 1996), pp. 180–183; and Sidney Blumenthal, *The Rise of the Counter-Establishment: From Conservative Ideology to Political Power* (New York: Times Books, 1986), pp. 292–295.

30. *New York Times* editorial page, February 3, 1985.

31. *New Republic*, March 25, 1985.

32. ABC News's *This Week*, November 28, 1993.

33. *Philadelphia Inquirer* editorial page, October 13, 1997.

34. Irene Sege, "'The Bell Curve': The Other Author," *Boston Globe*, November 10, 1994, p. 91.

35. Jean Stefancic and Richard Delgado, *No Mercy: How Conservative Think Tanks and Foundations Change America's Social Agenda* (Philadelphia: Temple University Press, 1996), p. 58.

36. DeParle, *New York Times Magazine*, p. 32.

37. www.slate.com, January 17, 1997.

38. Charles Murray and Richard Herrnstein, "Race, Genes, and IQ—An Apologia," *New Republic*, October 31, 1994.

39. Chester Finn, "For Whom It Tolls," *Commentary*, January 1995.

40. Leon Wieseltier, "The Lowerers," *New Republic*, October 31, 1994, p. 20.

41. Geoffrey Cowley, "Testing the Science of Intelligence," *Newsweek*, October 24, 1994, p. 56; Richard Lacayo, "For Whom the Bell Curves," *Time*, October 24, 1994; and Joel L. Kincheloe, Shirley R. Steinberg, and Aaron D. Gresson III, *Measured Lies: The Bell Curve Examined* (New York: St. Martin's Press, 1996).

42. Murray and Herrnstein, "Race, Genes, and IQ—An Apologia," *New Republic*, October 31, 1994.

43. DeParle, *New York Times Magazine*, p. 51.

44. David Brock, *Blinded*, p. 107.

45. Among other beliefs, Jefferson held that blacks "secrete less by the kidnies and more by the glands of the skin, which gives them a very strong and disagreeable odour. This greater degree of transpiration renders them more tolerant of heat and less so of cold, than the whites. . . . They seem to require less sleep. . . . They are at least as brave, and more adventurous. But this may proceed from a want of forethought which their seeing a danger till it be present. When present, they do not go through it with more coolness or steadiness than the whites. They are more ardent after their female; but love seems with them to be more an eager desire than a delicate mixture of sentiment and sensation. . . . In general, their existence appears to participate more of sensation than reflection." Thomas Jefferson, "Notes on the State of Virginia" (1787) in Thomas Jefferson, *Writings* (New York: Library of America, 1984), p. 265.

46. E-mail to the author, February 21, 2001.

47. This statement was developed by the [British] National Institutes of Health–Department of Energy (NIH-DOE) Joint Working Group on the Ethical, Legal, and Social Implications of Human Genome Research (ELSI Working Group) and was by the

National Society of Genetic Counselors. It was written by Lori B. Andrews and Dorothy Nelkin and published as a letter to the editor of *Science,* January 5, 1995.

48. Nicholas Lemann, "The Bell Curve Flattened," Slate.com, January 18, 1997.

49. Ibid.

50. Murray and Herrnstein, "Race, Genes," *New Republic.*

51. Jared Diamond, *Guns, Germs and Steel: The Fates of Human Societies* (New York: W. W. Norton and Co, 1997), p. 20.

52. *The Bell Curve,* p. 288.

53. Waqar Ahmad, "Race Is a Four-Letter Word," *New Scientist,* July 22, 1995, p. 44.

54. Nevertheless, Murray and Hernstein venture an estimate of African IQ, drawn mainly from an article by Lynn that appeared in *Mankind Quarterly* in 1991. It should be noted, for a start, that the authors of *The Bell Curve* misreport Lynn's data. They say he found a median IQ of 75 in Africa (p. 289). But in his article, "Race Differences in Intelligence: The Global Perspective," Lynn said that the mean African IQ—not the median—was 70 (p. 26).

55. For instance, Howard Gardner noted that the authors admit that IQ has gone up consistently around the world during this century—15 points, as great as the current difference between blacks and whites, which is obviously not a function of genetics. *The Bell Curve* does admit that when blacks move from rural southern to urban northern areas, their intelligence scores rise, which would seem to contradict their thesis as well, but they glide over this challenge. So too, the fact that when black youngsters are adopted in households of higher socioeconomic status, they demonstrate improved performance on aptitude and achievement tests. Again, this is an unanswered challenge. And the education professor Nathan Glazer pointed out that during World War II, a U.S. Army study found that Northern black recruits not only scored higher than southern black recruits on intelligence exams, they also scored higher than southern white recruits. The study was detailed in Otto Klineberg's easily available *Race Differences,* but nowhere is it mentioned in *The Bell Curve.* (See Nathan Glazer, "Scientific Truth and the American Dilemma" in Stephen Fraser, editor, *The Bell Curve Wars* [New York: Basic Books, 1995], p. 145.) Even Thomas Sowell, the conservative black sociologist writing in the conservative publication, *American Spectator,* while pointedly defending the authors against the charge of racism, found the book's scientific shoddiness impossible to defend. "Perhaps the most intellectually troubling aspect of *The Bell Curve,*" he wrote, "is the authors' uncritical approach to statistical correlations. One of the first things taught in introductory statistics is that correlation is not causation. It is also one of the first things forgotten, and one of the most widely ignored facts in public policy research. The statistical term 'multicollinearity,' dealing with spurious correlations, appears only once in this massive book." See Thomas Sowell, "Ethnicity and IQ," *American Spectator,* February 1995.

56. Michael Nunley, "The Bell Curve: Too Smooth to Be True," *American Behavioral Scientist,* September/October 1995.

57. Quoted in Tim Beardsley, *Scientific American,* 272, (1) January 1995: 244.

58. Leon J. Kamin, "Lies, Damned Lies and Statistics," in R. Jacoby and N. Glauberman (editors), *The Bell Curve Debate: History, Documents, Opinions* (New York: Times Books. 1995), pp. 81–105.

59. See Charles Lane, "The Tainted Sources of the Bell Curve," *New York Review of Books,* December 1, 1994; see also *New Scientist,* July 22, 1995, p. 44. According to *The Bell Curve's* bibliography and to back issues of the *Mankind Quarterly,* the seventeen are W. J. Andrews, Cyril Burt, Raymond B. Cattell (eight citations), Hans J. Eysenck, Seymour Itzkoff, Arthur Jensen (twenty-three citations), Richard Lynn (twenty-four citations), Robert E. Kuttner,

Frank C. J. McGurk (six citations), C. E. Noble, R. Travis Osborne (three citations), Roger Pearson, J. Philippe Rushton (eleven citations), William Shockley, Audrey Shuey, Daniel Vining (three citations), and Nathaniel Weyl. The ten who either are or were editors or members of the editorial board are: Cattell, Eysenck, Itzkoff, Kuttner, Lynn, McGurk, Noble, Pearson, Shuey, and Vining.

60. See Lane, *New York Review of Books*; also, Ahmad, *New Scientist*, July 22, 1995, p. 44.

61. Kamin, in Jacoby and Glauberman (editors), *The Bell Curve Debate*, pp. 81–105.

62. Mickey Kaus, "The 'It Matters Libble' Gambit," *The Bell Curve Wars*, p. 132.

63. The full title is Dinesh D'Souza, *The End of Racism: Principles for a Multiracial Society* (New York: Free Press, 1995).

64. Glenn C. Loury, "Perspective on Racism: A Well-Funded Entry in the Black Inferiority Sweepstakes: a New Book That Cites 'Pathological' Reasons for 'Black Failure' Threatens Yet Again to Sidetrack Serious Discusion," *Los Angeles Times*, September 24, 1995, p. 5.

65. See Dinesh D'Souza, *The End of Racism*, pp. 477–524, and Charles Johnson, "Widening the Racial Divide: Glib Proposals for Ending Racism Seem More Likely to Perpetuate It," *Los Angeles Times Book Review*, November 26, 1995, p. 4. The categorization belongs to Johnson.

66. *New York Times*, October 13, 1995, op-ed page.

67. Ibid.

68. See (http://www.salon.com/news/feature/2001/03/13/horowitz/index.html); *Washington Post*, March 28, 2001, p. C1; and www.kausfiles.com.

69. See Jack E. White, "A Real, Live Bigot: A Former Leftist Earns a Place on the Wild-Eyed Right," *Time*, August 30, 1999.

70. See Michael Lind, *Up from Conservatism: Why the Right Is Wrong for America* (New York: The Free Press, 1996), p. 201.

# Chapter Seven

1. See Louis Bolce and Gerald De Maio, "Our Secularist Democratic Party," *Public Interest*, Fall 2002, pp. 3–21.

2. Stephen L. Carter, *God's Name in Vain: The Wrongs and Rights of Religion in Politics* (New York: Basic Books, 2000), p. 13.

3. *Washington Post Book World*, June 30, 2002, p. BW03. See also Garry Wills, *Under God* (New York: Simon and Schuster, 1990).

4. Author's interview.

5. See Michelle Cottle's critique, "For Adults Only," *New Republic*, June 19, 2002 (http://www.tnr.com/doc.mhtml?i=life&s=life061902), and Tom Shales, "Don't Ask Don't Televise," *Washington Post*, June 18, 2002, p. C1.

6. Ibid.

7. Brent Bozell, "What Is the *New York Times* Promoting?" May 28, 2002 (http://www.townhall.com/columnists/brentbozell/bb20020529.shtml). Bozell is the president of Media Research Center.

8. Frank Bruni, *Ambling into History: The Unlikely Odyssey of George W. Bush* (New York: Crown Books, 2002). See also Eric Alterman, "Ambling into Nonsense," *American Prospect*, June 20, 2002 (http://www.prospect.org/print/V13/9/alterman-e.html).

9. Bruni, *Ambling*, p. 95.

10. Robert Samulelson, "A Liberal Bias?" *Washington Post*, August 29, 2001, p. A21.

11. Ken Auletta, "Annals of Communications: The Howell Doctrine," *New Yorker*, June 10, 2002, p. 66.

12. Shafer's piece appeared on July 3, 2002 (http://slate.msn.com/?id=2067699). The piece he criticizes appeared in the *New York Times*, on July 1, 2002, by Katharine Seelye.

13. See the *Washington Post*, June 24, 2002, p. C1.

14. This quote, and all of the quotes attributed to Shaw's study that follow, can be found in David Shaw, "Abortion Bias Seeps into News: A Comprehensive Times Study Finds That the Press Often Favors Abortion Rights in Its Coverage, Even Though Journalists Say They Make Every Effort To Be Fair," *Los Angeles Times*, July 1–4, 1990, p. 1.

15. *Washington Post*, July 24, 2002, pp. A4 and A18.

16. Michael Massing, "Market Driven: The (Liberal) Media Elite Have Acquired a New Tilt," *Columbia Journalism Review*, March/April 2001.

17. Author's interview.

18. William McGowan, *Coloring the News: How Crusading for Diversity Has Corrupted American Journalism* (San Francisco: Encounter Books, 2001), p. 10.

19. McGowan, p. 17.

20. McGowan, p. 18.

21. Ruth Shalit, "Race in the Newsroom: The *Washington Post* in Black and White," *New Republic*, October 2, 1995.

22. Ibid.

23. Quoted in Scott Sherman, "Donald Graham's *Washington Post*," *Columbia Journalism Review*, September/October 2002 (http://www.cjr.org/year/02/5/index.asp).

24. McGowan, *Coloring the News*.

25. Seth Mnookin, "Yellow Journalism," *Washington Monthly*, January/February 2002 (http://www.washingtonmonthly.com/features/2001/0201.mnookin.html).

26. See McGowan, p. 89, and Michael Hoyt, "The *New* New Republic," *Columbia Journalism Review*, March/April 1997 (http://www.cjr.org/year/97/2/kelly.asp).

27. Mnookin, *Washington Monthly*, January/February 2002 (http://www.washington-monthly.com/features/2001/0201.mnookin.html).

28. Mnookin. See also McGowan, p. 66, and the *New York Times*, December 16, 1995.

29. See Peter Johnson, "Press Club Defends Against Criticism," *USA Today*, July 23, 2002 (http://www.usatoday.com/usatonline/20020723/4297680s.htm).

30. PBS Online Newshour, July 11, 2000 (http://www.pbs.org/newshour/bb/media/july-dec00/race_7–11.html).

31. Richard Rodriguez, "How Race Is Really Lived in America," Salon, July 13, 2000 (http://www.salon.com/news/feature/2000/07/13/race/).

32. The study was undertaken by Media Tenor Ltd., a nonpartisan, German-based media analysis firm with an office in New York City. "Who's On the News?" *Extra!* June 2002, (http://www.fair.org/).

33. Robert M. Entman and Andrew Rojecki, *The Black Image in the White Mind: Media and Race in America* (Chicago: University of Chicago Press, 2000), pp. 53–54.

34. Ibid., p. 81.

35. Ibid., p. 74, and the *New York Times*, September 28, 2002 (http://www.nytimes.com/2002/09/28/nyregion/28JOGG.html).

36. *Milwaukee Journal Sentinel,* June 14, 2002 (http://www.jsonline.com/news/metro/jun02/51305.asp), *New York Times,* June 26, 2002 (http://www.nytimes.com/2002/06/27/national/27MISS.html).

37. Entman and Rojecki, pp. 64–66.

38. *Bias,* pp. 155–156.

39. Howard Rosenberg, "Insider's Edition of News Standards," *Los Angeles Times,* September 20, 2000, p. 1.

40. Richard Morin, "Misperceptions Cloud Whites' View of Blacks," *Washington Post,* July 11, 2001, p. A1.

## Chapter Eight

1. The president made these remarks in a speech called "The Press Under a Free Government," given before the American Society of Newspaper Editors in Washington, D.C., on January 17, 1925.

2. Author's interview.

3. Author's interview.

4. The journalist was Howard Fineman. The school was Sidwell Friends. See James Fallows, *Breaking the News: How the Media Undermine American Democracy* (New York: Pantheon Books, 1996), p. 78.

5. See Eric Alterman, *Who Speaks for America?: Why Democracy Matters in Foreign Policy* (Ithaca, N.Y.: Cornell University Press, 1998), pp. 105–116.

6. "NAFTA and National Interest," *New York Times,* November 17, 1993, p. A26.

7. "Which Direction for Post Cold War US? Trade Vote is a Vote for American Foreign Policy Continuity," *Los Angeles Times,* November 16, 1993, p. BG.

8. See Amy Waldman, "Class Not Race," *Washington Monthly,* November 1995, p. 26, and the *Washington Post,* November 16, 1993, p. A20.

9. James K. Glassman, *Washington Post,* November 11, 1997, p. A19.

10. Anthony Lewis, *New York Times,* November 14, 1997, p. A35.

11. David Broder, *Washington Post,* November 11, 1997.

12. *Washington Post,* November 12, 1997, p. A4.

13. The Bush administration has imposed duties ranging from 8 percent to 30 percent on a wide range of steel products. See the *Wall Street Journal,* September 13, 2002. For more information about the cost of farm subsidies, as well as their contradiction of the alleged rules of free trade, see the web site of the Environmental Working Group, at (http://www.ewg.org/issues/home.php?i=3), and this report by the Cato Institute, (http://www.cato.org/pubs/briefs/bp–070es.html). The latter notes that "Total direct subsidy payments to farmers have soared to more than $20 billion per year the past three years, up from an average of $9 billion per year in the early 1990s." For news of a WTO ruling against the United States for violating its global agreements re farm subsidies, as well as textile and other protectionist measures, see the *Wall Street Journal,* September 2, 2002 (http://online.wsj.com/article/0,,SB1030702909303753155,00.html?mod=article-outset-box).

14. Quoted in Eric Alterman, "Prattle on Seattle," *Nation,* January 3, 2000.

15. Quoted in William Greider, "Global Agenda," *Nation,* January 31, 2000.

16. Franklin Foer, "Buchanan's Surefire Flop," *New Republic* Online, July 11, 2002 (http://www.tnr.com/doc.mhtml?i=20020722&s=foer072202).

17. *New York Times*, July 6, 2002, p. A13.

18. See Partha Dasgupta, "Economic Pathways to Ecological Sustainability: Challenges for the New Millennium," revised, August 1999 (http://www.econ.cam.ac.uk/faculty/dasgupta/paths.pdf).

19. See Mark Weisbrot, Dean Baker, Egor Kraev, and Judy Chen, "The Scorecard on Globalization 1980–2000; Twenty Years of Diminished Progress," July 11, 2001 (http://www.cepr.net/globalization/scorecard_on_globalization.html/). See also Mark Weisbrot and Dean Baker, "The Relative Impact of Trade Liberalization on Developing Countries," Center for Economic and Policy Research, June 11, 2002 (http://www.cepr.net/relative_impact_of_trade_liberal.htm).

20. *New York Times*, June 9, 2002 (http://www.nytimes.com/2002/06/09/business/yourmoney/09SHEL.html?pagewanted=print&position=bottom). See also Joseph Stiglitz, *Globalization and Its Discontents* (New York: W. W. Norton, 2002).

21. *Washington Post Book World*, July 7, 2002, p. BW7.

22. *National Journal*, July 26, 2002 (http://nationaljournal.com/powers.htm).

23. *New York Times*, June 23, 2002 (http://www.nytimes.com/2002/06/24/business/24CEOS.html).

24. Here are a few of the gems Howard Kurtz collected:
- *Larry King Live*: "What's it like to have woken up in the morning worth, on October 19th, this is what we've learned, you woke up in the morning worth $250 million; went to bed worth $1.6 billion. What was that like?"
- *People* magazine in 1999: "Move over, pimply-faced Internet moguls: The ubiquitous cookie-maker has more dough than you do."
- *USA Today* in 2000: "A rainy breeze brushes past the open door as Martha Stewart whisks the warm, blue eggs she just filched from her Araucana hens. . . . Up since 4 a.m., Stewart has enjoyed the morning, from intense time with her personal trainer to serious time with company matters to quality time with her beloved menagerie."
- *Washington Post* in 2000: "You'd expect nothing less from the billionaire executive who handed out flaky brioche and fresh-squeezed OJ to Wall Street traders on the morning her company went public."
- *Business Week*, 2001: "She shows no signs of slowing as she cooks, plants and mushes her way to media moguldom." *Washington Post*, July 1, 2002, C1.

25. Quoted in the *Economist*, June 22, 2002, p. 80. See also Kevin Phillips, *Wealth and Democracy: A Political History of the American Rich* (New York: Broadway Books, 2002).

26. *Washington Post*, July 12, 2002, p. C7; *Wall Street Journal*, March 22, 2002; and *Los Angeles Times*, June 7, 2002.

27. Norman Solomon, "Money Makes Headlines in Today's News Coverage," *Nieman Reports*, Summer 2002.

28. *Washington Post*, July 11, 2002, p. A21.

29. See Alan Wolfe, "Idiot Time," *New Republic*, July 8, 2002 (http://www.tnr.com/doc.mhtml?i=20020708&s=wolfe070802). See also Kevin Philips, *Wealth and Democracy: A Political History of the American Rich* (New York: Broadway Books, 2002).

30. This statistic appears in *Harper's*, September 2002, p. 11.

31. *San Francisco Weekly*, June 5, 2002 (http://www.sfweekly.com/issues/2002–06–05/smith.html/1/index.html).

32. *Washington Post*, May 29, 2000, p. C1.

33. John Cassidy, "Striking it Rich," *New Yorker*, January 14, 2002, pp. 63–73.

34. Ibid.

35. *Los Angeles Times*, July 5, 2002.

36. Dow Jones Newswires, January 24, 2002.

37. Howard Kurtz, *Fortune Tellers: Inside Wall Street's Game of Money, Media, and Manipulation* (New York: Touchstone Books, 2001), p. 259; Gregg Easterbrook, "Greed Isn't Good," *New Republic* Online, July 1, 2002 (http://www.thenewrepublic.com/doc.mhtml?i=express&s=easterbrook070102); and *New York Times*, July 7, 2002, sec. 3, p. 1.

38. Kurtz, *Fortune Tellers*, p. 259.

39. John Cassidy, *Dot.con: The Greatest Story Ever Sold* (New York: HarperCollins, 2002), p. 179.

40. Nicholas W. Maier, *Trading with the Enemy: Seduction and Betrayal on Jim Cramer's Wall Street* (New York: Harper Business, March 5, 2002), pp. 124–125.

41. Kurtz, *Fortune Tellers*, p. 207.

42. James Cramer, *Confessions of a Street Addict* (New York: Simon and Schuster, 2002).

43. *New York Times*, May 13, 2002, p. C9.

44. *Wall Street Journal*, June 20, 2002, p. A1; *New York Times*, June 22, 2002, p. A1 (for Rite-Aid); *New York Times*, June 26, 2002, p. A1 (for Wal-Mart); *Washington Post*, June 26, 2002, p. A1; the *Wall Street Journal*, September 19, 2002 (http://online.wsj.com/home/us) for WorldCom; the *Wall Street Journal*, June 28, 2002, for Xerox; and *Wall Street Journal*, August 7, 2002, p. A1, for Tyco International.

45. Quoted in the *Washington Post*, July 1, 2002, p. C1.

46. See Greg Easterbrook, "Greed Isn't Good," *New Republic* Online, July 1, 2002, (http://www.thenewrepublic.com/doc.mhtml?i=express&s=easterbrook070102). See also Kurtz, *Fortune Tellers*, p. 113.

47. Scott Sherman, "Gimme an 'E'! ENRON: Uncovering the Uncovered Story," *Columbia Journalism Review*, March/April 2002 (http://www.cjr.org/year/02/2/sherman.asp).

48. Quoted in Sherman, *CJR*.

49. Quoted in Sherman, *CJR*.

50. Peter Behr, "Looking for Answers in the Enron Story," *Nieman Reports*, Summer 2002, p. 9.

51. For a host of examples, see Miles Maguire, "Business as Usual," *American Journalism Review*, October 2002 (http://www.ajr.org/Article.asp?id=2648).

52. Jeffrey Madrick, "A Good Story Isn't Always the Right One to Tell," *Nieman Reports*, Summer 2002, p. 7.

53. Ibid.

54. Phillip J. Longman, "Bad Press: How Business Journalism Helped Inflate the Bubble," *Washington Monthly*, October 2002 (http://www.washingtonmonthly.com/features/2001/0210.longman.html).

55. Eric Boehlert, "Andrew Sullivan's Selective Enron Outrage," Salon, Jan. 31, 2002.

56. Ibid.

57. Ibid.

58. *San Francisco Chronicle*, January 30, 2002, p. A1.

59. *Wall Street Journal*, June 5, 2002. Waxman is quoted by Joe Conason in the *New York Observer*, May 20, 2002, p. 5.

60. Quoted in the *New York Times*, July 6, 2002, p. A13.

61. "As first reported by the Center for Public Integrity in *The Buying of the President 2000*, Bush's top career patron was Enron. The company and its employees gave the Governor of Texas $550,000 in the six years before the January 2000 Iowa and New Hampshire caucuses and primaries. Enron later gave $300,000 for the Bush inaugural celebration alone. A few senior Bush administration officials today formerly worked for Enron, and at least 34 of them held Enron stock when they entered government last year. Bush's father, while Vice President and then President, received major campaign funding from Enron and assisted the company's Washington policy agenda in different, specific ways. Enron chairman Ken Lay was co-chairman of the Bush re-election campaign and chairman of the host committee of the Republican National Convention in Houston in 1992." Charles Lewis, "The Enron Collapse: A Financial Scandal Rooted in Politics," Center for Public Integrity (http://www.public-i.org/dtaweb/report. asp?ReportID=10&L1=10&L2=10&L3=0&L4=0&L5=0).

62. *New York Times*, May 25, 2001, p. A1.

63. *New York Times*, July 6, 2002, p. A13.

64. *New York Times*, January 30, 2002, p. C7.

65. Frank Rich, *New York Times*, February 2, 2002, p. A19.

66. *Wall Street Journal*, July 5, 2002, p. A1.

67. See Ned Stafford, "CNN's Lou Dobbs Lectures Reporter on Air About 'Balanced' Coverage," Press Watch (www.fair.org/views/2002.html).

68. *Wall Street Journal*, April 3, 2002 (http://online.wsj.com/article_email/ 0,,SB1017786407359564480,00.html).

69. Kurtz, *Fortune Tellers*, p. 103.

70. CNN's *Reliable Sources*, June 29, 2002.

# Chapter Nine

1. *New York Times Week in Review*, February 2, 1992, p. 1.

2. Quoted in Joan Didion, "Clinton Agonistes," *New York Review of Books*, October 22, 1998 (http://www.nybooks.com/articles/article-preview?article_id=699). See also Joan Didion, *Political Fictions* (New York: Alfred A. Knopf, 2001), pp. 215–249.

3. "Hit Parade Archive March 2002," www.kausfiles.com, March 17, 2002 (http://www. kausfiles.com/index.2002.march.html).

4. See Samantha Power, *A Problem from Hell: America in the Age of Genocide* (New York: Basic Books, 2002), pp. 329–390, and Chaim Kaufmann, "Why America Doesn't Stop Genocide," *Foreign Affairs*, July/August 2002, pp. 142–149.

5. *Washington Post*, March 30, 2000, p. A21.

6. *Washington Post*, March 27, 2002, p. A21.

7. This figure does not include HUD Secretary Henry Cisneros, who pleaded guilty to a misdemeanor for misstating to the F.B.I. the amount of money he gave his girlfriend, and Assistant Attorney General Webster Hubbell, who was convicted of embezzling funds from the Rose Law Firm before his federal appointment; that is, stealing from his law partners, including Hillary Rodham Clinton. Neither of these actions was taken while the person was in office or was in any way connected to his official duties.

8. Kalb, pp. 193–194.

9. Kalb, p. 130.

10. Kalb, pp. 146, 130.

11. Kalb, p. 23.

12. Kalb, p. 49.

13. *Washington Post,* October 7, 2000, p. A1.

14. *Washington Post,* October 9, 2000, p. C1.

15. Joseph Lelyveld, "Another Country," *New York Review of Books,* October 20, 2001 (http://www.nybooks.com/articles/14961).

16. Quoted in Joan Didion, "Clinton Agonistes," *New York Review of Books,* October 22, 1998 (http://www.nybooks.com/articles/article-preview?article_id=699).

17. Eric Alterman, *Sound & Fury: The Making of the Punditocracy* (Ithaca, N.Y.: Cornell University Press, 2000), p. 269.

18. Kalb, pp. 226–227.

19. *Sound & Fury,* pp. 272–273.

20. *Sound & Fury,* p. 270.

21. Michael Tomasky, "The Savaging of the President: His Terrible, Swift Sword: Raines on Clinton," *Nation,* January 4, 1999.

22. See Ted Gup, "Eye of the Storm," *Columbia Journalism Review,* May/June 2001 (http://www.cjr.org/year/01/3/gup.asp).

23. For the record: On the *McLaughlin Group,* John McLaughlin said the GOP would gain thirteen House seats; Pat Buchanan, twelve; Michael Barone, eight; former Gingrich spokesman Tony Blankley, seven; and Eleanor Clift, six. On ABC's *This Week,* George Will said six to twenty seats, Kristol said fifteen. On CNN's *Capital Gang,* Al Hunt and Robert Novak both saw the Republicans picking up five Senate seats.

24. Didion, *New York Review of Books* (http://www.nybooks.com/articles/article-preview? article_id=699).

## Chapter Ten

1. Joan Didion, *Political Fictions* (New York: Alfred A. Knopf, 2001).

2. Coelho is quoted in Eric Boehlert, "The Press vs. Al Gore," *Rolling Stone,* December 6–13, 2001.

3. www.Kausfiles.com.

4. Author's interview.

5. Pelosi is the daughter of Nancy Pelosi, the California congresswoman and top-ranking Democrat in the House of Representatives.

6. Eric Alterman, "Journeys with Fecklessness," *Nation,* June 3, 2002.

7. Didion, *Political Fictions,* p. 37. See also Joseph Lelyveld, "Another Country," *New York Review of Books,* December 20, 2001 (http://www.nybooks.com/articles/14961).

8. Howard Kurtz and Terry Neal, "Bush Team Devised Truth Trap That's Tripping Gore," *Washington Post,* October 15, 2000, p. A11.

9. See Jamie Malanowski, "Out on the Trail with an Informal, Playful George W.," *New York Times* Arts and Leisure Section, November 3, 2002 (http://www.nytimes.com/2002/11/03/arts/television/03MALA.html?pagewanted=all&position=top).

10. ABC's *The Note,* November 4, 2002.

11. Eric Alterman, "Ambling into Nonsense," *American Prospect,* May 20, 2002, vol. 13, no. 9.

12. Alterman, "Ambling."

13. Molly Ivins, "How Reporter's Fall in Love: A Campaign Trail Memoir," *New York Observer*, July 31, 2002.

14. Alterman, "Ambling."

15. See Project for Excellence in Journalism, "In the Public Interest? A Content Study of Early Press Coverage of the 2000 Presidential Campaign" (http://www.journalism.org/publ_research/election1.html).

16. See Project for Excellence in Journalism, "The Last Lap: How the Press Covered the Final Stages of the Presidential Campaign" (http://www.journalism.org/publ_research/campaign1.html).

17. Bill Kovach and Tom Rosenstiel, "Campaign Lite: Why Reporters Won't Tell Us What We Need to Know," *Washington Monthly*, January/February 2001, and *New York Times*, October 18, 2000, p. A1.

18. Eric Alterman, "Where's the Rest of Him?" *Nation*, March 27, 2000.

19. Quoted by Todd Gitlin on Salon.com, October 24, 2000.

20. ABC transcript, October 3, 2000.

21. Jonathan Cohn, "Sam and Cokie, This Weak: Yuck, Yuck," *New Republic*, November 6, 2000.

22. *Inside Politics*, October 4, 2000. See also Bob Somerby, The Daily Howler, August 1, 2002 (http://www.dailyhowler.com/dh080102.shtml).

23. *Hardball*, October 4, 2002. See also Bob Somerby, The Daily Howler, August 1, 2002 (http://www.dailyhowler.com/dh080102.shtml).

24. *Hardball*, October 4, 2002. See also Bob Somerby, The Daily Howler, August 1, 2002 (http://www.dailyhowler.com/dh080102.shtml).

25. Bruni, *Ambling*, p. 187.

26. *New York Times*, October 4, 2000, p. 1.

27. Kovach and Rosenstiel, *Washington Monthly*.

28. Project for Excellence in Journalism, "Question of Character: How the Media Have Handled the Issue and How the Public Has Reacted" (http://www.journalism.org/publ_research/character1.html) and (http://www.journalism.org/publ_research/character4.html).

29. Kovach and Rosenstiel, *Washington Monthly*.

30. Slate, August 1, 2000 (http://www.slate.msn.com/?id=87280).

31. CNN's *Reliable Sources* August 10, 2002 (http://www.cnn.com/TRANSCRIPTS/0208/10/rs.00.html).

32. *New York Times*, August 10, 2002, op-ed page.

33. Eric Boehlert, "Gore's Premature Obituary," Salon.com, October 10, 1999.

34. Online News Hour, New Hampshire Debates, January 27, 2000 (http://www.pbs.org/newshour/bb/politics/jan-june00/dems_debate_1–27.html).

35. Bob Somerby, The Daily Howler, August 7, 2002 (http://www.dailyhowler.com/dh080702.shtml).

36. David Maraniss and Ellen Nakashima, *The Prince of Tennessee: The Rise of Al Gore* (New York: Simon and Schuster, 2000), cited by Somerby, www.dailyhowler.com.

37. Eric Alterman, "The Seven-Year (Old) Snitch," *Nation*, November 22, 1999. Also Bob Somerby, The Daily Howler, October 20, 1999.

38. *Hardball*, November 12, 1999, and Bob Somerby, The Daily Howler, August 14, 2002. (http://www.dailyhowler.com/dh081402.shtml).

39. Bob Somerby, The Daily Howler, August 14, 2002 (http://www.dailyhowler.com/dh081402.shtml).

40. Eric Boehlert, "The Press vs. Al Gore," *Rolling Stone*, December 6–13, 2001.

41. *New York Times*, July 24, 1999, p. A8.

42. Dan Baltz, *Washington Post*, July 25, 1999, p. A6.

43. Howard Fineman, "A War Over Who Controls the Left," *Newsweek*, August 9, 1999, p. 33.

44. Walter Robinson and Ann Scales, "Gore Record Scrutinized for Veracity," *Boston Globe*, January 28, 2000.

45. Jill Zuckman and Bob Hohler, "Bradley Steps Up Attacks as Gore Quietly Plays the Front-Runner," *Boston Globe*, January 29, 2000.

46. Jill Zuckman and Michael Kranish, "Democrats Debate Abortion," *Boston Globe*, January 30, 2000.

47. Boehlert, *Rolling Stone*.

48. See Kathleen Hall Jamieson and Paul Waldman, *The Press Effect: Politicians, Journalists and the Stores That Shape the Political World* (New York: Oxford University Press, 2002), p. 49.

49. See Bob Zelnick, *Gore: A Political Life* (Washington: Regnery, 2000).

50. Boehlert, *Rolling Stone*.

51. Walter Shapiro, "'Untruthful' Label Could Dog Al Gore," *USA Today*, December 20, 2000, p. A15.

52. Richard Berke, "Tendency to Embellish Fact Snags Gore," *New York Times*, October 6, 2000, p. A26.

53. *USA Today*, December 26, 2000, p. A18.

54. For Somerby's detailed account, originally produced on (http://www.dailyhowler.com/dh110102.shtml) on November 3, 2002, see Appendix Four at www.whatliberalmedia.com.

55. Somerby, ibid.

56. Ibid.

57. Walter Robinson and Ann Scales, "Gore Record Scrutinized for Veracity," *Boston Globe*, January 28, 2000, and The Daily Howler, May 26, 2000 (http://www.dailyhowler.com/h052600_1.shtml).

58. Eric Pooley and Karen Tumulty, "Can Al Bare His Soul?" *Time*, December 15, 1997.

59. Eric Boehlert, "Gore's Too-Willing Executioners," Salon.com, October 27, 2000; Bob Somerby, The Daily Howler, March 30 and 31, 1999; Robert Parry, "He's Not Pinocchio," *Washington Monthly*, May 2000; and Sean Wilentz, "Will Pseudo-Scandals Decide the Election," *American Prospect* Online.

60. Bob Somerby, The Daily Howler, December 7, 1999 (http://www.dailyhowler.com/h120799_1.shtml).

61. Ibid.

62. Ibid. and Robert Parry, "He's Not Pinocchio," *Washington Monthly*, May 2000.

63. CNBC's *Hardball*, December 1, 1999.

64. *Washington Post*, December 2, 1999, p. A14.

65. ABC's *This Week*, December 5, 1999.

66. Boehlert, *Rolling Stone*.

67. Howard Kurtz and Terry Neal, "Bush Team Devised Truth Trap That's Tripping Gore," *Washington Post*, October 15, 2000, p. A11.

68. Jamieson and Waldman, pp. 64–66.

69. Ibid., pp. 59–60.

70. Ibid., p. 72.

71. Ibid.

72. Ceci Connolly, "First 'Love Story' Now 'Love Canal,'" *Washington Post*, January 2, 1999, p. A14.

73. *Washington Post*, April 14, 2000. See also Bob Somerby, The Daily Howler, August 13, 2002 (http://www.dailyhowler.com/dh081302.shtml).

74. *Financial Times*, August 17, 2000. See also Bob Somerby, The Daily Howler, August 13, 2002 (http://www.dailyhowler.com/dh081302.shtml).

75. AP, Dec. 14, 1999.

76. Ceci Connolly, "Evoking Memories of Reagan, Bush Melds a Jaunty Manner with Talk of Compassion," *Washington Post*, May 7, 2000, p. A11.

77. Ceci Connolly, "Al Gore Gets Jiggy, Talking Policy, Veep Morphs into a Giddy Wonk," *Washington Post*, June 23, 2000, p. C1.

78. Bill Sammon, *At Any Cost: How Al Gore Tried to Steal the Election* (Washington, D.C.: Regnery Publishing, 2001).

79. Eric Boehlert, "The Press vs. Al Gore," *Rolling Stone*, December 6–13, 2000.

80. Brit Hume, *Special Report*, Fox News Channel, September 24, 2002. See also Bob Somerby, The Daily Howler, September 26, 2002 (http://www.dailyhowler.com/dh092602.shtml), reprinted in Appendix Five at www.whatliberalmedia.com.

81. Slate, September 26, 2002 (http://slate.msn.com//?id=2071556).

82. Quoted in Eric Boehlert, *Rolling Stone.*

83. Eric Alterman, "Reporters Who Hate Al Gore's Guts," www.msnbc.com, October 31, 2000.

84. ABC's *The Note* (http://www.abcnews.go.com/sections/politics/DailyNews/The_Note.html).

## Chapter Eleven

1. Michael Kramer, "Bush Set to Fight an Electoral College Loss," New York *Daily News*, November 1, 2000, p. 6.

2. Ibid.

3. Eric Alterman, "Accuracy vs. Speed," *Nation*, November 24, 2000.

4. Ford Fessenden and Christopher Drew pointed this out in "Counting the Vote: The Mechanism," *New York Times*, November 17, 2000, p. A1.

5. John Lantigua, "How the GOP Gamed the System in Florida," *Nation*, April 30, 2001 (http://www.thenation.com/doc.mhtml?i=20010430&c=1&s=lantigua). For more details on Florida's "voter cleansing" program, see Gregory Palast, "Florida's Flawed 'Voter Cleansing' Program," Salon.com, December 4, 2000 (http://archive.salon.com/politics/feature/2000/12/04/voter_file/print.html).

6. Associated Press, August 27, 2002.

7. See Gregory Palast, "Florida's 'Disappeared Voters': Disenfranchised by the GOP," *Nation*, February 5, 2001; Lani Guinier, "Making Every Vote Count," *Nation*, December 4, 2000; and John Lantigua, "How the GOP Gamed the System in Florida," *Nation*, April 30, 2001. Also, Thomas B. Edsall, "Bush Far Outspent Gore on Recount," *Washington Post*, July 27, 2002, p. A4.

8. Jane Mayer, "The Talk of the Town—Dept. of Close Calls," *New Yorker*, November 20, 2000, p. 36.

9. Tom Rosenstiel, "One More Election Embarrassment for the Press: Bush Cousin," Committee of Concerned Journalists Web site, originally published in the *Los Angeles Times*, November 15, 2000.

10. Howard Kurtz, "Bush Cousin Made Florida Call for Fox News," *Washington Post*, November 14, 2000, p. C1.

11. Neil Hickey, "The Big Mistake," *Columbia Journalism Review*, January/February 2001.

12. Peter Grier, "Election 2000: Act II," *Christian Science Monitor*, December 15, 2000.

13. The Texas law, signed by Governor Bush, read, "If different counting methods are chosen under Section 214.042(a) among multiple requests for a recount of electronic voting system results, only one method may be used in the recount. A manual recount shall be conducted in preference to an electronic recount and an electronic recount using a corrected program shall be conducted in preference to an electronic recount using the same program as the original count." Bush signed the bill on June 20, 1997, and the bill was effective on September 1, 1997. [Bill Text, HB 331; Bill Actions, HB 331] See also Texas Secretary of State Election Rules (http://www.sos.state.tx.us/elections/laws/recounts.shtml).

14. Win McCormack, "Deconstructing the Election," *Nation*, March 26, 2001.

15. David S. Broder and Peter Slevin, "Both Sides Increase Legal Wrangling as Florida Begins Slow Hand Recount," *Washington Post*, November 12, 2000, p. A1.

16. NBC's *Meet the Press*, November 12, 2000, transcript and ABC's *This Week*, November 12, 2000, transcript.

17. Paul Gigot, "Burgher Rebellion: GOP Turns Up Miami Heat," *Wall Street Journal*, November 24, 2000, p. A16.

18. Tim Padgett, "Mob Scene in Miami," *Time*, December 4, 2000.

19. McCormack, *Nation*.

20. Only a handful of what Robert Parry calls "the Brooks Brothers rioters" were publicly identified, some through photographs published in the *Washington Post*. Jake Tapper's book on the recount battle, *Down and Dirty*, provides a list of twelve Republican operatives who took part in the Miami riot. Half of those individuals received payments from the Bush recount committee, according to the IRS records. The Miami protesters who were paid by Bush recount committee were: Matt Schlapp, a Bush staffer who was based in Austin and received $4,276.09; Thomas Pyle, a staff aide to House Majority Whip Tom DeLay, $456; Michael Murphy, a DeLay fundraiser, $935.12; Garry Malphrus, House majority chief counsel to the House judiciary subcommittee on criminal justice, $330; Charles Royal, a legislative aide to Rep. Jim DeMint, R-S.C., $391.80; and Kevin Smith, a former GOP House staffer, $373.23. Three of the Miami protesters are now members of Bush's White House staff, the *Miami Herald* reported in July 2002. They included Schlapp, a special assistant to the president; Malphrus, deputy director of the president's Domestic Policy Council; and Joel Kaplan, another special assistant to the president. [See *Miami Herald*, July 14, 2002.] For an overview, see Robert A. Parry, "Bush's Conspiracy to Riot," *Consortium News*, August 5, 2002 (http://www.consortiumnews.com/2002/080502a.html).

21. Jeffrey Toobin, *Too Close to Call: The Thirty-Six Day Battle to Decide the 2000 Election* (New York: Random House, 2001), p. 158.

22. www.abcnews.com, November 24, 2000.

23. Johnathan Chait, "Losing It: The Madness in the GOP's Method," *New Republic*, November 11, 2000.

24. Alterman, *Nation*, November 24, 2000.

25. Toobin, *Too Close to Call*, p. 82.

26. Michael Kelley, "Send in the Thugs," *Washington Post*, November 22, 2000, p. A27 (also in *Jewish World Review*, same date).

27. Tim Russert on NBC *Nightly News*, November 8, 2000. Also quoted in FAIR Media Advisory, "Media vs. Democracy," November 16, 2000.

28. Kathleen Hall Jamieson and Paul Waldman, *The Press Effect: Politicians, Journalists and the Stories That Shape the Political World* (New York: Oxford University Press, 2002), p. 118.

29. Ibid., pp. 121, 124.

30. Richard Reeves, "There's Always the Option of Giving In," *New York Times*, November 10, 2000, op-ed page. R. W. Apple Jr., "Recipe for a Stalemate," *New York Times*, November 9, 2000, p A1. William Safire, "The New 'Long Count,'" *New York Times*, November 9, 2000, p. A23. *Wall Street Journal*, November 10, 2000, editorial page.

31. R. W. Apple, "Recipe for a Stalemate" *New York Times*: "In his book, *RN, the Memoirs of Richard Nixon*, published 18 years later, Mr. Nixon wrote, 'There is no doubt that there was substantial vote fraud in the 1960 election. Texas and Illinois produced the most damaging as well as the most flagrant examples.' But he quickly accepted the verdict. Why? 'A presidential recount would require up to half a year, during which time the legitimacy of Kennedy's election would be in question,' Mr. Nixon explained in the memoirs. 'The effect could be devastating to America's foreign relations. I could not subject the country to such a situation.'"

32. David Greenberg, "Was Nixon Robbed?" Slate.com, October 16, 2000, and Gerald Posner, "The Fallacy of Nixon's Graceful Exit," Salon.com, November 10, 2000.

33. *Newsweek* and *U.S. News & World Report*, November 17, 2000.

34. Quoted in Hotline, November 18, 2000.

35. Toobin, *Too Close to Call*, p. 82.

36. ABC's *This Week* transcript, November 12 and November 19, 2000; CBS's *Face the Nation* November 19, 2000, transcript; and NBC's *Meet the Press* transcript, November 19, 2000.

37. For instance, according to a *Newsweek* poll published while these comments were being made, 72 percent of adults felt that making certain the count is fair and accurate was more important than getting matters resolved as quickly as possible. www.msnbc.com, November 11, 2000. And 69 percent said that the recount and the delay were proof that the U.S. electoral system is working, not a sign of weakness. On November 20, this number was still well above 50 percent. www.USAToday.com, November 20, 2000.

38. Gallup Poll, MSNBC.com, November 19, 2000.

39. David Broder, "Ruling Gives Democrats Seeds of a Comeback," *Washington Post*, December 13, 2000, p. A1.

40. Alicia Caldwell, "Challenges Dog Overseas Ballot Count," *St. Petersburg Times*, November 19, 2000, p. A9.

41. Michael Cooper, "GOP Drops a Suit," *New York Times*, November 26, 2000, p. A1.

42. David Barstow and Don Van Natta Jr., "Examining the Vote; How Bush Took Florida: Mining the Overseas Absentee Vote," *New York Times*, July 15, 2001, p. A1.

43. Paul Richter and Eric Bailey, "Unanswered Call on Military Ballots," *Los Angeles Times*, November 21, 2000, p. A1. See also Jamieson and Waldman, pp. 112–116.

44. For instance, Harris replied to one of the 250,000 e-mails she received during the recount, "Queen Ester Has Been a Wonderful Roll [sic] Model. Please Pray for the Nation and for Me." She told a group of reporters gathered at a college football game, "You know what I dreamed of today? I dreamed that I would ride into this stadium on a horse carrying the FSU

flag in one hand and the certification in the other—while everyone around me cheered." See Toobin, *Too Close to Call*, p. 129.

45. Frank Bruni, "Bush Claims Victory, Urging Gore to Bow Out," *New York Times*, November 27, 2000, p. A1.

46. NBC's *Meet the Press*, November 26, 2000.

47. Christopher Hanson, "All the News that Fits the Myth," *Columbia Journalism Review*, January/February 2001.

48. Eric Pooley, "Prime Time Battle," *Time*, November 27, 2000, p. 47.

49. Hanson, *Columbia Journalism Review*.

50. "'Awarding' Victory," *Washington Post*, November 10, 2000, p. A44, quoted in Eric Alterman, "Pundits, Media Favor Bush," www.MSNBC.com, November 13, 2000.

51. "A Gore Coup d'Etat," *Wall Street Journal*, editorial page, November 10, 2000, and Felicity Barringer, "Counting the Vote: The Editorials," *New York Times*, November 11, 2000, p. A13.

52. Juliet Eilperin and Matthew Vita, "GOP Leaders Back Plan to Block Gore; House Proposal Targets Military Votes," *Washington Post*, November 23, 2000, p. A1, and Eric Alterman for MSNBC.com, November 24, 2000.

53. George F. Will, "Gore Hungry for Power," *Washington Post*, November 12, 2000, p. B7.

54. George F. Will, "Slow Motion Larceny," *Washington Post*, November 14, 2000, p. A43.

55. Quoted in Eric Boehlert, "Out of Control," Salon.com, December 1, 2000.

56. Michael Kelly, "Burn that Village," *Washington Post,* November 29, 2000, p. A39.

57. Ibid.

58. Michael Kelley, "Send in the Thugs," *Washington Post*, November 22, 2000, p. A27 (also in *Jewish World Review*, same date).

59. Thomas B. Edsall, "Rage Sharpens Conservative Rhetoric," *Washington Post*, November 22, 2000, p. A19.

60. Willaim Kristol, "Judicial Tyranny," *Washington Post*, December 10, 2000, p. B7.

61. Edsall, *Washington Post*.

62. Toobin, *Too Close to Call*, p. 225.

63. Maureen Dowd, "Liberties; Sisyphus and Starbucks," *New York Times*, December 6, 2000, p. A33.

64. Toobin, *Too Close to Call*, p. 249.

65. John T. Noonan, Jr. *Narrowing the Nation's Power: The Supreme Court Sides with the States* (Berkeley: University of California Press, 2002).

66. See Win McCormack, "Deconstructing the Election," *Nation*, March 26, 2001.

67. David Greenberg, "Fishy Outcome: The Legend of Nixon's 1960 Loss," Tompaine.com, November 7, 2000 (http://www.tompaine.com/feature.cfm/ID/3851).

68. John DiIulio, "Equal Protection Run Amok," *Weekly Standard*, December 25, 2000.

69. Eric Alterman, "Farewell, My Cokie," *Nation*, August 5, 2002 (http://www.thenation.com/doc.mhtml?i=20020805&s=alterman).

70. Fred Barbash, " A Brand New Game; It Wasn't Pretty, It Wasn't Fair, but It Was Legitimate," *Washington Post*, December 17, 2000, p. B1.

71. Max Frankel, "Our System Leaves the Loser Standing," *New York Times*, December 15, 2000, p. A36.

72. "Colin Powell's Message," *Washington Post*, December 18, 2000, p. A26.

73. The political staff of the *Washington Post, Deadlock: The Inside Story of America's Closest Election* (New York: PublicAffairs, 2001), pp. 234–235.

74. Richard Berke, "Aftermath: It's Not Time for a Party but for How Long?" *New York Times Week in Review*, September 4, 2000, p. WR3.

75. Eric Alterman, "Florida Speaks, Media Spins, World Turns," MSNBC.com, November 12, 2001.

76. Howard Kurtz, "George W. Bush: Now More than Ever," *Washington Post*, November 12, 2001, p. C1.

77. "Katherine Harris: Gore's 'Dogs of War' Bit Him," CNN.com, August 26, 2002 (http://www.cnn.com/2002/ALLPOLITICS/08/26/harris.book.ap/).

78. David Damron and Roger Roy, "Both Sides Guessed Wrong," *Orlando Sentinel*, November 12, 2001.

79. On December 9, just as the U.S. Supreme Court stopped the counting, Lewis wrote a memo instructing canvassing boards to isolate "overvotes" that demonstrated clear intent. "If you would segregate 'overvotes' as you describe and indicate in your final report how many where you determined the clear intent of the voter," he wrote, "I will rule on the issue for all counties." Overvotes were clearly legal under Florida law, as a few counties had already included them in their counts. www.msnbc.com.

80. *The Economist*, November 17, 2001, www.economist.com.

# Chapter Twelve

1. Bush took this vacation while his daughter was undergoing emergency appendicitis surgery. www.inside.com, December 27, 2000.

2. David Brooks, *Weekly Standard*, January 22, 2001, www.weeklystandard.com.

3. Joshua Micah Marshall, "Confidence Men," *Washington Monthly*, September 2002 (http://www.washingtonmonthly.com/features/2001/0209.marshall.html).

4. ABC's *The Note*, September 26, 2002, (http://www.abcnews.go.com/sections/politics/DailyNews/TheNote.html).

5. Howard Kurtz, "Straight Man," *Washington Post Magazine*, May 19, 2002, p. W14.

6. Elisabeth Bumiller with Jim Rutenberg, "White House Memo: 'West Wing' Rides Coattails of the Real Thing," *New York Times*, January 23, 2002, p. A12.

7. Which, by the way, are absolutely amazing. She is very talented. No really, she is.

8. Dana Milbank and Dan Balz, "Behind Scenes, Bush Played Vigorous Role," *Washington Post*, April 12, 2001, p. A1.

9. Joshua Micah Marshall, "Wanted: A Vast Left-Wing Conspiracy," Slate.com, May 9, 2001.

10. Philip Pan, "China 'Concerned' by Bush Remarks," *Washington Post*, April 27, 2001, p. A19.

11. Norman Kempster, "Bush Gets High Marks for Low-Key Approach," *Los Angeles Times*, April 13, 2001, p. A12.

12. Robert Kagan and William Kristol, "A National Humiliation," *Weekly Standard*, April 16/April 23, 2001.

13. Jonathan Freedland, "Presidency of Dunces," *Guardian*, April 25, 2001.

14. Bruni repeated these phrases verbatim in *Ambling into History* (New York: HarperCollins, 2002), p. 237.

15. Bruni, *Ambling*, p. 223.

16. John F. Harris, "Mr. Bush Catches a Washington Break," *Washington Post*, May 6, 2001, p. B1.

17. Laurence McQuillan, "Bush Raises a Record $100 Million Today," *USA Today*, August 12, 2002 (http://www.usatoday.com/news/washington/2002–08–11-bush-usat_x.htm).

18. Sally Quinn, "Not in Their Back Yard: In Washington, That Letdown Feeling," *Washington Post,* November 2, 1998, p. E01.

19. Ibid.

20. George F. Will, December 20, 1998, p. C07.

21. Dana Milbank, "For Bush, Facts Are Malleable: Presidential Tradition of Embroidering Key Assertions Continues," *Washington Post,* October 22, 2002.

22. Press briefing by Ari Fleischer, September 26, 2001 (http://www.whitehouse.gov/news/releases/2001/09/20010926–5.html).

23. "The Ashcroft Smear," *Washington Post*, December 7, 2001, p. A40.

24. Quote in Brendan Nyhan, "Bully Brigade," Salon.com, March 5, 2002 (http://archive.salon.com/politics/col/spinsanity/2002/03/05/dissent/).

25. "Defending Civilization: How Our Universities Are Failing America and What Can Be Done About It," a project of the Defense of Civilization Fund and the American Council of Trustees and Alumni (www.goacta.org/Reports/defciv.pdf).

26. See Brendan Nyhan's energetic deconstruction, "The Big NEA-Sept. 11th Lie," on Spinsanity.com (http://www.spinsanity.org/columns/20020905.html), September 5, 2002.

27. (http://www.salon.com/politics/col/spinsanity/2002/09/18/nea/print.html).

28. Andrew Sullivan, "America at War: America Wakes Up to a World of Fear," *Sunday Times (London)*, September 16, 2001.

29. www.andrewsullivan.com, September 19, 2001.

30. See David Talbot, "The 'Traitor' Fires Back," Salon.com, October 16, 2002 (http://archive.salon.com/news/feature/2001/10/16/susans/index_np.html). Her original essay appeared in the *New Yorker*, September 24, 2001 (http://www.newyorker.com/talk/content/?010924ta_talk_wtc).

31. See, for instance, Eric Alterman, "Patriot Games," *Nation*, October 29, 2001 (http://www.thenation.com/doc.mhtml?i=20011029&s=alterman).

32. John F. Harris, "God Gave U.S. 'What We Deserve,' Falwell Says," *Washington Post*, September 14, 2001, p. C3.

33. Jacob Weisberg, "Left Behind," Slate.com, December 4, 2001.

34. *New York Times*, November 9, 2001 (http://query.nytimes.com/search/article-page.html?res=9E03E0D61638F93AA35752C1A9679C8B63).

35. Ibid.

36. Barbie Zelizer and Stuart Allen, editors, *Journalism After September 11* (New York: Routledge, 2002) p. 11.

37. Media Research Center, "Cyber Alert," October 31, 2001 (http://www.mediaresearch.org/cyberalerts/2001/cyb20011031_extra.asp).

38. Alex Beam, "Senseless Acts, Words of Nonsense," *Boston Globe*, September 27, 2001, p. D1.

39. Bernard Goldberg, *Bias* (Washington, D.C.: Regnery, 2001).

40. Alex Beam, "Senseless Acts, Words of Nonsense," *Boston Globe*, September 27, 2001, p. D1.

41. Charles Krauthammer, "To War, Not to Court," *Washington Post*, September 12, 2001, p. A29.

42. Eliot A. Cohen, "Make War, Not Justice," *New Republic*, September 24, 2001.

43. Seth Lipsky, "This Is War: Don't Treat It as a Law-Enforcement Problem," *Wall Street Journal*, September 13, 2001 (http://online.wsj.com/public/resources/documents/OJlipsky.htm).

44. Sir Michael Howard was speaking to the Royal United Services Institute.

45. Stanley Hoffmann, "On the War," *New York Review of Books*, November 1, 2001.

46. Elisabeth Bumiller, "America as Reflected in Its Leader," *New York Times Week in Review*, January 6, 2002, p. WR1.

47. Media Research Center, "Cyber Alert," September 18, 2001 (http://www.mediaresearch.org/cyberalerts/2001/cyb20010918.asp).

48. Howard Kurtz, "What Bush Said and When He Said It," *Washington Post*, October 1, 2001, p. C1.

49. Eric Boehlert, "All Bush, All the Time," Salon.com, April 18, 2002.

50. Maureen Dowd, "We Love the Liberties They Hate," *New York Times,* September 30, 2001, p. 13.

51. Alessandra Stanley, *New York Times*, October 12, 2001, p. B1.

52. "Mr. Bush's New Gravitas," *New York Times*, October 12, 2001, p. A24.

53. Robert Dallek, "Seeing Bush's Brains Despite Mangled Words," *New York Times*, March 20, 2002, p. E7.

54. Dana Milbank, "A Few Degrees Warmer for Bush: President Cheered at Commencement," *Washington Post,* June 15, 2002, p. A4.

55. David E. Sanger, "Skipping Borders, Tripping Diction," *New York Times,* May 29, 2002, p. A10.

56. Paul Krugman, "The Real Thing," *New York Times*, August 20, 2002, p. A19.

57. NBC's *Meet the Press*, December 23, 2001, transcript.

58. Frank Rich pointed this out in "The Jack Welsh War Plan," *New York Times*, September 28, 2002 (http://www.nytimes.com/2002/09/28/opinion/28RICH.html?pagewanted=print&position=top).

59. See Michael Getler, "Uncivil Wars," *Washington Post,* April 21, 2002, p. B6.

60. ABC News *The Note*, September 24, 2002 (http://www.abcnews.go.com/sections/politics/DailyNews/TheNote.html).

61. Micheal Kelly, "Look Who's Playing Politics," *Washington Post*, September 25, 2002, p. A27. See also "Hannity and Colmes," Fox News Channel, September 23, 2002.

62. Eric Alterman, "'Objectivity' RIP," *Nation*, December 24, 2001 (http://www.thenation.com/doc.mhtml?i=20011224&s=alterman), and *New York Post*, September 25, 2002 (http://www.nypost.com/postopinion/editorial/57795.htm).

63. Nicholas Confessore, "Beat the Press," *American Prospect*, March 11, 2002.

64. See, for instance, Dan Eggen and Bill Miller, "Bush Was Told of Hijacking Dangers," *Washington Post*, May 16, 2002, p. A1; Ed Vulliamy, "The White House and the Warnings: A Bad Call?" *Observer*, May 19, 2002, p. A19; Michael Hirsh and Michael Isikoff, "What Went Wrong," *Newsweek*, May 27, 2002 (http://www.msnbc.com/news/753689.asp); Michael Elliot, "Could 9/11 Have Been Prevented?" *Time*, August 4, 2002 (http://www.time.com/time/nation/article/0,8599,333835,00.html).

65. Tim Russert told him, "You're 69 years old and you're America's stud"—*Meet the Press*, January 20, 2002. Larry King told him, "You now have this new image called sex symbol"—*Larry King Live*, December 6, 2001. Fox's Jim Angle termed him "a babe magnet for the 70-year-old set)—Fox News Channel, December 11, 2001, while *Time's* Margaret Carlson cried,

"I love you, Donald" on CNN's *Capitol Gang* on December 23, 2001. Her colleague at the newsweekly, Mark Thompson, did not mind that Rumsfeld was not providing timely information to the media or the public about the war, because, as he put it, "Although he has not told us very much, he has been like a father figure."—*Chicago Tribune*, October 22, 2001. Fred Barnes, who must not be paying careful attention, asked, "Who would have thought a press corps filled with liberals would make Rumsfeld, the hardest of hard-liners, into the Backstreet Boy of the war against terrorism?"—*Weekly Standard*, December 3, 2001.

66. See Kathleen Hall Jamieson and Paul Waldman, *The Press Effect: Politicans, Journalists and the Stories That Shape the Political World* (New York: Oxford University Press, 2002), p. 138.

67. Bob Somerby, The Daily Howler, February 25, 2002 (http://www.dailyhowler.com/h022502_1.shtml); Joe Conason, "Press Falls for Lie About Clinton, Enron," *New York Observer*, March. 4, 2002, p. 5 (http://www.observer.com/pages/story.asp?ID=5532).

68. Brendan Nyhan, "Another Bedroom Farce," Salon.com, February 21, 2002.

69. Al Hunt, "A Presidency in Disarray," *Wall Street Journal*, quoted on ABC News, *The Note*, April 4, 2002 (http://abcnews.go.com/sections/politics/dailynews/TheNote_April4.html).

70. First quote: George W. Bush, in an interview with Britain's ITV, as reported by the Associated Press's Ron Fournier on April 5. Second quote: George W. Bush, at an April 6 press conference in Crawford, Texas, with British Prime Minister Tony Blair (http://usinfo.state.gov/regional/nea/summit/text/0406bshblr.htm). Also see Joseph Curl, "Bush to Sharon: Pull Troops Out," *Washington Times*, April 7, 2002.

71. ABC's *The Note*, September 17, 2002.

72. ABC News, *The Note*, May 14, 2002 (http://abcnews.go.com/sections/politics/dailynews/TheNote_May14.html).

73. Frank Rich, "How to Lose a War," *New York Times*, October 27, 2001, p. A19.

74. Joshua Micah Marshall, "Confidence Men," *Washington Monthly*, September 2002 (http://www.washingtonmonthly.com/features/2001/0209.marshall.html).

75. Ibid.

76. Nicholas Confessore, "Beat the Press," *American Prospect* 13 (5), March 11, 2002.

77. Doug Struck, "Casualties of U.S. Miscalculations, Afghan Victims of CIA Missile Strike Described as Peasants, Not Al Qaeda," *Washington Post* Foreign Service, February 11, 2002, p. A1.

78. Frank Rich, "Freedom from the Press," *New York Times*, March 2, 2002, p. A15.

79. See "Public's News Habits Little Changed by September 11, 2002. Americans Lack Background to Follow International News," a report by the Pew Research Center for the People and the Press, June 11, 2002, www.people-press.org.

80. Noted in the *Washington Post*, October 1, 2002, p. A19.

81. The *Atlanta Journal Constitution*, September 10, 2002 (http://www.accessatlanta.com/ajc/business/cnn/0902/10tough.html).

82. The column appeared in the *Nation* in the issue dated October 7, 2002, but was published on September 19, 2002, and on its website at (http://www.thenation.com/doc.mhtml?i=20021007&s=alterman). In its text I note my debt to Patrick Tyler and Jim Dwyer of the *New York Times*, Robert Kaiser of the *Washington Post*, Eric Boehlert of *Salon*, and Juan Gonzalez, author of the book *Fallout*.

83. Mike Allen, "Bush Knew Firm's Plight Before Stock Sale," *Washington Post*, July 21, 2002, p. A7.

84. Warren Vieth, "As a Board Member, Bush OKd a Deal Like Enron's," *Los Angeles Times*, July 12, 2002, p. 1.

85. Mike Allen, "Bush Took Oil Firm's Loans as Director; Practice Would Be Banned in President's New Corporate Abuse Policy," *Washington Post*, July 11, 2002, p. A1.

86. Ken Fireman, "He Promised Not to Sell: Bush Signed 'Lockup' on Stock," *Newsday*, July 17, 2002, p. A8.

87. David Teather, "Memo Emerges to Haunt President," *The Guardian*, November 2, 2002 (http://www.guardian.co.uk/usa/story/0,1227,824567,00.html).

88. Mike Allen, "Bush Took Oil Firm's Loans as Director; Practice Would Be Banned in President's New Corporate Abuse Policy," *Washington Post*, July 11, 2002, p. A1; Mike Allen, "Bush Uncooperative at First in '90 Probe, SEC Memo Suggests; Insider Trading Suspected in Sale of Stock; No Illegal Activity Found," *Washington Post*, July 12, 2002, p. A7; Frank Rich, "The Road to Perdition," *New York Times*, July 20, 2002, p. A13; *Dallas Morning News*, October 11, 1994.

89. *Washington Post*, July 16, 2002, p. A1.

90. Spencer Ackerman, "Where Was George?" *New Republic*, July 10, 2002.

91. *Fox on Media*, July 20, 2002, tape.

92. *Wall Street Journal*, July 10, 2002.

93. "The Harken Energy Distraction," *Washington Post*, July 12, 2002, p. A20.

94. Eric Boehlert in Salon, July 13, 2002, www.salon.com.

95. Cited in Joe Conason's Journal, July 12, 2002, www.salon.com.

96. Paul Krugman, "Succeeding in Business," *New York Times*, July 7, 2002, Sec. 4, p. 9.

97. Eric Boehlert in Salon, July 13, 2002.

98. Elizabeth Wilner and Marc Ambinder, "Vote First, Sentence Later," ABC's *The Note*, July 16, 2002 (http://abcnews.go.com/sections/politics/dailynews/thenote.html).

99. See John Harwood, "Bush, While Still Popular, Faces Grave Political Peril," September 11, 2002 (http://online.wsj.com/article/0,,SB1031692628413185235-search,00.html?collection=wsjie/30day&vql-string=%28%22Bush%2C+While+Still+Popular%2CFaces+Grave+Political+Peril%22%29%3Cin%3E%28article%2Dbody%29); *New York Times* September 25, 2002 (http://www.nytimes.com/2002/09/25/national/25POVE.html); *Washington Post*, September 30, 2001, p. 1; and Ronald Brownstein, "Like Father, Like Son: The Economic Indicators Head South," *Los Angeles Times*, September 30, 2002, (http://www.latimes.com/news/nationworld/nation/la-na-outlook30sep30004434,0,3851780.column? coll=la%2 Dheadlines%2Dnation).

100. Robert Pear, "Number of People Living in Poverty Increases in U.S.," *New York Times*, September 25, 2002, p. A1.

101. See, for instance, William Safire, *New York Times*, November 7, 2002 (http://www.nytimes.com/2002/11/07/opinioni/07SAFl.html).

## Chapter Thirteen

1. John F. Harris, "Mr. Bush Catches a Washington Break," *Washington Post*, May 6, 2001, p. B1.

2. Franklin Foer, "Kid Gloves," *New Republic* Online, May 8, 2001 (http://www.tnr.com/express/foer050801.html).

3. The description was used by Jude Wanniski, who was then an editorial page writer for the *Journal*, and is quoted in *Sound & Fury*, p. 165.

4. Thomas B. Rosentsteil, "*Wall St. Journal* Editorials Inspire, Anger," *Los Angeles Times*, March 12, 1989, p. 1.

5. PBS Media Matters, January 1997 (http://www.pbs.org/wnet/mediamatters99/transcript2.html).

6. PBS Media Matters, January 1997.

7. Among them, *Sound & Fury*, pp. 163–178.

8. See, for instance, "A Nation Transformed: Clinton-Gore Administration Accomplishments: 1993–1999" (http://clinton3.nara.gov/WH/Accomplishments/economy.html).

9. *Sound & Fury*, p. 166.

10. PBS Media Matters, January 1997.

11. *Wall Street Journal*, August 12, 2002, editorial page.

12. *Wall Street Journal*, August 13, 2002, p. 1.

13. Patrick E. Tyler, "Anti-Baghdad Talks Shunned by Top Kurd," *New York Times*, August 15, 2002, p. A10.

14. Quoted in the *Los Angeles Times*, March 12, 1989.

15. *Wall Street Journal*, October 20, 1998.

16. *Wall Street Journal*, March 18, 1993, editorial page.

17. Cockburn's appearance in the *Journal* during the 1980s infuriated its conservative contributors. For a brief time, Bartley even printed up "Alex Cockburn complaint cards" to give to the complainers. Cockburn's romance with Lally Weymouth, daughter of Katharine and Philip Graham, and his marriage to the novelist Katherine Kilgore, the granddaughter of Barney Kilgore, the famous *Journal* editor of the forties and fifties, inspired what must be the cleverest observation Joseph Sobran ever made: "Alex Cockburn's scorn for the men who created the wealth of America is exceeded only by his admiration for the women who inherited it." Quoted in Charlotte Hays, "Alex Cockburn's Popular Front: The Nation's Wittiest Soviet Apologist Has an Eye for Rich Men's Daughters," *Policy Review*, Summer 1984, p. 60. In a 1989 interview with the author, Bartley allowed that, personally, he found the column to be "not as interesting as [it] used to be." He discontinued Cockburn's column in January 1991.

18. Trudy Lieberman, "Bartley's Believe It or Not! The *Wall Street Journal*'s editorial page has plenty of clout. But what about credibility?" *Columbia Journalism Review*, July/August 1996 (http://www.cjr.org/year/96/4/wsj.asp).

19. See Letters, *Wall Street Journal*, June 14, 2002.

20. *Wall Street Journal*, March 25, 1994.

21. Robert Parry, "Hast Thou Seen the Whitewater Whale? The *Journal*'s Quest for Conspiracy," *Extra!* September/October 1995 (http://www.fair.org/extra/9509/whitewater-wsj.html).

22. Ibid.

23. *Wall Street Journal*, March 21, 1994, editorial page.

24. *Wall Street Journal*, March 21, 1994, editorial page; *New York Observer*, March 4, 1994.

25. Howard Kurtz, "Whitewater Weirdness; How a Four-Hour Gap in L. J. Davis's Life Became a Pause Celebre," *Washington Post*, April 23, 1994, p. G1.

26. *Wall Street Journal*, July 19, 1994, editorial page.

27. *Extra! Update*, June 2000 (http://www.fair.org/extra/0006/elian.html).

28. Mary Wakefield, "There Is No Alternative," *Spectator*, June 22, 2002 (http://www. spectator.co.uk/article.php3?table=old&section=current&issue=2002–06–22&id=1978).

29. Mark Helprin, "School for Scandal," *Wall Street Journal*, March 25, 1994.

30. Peggy Noonan, "The Man George Shultz Saw: Gov. Bush Is Reaganesque. Now America Knows It," *Wall Street Journal*, October 13, 2000.

31. Jonathan Chait, "How Peggy Noonan Sees Politics. Right Reverent," *New Republic*, May 35, 2002.

32. Wakefield, *Spectator*.

33. *Wall Street Journal* opinion journal, January 26, 2001.

34. *Wall Street Journal* opinion journal, November 1, 2002 (http://www.opinionjournal. com/columnists/pnoonan/?id–0002554).

35. Garry Wills, "Conjuring Evil," *New York Times*, April 25, 2000, p. A23, and Joe Conason, "The Elian Metaphor," Salon.com, April 25, 2000.

36. L. J. Davis, "World Class Tax Dodger!" *Mother Jones*, September/October 1998.

37. Russ Baker, "Murdoch's Mean Machine," *Columbia Journalism Review*, May/June 1998 (http://www.cjr.org/year/98/3/murdoch.asp).

38. Bill Hoffmann, "No. 1 'Titanic' Ready to Make Waves in China," *New York Post*, March 9, 1998, p. 3.

39. See Dan Barry, "The Post Reinvents Itself Again in the War of the Tabloids"; *New York Times*, July 8, 2001, p. A21; Felicity Barringer and Jayson Blair, "New Editor at Post Raised Sydney Paper's Influence," *New York Times*, April 25, 2001, p. B7; Gabriel Snyder, "Apparently the New Guy at the *Post* Doesn't Get the Joke," *New York Observer*, May 14, 2001, p. 6.

40. Quoted in Neil Chenoweth, *Rupert Murdoch: the Untold Story of the World's Greatest Media Wizard* (New York: Crown Books, 2002), p. 158.

41. Quoted in "Mr. Murdoch's Rage," *New York Times*, October 24, 1996, p. A26; *New Yorker*, November 11, 1995.

42. James, a college dropout whom Murdoch has since appointed to be the publisher of the *New York Post*, attacked the global media for its coverage of Chinese human rights abuses, insisting that "destabilizing forces today are very, very dangerous for the Chinese government." He instructed Hong Kong's brave young champions of democracy to accept the fact of an "absolutist" government. And he all but endorsed the persecution of what he called the "dangerous" and "apocalyptic" Falun Gong religious movement, which "clearly does not have the success of China at heart." (More than 150 adherents of the group had died in police custody at the time, and another 10,000 were imprisoned.) Evelyn Iritani, "News Corp. Heir Woos China with Show of Support," *Los Angeles Times*, March 23, 2001, p. 1; Bill Carter, "Murdoch Executive Calls Press Coverage of China Too Harsh," *New York Times*, March 26, 2001, p. C8; and *Wall Street Journal*, March 26, 2001.

43. Deng Maomao, *Deng Xiaoping: My Father* (New York: Basic Books, 1995). Advance: a reported $1 million. "[An] unrestrainedly adulatory piece of hagiography. . . . [She] bores her readers. . . . Were the publishers in such a rush to produce a scoop that they did not even bother to edit the 500-page manuscript? There is no end of mistakes of grammar and usage." Rene Goldman, "My Dad, China's paramount leader Deng's upheaval-filled life reflects the turmoil of the 20th century," *Toronto Star*, August 19, 1995, p. J15.

44. *Wall Street Journal*, March 26, 2001; and Uwe Parpart, "China's Oprah Winfrey," *Business Times Singapore*, September 20, 2001, pp. SS10, SS11.

45. What follows is a listing of the stories the *New York Post* did feature on its front page during the week of the China crisis, as compiled by Tunku Varadarajan of the *Wall Street*

*Journal:* "PLAY BALL! Yankee Fans Rooting for Another Subway Series." With a picture of Roger Clemens practicing. (The *Daily News* gave its front to the China story: "LET 'EM GO," it declared, with a picture of Admiral Dennis Blair pointing to a map of the area in which the collision occurred.) "Fans to Straw: YER OUT," on the drug saga, with a picture of Darryl Strawberry. "SLAIN FOR A SNACK," about the murder of a pizza deliveryman in Brooklyn, along with the victim's photograph. (On the same day, the *Daily News* gave its front page to the China crisis: "TIME'S UP," it said, sonorously, along with two pictures, one of a grim-faced President Bush and one of a detained serviceman's sister clutching a framed portrait of her brother.) "DOUBLE TROUBLE: Ricky Martin Lookalike Faces 30 Years in Rape Spree." "HILL NO!—Clinton says she'll NEVER run for Prez." *Wall Street Journal*, April 9, 2001, www.wsj.com.

46. He made this recommendation, telling President Bush to "Wag the dog already," on the *Post's* editorial page on July 17, 2002.

47. Steve Dunleavy, "Dollars and 'Sense' Will Prevail," *New York Post*, April 9, 2001.

48. Russ Baker, "Murdoch's Mean Machine," *Columbia Journalism Review*, May/June 1998 (http://www.cjr.org/year/98/3/murdoch.asp).

49. Quoted in www.salon.com, Feburary 24, 2000.

50. Burt Kearns, *Tabloid Baby: An Uncensored Account of the Revolution That Gave Birth to 21st Century News Broadcasting* (Nashville, Tenn.: Celebrity Books, 1999), pp. 55–60.

51. Marshal Sella, "The Red-State Network: How Fox News Conquered Bush Country—and Toppled CNN," *New York Times Magazine*, June 24, 2001.

52. Howard Kurtz, "Doing Something Right; Fox News Sees Ratings Soar, Critics Sore," *Washington Post*, February 5, 2001, p. C1.

53. Howard Kurtz, "Limbaugh, Post-Clinton: Dining Happily on What's Left," *Washington Post*, May 7, 2001, p. C1.

54. Seth Ackerman, "A Special FAIR Report: The Most Biased Name in News—Fox News Channel's Extraordinary Right-Wing Tilt," August 2001.

55. Eric Boehlert, "Rant: Fox Trot," www.salon.com, July 2, 2001.

56. Fox Network, March 25, 2001, and November 25, 1999.

57. See William A. Hammond, *Reporting Vietnam: Media and Military at War* (Lawrence: University Press of Kansas, 1998, originally published by the U.S. Army War College, Carlysle Barracks, Pa.).

58. Robert Kagan and William Kristol, "A National Humiliation," *Weekly Standard*, April 16, 2001/April 23, 2001, p. 11. See www.msnbc.com, April 10, 2001.

59. Author's interviews.

60. Eric Alterman, "Back into the Muck," *Nation*, March 7, 2002 (http://www.thenation.com/doc.mhtml?i=20020325&s=alterman)

61. William Kristol, "The Axis of Appeasement," *Weekly Standard*, 7 (47) August 26, 2002.

62. John B. Judis, "Below the Beltway: Neo-Cons vs. *New York Times*," *The American Prospect*, September 23, 2002 (http://www.prospect.org/print/V13/17/judis-j.html).

63. See David Nasaw, *The Chief: The Life of William Randolph Hearst* (New York: Houghton Mifflin, 2000).

64. See Matthew Engel, "Engel in America: Chicken Hawks,", *Guardian (London)*, August 20, 2002, p. 15.

65. See Michael Getler, *Washington Post*, November 3, 2002, p. B6; Greg Mitchell and Dave Astor, "Why Did 'NY Times' Run 2 Accounts of Anti-war Rally?" *Editor and Publisher*, November 1, 2002 (http://www.editorandpublisher.com/editorandpublisher/headlines/article

display.jsp?vnu content id=1753438); and Greg Mitchell, "Did 'New York Times' Blow Coverage of Antiwar March?" *Editor and Publisher,* October 30, 2002. As Mitchell and Astor note, "On Oct. 27, the day after the march, the *Times* ran a relatively short piece noting that the number of protesters in Washington was 'fewer' than organizers had hoped for. Since the organizers had only taken out a permit for 20,000—and the crowd, by police estimates, totaled 100,000—this was, of course, quite false. Three days later, as if to make amends, the paper ran a second, longer, 'make-up' story noting that the huge turnout 'startled event organizers,' who hailed it as the biggest antiwar rally since the Vietnam war."

66. Dana Milbank, "Cheney Says Iraqi Strike Is Justified; Hussein Poses Threat, He Declares," *Washington Post,* August 27, 2002, p. A1.

67. Howard Kurtz, "The Resurrection of Jeb Bush," *Washington Post,* August 29, 2002 (www.washingtonpost.com).

68. *Washington Post,* August 27, 2002, p. 1, and (http://rittenhouse.blogspot.com).

69. The Forbes 400, September 13, 2002 (http://www.forbes.com/2002/09/13/rich400land.html).

70. Robert G. Kaiser, "An Enigmatic Heir's Paradoxical World," *Washington Post,* May 3, 1999, p. A1.

71. Sidebar to Karen Rothmyer, "Citizen Scaife," *Columbia Journalism Review,* July/August, 1981 (http://www.cjr.org/resources/scaife/scaife_sidebars.asp).

72. Kaiser, "An Enigmatic Heir."

73. Robert G. Kaiser and Ira Chinoy, "How Scaife's Money Powered a Movement," *Washington Post,* May 2, 1999, p. A1.

74. Burton Hersh, *The Mellon Family: A Fortune in History* (New York: Morrow, 1978).

75. Kaiser and Chinoy, *Washington Post.*

76. Ibid.

77. The importance of outdoor peeing was the reason given by club members for the necessity of the exclusion of women.

78. See Rick Perlstein, *Before the Storm: Barry Goldwater and the Unmaking of the American Consensus* (New York: Hill and Wang, 2001), pp. 511–516.

79. Karen Rothmyer, "The Small Bore Publisher," *Columbia Journalism Review,* July/August 1981 (http://www.cjr.org/year/81/4/scaife_part2.asp).

80. For instance in 1999, Scaife ordered a reporter to investigate a rumor that Russian soldiers had landed in the Allegheny National Forest. After Pennsylvania Republican Senator Arlen Specter voted to oppose the nomination of Robert Bork to the U.S. Supreme Court, Scaife issued a blanket coverage that the hometown senator—one of only two, naturally—would receive no coverage whatsoever in his newspaper. In 1998, he ordered all mentions of the local baseball franchise, the Pirates, off of the newspaper's front page and fired the editor who allowed one there while the editor was recovering on medical leave for triple bypass surgery. During the 2000 presidential election, Scaife barred all photographs of Democratic candidate Al Gore from page one. See Kimberly Coniff, "All the Views Fit to Print," *Brill's Content,* March 2001.

81. Rothmyer, "Citizen Scaife."

82. Kaiser and Chinoy, *Washington Post.* See also www.mediatransparency.org.

83. www.mediatransparency.org.

84. Robert G. Kaiser and Ira Chinoy, "Scaife: Funding Father of the Right," *Washington Post,* May 2, 1999, p. A1.

85. www.mediatransparency.com.

86. Chris Mooney, "Losers: Bush's Ally, the Federalist Society, Resurrects the Views of the Vanquished in the Constitutional Debate—the Anti-Federalists," *American Prospect* Online, April 25, 2001 (http://www.prospect.org/webfeatures/2001/04/mooney-c-04-25.html). See also Garry Wills, *A Necessary Evil: A History of American Distrust of Government* (New York: Simon and Schuster, 1999) and Jonathan Mahler, "The Federalist Capers: Inside Ken Starr's Intellectual Auxiliary," *Lingua Franca*, September 1998, pp. 38–44.

87. Thomas B. Edsall, "Federalist Society Becomes a Force in Washington: Conservative Group's Members Take Key Roles in Bush White House and Help Shape Policy and Judicial Appointments," *Washington Post*, April 18, 2001, p. A4.

88. Ibid. See also Neil A. Lewis, "A Conservative Legal Group Thrives in Bush's Washington," *New York Times*, April 18, 2001, p. A1.

89. Ibid.

90. Ira Chinoy and Robert G. Kaiser, "Decades of Contributions to Conservation," *Washington Post*, May 20,1999, p. A25.

91. Ibid.

92. See Jacob Weisberg, "NAS: Who Are These Guys Anyway?" *Lingua Franca*, April 1991, pp. 34–39.

93. Bradlee is proudly quoted in Reed Irvine, *Media Mischief and Misdeeds* (Chicago: Regnery, 1984) and can be found at (http://my.ohio.voyager.net/~dionisio/queer/database/a.html) and (http://www.mountnixon.com/bradlee.html). The word "retromingent," which my spelling checker does not recognize, according to Bradlee, "describes that subspecies of ants (and other animals) that urinate backwards."

94. Robert G. Kaiser and Ira Chinoy, "How Scaife's Money Powered a Movement," *Washington Post*, May 2, 1999, p. A1.

95. Nurith C. Aisenman, "The Man Behind the Curtain," *Washington Monthly*, July/August, 1997 p. 34.

96. See Trudy Lieberman, "The Vincent Foster Factory," and "Courage in Journalism," *Columbia Journalism Review*, March/April 1996; and Joe Conason and Gene Lyons, *The Hunting of the President: the Ten-Year Campaign to Destroy Bill and Hillary Clinton* (New York: St. Martin's Press, 2000), pp. 310–311.

97. Robert G. Kaiser and Ira Chinoy, "How Scaife's Money Powered a Movement," *Washington Post*, May 2, 1999, p. A1.

98. The most informative discussion of the genesis of the Arkansas Project can be found in Conason and Lyons, especially chapter 10. Much of the information cited here is drawn from their account and from Jonathan Broder and Joe Conason, "The *American Spectator*'s 'Funny Money,'" Salon.com, June 8, 1998, along with Conason and Lyons, *Hunting*. Other useful background sources on this episode include: Jeffrey Toobin, *A Vast Conspiracy* (New York: Random House, 2000), Michael Isikoff, *Uncovering Clinton* (New York: Three Rivers Press, 1999), and Susan Schmidt and Michael Weisskopf, *Truth at Any Cost: Ken Starr and the Unmaking of Bill Clinton* (New York: HarperCollins, 2000). The latter book is generally understood to represent events through the prism of Ken Starr's prosecutor's office.

99. David Brock, *Blinded by the Right* (New York: Crown Books, 2001) p. 101.

100. Jane Mayer, "True Confessions," *New York Review of Books*, June 27, 2002 (http://www.nybooks.com/articles/15522).

101. Mayer, "True Confessions."

102. Jonathan Broder and Joe Conason, "The *American Spectator*'s 'Funny Money," Salon.com, June 8, 1998.

103. Ibid.

104. *Boston Globe*, August 7, 2002.

105. See Jake Tapper, "Olsen Under Fire," Salon.com, May 11, 2001 (http://archive. salon.com/politics/feature/2001/05/11/olson/); Daryl Lindsey and Kerry Lauerman, "Smearing David Brock," Salon.com, May 17, 2001 (http://archive.salon.com/politics/feature/2001/05/17/ brock/print.html); and the *Washington Post*, May 10, 2001, p. A29.

106. Howard Kurtz, "Right and Wrong; David Brock Went After Liberals With Zeal. He Made Money, Friends. Then, He Says, He Had an Attack of Conscience," *Washington Post*, February 26, 2002, p. C1.

107. David Horowitz, "Believe David Brock at Your Own Risk," Salon.com, April 17, 2002 (http://www.salon.com/news/col/horo/2002/04/17/brock/index1.html).

108. Ramesh Ponnuru, "The Real David Brock," *National Review* (Flashback from the *NR* Archives), April 6, 1998 (http://www.nationalreview.com/flashback/flashback-ponnuru 051001.shtml).

109. Hendrik Hertzberg, "Can You Forgive Him? A Right-Wing Conspirator Comes Clean," *New Yorker*, March 11, 2002, p. 85.

110. Jacob Weisberg, "The Conintern: Republican Thought Police," Slate.com, June 29, 1997 (http://slate.msn.com/?id=2280).

111. Hertzberg, *New Yorker,* p. 85.

112. For details on the low opinion held of him by his own colleagues, as well as Stossel's many questionable journalist practices, see Mark Dowie's report in the January 7, 2002, issue of the *Nation*, "A Teflon Corespondent."

113. Timothy Noah, "Did David Brock Lie About Appearing on Fox? A Chatterbox Investigation," April 26, 2002 (http://slate.msn.com/?id=2064849).

114. Kurtz, "Right and Wrong."

115. Richard Cohen, "Gore Can't Heal the Hurt," *Washington Post*, November 24, 2000, op-ed page, p. A43.

116. See Chapter 12.

117. John Podhoretz, "So Let Gore Have It," *New York Post*, December 10, 2000, p. 55.

# Conclusion

1. *Los Angeles Times*, September 29, 2002, (http://www.latimes.com/news/specials/enrique/ la-enrique-footnotes-ch1.story).

2. Frank Rich, "Slouching Towards 9/11," *New York Times*, August 31, 2002, p. A15 (http://www.nytimes.com/2002/08/31/opinion/31RICH.html).

3. Michelle Goldberg, "Summer Kidnapping Panic," Salon.com, August 7, 2002 (http://archive.salon.com/news/feature/2002/08/07/kidnapping/print.html).

4. Sarah Wildman, *New Republic*, September 9, 2002, and "Public's News Habits Little Changed by Sept. 11: Americans Lack Background to Follow International News," a report by the Pew Research Center for the People & the Press, June 11, 2002, www.people-press.org.

5. Wildman. See also "Public's News Habits Little Changed by Sept.11: Americans Lack Background to Follow International News," a report by the Pew Research Center for The People & the Press, June 11, 2002, www.people-press.org; and Michael A. Dimock, Peyton M. Craighill, and Melissa Rogers, "Temporary Turnabout: Religion and the Crisis," *Public Perspective,* September 2002, pp. 29–33.

6. Ibid., "People and the Press."

7. *Washington Post*, September 2, 2002, p. A1.

8. Ibid.

9. John H. Cushman Jr., "To Obey, or Not to Obey, Orders," *New York Times*, February 10, 2002, sec. 4, p. 3.

10. Kovach delivered this address at the annual meeting of the Organization of News Ombudsmen on April 30, 2002, at Salt Lake City, Utah (http://www.newsombudsmen. org/kovach.html).

11. Robert N. Entman, *Democracy Without Citizens: Media and the Decay of American Politics* (New York: Oxford University Press, 1989), p. 17.

12. Hendrik Hertzberg, "The Talk of the Town—Sins," *New Yorker*, April 1, 2002, p. 35.

13. E. J. Dionne, "A Cleric Gets It All Wrong," *Washington Post*, June 11, 2002, p. A25.

14. Salon, March 29, 2002.

15. Wendy Kaminer, "On the Contrary: Secrets and Lies," *American Prospect*, May 25, 2002.

16. Quoted in Eric Alterman, "The Liberal Media, RIP," *Nation*, March 13, 2000.

17. Quoted in Scott Sherman, *Columbia Journalism Review*, September/October 2002 (http://www.cjr.org/year/02/5/sherman.asp).

# Afterword

1. Wolf Blitzer is quoted on (http://www.atrios.blogspot.com/), September 7, 2003.

2. See Michael Wolff, *Autumn of the Moguls* (New York: HarperCollins, 2003), pp. 351-355.

3. CNBC's *Topic A with Tina Brown*, September 10, 2003, transcript.

4. Michael Getler, "Connecting the Blips," *Washington Post*, March 16, 2003, p. B6.

5. Ari Berman, "The Postwar Post," *The Nation* Online, September 17, 2003 (http://www.thenation.com/doc.mhtml?i=20030929&s=berman).

6. Todd Gitlin, "The Pro-War *Post*," *American Prospect*, 14 (4), April 1, 2003.

7. Fareed Zakaria, "The Arrogant Empire," *Newsweek*, March 24, 2003 (http://www. fareedzakaria.com/articles/newsweek/032403.html).

8. Susan Schmidt and Vernon Loeb, "Rescued POW Put Up Fierce Fight," *Washington Post*, April 3, 2003, p. A1.

9. Jose Martinez, "Inside the Daring Nighttime Rescue," *New York Daily News*, April 3, 2003 (http://www.nydailynews.com/news/wn_report/story/72419p–67099c.html).

10. See Bryan Nyhan and Bryan Keefer, "More Myths, Misconceptions and Unanswered Questions About the War in Iraq," May 28, 2003 (http://www.spinsanity.com).

11. See Nancy Gibbs, "The Private Jessica Lynch," *Time*, November 9, 2003; and Michael Getler, "Capturing the Faces of War," *Washington Post*, November 23, 2003, p. B6.

12. Michael Getler, "A Long, and Incomplete Correction," *Washington Post*, June 29, 2003, p. B6.

13. Michael A. Gordon and Judith Miller, "Threats and Responses: The Iraqis: U.S. Says Hussein Intensifies Quest for A-Bomb Parts," *New York Times*, September 8, 2002, p. A1.

14. Walter Pincus, "Bush Faced Dwindling Data on Iraq Nuclear Bid," *Washington Post*, July 16, 2003, p. A1.

15. Howard Kurtz, "Embedded Reporter's Role in Army Unit's Actions Questioned by Military," *Washington Post*, June 25, 2003, p. C1.

16. Douglas Jehl, "Agency Belittles Information Given by Iraq Defectors," *New York Times*, September 29, 2003, p. A1.

17. See Eric Umasky, "Today's Papers," September 25, 2003 (http://www.Slate.com).

18. Michael D'Antoni, "Sneer When You Say 'Journalist'," *Los Angeles Times Magazine*, August 24, 2003 (http://www.latimes.com/features/printedition/magazine/la-tm-journalist34aug24,1,1174301.story).

19. Lisa de Moraes, "TV," *Washington Post*, April 3, 2003, p. C1.

20. Peter Johnson, "Who Won, and Who Lost, in the Media Battle: Koppel and Rather Go the Distance; Arnett Digs His Own Hole," *USA Today*, April 13, 2003, p. 1A.

21. Mark Jurkowitz, "With a Mix of Reporting and Cheerleading, Fox News Stays Ahead of Cable Pack," *Boston Globe*, March 30, 2002.

22. David Folkenflik, "Fox News Defends Its 'Patriotic' Coverage: Channel's Objectivity Questioned on Iraq," *Baltimore Sun*, April 2, 2003.

23. See Dan Kennedy, "Picture Imperfect: From Bombs Away to Embedded Reporters, the Media War Has Provided Some Striking Images—But Not Much Context," *Boston Phoenix*, March 27–April 3, 2003 (http://www.bostonphoenix.com/boston/news_features/dont_quote_me/multi-page/documents/02781708.htm).

24. Peter Ames Carlin, "Bush Can Wage War, But If CNN Does So, News Balance Suffers," *Portland Oregonian*, March 19, 2003.

25. Kennedy, "Picture Imperfect."

26. Howard Kurtz, "Protest Letters to MSNBC Draw Savage Response," *Washington Post*, March 5, 2003, p. C1.

27. Norman Solomon, "Unmasking the Ugly 'Anti-American'," October 2, 2003 (http://www.fair.org/media-beat).

28. David Bauder, "MSNBC Fires Savage on Anti-Gay Remarks," Associated Press, July 7, 2003.

29. D'Antoni, "Sneer When You Say 'Journalist'."

30. Ben Fritz, "Savage with the Truth: The Man Who Makes Limbaugh Look Sane and Logical," *Salon*, February 19, 2003.

31. See James Wolcott, "MSNBC's Fox Hunt," *Vanity Fair*, October 2003, p.140–146.

32. Steve Rendall and Tara Broughel, "FAIR Study Finds Democracy Poorly Served by War Coverage," *Extra!*, May–June 2003.

33. Center for Media and Public Affairs, "Surprise! TV's War News Was Fairly Balanced," Washington, DC, September 2003.

34. Rendall and Broughel, "FAIR Study Finds Democracy Poorly Served."

35. Steve Rendall, "Dissent, Disloyalty Double Standards: Kosovo Doves Denounced Iraq War Protest as 'Anti-American'," *Extra!*, May–June 2003.

36. Howard Kurtz, "For Media After Iraq, a Case of Shell Shock Battle Assessment Begins for Saturation Reporting," *Washington Post*, April 28, 2003, p. A1.

37. Zoe Heller, "TV Anchors Choke Back Tears: I Gag," *The Telegraph* (London), March 29, 2003.

38. "The Media at War," conference, New School University, July 24, 2003, New York City, author present.

39. Josh Getlin and David Wharton, "War with Iraq/Media: With Media in Tow, Does Objectivity Go AWOL?" *Los Angeles Times*, March 22, 2003, p. A1.

40. "Media at War," July 24, 2003.

41. Howard Kurtz, "Reports with a Troop's-Eye-View: For Embedded Correspondents, the Small Picture Is Big News," *Washington Post*, March 22, 2003, p. C1.

42. Howard Kurtz, "For Media After Iraq, a Case of Shell Shock."

43. Howard Kurtz, "Reports with a Troop's-Eye-View."

44. Jake Tapper, "Weapons of Mass Deception," June 6, 2003 (http://www.salon.com).

45. Dan Plesch and Richard Norton-Taylor, "Straw, Powell Had Serious Doubts over Their Iraqi Weapons Claims; Secret Transcript Revealed," *Guardian*, May 31, 2003, p. A1.

46. Charles J. Hanley, "U.S. Justification for War: How It Stacks Up Now," *Seattle Times*, August 10, 2003 (http://seattletimes.nwsource.com/html/nationworld/2001461070_the-case10.html).

47. Gilbert Cranberg, "Bring Back the Skeptical Press," *Washington Post*, June 29, 2003, p. B2.

48. For a lengthy discussion of this topic, see Eric Alterman and Mark Green, *The Book on Bush: How George W. Misleads America* (New York: Viking Books, 2003), p.266–302.

49. See Eric Alterman, "Patriotic Gore," *The Nation*, September 1, 2003, p. 9.

50. Barton Gellman and Walter Pincus, "Iraq's Nuclear File, Inside the Prewar Debate: Depiction of Threat Outgrew Supporting Evidence," *Washington Post*, August 10, 2003, p. A1.

51. See Alterman, "Patriotic Gore."

52. Author's interview, July 24, 2003. See also Rachel Smolkin, "Are the News Media Soft on Bush?" *American Journalism Review*, August–September 2003.

53. Smolkin, "Are the News Media Soft on Bush?" As Bush told a reporter of his cushy stint flying airplanes at home during Vietnam, "I was not prepared to shoot my eardrum out with a shotgun in order to get a deferment. Nor was I willing to go to Canada. So I chose to better myself by learning how to fly airplanes." Even with that good fortune, made possible by special treatment accorded to him by his famous father's friends, Bush managed to disappear from his reserve unit for his final eighteen months of service. Normally, this would be called desertion, but with Bush it is usually treated by a compliant media as nothing more than a curious gap in his autobiography as well as the record-keeping abilities of the U.S. military. See David Corn, "See Now They Tell Us," *The Nation*, May 19, 2003.

54. Anne E. Kornblut, "Bush Proclaims a Victory," *Boston Globe*, May 2, 2003, p. A1.

55. Richard A. Oppel, "G.I. Killed and 6 Are Wounded in Stepped-Up Attacks," *New York Times*, July 17, 2003, p. A7.

56. Michael O'Hanlon, "Breaking the Army," *Washington Post*, July 3, 2003, p. A23. See also "The Cost of Empire," *Newsweek*, July 17, 2003, p. 27.

57. Russ Bynum, "U.S. Troops to Get Longer Stay in Iraq," Associated Press, July 15, 2003.

58. John B. Judis and Spencer Ackerman, "The First Casualty," *The New Republic*, June 30, 2003, p. 14.

59. Seymour M. Hersh, "Selective Intelligence: Donald Rumsfeld Has His Own Special Sources. Are They Reliable?" *The New Yorker*, May 12, 2003, p. 44.

60. See Eric Alterman, "'Lyndon B. Bush'?" *The Nation*, August 4, 2003, p. 9.

61. CNN's *Reliable Sources*, July 20, 2003 (http://www.cnn.com/TRANSCRIPTS/0307/20/rs.00.html).

62. Ari Berman, "Polls Suggest Media Failure in Pre-War Coverage: Public Believed Saddam Was Behind 9–11, Has Nukes," *Editor and Publisher*, March 26, 2003.

63. See Steven Kull et al., "Misperceptions, the Media, and the Iraq War," Program on Policy Attitudes, October 2, 2003 (http://www.pipa.org/OnlineReports/Iraq/Media_10_02_03_Report.pdf).

64. NBC's *Meet the Press*, September 10, 2003 (http://www.msnbc.com/news/966470.asp?0dm=C21AV). For details, see the Iraq chapter of Eric Alterman and Mark Green, *The Book on Bush* (New York: Viking Books, 2003).

65. "Cheney in Wonderland," *Los Angeles Times*, editorial, September 16, 2003.

66. Richard Cohen, "Never Mind the Weapons," *Washington Post*, May 7, 2003, p. A31.

67. "Cheney in Wonderland."

68. Dana Milbank and Claudia Deane, "Hussein Link to 9/11 Lingers in Many Minds," *Washington Post*, September 6, 2003, p. A1.

69. Matthew Yglesias, "TV Guided How the Networks Did Bush's Bidding in Their Second-Anniversary Coverage of 9–11," *American Prospect* Online, September 12, 2003.

70. Terence Hunt, "Bush Says No Evidence that Saddam Hussein Involved in Sept. 11 Attacks," Associated Press, September 17, 2003.

71. Robert Scheer, "When Corrections Need Correcting . . . ," September 17, 2003 (http://www.salon.com).

72. Greg Miller, "No Proof Connects Iraq to 9/11, Bush Says," *Los Angeles Times*, September 18, 2003, p. A1.

73. Eric Alterman, "Colin Powell and 'The Power of Audacity'," *The Nation*, September 22, 2003, p. 9.

# INDEX

# READER DISCUSSION GUIDE

## About the Author

Termed "the most honest and incisive media critic writing today" by the *National Catholic Reporter*, Eric Alterman is media columnist for *The Nation*, the "Altercation" weblogger for MSNBC.com (www.altercation.msnbc.com), and a fellow of the Center for American Progress. His *Sound & Fury: The Making of the Punditocracy* (1992, 2000), won the 1992 George Orwell Award and his *It Ain't No Sin to Be Glad You're Alive: The Promise of Bruce Springsteen* (1999, 2001), won the 1999 Stephen Crane Literary Award. He is also author of *Who Speaks for America? Why Democracy Matters in Foreign Policy* (1998), *The Book on Bush: How George W. (Mis)leads America* (with Mark Green, 2004), and *When Presidents Lie: Deception and Its Consequences* (forthcoming in 2004). In recent years, he has been a contributing editor to, or columnist for: *Worth, Rolling Stone, Elle, Mother Jones, World Policy Journal*, and *The Sunday Express* (London). A senior fellow of the World Policy Institute at New School University, and Adjunct Professor of Journalism at Columbia University, Alterman received his BA in History and Government from Cornell, his MA in International Relations from Yale, and his Ph.D. in U.S. History from Stanford. He lives with his family in Manhattan.

## About the Book

The question of whose interests the American news media protects and serves—in short, the question of bias—is hotly contested. Is bias in the media keeping us from getting full and accurate reporting of the stories that count? If so, who is at fault? Is it the "liberals" purported to control the nation's newsrooms and television and radio stations? Or is it the "conservatives," whose reliably belligerent rallying cry of a liberal media bias serves to consolidate their political base?

The answers are critical not only for media watchers, but for everyone concerned about the potentially disastrous consequences of media bias on the future of American democracy. In *What Liberal Media?*, journalist and historian Eric Alterman offers a keen, passionate, persuasive—and copiously documented—assessment of the nature and quality of our news, and dispels the smoke screens of inflammatory rhetoric once and for all.

Alterman's head-on confrontation with the Right's repeated charges of a liberal bias constitutes an utterly convincing evaluation of the realities of politics and the news. In distinct contrast to the allegations churned out by Coulter, Goldberg, O'Reilly, Hannity, and others, Alterman finds the media to be, on the whole, far more conservative than liberal. His primary concern, however, is not with whether this newspaper, or that news anchor, is biased, but rather with the extent to which the entire news industry is organized to push American politics to the right.

How does he do? The reviews have answered that question. *The Columbus Dispatch*: "A welcome, lonely voice in our current political and media climate." *The Santa Fe New Mexican*: "Fair-minded and persuasive." *The Orlando Sentinel*: "Thoroughly researched and passionately argued. . . . Alterman lights a candle in the darkness of American punditry." *The New Yorker*: "The meticulous care with which his arguments are sourced and footnoted is in commendable contrast to efforts of some of his more fire-breathing opponents." *The Florida Sun-Sentinel*: "Not only a superb piece of polemical reporting . . . Alterman, who ends with an impassioned essay on the crucial importance of high-quality journalism in a democratic society, shows that much more than liberal or conservative victory is at stake."

The following questions are intended to facilitate your discussion of *What Liberal Media?* and the critical points it raises. For regular updates on this ongoing conversation, please also visit www.whatliberalmedia.com.

## For Discussion

1. Whose interests—or what interests and powers—do the media serve, in what ways, and to what ends? In addition to political and economic interests, what other interests or powers (cultural and religious, for example) come into play? How do these interests appear to be interrelated, in terms of their impact on the media?

2. Alterman laments "the moral and intellectual bankruptcy of a journalistic culture that allows [Ann Coulter] near a microphone, much less a printing press." (4) How successful is Alterman in showing that bankruptcy? Why might his attacks on Ann Coulter, Bernard Goldberg, and other "conservative" pundits be so vigorous? How successful is Appendix 1 of Alterman's Website, www.whatliberalmedia.com—"Fact Checking Ann Coulter"—in undercutting Ms. Coulter's claims and accusations in her books, columns, and television appearances? Why might the media continue to publish and broadcast her and similar commentaries?

3. What might comparative lists of "liberal" and "conservative" media outlets, both print and broadcast, reveal about "bias" in the media? What criteria might one use to label a media outlet liberal or conservative? How does Alterman use these terms in his discussion? How substantial, in respect to both news presentation and consequences, are these labels? To what extent is much of what now passes for political

commentary and debate distorted by a looseness of terminology, a lack of precision, and disrespect for accuracy?

4. What substantive definitions of "liberal bias" have the media offered, as reported by Alterman? He argues that "the right's ideological offensive of the past few decades has succeeded so thoroughly that the very idea of a genuinely philosophically [sic] 'liberal' politics has come to mean something quite alien to American politics." (19) What might a "genuinely philosophical liberal politics" consist of, and what might be its distinctly *American* components?

5. Alterman contends that the pundits—on television, the radio, and the Internet and in newspaper opinion pages—"together with the White House, define the shape and scope of public debate in the elite media. . ." (28) He further contends that, as a group, they are "dominated by two qualities: ignorant belligerence and sitcom-like silliness." (28) What specifics does he present in support of these statements? What specifics would you present either in support or in rebuttal of the statements?

6. How would you characterize the nature and quality of political debate in the United States today, particularly as it is reflected in, and influenced by, the media? What might be done to improve the quality of that debate, in order to enhance everyone's understanding of political events, personalities, and issues, and of the American political process on the whole?

7. What instances of "ideological extremism, false information, and accusation" can you cite in the print, broadcast, and electronic media? What indications are there that these factors are as widespread and influential as Alterman claims? What indications are there that his claims may be exaggerated?

8. At the end of his chapter on the Web punditocracy, and with specific reference to Matt Drudge and Rush Limbaugh, Alterman writes of "conservatives and scandal-mongers . . . who seek to poison our political discourse with a combination of character assassination, ideological invective, and unverified misinformation." (80) What impact on the quality and usefulness of political discourse in this country do people like Drudge and Limbaugh, in fact, have?

9. What effects and consequences has the money of Richard Mellon Scaife and other conservative millionaires and of conservative foundations had on American politics and jurisprudence and related media coverage over the past several decades? To what extent might their influence be beneficial or detrimental to the American political process and American democracy? How might the link between conservative money and the conservative punditocracy be further reflective of the political power enjoyed by wealthy individuals and organizations in the U.S.?

10. "The key question to ask is not whether examples of bias can be found" in the mainstream media, Alterman contends, "but exactly where is bias pervasive and what is its effect on the news and American public life?" (104) On the basis of the evidence documented in *What Liberal Media?*, what biases—political, religious, racial, issue-related, and others—appear to be most prevalent? How do they impact the presentation of the news, our reception of and responses to the news, and the quality of life in America?

11. "Contempt for the questioning of the fundamentals of globalization and free investment is of a piece with the media's total embrace of corporate values in virtually all matters of political economy," writes Alterman. (122) What do you observe as the influence on national economic policy of strictly corporate values and objectives, short-term and long-term? To what extent might corporate values and goals be counter-productive in relation to the common good? How have the mainstream media covered related issues and events?

12. To what does Alterman refer when he writes of "the journalistic rubble left in the wake of Enron's collapse"? (129) What conclusions concerning the relationship between the media and big business might we draw from his account of the business media's coverage of corporate growth and activity before and after the Enron, WorldCom, Tyco, and other corporate failures and scandals? To what degree is Alterman accurate in stating that journalists "played patsy to" Enron's "plots of deception"? (132)

13. Alterman writes that "most independent observers would grant that the Clinton [White House] team just could not catch a break from the media." (140) To what extent might this observation be appropriate? To what degree were ideologically hostile media responsible for the constitutional crisis that emerged from the Lewinsky affair? To what extent has Alterman's examination of the media's coverage of Clinton, his policies, and his peccadilloes changed your own view of the Clinton presidency, if not of Clinton the individual?

14. How persuasive is Alterman in his account of the 2000 presidential election, media coverage of the two candidates, and the outcome of the election? To what extent do you think Gore's "loss" resulted from "the almost universal hostility he inspired in the reporters and editors who covered the race"? (149) To what extent has Alterman's account of the 2000 election modified your judgments concerning the campaign and its outcome? How might the media's "refusal to pay attention to the many substantive issues that separated the two candidates" (157) contributed to the way in which the campaign unfolded, as well as the ultimate outcome?

15. How might the media's coverage of the 9/11 attacks have confused the ramifications of the event itself and the debate concerning the appropriate response?

16. What might have been—and what might be now—the significance of the fact, as reported by Alterman, that "wholly missing from the media's endless regurgitation of the horrific events" of 9/11 "were voices of scholars who, while not pacifists or even . . . leftists, knew enough about history and diplomacy to ask at least some difficult questions about whether 'war' in the traditional sense would be the most effective response to achieve our purposes and defend our country"? (205) What distinctions and options may have been ignored in the administration's rush to declare war on Osama bin Laden and his supporters? What might be the consequences of failing to address those distinctions and options?

17. "By September 2002," writes Alterman, "the costs of the media acquiescence to the atmosphere of conservative superpatriotism were everywhere evident." (216) What have been some of those costs? Which of them continue today? Which of the issues that Alterman identified in *The Nation* in September 2002 as among those "for which Americans still did not have answers—and for which the media, with a few significant exceptions, had all but given the Bush administration a pass . . . " (216) are still unanswered? What issues since September 2002 might be added to that list?

18. To what extent do the media today fulfill "their fundamental constitutional charge to help create an informed citizenry in both war and peace"? (216) To what extent do they fail in that responsibility? What might their failings reveal about the attitudes of the media owners and managers, our politicians, and corporate and other special interests regarding an informed citizenry? To what extent might the media actually prevent us from receiving a balanced and thorough understanding of events and developments?

19. In what ways do the various contributory forces—corporations, the administration, politicians, conservative organizations, and the media themselves, and the public, for example—contribute to "a media culture that is increasingly giving itself over to tabloid fluff that distracts as it simultaneously disinforms"? (262) Why does each of these forces behave in a manner that encourages this media culture of fluff, distraction, and disinformation?

20. Why do we need honest, thorough, accurate, truthful, intelligent, ethical, and independent journalists?

This discussion guide has been prepared by Hal Hager, Hal Hager & Associates, Somerville, NJ.